Venice

Venice

A Contested Bohemia in Los Angeles

ANDREW DEENER

THE UNIVERSITY OF CHICAGO PRESS   CHICAGO AND LONDON

ANDREW DEENER is assistant professor of sociology at the University of Connecticut.

The University of Chicago Press, Chicago 60637
The University of Chicago Press, Ltd., London
© 2012 by The University of Chicago
All rights reserved. Published 2012.
Printed in the United States of America
21 20 19 18 17 16 15 14 13 12   1 2 3 4 5

ISBN-13: 978-0-226-14000-1 (cloth)
ISBN-13: 978-0-226-14001-8 (paper)
ISBN-10: 0-226-14000-8 (cloth)
ISBN-10: 0-226-14001-6 (paper)

Library of Congress Cataloging-in-Publication Data

Deener, Andrew, 1976–
    Venice : a contested Bohemia in Los Angeles / Andrew Deener.
      pages ; cm
    Includes bibliographical references and index.
    ISBN-13: 978-0-226-14000-1 (cloth : alkaline paper)
    ISBN-10: 0-226-14000-8 (cloth : alkaline paper)
    ISBN-13: 978-0-226-14001-8 (paperback : alkaline paper)
    ISBN-10: 0-226-14001-6 (paperback : alkaline paper)   1. Venice (Los Angeles,
Calif.)—Social conditions.   2. Venice (Los Angeles, Calif.)—Social life and customs.
3. Neighborhoods—California—Los Angeles.   4. City and town life—California—
Los Angeles.   5. Urbanization—California—Los Angeles.   6. Bohemianism—
California—Los Angeles.   I. Title.
    HN80.L7D44 2012
    306.09794'94—dc23
                                                                    2011044278

⊚ This paper meets the requirements of ANSI/NISO Z39.48-1992 (Permanence of Paper).

FOR ALANA AND AZALEA

Contents

List of Tables and Figures ix

Preface xi

Acknowledgments xvii

Introduction: Welcome to Venice 1

CHAPTER 1.   A Beach Town in Transition 19

CHAPTER 2.   The Transformation of a Black Neighborhood 44

CHAPTER 3.   People out of Place 86

CHAPTER 4.   Scenic Neighborhood 124

CHAPTER 5.   Bohemian Theme Park 164

CHAPTER 6.   Fashionable Bohemia 204

CHAPTER 7.   The Future of the American City 235

Notes 251

Bibliography 283

Index 301

Tables and Figures

TABLES

Table 1   Growth of African American population in Oakwood / 33
Table 2   Growth of Latino population in Venice and Oakwood / 35

FIGURES (MAPS AND PHOTOGRAPHS)

Figure 1   Map of Venice tour / 2
Figure 2   Oil derricks on the beach / 25
Figure 3   Map of the distribution of housing projects in Oakwood / 53
Figure 4   Oakwood Recreation Center with Shoreline Crip tag / 57
Figure 5   Oakwood alleyway / 62
Figure 6   Map of Latino residents' church and park routes / 66
Figure 7   Fence surrounding a house / 80
Figure 8   Gates in front of boardwalk businesses / 100
Figure 9   Sponto Gallery / 112
Figure 10   RVs near Rose Avenue / 114
Figure 11   Homeless encampment / 118
Figure 12   Canal sidewalks prior to redevelopment / 127
Figure 13   Canal cleanup campaign on empty lot / 136
Figure 14   Scenic Venice Canals / 153
Figure 15   Venice Boardwalk scene / 168
Figure 16   Venice Beach carnival performer / 172
Figure 17   Homeless performer / 201
Figure 18   Abandoned storefront / 214
Figure 19   Thrift shop / 221
Figure 20   High-end shop mimicking thrift presentation / 222
Figure 21   New artist lofts / 225

Preface

I moved to Los Angeles from New York in 2002 with a strong East Coast bias. I had already heard about the stereotypical reputation of L.A. as superficial, filled with countless Hollywood types; and I read critical treatises about the city's sprawling and sanitized spaces that keep racial, ethnic, and socioeconomic differences at bay. When I came across the palm-tree-lined Venice Boardwalk, the famed public space located just south of Santa Monica along the Pacific coast, I found a dynamic attraction that represents the exact opposite of these stereotypes. The boardwalk is diverse beyond imagination. Tourists speaking dozens of languages enjoy the pulsating spectacle with roller skaters and bicyclers speeding past, hulking and bronzed bodybuilders pumping iron on the beach, carnival performers and artists entertaining passersby, and restaurants and cafés interspersed between ragtag tourist shops.

I also realized that the boardwalk is filled with inherent contradictions. As one of thousands strolling along the pedestrian walkway, I initially shared in the unstated collective agreement that allows everyone to find pleasure in the surroundings while ignoring the poverty and hardship underlying its theme park persona. Filtered through the salty air, a pungent blend of body odor is masked by patchouli oil; flowery incense and coconut suntan lotion mix with marijuana, tobacco, and burning sage; and kettle corn and barbeque smoke blend together with the fumes of urine and sun-rotted garbage overflowing out of trash cans. Homeless men and women are sleeping on the beach. People throughout Los Angeles without formal jobs—mostly Latino, African, and Asian immigrants, as well as African Americans—show up before sunrise to claim a space on the boardwalk and sell a wide variety of paintings, photographs, incense, jewelry, T-shirts, bumper stickers, and other odds and ends. Others who live in ramshackle RVs on the streets of Venice drive into the beachfront parking lot and set up for a day of selling their wares. As I looked closer, I found that poverty and economic exclusion stabilize the reputation of the boardwalk while city politicians, real estate developers, retailers, and homeowners repeatedly step in to try to alter it.

I began ethnographic research on the boardwalk in early 2003, thinking that I was exploring the intersection of homelessness and the arts. Like most ethnographers, I adopted a research stance of looking at the world from the points of view of the people I was studying. I got to know the ins and outs of the boardwalk's vending culture, directly asking people if I could spend my days "hanging out" with them. This strategy worked well in a public space where people had little else to do but sell objects to tourists and talk to others nearby. I learned about how people end up selling their wares on the boardwalk, what they do to create their vending identities, how they contribute to the vibrant tourist attraction, and what happens to the boardwalk and the vendors when the sun goes down and visitors go home. I also could not avoid the aggressive attempts to regulate this informal economy. New city ordinances are passed to control the vending and old ones are tossed into the garbage, along with forty years of other failed regulations.

I went to neighborhood meetings to make sense of the political conflicts over the control of the boardwalk and met a number of homeless activists worried about similar restrictions regarding where homeless men and women could sleep or park their RVs and vans in other sections of Venice. I found out that African American activists and white countercultural activists were concerned about loss of affordable housing and conflicts over the uses of public spaces in other areas. Continuing my research on the boardwalk, I wandered around Venice, walking up and down every single street. My early explorations made me realize that the Venice Boardwalk is not an isolated zone. It is wedged into a coastal community undergoing marked shifts; and struggles are taking place over what distinct neighborhoods should become and who should have a say.

Venice is not a single place, as one might see it labeled on a Los Angeles city map. It is a community made up of different neighborhoods, each with its own identity, history, and struggles between groups. While some adjacent neighborhoods are filled with racial, ethnic, and socioeconomic diversity, others are more exclusive and homogeneous. Much like Harvey Zorbaugh's (1929, 4–6) classic study of the Near North Side of Chicago during the early twentieth century, *The Gold Coast and the Slum*, Venice is a twenty-first-century setting "of high light and shadow, of vivid contrasts . . . between the old and the new, between the native and the foreign . . . between wealth and poverty, vice and respectability, the conventional and the bohemian, luxury and toil." If I wanted to make sense of this Los Angeles community where immigration, homelessness, countercultural movements, gentrification, and African American segregation have converged in close proximity, I needed to study different neighborhoods, think more clearly about what is happening in each one, and examine the relationships between them.

I extended the scope and geography of my project. I spent time in various places throughout Venice and gradually got to know many people living and working in five of Venice's adjacent neighborhoods. Later, in 2003, my wife and I moved to Venice, five blocks inland from the boardwalk, in order to better understand how people experience and understand their relationships to others in their daily lives. We rented a dark and damp beach apartment in a small eight-unit building with warped wooden floors and loose and cracked kitchen tiles, one of a few apartment buildings like it on our street, increasingly surrounded by nouveau solar-powered single-family homes and artist lofts.

Proximity and constant interactions with my surroundings proved to be the single most important method in conducting a community study.[1] As a resident for five years, I walked through the various neighborhoods of Venice countless times, at all hours of the day and night. I bought my coffee at local cafés, shopped at nearby grocery stores, ate at local restaurants, and watched the surroundings change before my eyes: new buildings, stores, conflicts, and organizations often emerged. I continued to meet a number of people in meetings, but I also became acquainted with locals in more spontaneous ways. I engaged in countless informal conversations in coffee shops, grocery stores, parks, sidewalks, and alleyways, which taught me new perspectives and provided me with new avenues of research.

I attended over 150 community meetings, festivals, protests, and other events, often spending days and evenings at neighborhood functions. I participated in or observed meetings of the Venice Neighborhood Council, homeowner and tenant associations, homelessness and poverty organizations, Boardwalk Free Speech and other commercial organizations, police advisory board meetings, park advisory board meetings, and public forums held by L.A. City Council members, LAPD officers, the city's

Human Relations Commission, and city attorneys that focused on gang violence, race relations, new regulations of the boardwalk, and homelessness. This multifaceted exploration of community, diversity, and the politics of urban change required me to continue relationships with dozens of groups and follow the development of cultural events, legal battles, and intergroup conflicts over the course of years in these five adjacent neighborhoods.

I continued to incorporate an ethnographic perspective, trying to identify competing points of view and locate as much variation as I could find in these different neighborhoods. Being present with others helped me to make fine-tuned distinctions and see the relationships between individuals and groups in action. But I also realized that the participant and observational methods I was using focused squarely on the present conditions, and that I was also interested in figuring out how the relationships between individuals, groups, and neighborhoods changed over time. I needed to delve into the past. I recorded and transcribed 145 life-story and oral history interviews with people of all different backgrounds, who came to live in Venice at different periods of time, and who lived and worked in the different neighborhoods. During these interviews, most of which were open-ended and lasted between one and three hours (although several lasted over six hours), we discussed how people first came to live or work in Venice, how they constructed their local attachments to the place and came to associate with others, and how they perceived changes over the course of time they had spent in the area.

I interviewed some people on sidewalks and in coffee shops, restaurants, and parks. Those who had homes or stores were often kind enough to invite me over in order to share a piece of their private lives. I had the good fortune of getting to know individuals with diverse social networks who advocated on my behalf, invited me to neighborhood events, told me about their biographies and family histories, and vouched for me with friends, family members, neighbors, and other acquaintances. Living in Venice and participating in so many aspects of community life, I frequently ran into people who updated me about ongoing events, experiences, and changes in their own lives. In each neighborhood, I developed key informants whom I followed up with over the course of this research, in some circumstances sitting down and formally interviewing individuals multiple times. Twenty-five people provided me with personal tours of their neighborhoods, a key method that helped me to see how individuals understand their places in their neighborhoods relative to others and make sense of changes to their surroundings.[2]

At the same time, I paired these methods with other historical findings. I dug through archived collections at the Los Angeles Public Library; California State University, Long Beach; and University of California, Los Angeles. Some residents gave me access to their personal collections that characterized their histories and relationships with others in Venice, which included photographs, documents, pamphlets, and other memorabilia. In addition, I read a wide range of secondary sources that included books by local historians, master's theses, doctoral dissertations, memoirs, hundreds of newspaper articles from the *Los Angeles Times*, the *Argonaut*, the *Free Venice Beachhead*, and the *Venice Paper*, and I followed a range of online discussions, all of which helped me to better contextualize and understand the historical processes and changing political conflicts that have made Venice what it is.

I often examine the history and current circumstances of this community through the words and experiences of people whom I came to know. Anytime I use a quotation in the following chapters, it is from something that someone said directly in front of me, either to me or to others present at the time, unless I note it otherwise. I recorded and transcribed all of the interviews myself. It is always beneficial, although exhausting and tedious, to listen to recordings as an exercise in making sense of competing meanings of change and community. If recording an interview was not possible, either because I did not have my tape recorder available or in rare circumstances because someone was opposed to it, I took detailed handwritten notes either during the interaction or directly afterward. In some circumstances throughout these chapters, I draw quotations from recordings and transcriptions that I found in one of the archives or from various media sources to demonstrate the everyday texture of a particular period. I identify these instances in the notes.

I follow sociological convention of using pseudonyms so as not to contribute to already contentious relationships, but if I draw upon historical documents, media accounts, or interviews with individuals working in official city capacity or with individuals who passed away before the book's publication, I use their real names to accurately reflect the sources from which they came. While pseudonyms protect respondents, I believe it is an enormous disservice to any future researchers and observers to mask the identities of particular places. Identifying Venice and its various neighborhoods and public spaces will allow those in the future to make sense of my findings and compare their own observations against the ones presented here, hopefully as a historical resource that further highlights the transformation of neighborhoods.

Locals often joke that if there are three Venetians in a room, they will have at least four opinions. Venice is known for its independent spirit, where agreement is difficult to find. It is a stressful task to report on competing sides in such a place, especially when each has come to trust that you will make objective interpretations about situations and events, but ultimately hopes that you agree with them. I try not to agree or disagree with anyone's assumptions, but rather strenuously examine how different perspectives came about, how different people have become positioned against others, and how conflicts emerged and changed over time. Although the details discussed in this book take place in Venice, I believe the themes and explanations will resonate beyond it and likely beyond the city of Los Angeles. I hope in the end they provoke dialogue and debate about the future of the American city.

Acknowledgments

The research and writing of this book took me on a long journey, if not always in distance, than certainly in terms of the wide range of people who helped to make it possible. I could never have developed this project if it were not for the enthusiasm of the people of Venice. Those living and working in this community have one clear thing in common: a passion for this place.

A number of people put up with me for years on end, many sat down for interviews and regular conversations, others pointed me to key historical and political resources, and some simply liked the idea of the book and invited me to meetings and festivities. While I cannot thank each of you by name, I hope that this work helps you to see Venice in a new light.

This project began when I was a graduate student in the sociology department at UCLA, and I owe a special debt of gratitude to David Halle and Gail Kligman. Always willing to share his extensive knowledge of cities, politics, and culture, David was an early and enthusiastic supporter of this project and gave ongoing advice about how to expand and improve it. Gail's masterful readings of so many chapter drafts and brainstorming sessions at the French Market consistently left me with much more to think about. I am lucky to count them both as my mentors and friends.

Sherry Ortner and Bill Roy provided guidance, encouragement, and wonderful feedback along the way, forcing me to think beyond Venice and Los Angeles more generally. I was fortunate to have research training by Jack Katz and Maurice Zeitlin, both masters of their respective trades. I reserve a special thanks to Jack for opening up my eyes to the importance of seeing social processes and for his incisive comments on an early draft of the manuscript, and to Mitchell Duneier for regularly joining our ethnography seminar and offering advice that helped to make a novice field-worker a bit more at ease. Rene Almeling offered her sharp eye on multiple chapter revisions, always with the aim of improving the book. Adrian Favell, Pepper Glass, Darnell Hunt, Rob Jansen, Jooyoung Lee, Justin Lee, Jeff Prager, Steve Sherwood, and Jon Sigmon all provided valuable feedback on chapters, talks, or simply in one of many thought-provoking conversations about a kernel of an idea.

I started to rework the manuscript at the University of Connecticut. Claudio Benzecry and Gaye Tuchman both read it in its entirety and provided insightful advice that helped me to get the ball rolling again. Claudio's intellectual curiosity and willingness to think through new ideas—sometimes on a daily basis—were central to bringing out the very best in the book. Thanks also to Clint Sanders for always-engaging conversations about the meaning and history of ethnography in sociology.

A number of friends and colleagues read chapters, challenged me during talks, or simply listened to me ramble on about Venice. Thanks to Gabi Abend, Mike Bader, Ryan Centner, Frank Esposito, Colin Jerolmack, Erin O'Connor, Van Tran, Owen Whooley, and Jon Wynn. Workshops, classes, and discussions at the University of Pennsylvania, Yale University, and City University of New York were extremely helpful. I am especially grateful to Elijah Anderson, Philip Kasinitz, Michael Katz, and Annette Lareau for providing me with the space to try out new frameworks and entertain stimulating discussions, and to Philippe Bourgois, for challenging me to reconsider some of my conclusions by thinking about Los Angeles as a particular type of American city.

Research support from the John Randolph Haynes and Dora Haynes Foundation and the Department of Housing and Urban Development provided me with time to conduct research and write chapters. A fellowship with the Robert Wood Johnson Foundation Health & Society Scholars Program provided time to bring the book to its completion, and I thank the directors of the program at the University of Pennsylvania, Robert Aronowitz, David Asch, and Jason Schnittker. Parts of chapter 2 previously appeared in *Ethnography* 11, no. 1, and in a volume edited by Darnell Hunt and Ana-Christina Ramón, *Black Los Angeles: American Dreams, Racial Realities*, published by New York University Press; and a portion of chapter 6 appeared in *City and Community* 6, no. 4. Thanks to their editors and reviewers.

Librarians, archivists, and staff at UCLA Library, the Abbot Kinney

Memorial Branch of the Los Angeles Public Library, and the Los Angeles Public Library's History and Genealogy Department's Photo Collection were extremely helpful. I owe a special thanks to Kristie French at the library of the California State University, Long Beach, for her extensive knowledge and assistance using their Venice archives. I am also grateful to Darryl DuFay for permission to use his photograph in chapter 4.

It has been a great pleasure to work with Doug Mitchell at the University of Chicago Press. Doug's enthusiasm for a book about Venice started with our very first encounter and was felt at each successive stage of the publication process. Thanks also to Tim McGovern, Andrea Guinn, Jennifer Rappaport, Carol Saller, Aaron Schielke, and Jeffrey Waxman for their commitment to ushering the book into print, and to Grey Osterud for her astute and critical reading of the manuscript. Book reviewing can be an arduous task, and I was fortunate to have two reviewers—one remained anonymous—who provided incredibly useful feedback. Harvey Molotch set the bar extremely high. His detailed comments on every single chapter, along with his generosity in subsequent conversations, enabled me to move beyond some of my old ideas and develop new ones.

My parents, Mal and Debbie, both lifelong residents of New Jersey, moved to Southern California not that long after I did. It was a stroke of good fortune having them nearby for so many years as a source of support and an occasional escape from Venice. I also want to thank Frank Dlubak, Ave Maria Dlubak, Alyssa Bodiford, Rick Bodiford, Amy Kim, Sung Hoon Kim, Damon Dlubak, Rocio Martinez Dlubak, David Deener, and Alan Bitterman for their encouragement and always stimulating conversations.

Alana Dlubak experienced Venice with me in countless ways. Without having her in my life, this book would never have seen the light of day, as I probably would have moved back to New York. Alana's unparalleled ability to connect with people in the most unexpected places and uncover a city's hidden gems has taught me more about how to appreciate life than anything or anyone else. When the research for this book began, it was just the two of us, and upon its completion, we now number three. I dedicate this book to Alana and Azalea for making my life more colorful and for showing me the meaning of joy.

Introduction

Welcome to Venice

Nestled between Santa Monica and Marina del Rey along the Los Angeles coast, Venice is a vibrant community where contrasts between cultures and classes are seemingly everywhere. Most think of it as a quirky beach town and enclave for artists, beatniks, and hippies; and visitors from near and far come to its boardwalk, one of the most eclectic and iconoclastic public spaces in California. Yet Venice also has so many elements that make urban living attractive: racial, ethnic, and socio-economic diversity; artistic and architectural creativity; interesting commercial amenities, ranging from the boardwalk's raucous vending culture to the restaurants, coffee shops, and boutiques on other nearby commercial strips; and it has residents consumed by a spirited political dialogue about its future.

Venice represents the dynamism and contradictions that diversity brings. It reveals the cultural richness and creative nuances that emerge when people seek out proximity to differences; but it also shows that even as individuals of different backgrounds idealize diversity as a concept, inequalities and conflict are a persistent thorn in the pursuit of a new age of neighborhood integration.[1] Widely hailed as a Southern California bastion of liberal culture and politics, Venice is a community divided. It is broken up into more than a dozen smaller neighborhoods where competing groups struggle to control distinct collective representations through architectural styles, commercial trends, uses of public spaces, symbolic commemorations, and the formation of political, religious, social service, and other types of organizations.[2] The identities of some neighborhoods have remained ambiguous for decades due to the competing influences of diverse racial, ethnic, or socioeconomic groups. Other neighborhoods have become more exclusive after years of contestation have withered away and displaced the presence of less influential groups.

This book focuses on five of Venice's adjacent neighborhoods—three residential and two commercial neighborhoods—chosen because of what they can tell us about how diversity and exclusivity coexist in constant tension. In order to further examine these tensions, I first describe what we would see if we walked around. A typical tour would certainly introduce visitors to the boardwalk and to the scenic canals. I will bring you to these sections, but I will also show you neighborhoods and point out themes that other tour guides may not. Outlined in figure 1, this three-mile walk-around will take us about half a day and call attention to the ways that diversity and exclusivity are organized, cheek by jowl, into contiguous spaces.[3]

We begin our tour on the Venice Boardwalk, formally known as Ocean Front Walk, where the Pacific Ocean is directly to the west and the Santa Monica Mountains are in our distant view to the north. The former site of lively beatnik cafés and kosher bakeries during the decades

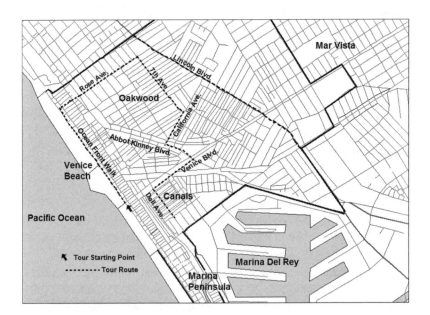

FIGURE I. Map of Venice Tour

between 1950 and 1970, the boardwalk has become a world-renowned tourist destination with a unique commercial identity. On any given day, up to two hundred people set up shop on the beachside of the boardwalk in a rent-free vending economy called the Free Speech Zone. While most cloak their sales and performances with some element of "free speech," incorporating some artistic, religious, or political emblem, they blur the boundaries between this presentation and economic ambitions.

An African American artist with chin-length dreadlocks, who has been homeless on and off for four decades, preaches about his display of shattered television screens painted over with the phrase Axis of Evil. He also sells color-copied prints of paintings of the boardwalk scenery. Curious about the peppery scent of burning sage, tourists listen to a tall and lanky black man with a silver beard peddle the herb tied in bundles, promising them that burning it like incense will ultimately rid their homes of demons. A middle-aged Asian artist strains to express his point in English to a white teenage girl posing for her portrait, with posters labeled "Chinese Paintings for Sale" stacked beside him. A Latina woman in her midtwenties originally from Mexico City beads jewelry on hemp, adding a crucifix to each piece. An elderly homeless poet leftover from Venice's beat scene of the late 1950s, sporting a red beret and a thick gray beard, writes his treatises on cardboard cutouts and places them on a bed sheet for sale to the public. A large crowd gathers around a Salvadoran man who walks shirtless and barefoot with a woman sitting on his shoulders over the crushed remains of hundreds of glass bottles, with each step leaving behind bloodstained footprints on the concrete. The crowd, enthralled by his performance, throws dollar bills into a straw hat. In the background, the sounds of competing musical performances come from multiple directions: a jazz ensemble and a folk duo are barely audible over the rhythms of conga drums coming from the Venice Drum Circle located in the center of the beach.

The mob packing into Ocean Front Walk divides the informal economic attachments from the formal ones. Opposite the Free Speech Zone are beach bungalows, weather-worn apartment buildings, shiny new multilevel loft and condominium developments, as well as rent-paying businesses where one can buy a $2 coffee or a $5 sandwich, get a tattoo, cheap sunglasses, or a touristy T-shirt. Some residents, store-owners, and landlords complain to the police about competition over vending spaces and noise from amplified music coming from the Free Speech Zone. Rent-paying business owners object to those on the rent-free side selling similar products as the ones they carry in their stores. Police officers move up and down the boardwalk on foot, by bicycle, or in slowly maneuvering cars and SUVs through the masses, trying to mediate between these competing interests.

We walk toward the northern end of the boardwalk and stop at the corner of Rose Avenue. In the mid-1980s, a homeless tent city took over this section of the beach, leading to an intense conflict between residents and homeless activists. The tent city is long gone, but hidden behind the string of vendors are dozens of people sleeping on a grassy mound shaded by towering palm trees. If we return the next day, this group may have suddenly disappeared, the outcome of a homeless sweep. Awakened by LAPD officers at 5:00 a.m., many are hauled away to jail only to return the following week to begin accumulating their modest possessions from scratch.

As we continue up Rose Avenue away from the boardwalk, homelessness is even more pronounced, differentiating this section as a separate neighborhood. Lining Rose and its intersecting streets are dozens of rundown RVs. Those who live in them are outside talking with friends, many of whom live directly on the streets without a vehicle, some smoking hand-rolled cigarettes and others smoking pot. Several homeless men and women stand on the corner, watching a parade of tourists park their cars and saunter toward the beach. A few in a far worse state of mind appear disconnected from their surroundings and hold elaborate conversations with themselves. They rummage through trash cans, picking apart Styrofoam packages to look for intact leftovers. One woman with thinning, disheveled hair wildly yells at a man walking by, showing off her missing teeth with each insult; a burly man with a dark brown beard, raggedy trucker's hat, and broken sunglasses held together by masking tape politely asks pedestrians for money; and others bury themselves under blankets on the sidewalks of less trafficked streets perpendicular to Rose.

On Rose Avenue, several social service agencies stand opposite retail businesses, condominiums, and recently remodeled homes. While these agencies started as a support system for poor housed families in Venice, they have since expanded to incorporate many different programs that address the rapidly growing number of homeless people in the area. A mix of older hippies, younger professionals, and stay-at-home moms and dads navigate a path up the street from their quaint single-family homes in and out of sleeping bags, panhandlers, and garbage remains to Groundwork, a small organic coffee shop. Others meander past to Whole Foods, located on the corner of Lincoln and Rose, directly across the street from an affordable housing organization.

Walking inland from the beach along Rose Avenue, a right turn on Seventh Avenue takes us into another distinct neighborhood that locals call Oakwood. We pass by one of five historically black churches, the First Baptist Church, with roots dating back to the early 1900s when Venice was first developed and the earliest African Americans moved in. Across from the church is a park that operates as the neighborhood center, marked by a sign honoring a onetime influential African American activist, one of many visible tributes to the black community in Oakwood. On the northern end of the park, retired African American men sit at picnic tables playing dominoes and reminiscing about the way things used to be. Younger black men in their twenties and thirties congregate by the fence near the picnic tables, listening to music played from cars parked in the street. One of the young men moves away from the group toward a slow-moving vehicle driven by a middle-aged white man and holds a small bag out in the open during daylight hours without even trying to disguise his action. After making an exchange, the car speeds off and he returns to his friends.

Formerly part of a massive operation on many street corners throughout Oakwood, the drug distribution ring has been steadily pushed by LAPD officers into the vicinity of the park, where surveillance cameras now monitor every move. Only a few of the young men engage in illicit activities, but the friendships between dealers and nondealers have complicated histories, as many grew up together in Oakwood and family members have known each other for decades. On the opposite end of the park a different type of lawlessness takes place: newer residents— white men and women in their thirties and forties—let their dogs run off their leashes, disregarding a city ordinance that restricts this activity and runs at cross-purposes with the interests of older residents whose children and grandchildren also use the park to play.

Most of the streets surrounding Oakwood Park follow a grid pattern and are lined with multiple housing types. Neglected apartment buildings and well-kept Section 8 housing projects sit on the same blocks as aging stucco cottages and recently remodeled Craftsman and Spanish-style homes, new innovative barnlike condominiums made of shimmering steel, and a few much larger fortresses made of corrugated metal. Some of the new remodeled homes have solid wooden, metal, or concrete fences surrounding their properties, but when an electric gate opens and a luxury sedan pulls out, we catch a glimpse of high ceilings, ample skylights, and exposed beams that represent an attention to detail only allowed by a more opulent lifestyle. The low-income housing projects located just a few steps away are not labeled in any way, but fourteen almost identical boxlike buildings are scattered throughout this one square mile area.

With the exception of the park and its immediate surroundings, Oakwood's streets are relatively quiet. Occasionally, we pass individuals, couples, and families walking on the sidewalks. African American women, many of them seniors, sit outside of their small and simple but neatly organized homes in which multiple generations of family members have lived. Latina women wait with their children outside a grocery truck with fresh fruits and vegetables for sale, making friendly banter with the driver who only speaks Spanish. White women pushing vibrant-colored designer baby strollers cross the street without breaking stride in order to avoid an African American homeless man stumbling toward them from a desolate alleyway.

Walking on Seventh Avenue toward California Avenue, a right turn brings us to Abbot Kinney Boulevard, a diagonal retail artery that runs through the center of Venice and operates as a clear neighborhood boundary. A local coffee shop called Abbot's Habit is on the corner. Opened in the late 1980s, it is one of the "old spots" on the street, where gray-haired hippies, sunglass-wearing hipsters, as well as up-and-coming professionals in "the industry" (i.e., the entertainment business), all make use of this small social space, one of the few remaining integrative spots on the street. At one time, Abbot Kinney Boulevard was the site of African American community organizations, left-wing political groups, artist studios, thrift stores, abandoned lots, and graffiti-covered buildings. In recent years, it has become filled with high-end shops and eateries.

Successful artists who have lived in Venice for decades meet in the evenings at Hal's Bar and Grill, a longtime local favorite. Closer to Main Street, people from all over Los Angeles flock to a strip of expensive restaurants, giving rise to the label "Restaurant Row." Strolling along, we witness people parking hybrid cars, getting ready to shop at trendy boutiques and antique furniture stores. Some are donning the latest designer fashions: $200 skinny jeans, $350 oversized sunglasses, and one woman drapes a $3,000 bag over her forearm, large enough to fit her toy

dog. Others purposely present themselves as beach bums and bohemians, wearing ripped jeans, flannel shirts, flip-flops, and fedoras. Regardless of how they stage themselves, they walk in and out of upscale stores,
sometimes spending much more money on lavish items than it seems
they can afford from the way they dress.

Continuing up Abbot Kinney Boulevard away from Main Street, we
reach Venice Boulevard, where a right turn once again leads us in the
direction of Venice Beach. On the way, Venice Boulevard meets Dell
Avenue, and a left turn directs us toward the Venice Canals. Along
Dell Avenue, the only car-accessible road through the Canals, a series
of arched bridges pass over four successive waterways running east to
west. Six man-made waterways in total—four running east/west and two
running north/south—physically demarcate the neighborhood from its
surroundings. At one time rundown with stagnant, foul-smelling waterways and caved-in sidewalks, it was the home of beatniks, hippies, artists, and bikers living in cramped and poorly constructed bungalows.
In sharp contrast, we now witness some of the most pristine living conditions in Southern California. Refurbished 1920s California bungalows and 1960s duplexes rest between large, two-and-three-story single-
family homes, many of which were designed by cutting-edge architects
to maximize internal square footage under the restrictions of small lot
sizes and densely packed conditions. Day and night, many of the houses
remain dark, abandoned by wealthy homeowners with no financial need
to supplement their incomes by renting out properties, only using them
as temporary or summer dwellings. Those in residence, however, often
sit outside on their decks or in their gardens, watching small groups of
people, including various tour groups, trek up and down the sidewalks.
After more than four decades of political controversies, the infrastructure was remodeled in the mid-1990s, with stylish new canal walls, sidewalks, and wooden footbridges. Occasionally, someone paddles by on a
kayak, swerving out of the direction of the mallards, egrets, and herons
that have turned these man-made waterways into a natural habitat.

As the sun sets, our tour comes to a close and we meander back to the
boardwalk only to find that the vibrant daytime attraction has vanished.
A cover band playing the music of the Doors, the iconic rock group that
formed in Venice in the 1960s, blasts out of a local bar. Older homeless men and women dance outside, sharing memories—no one knows
whether they are fact or fiction—of past friendships with Jim Morrison, the Doors' rambunctious lead singer who died in 1971 at the age of

twenty-seven. Some of the younger homeless are sitting in the distance on the beach smoking anything they were able to get their hands on, from methamphetamines to marijuana. Others congregate with friends to fend off potential dangers of the night, waiting for the sun to rise and the bustling crowd to return when they will once again try to get a piece of the economic action.

Neighborhood Public Cultures

During our tour, I purposely present readers with an account of what we might see as we pass through these five neighborhoods. My emphasis on the visual is not only an exercise in describing the setting. The visible contrasts between diversity and exclusivity operate as a relevant force in urban development. As we walk around cities, we observe neighborhood public cultures, that is, the visible cues that allow us to distinguish the identities of adjacent places from one another. We take notice of commercial amenities, various organizations and services, housing sizes and styles, types of people walking around, activities in parks and on street corners, and any other public actions, rituals, and symbols. We also make judgments about these distinct public cultures: we determine what looks good to us, where we want to spend our time, and even if we do not have the resources, we fantasize about where we would like to live. But how do these neighborhood public cultures come into being? What groups stake claim to, and influence, these neighborhood identities? And why do we interpret some as ambiguous and diverse, while we interpret others as more exclusive and homogeneous?

For well over a century, scholars have been trying to make sense of the connections between urban diversity and the distinct identities of places. One of the most well-known sociological stories focuses on the mass movement of people from the rural hinterlands to the crowded industrial spaces during the period of the late nineteenth and early twentieth centuries. Along with industrialization came European immigration, African American migration from the South, new forms of bohemianism, and increasing suburbanization. The dense and diverse conditions of early twentieth-century cities motivated a continuous academic interest in their unique social problems.

In order to study urban development during the first half of the 1900s,

Robert Park, a University of Chicago sociologist, prompted his students to go out into the city and conduct research by directly observing people in a wide variety of settings. He urged them, "Go sit in the lounges of luxury hotels and on the doorsteps of the flophouses; sit on the Gold Coast settees and on the slum shakedowns; sit in the Orchestra Hall and in the Star and Garter Burlesque."[4] Based on their observations of how separate classes, cultures, and spaces were organized in Chicago, Park described the city as a "mosaic of little worlds which touch but do not interpenetrate."[5] This metaphor of the urban mosaic—a series of interconnected but homogeneous social spaces—has remained a guiding framework for American urban ethnographers despite ongoing changes to cities across the nation. Researchers continue to define diversity as a series of occasional contacts at the edges of distinct racial, ethnic, and socioeconomic zones. From this point of view, temporary alliances and intergroup conflicts ultimately lead individuals back into their more homogeneous, defended territories.[6]

Yet population movements of the late twentieth century have layered new groups onto the urban map, forcing us to rethink our classifications of neighborhood public cultures.[7] Since the 1970s, three simultaneous shifts have reorganized the racial, ethnic, and socioeconomic composition of Los Angeles, leading to emerging struggles over space. Multiple waves of Latin American and Asian immigration transformed the sprawling metropolis into one of the most ethnically diverse cities in the United States, transcending the historic color line between African Americans and whites. An unprecedented growth in homelessness has marked L.A. as the city with the largest homeless population in the nation, giving rise to the presence of poverty in many public spaces. And the proliferation of gentrification has increasingly led wealthier people, no longer simply opting to reside in the most exclusive residential enclaves, to inhabit areas with cultural diversity and dramatic income divisions.[8]

A team of sociologists, Bobo, Oliver, Johnson, and Valenzuela, describe Los Angeles as a "prismatic metropolis." They argue that, like a glass prism that reflects and differentiates the spectrum of colors out of a stream of light, the city "captures and refracts" the complex racial, ethnic, and socioeconomic changes in the United States and positions them in relation to one another throughout its vast landscape.[9] Likewise, Venice is a prismatic community. The diversity found throughout the city is thrust together in even closer proximity, magnifying the spectrum of demands that people make about access to, and control of, the Los Angeles coast.

In contemporary Los Angeles, the static classifications that have historically guided sociological interpretations of urban neighborhoods as rich *or* poor, black *or* white, ethnic *or* Wasp, and working class *or* professional do not consistently hold. How should we label Oakwood: Is it a black, Latino, or white neighborhood? Is Rose Avenue a skid row for the homeless and the down and out, or is it a middle- and upper-income residential locale? Should we interpret the boardwalk as an up-and-coming shopping district, a free attraction for the masses, or a space of economic opportunity for the most destitute? Furthermore, how did the Canals and Abbot Kinney Boulevard, neighborhoods once deemed as centers of cross-cultural contact, become more exclusive when they are located directly on the boundaries of these other highly diverse spaces?

Just as we have to be careful not to automatically adopt static classifications of distinct neighborhood public cultures, we have to be careful not to oversimplify the place of gentrification in the process of neighborhood change.[10] We can certainly see the everyday performances, housing infrastructures, and iconic representations of wealth in all five of the neighborhoods making up this study, but the pathways of neighborhood change are not empty conduits between central power holders, local neighborhood groups, and any given set of neighborhood conditions. Wealthy developers, influential architects, new retailers, and new homeowners are present in this discussion about urban change, but not in a way that makes these adjacent neighborhoods look the same. Venice has emerged over the last four decades as a coastal community in extremely high demand where everyone wants a piece of the property, from long-standing African American residents and bohemians to homeless men and women, Latino immigrants, and wealthier homeowners.

Under such conditions, the concept of the "local" serves as a multi-sided and contested sociological category. The interactions between broader forces transforming Los Angeles and collective actions in specific neighborhoods give rise to what Elias and Scotson call social configurations between groups, where the more "established" residents continue to shape neighborhoods by drawing upon local resources and distinguishing their interests and identities from newcomers whom they define as "outsiders."[11] Molotch, Freudenburg, and Paulsen further argue for the importance of studying the histories of places, their economic and material infrastructures, and their political organizations to understand how places remain "durably distinct." They argue that people actively draw upon these existing conditions to reinforce and reproduce the divergent character of places over time.[12] We can extend these frameworks into our investigation of distinct neighborhood public cultures in Venice. As neighborhoods change and newcomers move in, stabilizing forces counter the constant flow of transition. People work within the confines of economic and material infrastructures, community organizations, political associations, interactions in public spaces, and symbolic representations of distinct group identities, collectively influencing public cultures into the present and the future. A competing logic of consistency exists side by side with the influx of newcomers, such that two or more groups can simultaneously shape a neighborhood public culture for a period of decades.

Stability and change are intertwined processes in neighborhood development. We need to think of neighborhoods and the people who occupy them in medias res, as part of a continuous history of creating, maintaining, and transforming public cultures. As newcomers move in, they sometimes construct their own organizations, import or generate their own building stocks and aesthetic codes, engage in their own ways of defining public spaces and social order, and establish their own forms of neighborhood attachment. In other words, newcomers build stability over time. They take part in the historical transformation of inter- and intragroup relationships, in some circumstances becoming perceived (and even coming to perceive themselves) as old-timers when additional sets of newcomers follow them into their neighborhoods. To make sense of the stability and transformation of neighborhood public cultures in Venice, we need to examine how people become repositioned against one another over time; how some maintain their connections to certain neighborhoods in the face of ongoing changes; and how these changes lead to the development of more exclusive neighborhoods that remain in direct geographic contact with more diverse ones.

The Social and Symbolic Order of Neighborhoods

Public cultures take form as a structure of oppositions within and between neighborhoods. As people become configured against others within their neighborhoods, they establish competing and complementary positions.[13] In diverse neighborhoods, configurations emerge between people competing over shared space; whereas in exclusive neighborhoods, the public cultures of successive waves of newcomers complement one another and come together like a jigsaw puzzle, pushing aside competing interests. The relationship between these adjacent spaces, some with competing positions and others with complementary positions, generates the social and symbolic order of diverse and exclusive neighborhoods.

The public cultures of diverse neighborhoods remain ambiguous, because competing visible cues, uses of public spaces, and collective interests challenge any overarching representation. Differences of race, ethnicity, and class converge in the neighborhoods of Oakwood, Rose Avenue, and the Venice Boardwalk. Yet sharing proximate spaces with others of different backgrounds does not automatically translate into neighborhood integration. Instead, people often develop social and cultural distances, feelings of distrust, and intense political conflicts about definitions of quality of life and plans for the future of their neighborhoods. When individuals fail to establish durable interpersonal ties with those living and working in their immediate surroundings, they become cautious and critical of discernible differences and develop stereotypes that overshadow the texture of diversity within distinct racial, ethnic, and class categories.[14] Longtime African American residents in Oakwood believe that incoming white residents are overtly private; homeless people living in RVs and on the streets surrounding Rose Avenue are convinced that housed residents are extremely affluent; and boardwalk vendors commonly label any political action that opposes the Free Speech Zone as stemming from the corrupted interests of developers.

Not all labels carry equal weight, however. A pervasive middle- and upper-class quality of life narrative has put some urban dwellers in a better position to stigmatize less powerful people. Middle- and upper-class conventions overlap with political authority to create official classifications of people and their uses of public spaces according to the division between "order and disorder."[15] Some rent-paying business owners, newer homeowners, and wealthier real estate brokers and developers employ *power labeling*. They mark certain types of people as threats to their personal safety and the security of their property, and these labels gain official political and law enforcement traction.[16]

Power labeling begins as a reaction to recurring transgressions that challenge newcomers' feelings of safety and perceptions of order. Individuals respond to real and immediate concerns such as gang violence, graffiti on private property, or drug dealing in Oakwood; informal and illegal economic activities and early morning clamoring on the Venice Boardwalk; and public defecation, urination, or drug use among homeless individuals on Rose Avenue. As regular witnesses to, and subjects of, breaches to their own safety thresholds, newcomers become directly positioned against those who conduct these offenses. They do not necessarily know the exact individuals committing the crimes and interrupting their quality of life, which makes it very difficult to identify perpetrators and address their neighborhood issues. Yet even in cases where they can make these identifications, they do not confront offenders in face-to-face interactions. They link up with police officers, city attorneys, city council members, and other city officials who provide bureaucratic backing to the stigmatization process. New official organizations are created where residents and business owners interact with city representatives to identify neighborhood problems; new legal codes are written and old ones enforced to restrict the uses of public spaces by certain types of people; and new surveillance methods are set up to monitor and uproot those perceived as threatening to their daily lives. Neighborhoods with frequent infractions against middle- and upper-class neighborhood norms lead African Americans, homeless people, countercultural groups, and boardwalk vendors to become viewed as problem populations.

Still, some newcomers, particularly enamored with the unconventional and artistic lifestyles that made Venice famous, continue to romanticize Venice's bohemian history. They also cherish their proximity to race and class diversity. Even then, they do not stand outside of the neighborhood transition process. They contribute to it by reinforcing class differences through the daily performances of cultural practices and techniques of political involvement. They share a standard of living that reflects a distinct social position: higher-status jobs, more private lifestyles, shopping at more expensive stores, driving newer and more fashionable cars, eating at trendy restaurants, associating and networking with those of like mind and taste, and taking distinct modes of political intervention for granted, in which they readily accept and rely upon the roles taken by politicians, law enforcement officers, and other city officials in their own neighborhoods.

Economic advantages and power labeling do not instantly grant newcomers with special powers to remove so-called problem populations. It is not until successive waves of newcomers form complementary relationships within their neighborhoods that they erode and sometimes eliminate less influential groups. Abbot Kinney Boulevard and the Venice Canals are now more easily identifiable as exclusive neighborhoods, because successive waves of middle- and upper-class residents, business owners, real estate brokers, and developers have established complementary positions between them, in each case generating a *neighborhood homology* between groups, symbols, and spaces that represents the appearance of a coherent public culture.[17]

Neighborhood homologies begin to take form when people are attracted to recognizable cues. Adventurous "pioneers"[18] contribute early pieces of a visible symbolic code—remodeled houses, freshly painted fences, and newer cars in driveways—but public cultures accumulate over time. Successive waves of newcomers fit together through shared norms about property upkeep, architectural innovations, etiquette about the meaning of being a neighbor and using public spaces, specific commercial trends that signify shared values about the types of products and stores worthy of support, and approaches to political interventions that represent their collective interests.

In neighborhoods with more ambiguous public cultures, people disagree about how to define problems, as well as how to practically address and organize their interests against these problems. Conflicts over housing affordability and uses of public spaces stand alongside conflicts over how people ought to intervene into everyday affairs and engage an opposing side. At one time, competing cultural and political assumptions existed in the Venice Canals and on Abbot Kinney Boulevard. Over time, people with complementary interests altered the nature of the political debates about belonging in these neighborhoods. They established a critical mass of people who hold similar assumptions about local politics, including a common language for debating about the future of their neighborhoods and a fundamental belief that it is the duty of public officials to address their concerns. Although different groups may form within exclusive neighborhoods, continuing mild confrontations over planning codes, parking shortages, and the aesthetic façades of new buildings, they share familiar conventions about political decision making and collective action that enables them to compromise over definitions of neighborhood problems and exclude those with radically different perspectives, concerns, and needs.

Complementary and competing positions within neighborhoods reinforce the boundaries between diverse and exclusive public cultures. Although these boundaries are potentially porous due to sheer physical proximity, the coherent logic of an exclusive neighborhood makes the presence of people perceived as "outsiders" more noticeable and easily contested if necessary.[19] In such cases, power labeling is rarely called into practice. The power of a neighborhood homology is revealing in this respect: some people have been persuaded over time that they do not belong and therefore rarely challenge the prevailing public culture. Longtime Oakwood residents are aware of the social and economic distances between them and the commercial amenities on bordering Abbot Kinney Boulevard; and homeless men and women rarely set up encampments in the Venice Canals because it makes more sense for them to establish themselves in other nearby neighborhoods, like Rose Avenue, where they can more easily fit in.

Residential and Commercial Neighborhoods

Venice: A Contested Bohemia in Los Angeles examines the configurations within five adjacent neighborhoods and the tensions that have materialized between diverse and exclusive public cultures in residential and commercial neighborhoods. To this end, both neighborhood histories and comparisons serve as valuable sociological tools. Chapter 1, "A Beach Town in Transition," provides the background story about Venice by situating the coastal community in the context of Los Angeles urban development, cultural movements, and population settlements. In particular, it explores how and why a severe economic decline between 1920 and 1950 attracted African Americans and successive bohemian groups to Venice, giving way to the influx of immigrants, homeless men and women, and wealthier residents between the 1970s and the present day.

These population shifts set the stage for ongoing neighborhood battles over public cultures discussed in closer detail in the following chapters. Because Los Angeles is a city where residential and commercial spaces have a history of planned separation, I examine both types of neighborhoods.[20] I focus on contrasting cases of diversity and exclusivity in both residential and commercial neighborhoods as a way to develop a more sound sociological theory of how neighborhood stability and neighborhood change become intertwined and reinforce the social and symbolic order of neighborhoods.

I examine three residential neighborhoods. Chapter 2 addresses competing demands over space through a lens of race and ethnic relations. I show how African Americans established a lasting influence over Oakwood's public culture despite their demographic decline. A history of segregation gave rise to durable political organizations, streets and buildings named after residents, and a vibrant public social life in Oakwood. The ways in which Latinos became localized in this setting further contributed to African Americans' enduring influence. Latinos became the largest demographic group, but they were historically unable to establish comparable institutions, organizations, or neighborhood representations *within* Oakwood, often establishing a vibrant public life outside of the neighborhood. The influx of white gentrifiers, however, has since produced a competing public culture, adding to a new wave of conflicts over lifestyle and urban space. In efforts to curb severe gang violence and drug dealing that plagued the neighborhood for decades, African Americans often become stigmatized in their continuing visibility.

Chapter 3 focuses on how neighborhood change becomes filtered through conflicts between the housed and the homeless. As Rose Avenue emerged as a "home for the homeless" in the 1970s and '80s, newer residents also moving in during that time came to define the homeless population as "people out of place." Social service agencies on Rose Avenue have supported the homeless for several decades, also playing a prominent political role. With multimillion-dollar budgets, they are wealthier than most housed residents and their function is equally important to the city's overall political landscape, in that they pick up the slack for a government system that has consistently failed to resolve persistent homelessness over the last four decades. The boardwalk's informal economy, state coastal commission protections on public parking, social support from long-standing countercultural activists, and collective actions among the homeless themselves further stabilize the connections of the homeless in the area. At the same time, recurring problems with public defecation, urination, drug use, and dumping of litter and waste from RVs onto surrounding streets generate a cycle of conflicts about the place of homelessness in the neighborhood.

Chapter 4 emphasizes how gentrification produces residential exclusivity by successive waves of newcomers reconfiguring the relationships between groups and establishing a cohesive public culture. Lower-income bohemian renters of the Canals were able to hold on to the neighborhood's public culture as "unconventional" for almost two decades, well into the 1970s, even as speculators tried to restore the district into an upscale haven. The influx of the middle class as live-in residents slowly diluted the neighborhood's reputation for unconventionality, as they altered the everyday culture of the setting and unintentionally redirected the politics of urban change. Instead of joining the ongoing resistance by countercultural activists against all development whatsoever, they advocated for "sensible development." A new complementary political configuration between middle-class homeowners and speculative developers pushed aside the radical interests of the more established countercultural renters. These two property-owning segments changed the nature of local conversations by compromising about aesthetic preferences, overshadowing the former renter-owner class conflict, and reshaping the public culture of their neighborhood as more exclusive and homogeneous.

Commercial neighborhoods also develop distinct public cultures in cities. Melrose Avenue, Hollywood Boulevard, Rodeo Drive, and the Venice Boardwalk most famously represent these iconic distinctions in Los Angeles. Yet commercialism does not follow one uniform path, not even on commercial streets located in direct walking distance from one another in the same community. Focusing on the contrasting cases of the Venice Boardwalk and Abbot Kinney Boulevard details two ways in which Venice's historic bohemianism, once defined as an alternative and artistic lifestyle, became commercialized through the use of distinct economic symbols and performances. Whereas the boardwalk has emerged as a bohemian theme park and an integrative milieu for the masses, nearby Abbot Kinney Boulevard has become a fashionable bohemia, incorporating amenities for the wealthy at the direct exclusion of lower-income groups.

Chapter 5 examines a case where racial, ethnic, and socioeconomic diversity has been stabilized through a public-space informal economy. On the Venice Boardwalk, homeless men and women, immigrants of different racial and ethnic backgrounds, African Americans, artists, and carnival performers collectively uphold an economic role in the boardwalk's identity as a Free Speech Zone, notwithstanding forty years of political and legal battles to restrain public space vending to no avail by politicians, police officers, district attorneys, rent-paying merchants, developers, and homeowners.

Chapter 6 examines how commercial gentrification produces spatial exclusivity and redraws neighborhood boundaries. Abbot Kinney Boulevard was a mixing ground for distinct racial, ethnic, and socioeconomic groups for several decades. The complementary actions of a new merchants association, savvy real estate brokers, new developers, creative retailers, and a growing supply of upscale clientele blended together into the street's new fashionable bohemianism, constituted by independent stores, ethically produced goods, and an overarching arts and crafts ideal. Their parallel actions reinforce a new symbiotic relationship between Oakwood and Abbot Kinney Boulevard. The thriving retail artery has served as a symbolic force in Oakwood's gentrification, and new wealthier residents have participated in the street's commercial revival, normalizing the exclusion of Oakwood's more established and lower-income residents from the upscale commercial setting.

In the concluding chapter, "The Future of the American City," I review the central themes of the book and draw wider implications from this study. I discuss how demographic, political, and economic forces specific to metropolitan regions become compressed into local neighborhood public cultures. This approach to neighborhood stability and change highlights the intersections of both macro- and microprocesses that shape the distinctions within and between cities. This chapter ends by addressing the contradictory narratives about contemporary urban life in places like Venice, where the celebration of diversity takes hold at the same time that middle-class definitions of urban order promote new definitions of quality of life.

CHAPTER ONE

A Beach Town in Transition

A t the turn of the twentieth century, private developers transformed
Los Angeles from rural settlements, marshlands, valleys, and hills
into named subdivisions where they saw economic potential.[1] By the
1920s, the construction of interurban and streetcar lines opened up a
new possibility for dispersed communities built upon a "suburban ideal"
of the single-family home.[2] The demise of L.A.'s public transportation
system over the next three decades further distanced the relationship between the center of the city and its periphery.[3] While annexation of independently planned communities geographically expanded municipal
authority, communities were still differentiated by varied natural landscapes of beaches, foothills, and valleys, all of which became loosely integrated into an ever-expanding regional freeway system.[4]

Geographers of Southern California have repeatedly drawn attention
to the region's sprawling spatial organization.[5] However, as Los Angeles increased in territory during the second half of the twentieth century,
large-scale population shifts, influential countercultural movements, and
political-economic power brokers also transformed how people became
positioned against others within neighborhoods and between them. In
particular since the 1970s, immigration, homelessness, and gentrification solidified the diverse composition of Los Angeles as a sprawling and
scattered urban ecology of competing interests over space and over the
control of neighborhood public cultures.

This chapter addresses two historical tensions between the macrotran-
sitions of Los Angeles in general and the microtransitions of Venice in
particular. The first part of the chapter details the rise and fall of Venice
as an independent municipality in the context of the mounting power of
the city of L.A. During the early 1900s, Venice developed a reputation

for seaside amusements and was a key part of a growing commercial and entertainment ecology of independent communities along the coast.[6] Yet after consolidation with the city of Los Angeles and the overwhelming effects of the Great Depression, Venice fell into a period of disinvestment and decline, leading its reputation to transform from the "Coney Island of the Pacific" into the "slum by the sea." The second part of the chapter outlines how this economic decline created new opportunities for different groups to converge in Venice and define neighborhood public cultures. Although Venice became widely recognized for countercultural trends and bohemian lifestyles, it was also a rapidly changing coastal community where many different groups vied for prominence. More accurately, Venice transformed into a contested bohemia, a site of major confrontations over development, uses of public spaces, and ongoing tensions between sustaining diversity and generating exclusivity.

The Coney Island of the Pacific

Venice began as an independently planned and financed community. Abbot Kinney, born in 1850 into a wealthy tobacco family, inherited a substantial fortune. As an asthmatic, he followed a trend of moving to Southern California in hopes of improving his health. In Los Angeles, Kinney immersed himself in several different ventures, ranging from scientific to economic. He was an agriculturalist, served as the president of the Southern California Academy of the Sciences, and bought and sold property in downtown Los Angeles.[7] After convincing the Santa Fe Railroad to open up a terminal in the southern end of Santa Monica, Kinney sought to develop the coastal area.[8]

Kinney's inheritance coupled with subsequent successes buying and selling property enabled him to make an indelible mark on the Southern California coastline. He and partner Francis G. Ryan purchased a tract south of the city of Santa Monica and developed property to attract buyers. They called it Ocean Park, a label that remains today as the section of Santa Monica that borders Venice. After Ryan's death, Kinney and a new set of partners disagreed over the future direction of the area. They split the land and parted ways. Kinney controlled an undeveloped section of the Ballona Wetlands, a coastal marshland south of Ocean Park.[9]

Abbot Kinney had big dreams. He hired architects Norman Marsh and Clarence Russell, who modeled a new city after Venice, Italy. They planned to drain the marshes, create an extensive canal system, and construct buildings with arches and columns. Kinney hoped to make this seaside attraction the "Venice of America," a center of high culture where the Chautauqua, a popular educational and cultural movement of the late nineteenth and early twentieth centuries that originated in upstate New York, would serve as a model for organizing musical performances, artistic exhibits, and noted speakers for a creative and intellectual community.[10] An astute capitalist looking to increase his wealth, Kinney pursued alternatives when his cultural assemblies lost money.

During this period, white working- and middle-class people, not the cultural elites to whom Kinney hoped to appeal, were flocking to Los Angeles. In the early 1900s, Los Angeles mostly lured white migrants from the Midwest looking for new financial opportunities. Between 1900 and 1930, Los Angeles County grew in territory at a rate of 40 percent per year and its total population multiplied by thirteen. With such a vast expansion, Los Angeles became the most Anglo metropolis in the United States.[11] Two amusement hubs built in the area, the Ocean Park Pier, directly north of Venice, and the Pleasure Pier in Santa Monica, just north of Ocean Park, were meeting the cultural demands of this growing population of working- and middle-class whites.

Kinney altered his themed focus to satisfy the tastes of the masses and compete with nearby beach attractions in an emerging commercial ecology. He brought in the Lewis and Clark Centennial Exposition with roller coasters, a fun house, a Ferris wheel, an indoor swimming pool, and a range of carnival sideshows.[12] The amusement atmosphere also became an emblem of popular culture, commonly serving as the setting for major silent films of the era. Charlie Chaplin's first performance of what would eventually become his famed Little Tramp persona took place in the comedy short *Kid Auto Races at Venice*, while parts of his more critically acclaimed film *The Circus* were shot on the Venice Amusement Pier a decade later. Mack Sennett, Buster Keaton, and many of the Keystone Comedy capers were also recorded in the vicinity of the Venice Boardwalk.[13]

During this period, Venice had such a high degree of homogeneity that it did not even house a Catholic church. Most people who lived along the sixteen miles of canals in the early 1900s, a much more elaborate system of man-made waterways than the six waterways that remain today, were either proprietors of businesses on or near the pier or were vacationers who stayed in small, inexpensive, and poorly constructed wooden bungalows. Many stayed only during the summer months, as houses had poor insulation, and commuted to their jobs downtown along the Venice Short Line of the Pacific Electric Railway.[14]

The only site of nonwhite residents was a small area north of the canals. It was a mostly undeveloped section that lacked waterways and public attractions and received little public attention. Abbot Kinney welcomed several African American families to settle in this tract, because they could serve as a nearby labor pool. He permitted them to build houses and open up small service businesses, and in doing so, established early conditions for the growth of a home-owning black community, anchoring what would become a persistent trend toward racial diversity in this section of Venice that eventually became the neighborhood of Oakwood. Allowing the settlement of African Americans was a basic economic investment for Kinney, as many were influential in shaping Venice's carnival identity.[15] Nonetheless, African Americans, whose sweat and ingenuity helped build Venice's infrastructure and propel its popular identity, were still not welcome to participate in public events on the famous amusement pier due to the racial climate of the time.[16]

"Place entrepreneurs" like Kinney, wealthy men who were seeking to maximize profits by creating distinct towns in Southern California,[17] transformed the Los Angeles coastline into a competitive seaside commercial ecology, marketing their beachfront entertainment resorts to the public. In weekly flyers and newsletters, the Kinney Company pitched Venice as "a picturesque, modernized replica of the ancient Italian Venice," "the acropolis of fun seekers," and "Atlantic City's only rival."[18] As owners of amusement piers vied for the biggest and best rides, games, and contests, the media labeled Venice as "The Coney Island of the Pacific." Historian Kevin Starr notes that Venice was the earliest themed environment in a metropolis that greatly popularized this urban planning genre in following decades.[19] But even with Italian-style architecture, miles of canals, and a Coney Island–like boardwalk, popular enthusiasm for Venice of America soon faded.

Annexation and Decline

Los Angeles continued to grow in population and territory. Between 1906 and 1930, the city held seventy-three annexation elections and increased its size from 43 to 442 square miles.[20] Ocean Park consolidated with the growing city of Santa Monica, but Venice remained an independent town. In search of a beach within its official limits, Los Angeles city officials urged the Venice community to join the expanding metropolis. Residents and merchants, having experienced substantial economic setbacks, considered the possibility. Prohibition instituted in 1920 generated a great deal of turmoil, forcing a number of establishments out of business.[21] In the same year, Abbot Kinney died. The president and major financier of the Abbot Kinney Company, he had invested a fortune in building and maintaining Venice, remaining central in almost all local operations, including the organization of municipal needs. Kinney's death created a great deal of uncertainty and turmoil about how to finance and manage existing conditions. Several weeks later, the Windward Avenue Pier, a main source of income and employment in Venice, was destroyed in a fire that resulted in $1.5 million in property damages.[22]

These setbacks aggravated an already complex set of municipal problems. Residents had limited access to drinkable water—a common complaint made by dwellers in independent towns—attributed to the expensive and complex irrigation engineering required in Southern California. They faced complications with waste disposal, as Venice's private sewage plant, initially constructed for a much smaller population, often overflowed and forced the state to quarantine the beach and ocean. In addition, the city of Los Angeles dumped untreated sewage along the coast, which exacerbated health risks at Venice Beach.[23]

A number of local interest groups believed that annexation with Los Angeles would alleviate these problems, but a powerful few wanted to preserve Venice's independence because they were still profiting from the control of local resources and feared that enforcement of L.A.'s blue laws on amusements, cafés, and dance halls would put an end to their dominance. Between 1919 and 1925, a battle ensued over the future of Venice, with residents considering three possibilities: remaining independent, consolidating with Santa Monica, or consolidating with Los Angeles. Movements and organizations waxed and waned during this period, leading to major confrontations about how to move forward. On one hand, residents feared that consolidation with Santa Monica would create backroom compromises between commercial entities in each of the two cities that would ultimately keep Venice's power structure in place and overlook residential demands. On the other hand, they

thought Los Angeles was big enough that Venice's commercial interests would be unable to manipulate city officials. Instead, they believed
Los Angeles leaders would alleviate many of the local problems through
a fairer government system, strict moral laws on commercial activity,
and substantial resources to improve quality of life. After years of conflict, residents voted narrowly for annexation to the city of Los Angeles
in 1925.[24]

Following annexation, Los Angeles city officials failed to follow
through on extensive promises to resolve resident concerns, and the
community's infrastructure further deteriorated. With the Los Angeles
rail system in decline, the city hired a contractor to pave over the canals,
Venice's most distinctive planning feature, in order to make room for au-
tomobiles.[25] During the Great Depression, the remaining mostly undeveloped tract of canals was unable to support a tax assessment and the
contractor never finished the job.[26] Leaving the southern subdivision of
canals in place has continued to demarcate this series of six waterways
from its surroundings as a distinct neighborhood.

By 1929, Venice residents, like people across the nation, were suf-
fering monumental economic setbacks that eventually turned into the
Great Depression. A string of economic responses and government failures pushed Venice's infrastructure and natural resources into a state of
disrepair. At the tail end of an enthusiastic oil rush in Southern California, with successful drilling along the coast at Huntington Beach, Long
Beach, and Ventura, the Ohio Oil Company drilled directly beyond Venice's barren southern border, the future site of Marina del Rey.[27] Striking
oil led to a mad rush to profit under harsh economic circumstances. It was
devastating to the natural scenery and to the popular amusements, and it
also provided little economic security for locals. Most of the oil dried up
quickly and the derricks furnished the beachfront with a noisy and pol-
luting eyesore for the following four decades (see figure 2).[28] Moreover,
sewage dumping continued to contribute to ocean and beach contami-
nation. To cap it off, Venice's housing stock and public structures were
poorly maintained. By the 1940s, the sidewalks in the neighborhood of
the Venice Canals were caving into sluggish waterways, leading the city
to post signs that prohibited public access. These sidewalk conditions
would remain until the 1990s. The amusement pier, reconstructed after
the 1920 fire, was also officially declared unsafe by the city.

Whereas the amusement environment was the backdrop of a new age
in silent films, the deteriorating conditions of the 1940s and '50s emerged

FIGURE 2. Oil derricks on the beach. Photograph by Herman Schultheis. Copyright Los Angeles Public Library.

as a perfect setting for noir film and literature. Orson Welles's classic *Touch of Evil* was filmed throughout Venice. The acclaimed author Ray Bradbury, who initially moved to Venice with his family as a teenager in the 1940s, portrayed the waning coastal theme park in the vivid opening description of Venice, the setting of *Death Is a Lonely Business*:

> Venice, California in the old days had much to recommend it to people who liked to be sad. It had fog almost every night and along the shore the moan-

ing of the oil machinery and the slap of dark water in the canals and the hiss of sand against the windows of your house when the wind came up and sang among the open places and along the empty walks.

Those were the days when the Venice pier was falling apart and dying in the sea and you could find there the bones of a vast dinosaur, the roller-coaster, being covered by the shifting tides.

At the end of the one long canal you could find old circus wagons that had been rolled and dumped, and in the cages, at midnight, if you looked, things lived—fish and crayfish moving with the tide; and it was all the circuses of time somehow gone to doom and rusting away.[29]

When the Kinney Company's lease on the pier ran out in 1946, having lost their clout to control the future of the local environment, the pier was condemned and demolished.[30] Left behind were crumbling remnants of a popular themed environment. These conditions were not particular to Venice. Abandonment and decay were sweeping through American urban neighborhoods, leading city leaders and urban planners to call such places "urban slums." Public financing of housing developments and highways gave way to the massive new residential construction of modern suburbs and lured the middle classes away from places like Venice. As many departed, others without the same resources, including those opposed to the popular suburban lifestyle, moved into the dilapidated housing structures. Bohemian groups, made up of artists, poets, musicians, and others defining themselves in contrast to their own stereotypes of American middle-class conformity, sought out places where rent was cheap and moral constraints over presentation of self were few. As vibrant countercultural movements seeped into the American consciousness— beat and hippie movements the most visible—specific locales like Venice offered nurturing habitats as bohemian enclaves.

Three Successive Bohemian Movements

One of the opening scenes of Oliver Stone's film *The Doors* introduces viewers to Venice Beach of the early 1960s, where a young Jim Morrison sits on the sand talking with keyboardist Ray Manzarek. Living near the beach, Morrison had been greatly influenced by the local beat culture, transitioning from a wannabe filmmaker who attended UCLA film school into an invisible poet along the coast. Morrison recites a verse of "Moonlight Drive" to Manzarek, who is immediately enamored with his friend's writing and singing ability. One of the most influential musical groups of the era was born out of this interaction, made possible by the concentration of the Southern California bohemian lifestyle in this beachfront setting.

The California coastline became a sought-after bohemian destination a decade earlier, beginning in the 1950s.[31] Although San Francisco was synonymous with West Coast countercultural movements, it was the coastline itself and, perhaps more significantly, the movement between various locales that most signified the bohemian lifestyle. Mobility has always been a central feature of American bohemianism. Hobos of the late nineteenth and early twentieth centuries lived a mobile existence, hopping freight trains and constructing squatter settlements around railroad work sites. The beat culture of the '50s, most famously represented in Kerouac's *On the Road*, was similar to the hobo way of life in that it incorporated transience, temporary employment, and the cultivation of a philosophical and creative expression that countered mainstream norms.[32]

People hitchhiked and traveled up and down the West Coast. Places such as Topanga, Ocean Park, and Venice were centers of a new Southern California standard of living structured around the scenic if dilapidated oceanfront scenery. Between the 1950s and 1970s, hitchhikers, rubber tramps (those living in their vehicles), musicians, poets, activists, artists, free-spirited hippies, and others opting at least temporarily to live outside of the American mainstream developed cultural attachments to the Pacific Coast. Venice, with its abandoned boardwalk and deteriorating infrastructure, was also a major stopping point for students, young dropouts, and veterans of the Korean War and subsequently Vietnam War. They "crashed" at strangers' "pads" or found other temporary arrangements, sleeping in garages, crowding into run-down beach cottages, setting up tents in parks, on the beach, or in one of the many abandoned lots along the canals, or living in cars, vans, buses, and RVs.

The transient way of life did not stop bohemian writers, artists, and activists from promoting their status to others, stabilizing their attachment to certain places. Three successive movements, employing grassroots cultural and political activities, solidified Venice's popular bohemian identity. The first was the beat movement, which spread across the nation in the 1950s. Beatnik enclaves were comparable to the Hobohemias of earlier decades, where a noticeable concentration of services and resources met the interests and needs of transient hobos in the ur-ban center.[33] Famous beatnik enclaves surfaced in San Francisco's North Beach, New York's Greenwich Village, and Venice in Los Angeles. In Venice, resistance against mainstream ideals and economic trends was recognizable to visitors and newcomers through coffee shops and cafés, jazz performances, poetry readings, and other organized cultural events, public interactions on the boardwalk, and the publishing of local news-papers, leaflets, and books.

Writer Lawrence Lipton, the author of *The Holy Barbarians*, a de-tailed account of the beatnik lifestyle and identity in Venice published in 1959, brought many of the young local talent together through discus-sions and poetry readings at his home near the Venice Boardwalk.[34] Ac-cording to historian John Arthur Maynard, Lipton promoted "Venice West" on the radio and helped launch the opening of the Gas House in a former bingo parlor on the Venice Boardwalk, which served as an art gallery, coffee house, community center, and performance space that at-tracted as many as two thousand people to open poetry readings and jazz sessions.[35] The Gas House and subsequently the Venice West Café, located closer to the northern end of the boardwalk on Dudley Avenue and a popular haunt for Jim Morrison and Ray Manzarek in the '60s,[36] were centers of bohemian culture. The *Los Angeles Times*, *Newsweek*, *Time*, and *Life* magazines, and Lipton's controversial book, attracted national attention and popularly redefined Venice as a locale for the unconventional.

After the beatniks, individuals continued to find solace in Venice's scenic coastal location, inexpensive rent, and lively public cultures along what Lawrence Lipton described as "green-scum-covered canals" and a "sea-rotted" boardwalk.[37] The beat movement, largely built upon a phi-losophy of disengagement, faded with the rise of the '60s counterculture, as a new search for equal rights, built upon ideals promulgated by civil rights, feminist, and antiwar movements, made protest the centerpiece of a new cultural and political opposition against the status quo. According to Rick Davidson, a Venice activist during the '60s, there was a symbi-otic relationship between the larger national movements and grassroots activism to fight against inequality in local neighborhoods. He said, "As soon as we decided to take the question of war into the neighborhoods we immediately found you then have to be involved in local areas. The first thing you have to do is sort of deal with where they are at that time, which is wanting to fight a freeway or dealing with code enforcement."[38]

Activists like Davidson and John Haag, along with a number of other men and women, created the Peace and Freedom Party in Venice in 1968, a radical left-wing political organization "opposed to war, racism, and poverty."[39] With headquarters on West Washington Boulevard, renamed Abbot Kinney Boulevard in the late 1980s, "a small group of civil rights and anti-Vietnam War activists did much of the work that began the ambitious task of putting a new political party on the ballot."[40] Turning to local affairs, this group established the *Free Venice Beachhead*, an independent neighborhood newspaper comparable to the more widespread *Los Angeles Free Press*, to expose local social and political inequalities. The Peace and Freedom Party and the *Beachhead* quickly materialized as important local institutions, criticizing the Vietnam War, opposing incoming economic development along the coast, supporting artistic causes, and pushing a "Free Venice" movement for "community control of community affairs."[41] Still in existence today, the party and its paper have provided enduring outlets for a relatively small number of Venice activists to promote anticapitalist, socialist, and pacifist agendas to the rest of the community and integrate newcomers sympathetic to their causes.

Many of the hippies were artists who linked together art and politics. For example, the Fine Art Squad created political murals that still color buildings throughout Venice. These artists were not integrated into the art world nor did they pursue a status-seeking career that contributed to national and international dialogue. Nevertheless, as these politically oriented bohemians continued their work, well-connected and influential artists also moved in and reinvented Venice's bohemian stage once more.

By the early 1960s, the Ferus Gallery on La Cienega in Hollywood had gained a foothold in the national and international visual art circuit. In addition to launching the careers of Los Angeles artists such as Robert Irwin, Edward Kienholz, Ed Moses, and Edward Ruscha, it was the site of Andy Warhol's first solo exhibition in 1962. The Ferus was the promotional core of the Los Angeles "Cool School,"[42] but the cheap rent for large inexpensive lofts and reasonable living costs of Venice made it a residential haven for artists who wanted to live a bohemian life. Artist Chuck Arnoldi recounted, "Downtown, all I got was cheap rent—no street life. I suffocated in summer and froze in winter. In Venice, the air was fresh, I rented a 12,000-square-foot loft for almost nothing, and it was a place beyond the law. The more space the more freedom. Big lofts have an influence on what you produce."[43]

In addition to Arnoldi, artists such as Billy Al Bengston, Robert Graham, Robert Irwin, Ed Moses, Edward Ruscha, Guy Dill, and Laddie John Dill established a prominent, albeit very masculine, art community by the beach. These artists were connected to the biggest names in the art world. Laddie John Dill relocated to Venice during the late '60s. Soon after, he met Jasper Johns while working at the Gemini publishing workshop in Hollywood. Dill moved to New York where he initially stayed in Johns's studio, and then lived with Robert Rauschenberg before returning to Venice where he settled. As local artists became more famous, many like Dill purchased larger studios, continued to work in Venice, and reinforced the area's artistic identity as their own reputations transcended local and even national boundaries.[44]

Artists living in Venice during the 1970s played a part in shaping the Light and Space movement in Southern California, and galleries such as ACE and L.A. Louver, still a top gallery today, promoted Los Angeles artists and strengthened connections to New York and pop art.[45] These up-and-coming visual artists brought a great deal of recognition to this struggling area, becoming known as the "Venice Beach mafia."[46] The *Los Angeles Times* reported in 1976,

> If anyplace can be considered the art capital of Los Angeles, this is it. There are dozens of painters and sculptors working away in their lofts and studios, some of them among the top artists in the West. Some of these artists are a little bit like the old Hole in the Wall Gang. They're hard to find if you don't have an invitation. And they don't take too kindly to strangers. . . . In Venice, what appears to be a deserted warehouse, or an old auto repair shop destined for merciful demolition, frequently turns out to be both home and workshop for a highly successful artist.[47]

During this period of Venice's reinvention of the meaning of bohemianism, Los Angeles's population continued to grow. Beginning in the '70s, a massive influx of Latino and Asian immigrants converted Los Angeles into one of the most racially and ethnically diverse cities in the world. Yet a prior history of restrictive housing covenants, white flight, and redlining practices continued to influence the segregation of African Americans, even after the passing of the Fair Housing Act in 1968. Moreover, by the early '80s, the rapidly growing homeless population throughout L.A. made encounters with visible poverty on the street a common experience. Later chapters will discuss how new associations, separations, and tensions between different populations became central to the specific neighborhood public cultures of Venice, exploring these changes through the voices and life experiences of local African Americans, Latinos, countercultural residents, homeless men and women, and gentrifiers alike. The remainder of this chapter provides a more general outline of how key demographic forces affected both Los Angeles and Venice and set the stage for neighborhood divisions and intergroup configurations that I explore in closer detail throughout the remainder of the book.

Race, Ethnicity, and Poverty

Bohemian countercultures have historically and strategically stood ideologically opposed to conventional professional careers, while racial and ethnic minorities have been disproportionately excluded from these same paths to success. Yet because of the similar class positions of bohemians and racial-ethnic minorities in the United States, bohemian cultures are commonly located close to African American and immigrant residential settings. The postwar period, up until the 1970s, re-created Venice as bohemian and black, a "run-down" district that was "something between a ghetto and a hippie haven, with social problems on both counts," as architectural critic Reyner Banham once described it.[48] Bohemianism drove Venice's popular reputation as African Americans became concentrated in a neighborhood in the center of Venice ultimately known as Oakwood.

African Americans

Population expansion and industrial growth after the Great Depression altered L.A.'s demographic and economic landscape. Between 1930 and 1940, the city's population increased by almost 600,000, and its aircraft industry provided Los Angeles with an early advantage in the growth of a wartime economy during World War II. According to sociologist Janet Abu-Lughod, "[By] 1939 Los Angeles County not only remained the first-ranking county in the country in agricultural wealth and income, but stood first in the production of airplanes and motion pictures, second in auto assembling and rubber tires and tubes, third in furniture production and retail trade, fourth in women's apparel, and fifth in overall value of industrial production."[49]

Los Angeles witnessed a dramatic transition in its demographic composition as people of color escaped the hostile racial climate of the South in search of newfound opportunities and freedoms. The African American population of Los Angeles numbered about 39,000 in 1930, quadrupled to over 171,000 by 1950, and quadrupled again to over 760,000 by 1970.[50] During this period, restrictive covenants and white flight forced most African Americans to settle in segregated residential districts. By the 1940s, for instance, Watts in South Central transformed from a white neighborhood into the most prominent black section of Los Angeles.[51]

According to historian Eric Avila, white flight was a key source of this transition, producing highly segregated black neighborhoods in Los Angeles by the 1950s. He quotes a Los Angeles County Commission of Human Relations report conducted during this time: "Of the 334,916 Negroes living in the city of Los Angeles . . . 313,866 or 93.7 percent live in the Central District." In addition, "of the 12,297 blacks who lived outside of Watts, 10,860 'have simply joined members of their race in the segregated areas of San Pedro, Venice, and Pacoima.'"[52] The combination of continuing residential segregation, population growth, white flight, and its relationship to surrounding white neighborhoods along the coast transformed Venice's Oakwood neighborhood into L.A.'s most visible black locale along the coast.

When the Douglas, North American, and Hughes aircraft companies opened factories on the West Side of Los Angeles, the increase in available jobs resulted in the rise of a working-class population in Venice, including a significant growth in the number of African Americans. Due to restrictive housing covenants, African Americans were limited in where they could reside on L.A.'s West Side. Abbot Kinney had already permitted a number of African American families to build houses and move into a subsection of the community, now called Oakwood, which served as a foundation for black population growth in the neighborhood. In 1912, there were only 33 African Americans living in this section of Venice. The black population increased to 330 by 1940, tripled to 1,133 by 1950, and tripled again to 3,191 by 1960. The number of African Americans residing in Oakwood continued to increase until 1970. Although this two census tract area of Oakwood never became a majority black neighborhood, multiple streets were predominantly filled with

TABLE 1. **Growth of African American population in Oakwood in relation to total Venice population, 1940–2009**

Year	Venice population	Oakwood population	Oakwood African American population
1940	23,263	7,741	330 (4.3 %)
1950	28,891	9,004	1,133 (12.6%)
1960	38,365	8,228	3,191 (38.8%)
1970	35,868	8,152	3,660 (44.9%)
1980	36,553	8,962	2,675 (29.9%)
1990	40,040	9,216	2,041 (22.2%)
2000	37,758	8,536	1,371 (16.1%)
2005–2009	36,373	7,299	1,184 (16.2%)

Source: United States Census, 1940–2000; American Community Survey 2005–2009.
Note: In 1960, the geographic division of census tracts was slightly changed and the tracts were renumbered. The years 1940 and 1950 constitute a larger area and population than existed in the section now called Oakwood. I include these numbers to reflect an approximate transition in the size of Oakwood's African American population. Beginning in 1980, I use the category non-Hispanic black/African American to count African Americans, taking into account the shift in census classifications to distinguish between Hispanic and non-Hispanic populations. Data from 1940 to 2000 are from the United States Decennial Census. The 2005–2009 data are from the American Community Survey 5-Year Estimates, which relies upon responses collected from a random sample over a five-year period between January 2005 and December 2009 and represents the average characteristics over this period.

African American residents, leading city leaders, law enforcement officials, and the media to regularly refer to this area as the black section of Venice (see table 1).

Venice's status as a bohemian community with a historic black neighborhood set the stage for additional population shifts. A vast sea change in Los Angeles's ethnic composition followed the postwar expansion of the black population. The more recent arrival of Latino and Asian immigrants has complicated the historically pervasive black/white racial classification system in the United States.[53] Latinos moved into Venice, and particularly into Oakwood, in larger numbers than African Americans, and a wide range of immigrants from various nations became central to the boardwalk's newfound popularity, playing a key role in commercializing the area's bohemian public culture as entrepreneurs on both sides of the boardwalk.

Immigrants

Domestic migrants from outside of California, including many African Americans, were the main source of demographic change in Los Angeles prior to 1970. In 1970, while 43 percent of Los Angeles residents had been born in states other than California, only 11 percent were foreign born.[54] The demographic composition of Los Angeles was significantly transformed during the '70s. Once the most Anglo metropolis in the United States, the expanding foreign-born population turned Los Angeles into a "prismatic metropolis," where racial and ethnic diversity became one of the city's most defining characteristics.[55]

The relationship between immigration and Southern California is part of a complicated history that is well documented by sociologists and historians. Legal pathways were opened to Mexican refugees during the Mexican Revolution in the early 1900s. Mexican laborers entered into the United States through the Bracero Program between the 1940s and 1960s, many staying and bringing family members with them. And immigrants and their families, especially skilled professionals, came into the country through the Hart-Celler Immigration and Nationality Act of 1965, which brought an end to long-standing quotas. In addition, social networks between immigrants and their native towns, cities, and villages led to escalating flows of undocumented men and women into the United States, especially from Mexico and Central America.[56]

Between 1970 and 1990, the proportion of foreign born in L.A.'s population tripled from 11 to 33 percent, as both Latino and Asian immigrants took advantage of new openings.[57] The Hispanic population increased from 400,000 to 2.8 million, likely an underestimate given the steady stream of undocumented immigrants. Three-quarters of them were of Mexican origin, and most other Latinos came from El Salvador or Guatemala.[58] By 2000, Latinos had grown to 47 percent of the city's population and outnumbered African Americans by three to one.[59]

Latinos have settled in a wide range of districts throughout the city. Nonetheless, the poorest immigrants have historically moved into low-income African American neighborhoods.[60] Despite the fact that Latinos are the largest minority group in L.A., they have not always been able to translate numerical gains into political influence. For instance, as urban policy expert Dowell Myers explains, "In a demographic twist of voting power, the African American residents of Compton who had been dominated earlier by a white minority of the local population were now a minority themselves, and in similar fashion, they were dominating the rising Latino majority."[61] Even as Latinos flooded the region and Los Angeles elected its first Latino mayor since the early twentieth century, the public continues to identify Latino majority neighborhoods such as Watts and Compton as "black."

Oakwood provides a microcosm of this changing racial-ethnic para-

TABLE 2. **Growth of Latino population in Venice and in the Oakwood neighborhood,**
1970–2009

Year	Venice population	Venice Latino population	Oakwood population	Oakwood Latino population
1970	35,868	8,145 (22.7%)	8,152	2,635 (32.3%)
1980	36,553	8,759 (24.0%)	8,962	4,032 (45.0%)
1990	40,040	9,445 (23.6%)	9,216	4,570 (49.6%)
2000	37,758	8,195 (21.7%)	8,536	4,065 (47.6%)
2005–2009	36,373	5,756 (15.8%)	7,299	2,388 (32.7%)

Source: United States Census, 1970–2000; American Community Survey 2005–2009.

digm, comparable to these more famous historic African American places. The Latino population, the largest minority population in overall Venice at least dating back to the 1960s,[62] multiplied over the course of several decades as shown in table 2. By 1980, Latinos overtook African Americans as the largest segment of the population in Oakwood, but were still unable to translate their sheer numbers into collective influence over the neighborhood public culture.

Latinos have been unable to exert collective influence in nonblack residential neighborhoods as well. In 1980, the city designated a neighborhood filled with Korean businesses along Olympic Boulevard as Koreatown even though Koreans only comprised a small proportion of the residential population compared to Latinos.[63] Despite their smaller numbers, Asians have emerged as a major component in the Los Angeles economic landscape.

Unlike Latinos, many Asians have arrived to the United States as members of the middle class, which gives them a more immediate advantage in developing entrepreneurial opportunities.[64] Korean small family businesses, for example, grew rapidly after 1970. According to sociologists Light and Bonacich, the 1980 census showed that "22.5 percent of Koreans in Los Angeles were self-employed or unpaid family workers," which made them three times more likely to be entrepreneurs than non-Koreans.[65] This high rate of self-employment has served as the foundation for the growth of Korean businesses in low-income neighborhoods traditionally abandoned by large commercial investors.[66]

The boardwalk, which for decades was a site of unstable rent-paying businesses and high crime rates, has become a place where the Los Angeles immigrant economy is on display. Korean businesses have prospered and multiplied on the inland side of the boardwalk since the 1980s, often employing Mexican workers. The beach side of the boardwalk has since grown into a world-famous informal economy that integrates many different groups, including Asian, African, Latino, and Caribbean immigrants, as well as African Americans trying to make money from the rent-free business opportunities. But it is not only immigration and racial-ethnic disparities that shape the boardwalk's identity. Homelessness has also emerged as a central characteristic of the boardwalk and the adjacent Rose Avenue section of Venice.

Homelessness

The Los Angeles landscape is one of the many stars of the film *The Soloist*, based upon a book of the same name by *Los Angeles Times* reporter Steve Lopez. The film follows the unlikely connection between Lopez and schizophrenic, homeless musical prodigy Nathaniel Anthony Ayers. Besides providing a glimpse into the difficulties of a man with a mental disorder living on the street, the film offers viewers unfamiliar with the city and its vast homeless population some of the most striking footage. Thousands of homeless people are pressed together into a few city blocks in downtown L.A. In a 2005 visit to skid row, Los Angeles mayor Antonio Villaraigosa described the look and feel of this area to Lopez: "I mean, that almost looked like Bombay or something, except with more violence. . . . There is no place [in the city] where the chaos and the degradation are as pronounced. You see a complete breakdown of society."[67]

The homeless population in the region has multiplied since the late 1970s, readily exposing people to the daily conditions of poverty. During the '80s, when people started to pay more attention to the street presence of the homeless in the United States, estimates of the number of people across the nation living without a home ranged from 350,000 to 3 million.[68] This range demonstrated the difficult task of accurately calculating how many people are homeless on any given night. Despite the imprecision of this count, researchers uniformly agree that the United States witnessed a dramatic increase in the number of people living on the streets as well as a far greater demand for social services beginning in the 1980s.[69]

According to urban planner Jennifer Wolch, the '80s brought about seismic shifts in how federal, state, and city governments dealt with the poor in general, making them more likely to become homeless. It transformed Los Angeles into the city with the largest homeless population in the nation. Wolch shows how social spending greatly declined in the early '80s, as tens of thousands of welfare recipients lost their benefits. Health care and mental health services were also cut significantly. She finds that 43,000 patients lost health care services when the Los Angeles County Board of Supervisors restricted millions of dollars of support. Mental health clinics and federal welfare programs administered by the state were also closed during this time.[70]

Just as the need for more affordable housing monumentally increased in the '80s and '90s, its availability greatly diminished and public housing funds all but disappeared. The loss of public support combined with the decline of affordable housing options gave rise to a homeless crisis in Los Angeles. Wolch and Dear note that as early as 1984, the U.S. Department of Housing and Urban Development labeled L.A. the nation's "homeless capital," counting somewhere between 31,300 and 33,800 homeless people.[71] According to the 2007 Los Angeles Homeless Services Authority Homeless Count, 40,144 people are homeless on any given night within the city and over 68,000 in the county. Estimates from the Los Angeles City Council during the mid-2000s put the number at closer to 90,000.

Most homeless have historically congregated in a single urban district known as skid row. Skid row in downtown L.A. is the site of Lopez's reporting, where a confluence of resources and institutions have provided aid to people living on the streets, drawing them to this area and keeping them out of other higher-income neighborhoods.[72] Yet the national, state, and local funding infrastructures for social services have increasingly relied upon decentralized private and nonprofit organizations, promoting the dispersion of homeless people throughout the city.[73]

In Los Angeles, the privatization of services coupled with recent economic renewal pressures in the blocks surrounding skid row forced many of the homeless to seek refuge beyond the traditional core, ending up on the streets of West Side communities such as Venice, Santa Monica, and Hollywood. Skid row still maintains the largest homeless concentration with 5,131, but this figure is just below 8 percent of the total homeless count. City Council District 11, which includes Venice, has 2,799 homeless people, a somewhat misleading number in that it does not include those in the independent city of Santa Monica—another 1,506—who readily move back and forth between there and Venice.[74]

Whereas bohemian transients have sought out Venice's coastal location, some identifying with its reputation for art and tolerance, most of the homeless in Venice are drawn to a combination of limited restrictions on overnight parking for those living in vehicles and expanding nonprofit social service agencies in the vicinity that receive both public and private funding. Others are drawn to economic opportunities in the boardwalk's complex tourist economy, which has further contributed to the rise of Venice as a homeless center. The public culture between the Venice Boardwalk and Lincoln Boulevard along Rose Avenue has most noticeably emerged as the focal point for the homeless debate in Venice, leading some locals to label the area "Skid Rose."[75] Even as racial, ethnic, and socioeconomic diversity became central to Venice's identity, people rediscovered the economic potential of the coast. From urban renewal programs to residential and commercial gentrification, the rich and poor have become increasingly positioned in close proximity to one another.

Rediscovering the Coast

The wealthy residents of Los Angeles have historically concentrated in its scenic hills communities. Most famous is Beverly Hills, but Hollywood Hills, Holmby Hills, Bel Air, Brentwood, Pacific Palisades, and more recently Malibu rival this historic center for the rich and famous, giving rise to a complex ecology of affluence. As urban historian Robert Fishman points out, class distinctions in L.A., unlike in Chicago and New York, were not organized by the distance between the center of the city and its periphery. Instead, in a decentralized "suburban metropolis" with no cohesive connection between the periphery and the urban core, class distinctions were in large part characterized by elevation, or as Banham asserts, "the higher the ground the higher the income."[76] The scenic vistas, the mix of nature and proximate amenities, and the better air quality gave rise to some of the most exclusive and famous communities in the world, as the home to countless celebrities and entertainment moguls.

Many people might expect Southern California's coastal communities to correspond to wealth in a similar fashion as its picturesque hills, given the current status of such places as Newport Beach, Laguna Beach, and parts of Venice, Santa Monica, and Santa Barbara as homes to the rich and famous.[77] Most take it as a given that coastal land is now in high demand, believing that the current "limited supply" of coastal property is what caused its "higher values." Yet social scientists have repeatedly demonstrated that social and political processes create the symbolic and material designs of places that shape public perceptions of them as "in demand."[78]

For decades, Los Angeles coastal areas suffered from political disregard, economic disinvestment, and infrastructural decay. Demand for L.A.'s beachfront property required that middle- and upper-income people "rediscover" the benefits of living by the beach, which depended upon developers and politicians transforming coastal communities into an enticing habitat that met their standards of living. City officials took little interest in maintaining the Coney Island imagery of a coastal zone for the masses and instead began to envision and adopt new emblems of the Pacific Coast's economic potential.

In 1938, the Los Angeles Regional Planning Commission first proposed the construction of a pleasure boat harbor as a regional park located south of Venice. The plan did not come to fruition until the 1950s, when L.A. County officials adopted a proposal that would greatly accelerate revenue along the coast. The new Marina del Rey plan consisted of 4,700 high-density multiple-unit dwellings instead of a regional public park with widely available beach access.[79] The marina development was finally dedicated in 1965, having emerged out of barren marshes into a young-professional enclave, a tourist destination due to the construction of high-density hotels, and the largest man-made leisure boat harbor in the world.

The development of Marina del Rey coincided with a new shift in thought about solving problems of urban decay. The urban renewal programs that were becoming increasingly common throughout the United States during the 1940s and '50s generated serious controversy. Sociologist Herbert Gans's study of Boston's West End pointed out ulterior motives guiding city-instigated redevelopment programs that overshadowed the successful qualities of an "urban village" already in place.[80] Urban planners labeled such areas as "slums," using public resources to officially classify places with their negative attributes without taking into account that most urban dwellers, as Gans demonstrated, were hardworking, trying to make ends meet, and existing in social and economic orders that made such places safe and congenial to live in.

The Los Angeles coastline, after undergoing a dramatic process of economic disinvestment and infrastructural decay, but now incorporating a new marina development, was ripe for political and economic intervention. It is much easier, however, to construct a new community identity out of barren land, as was the case with Marina del Rey or for that matter the initial development of Venice in the early 1900s, than it is to reconstruct a community out of its existing infrastructure. In order to redevelop this segment of the Los Angeles coastline, political and economic interest groups first had to redefine Venice as a "slum by the sea" and argue that it operated below its economic potential.[81] Focused on the areas in Venice located west of Lincoln Boulevard, the Community Redevelopment Agency, the Los Angeles Department of City Planning, and the Haynes Foundation all conducted studies about renewal potential and reached similar conclusions. According to a 1947 Los Angeles Department of City Planning report,

> There are several blocks in the Venice section of Los Angeles close to the beach in which the housing is largely sub-standard. These flimsy structures were presumably built for summer vacation occupancy but for some years they have been used as permanent homes. The housing is not only sub-standard, in serious danger from fire and badly overcrowded . . . but the land is badly used because of the narrow lots, poor street layout, and its under-use in relation to its potentiality for beach rental property. Parts of the Venice area and the adjacent city of Santa Monica [particularly, Ocean Park], similarly jammed with shanties, are actually the most valuable tracts in the county.[82]

Using the term *shanties* to describe the insufficient housing infrastructure is striking in its class and race resonances. This bias became even more apparent by the 1960s, as real estate interests and city politicians united to establish a code enforcement program along the coast as a way to condemn older buildings, advocate for new aesthetic designs, and target specific local populations. Code enforcement filtered its way through Venice, impacting bohemian groups in the Canals and along the boardwalk, African Americans in Oakwood, and elderly Jewish residents of the north beach bordering Ocean Park. Between 1960 and 1965, the city condemned 446 buildings, including the beatnik gathering place, the Gas House, which was the very first building inspected.[83] The city required building owners to make over one thousand repairs, and officials distributed an additional ninety permits for new development projects, beginning an economic upgrading process.[84] In her celebrated ethnography of elderly Eastern European Jews, anthropologist Barbara Myerhoff recounts her subjects' description of this urban renewal process as a "second Holocaust."[85]

The code enforcement program brought together political and economic interests in an attempt to reshape Venice's image, targeting certain populations perceived to be damaging to it, especially countercultural and bohemian groups, while also directly affecting other lower-income populations, including African Americans, Latinos, and elderly Jews on fixed incomes. Yet urban renewal programs did not immediately revolutionize Venice's demographic makeup. Instead, grassroots activists— white countercultural residents and African Americans in particular— fought against the city's attempts to regulate housing and public activity, foreshadowing the way antigrowth resistance would stall the growth machine in Venice during the next several decades.

As new high-rise apartment and condominium developments in Marina del Rey and Santa Monica, bordering Venice to the south and north respectively, invigorated an ongoing interest in development along Venice's oceanfront, political organizing brought continued attention to a local antigrowth agenda. The Venice Town Council, which was created in the early 1970s by City Councilwoman Pat Russell, served the purpose of giving local residents a voice in the process of coastal change, and left-wing activists and other proponents of antidevelopment and antigrowth strategies joined forces and quickly took control.[86]

During the '70s, the state government also passed the California Coastal Act and created the California Coastal Commission in order to protect the state's coastal zone, an area one mile inland from the Pacific Ocean. In Venice, this area consists of the subdivision west of Lincoln Boulevard, the same area targeted by urban renewal efforts in prior decades. Local activists fought successfully for several years to halt large-scale development projects and make economic diversity and small-scale development a central priority of the coastal commission's decisions in Venice.

At the same time that high-density luxury development was being stalled by antigrowth activists, affordable housing advocates secured major victories and social service organizations expanded. During the 1970s, an African American community organization called Project Action received economic backing to construct and manage fourteen housing projects in Oakwood. Another nonprofit community housing developer, the Venice Community Housing Corporation, an organization that grew out of the countercultural activism of the 1960s and 1970s, constructed additional affordable housing complexes over the next two decades.

When the state's coastal commission first came into existence, affordable housing advocates tried to leverage collective momentum to protect housing prices and push for additional affordable housing projects. However, federal cuts in housing programs made it almost impossible to garner public resources. Moreover, the passing of the Mello Act in the early 1980s further complicated affordable housing debates. The 1982 Mello Act is a California state law set up to preserve affordable housing in the coastal zone by requiring the inclusion of affordable units below market rate in future development sites with more than ten units. Essentially mandating mixed-income development, the new legal standards have been difficult for city leaders to enforce. City authorities must review every project, and when development runs rampant, many go unchallenged. Under certain circumstances, developers claim that the inclusion of affordable units is simply not feasible. Hiring consultants to write reports to justify these claims, they negotiate with city council members to add extra lower-income apartments off site in future buildings, sometimes never following through on their promises.[87]

In addition, small-scale condominium conversions and the construction of single-family houses have been largely exempted from state and city planning regulations. This pattern of development has not produced the rapid influx of wealthier residents, as had occurred with the construction of high-rise buildings in bordering Marina del Rey and Santa Monica. Instead, the remaining single-family housing ideal coupled with smaller condominium conversions has changed Venice one building at a time, block by block, street by street, and neighborhood by neighborhood. New houses, condominiums, and retail spaces have gradually generated the living, working, and consumption conditions for a different class of residents.

Such changes to the area's infrastructure have propelled transitions in the social configurations within and between neighborhoods. Developers, real estate brokers, retailers, middle-class homeowners, and newer affluent residents have established the conditions for a slow economic upgrading process that has accumulated over time and crept its way across Venice. Nevertheless, instead of adjacent neighborhoods replicating the creation of the more exclusive public cultures of the Canals and Abbot Kinney Boulevard, a confluence of historical forces, stabilizing mechanisms, and demographic changes has sustained visible differences in the social and symbolic order of neighborhoods.

Conclusion

This chapter has focused on the social, economic, political, and cultural conditions that made it possible for Venice to become a prismatic community in a prismatic metropolis. The early decentralization of Los Angeles may have led observers to view it as a sprawling urban anomaly, but more recent cultural movements, population settlements, and political-economic interests have motivated ongoing social and political configurations within neighborhoods and between them. Venice is one place to explore the ongoing tensions between diversity and exclusivity on the ground.

Ethnographic and historical research on adjacent neighborhoods calls attention to how and why such places have changed in similar and different ways. The remainder of the book examines how historical shifts have shaped ground-level meanings and collective practices and given rise to political configurations between competing groups. While neighborhood stability operates as an alternative logic of consistency, power labeling by more affluent residents linking up with city administrators and law enforcement officers stigmatizes entire populations who occupy public spaces. In some cases, successive waves of newcomers redefine neighborhood public cultures by establishing neighborhood homologies between groups, symbols, and spaces that are built upon a cohesive logic of exclusivity. The next three chapters focus on distinct residential settings in Venice, beginning with the case of Oakwood, where African Americans have historically influenced the local territory even as the area has become increasingly Latino and white in its demographic composition.

CHAPTER TWO

The Transformation of a Black Neighborhood

A s I sit in the kitchen of my Venice apartment drinking coffee and reading a book, a deafening roar shakes the floors and walls, jarring me out of my concentration. At first, I am unsure if these are signs of an earthquake. The vibrations and racket continue, and I cautiously open the front door to see what is going on. I notice the shadow of a helicopter on the ground, and when I look up, one is flying so low that I can feel the breeze that it gives off and clearly read the letters L-A-P-D as it circles around.

Media helicopters soon join the LAPD air unit hovering over Venice, although they remain at a higher altitude. I walk several blocks, following the sound of police sirens that blast from the Oakwood area. By the time I arrive, officers have already set up blockades at each intersection. Cars are unable to travel into the area, and police officers stop those trying to leave, inspecting their trunks before they permit them to cross the police line. I walk along Fourth Street, the western perimeter of Oakwood, from California Avenue to Rose Avenue. On each corner I witness the same thing: small groups of white people congregating and observing from the periphery.

One woman waiting with her daughter is on her way back from the grocery store but has been forced to leave her packages in the car, which she parked on nearby Abbot Kinney Boulevard. Some take in the scene by photographing the swirling helicopters and police lines, radiating nervous excitement about their proximity to something potentially dangerous happening in their own neighborhood. As time wears on, some transform the event into a social activity and catch up with neighbors and friends.

People speculate as to the cause of this intense commotion disrupting the rhythm of daily life in Oakwood. I walk block by block, catching snippets of conversations. "Do you think someone was killed?" asks a white woman in her forties wearing a silky purple and pink flowered dress. "It wouldn't surprise me," responds a white man in his twenties, carrying a glossy blue and white fiberglass surfboard under his arm. "I've heard gun shots before. This used to be a violent place a bunch of years ago."

As I continue walking, I eventually encounter an officer whom I know and ask him about the situation. He says that a "male Hispanic student" was shot and killed near the Venice High School campus, and witnesses at the scene of the crime alleged that the shooter is an "African American male teenager" around the age of seventeen. Police officers immediately began searching Venice for the suspect, both through air surveillance and on the ground. Although the crime took place about two miles from Oakwood, they directed most of their attention on this neighborhood. While white and Latino residents are inconvenienced by the LAPD takeover of the neighborhood and concerned about its meaning, young African American men are the focus of the search. Lakesha Holt, an African American resident, said that she was at work and saw her house on television. She watched police officers rappel out of helicopters onto her roof and surround her house on all sides with guns drawn in search of her nephew whom they believed fit the description, despite the fact that the alleged shooter is seventeen and her nephew is in his thirties. Her youngest daughter, already home from school, was subjected to a military-style invasion of her house.

Coincidentally, Los Angeles city councilman Bill Rosendahl had already scheduled a town hall meeting at the Oakwood Recreation Center for that very evening to address issues stemming from race and class tensions. Modifying the program as a result of the shooting, he invites the Los Angeles Human Relations Commission, high-ranking officials from the LAPD Pacific Division, and gang intervention activists from Latino and African American community organizations throughout Los Angeles to join him at the meeting and quell rumors spreading on the streets of a possible racial conflict and gang war, a fear that sends shivers down the spines of residents who lived in Oakwood during the early 1990s when a ten-month war between African American and Latino gangs left seventeen dead and over fifty more shot and injured in this one-and-a-half-square-mile neighborhood.[1]

The meeting quickly becomes a space for African American residents to reaffirm their distrust of the LAPD. Of approximately one hundred people at the town hall meeting, about 70 percent of them are African American. There are fewer than ten Latinos, and those present are mostly activists from elsewhere in L.A. Remaining audience members are white residents. Dozens of people, all African Americans except for two, wait in line to address the panel of city officials. Elderly black men step up to the podium first. One after another, they call attention to emotional scars lingering from previous decades, publicly declaring that they were beaten and harassed by police officers. They condemn the current LAPD officials for these past attacks. Younger black activists, midthirties and early forties, follow them. Having grown up in Oakwood, they emphasize their distress about the lack of jobs and opportunities for African American youth, which, they contend, leads many to engage in a self-destructive street life. The crowd cheers enthusiastically what they believe is an important point, presenting a unified front of support for these public appeals.

In the midst of the proceedings, several outbursts heighten the possibility of full-fledged unrest, yet the combative tone is not between black and Latino attendees, but between white and black men. A black man in his thirties walks around the meeting with a video camera following a newer white resident in his forties, whom he accuses of racism. Lila Riley, an African American woman in her sixties with long gray dreadlocks, leans over to me and says that the white man is known as someone who regularly calls the police to complain about the gatherings of African Americans in Oakwood Park. The African American man holds the camera up to the white man and yells, "What do you think, white boy? What do you think now, white boy?" The latter, trying to escape the focus of the camera, scurries around the gym, yelling back at him, "Fuck you!" The tension escalates to pushing and shoving, but a few people jump up, including Lila, who quickly steps in and helps to break it up. LAPD officers request that the black man stop filming the event and ask the white man to leave.

About 7,300 people live in Oakwood.[2] For decades, residents and city officials have defined it as a black neighborhood. This public culture, cemented in community events like this one, masks a dramatic demographic transition that took place there between 1970 and 2010. In 1970, African Americans made up the largest racial-ethnic group in Oakwood at 45 percent of the population, with Latinos following at 32 percent.[3] By 1980, those proportions had been inverted. Latinos made up 45 percent of the population, followed by African Americans at 30 percent and non-Hispanic whites at 24 percent. The 2000 census showed that Latinos still made up the largest racial-ethnic group at 48 percent, but non-Hispanic whites now followed them at 33 percent, trailed by African Americans at 16 percent. According to the most recent census estimates (2005–2009), non-Hispanic whites have become the largest racial-ethnic group in Oakwood, making up 44 percent of the population, followed by Latinos at 33 percent and African Americans at 16 percent.

This chapter examines Oakwood's changing neighborhood public culture through the lens of race and ethnic relations. It looks at how African Americans stabilized a public culture in the face of Latino immigration and white gentrification. A history of residential segregation during the early twentieth century laid a foundation that later generations of African Americans built upon, sustaining and reinforcing the public culture through a solid institutional infrastructure, a culture of public interaction, labeling of spaces in honor or memory of community members, ceremonial and festive events, as well as other forms of political organizing and symbolic practices.

Focusing on the history of constraints and opportunities facing African Americans only addresses part of Oakwood's complicated story, however. Because Latinos made up the largest segment of the neighborhood for several decades, this chapter considers why they have not established control over the public culture in the same way. A different set of historical conditions has constrained a collective Latino presence within Oakwood's boundaries: a history of state-authorized harassment of undocumented immigrants; interactions with, and perceptions of, a changing African American community; the geographic diversity of Latinos' origins; and public participation in community spaces beyond Oakwood's boundaries.

More recently, wealthier people, most of whom are white, have moved into Oakwood in larger numbers. Unlike Latinos, they are mounting a challenge to the area's historic black identity. Many have purchased aging homes and remodeled them or even had them torn down in order to build sleek, multilevel dwellings. Some have acquired adjoining lots in order to construct standout homes that loom large over smaller, aging structures. A number of newcomers have erected tall fences around their homes that exceed the city's legal limit in order to manufacture a feeling of security and privacy. In addition, newcomers have adopted more formal methods of neighborhood intervention, addressing social problems through official political and law enforcement avenues, stigmatizing African Americans' uses of public spaces. Over time, Oakwood's public culture has become more ambiguous and diverse due to competing stabilizing forces.

The Rise of a Black Neighborhood

The origins of Oakwood's black public culture begin with one extended family's relationship with Abbot Kinney during a period of pervasive residential segregation. Kinney permitted servants and laborers, some of them African American, to build houses in a mostly undeveloped area north of the elaborate canal system during the early 1900s. What started as a few blocks occupied by African American residents extended into two census tracts known as a black neighborhood over the next six decades. Intergenerational ties, population growth, a culture of public interaction, institution building, and political organizing under continuing spatial constraints strengthened the neighborhood's public culture over time.

Arthur Reese moved from Louisiana to Los Angeles in 1903, becoming the first African American to live in Venice. Navalette Tabor Bailey, who passed away in 2010 at ninety-five, was the oldest surviving member of Reese's extended family during the course of my research. She said that when Reese first came to Los Angeles, "[h]e ran on the railroad and he heard about this area, with the canals being put in. . . . One of his stops out here, on the railroad, he met Kinney. . . . He made suggestions, and Kinney was interested in him. He needed someone to clean the pier, and different jobs, and there was nobody to do it. The blacks that were here [in Los Angeles] were living in [central and downtown] Los Angeles mostly and they didn't want to come down here [to Venice] because it was a long distance for them to come to work every day. So [Kinney] wanted somebody to come and settle."

Reese bought a parcel of land and built a house. Because no one would rent property to African Americans, Reese's son Mercier recounts, "Dad bought another piece of land at Sixth Avenue and Santa Clara Avenue. . . . He told [his cousins] Charlie and Quincy Tabor that they could build on the back of the lot. They constructed the floor of the house first, so they would have a place to sleep."[4] Reese's granddaughter, Sonya Reese Davis, says, "Each one in secession would build houses on the back of their houses and bring more relatives. So they kind of started the black community that way."[5]

Before the beachside amusement park opened to the public in 1905, Kinney employed Reese in his company's janitorial department. Reese was also a brilliant decorator, and Kinney came to rely on him to invent floats, banners, and festival themes that attracted people to the fantasy environment. At the same time that African Americans were forbidden from participating in public events on the Venice Pier, Reese and his team, comprised mostly of African American men, worked to construct its identity as a leisure-time destination.

One of Reese's cousins, Irvin Tabor, initially took a job sweeping the pier. Kinney was impressed by his work ethic and offered him a position as his personal chauffeur. Although Tabor had never before driven a car, he jumped at the opportunity. The two men became quite close, and when Kinney died in 1920 he left Tabor his house located on the Grand Canal, the central waterway and the most luxurious residential setting in Venice. As a black man in the early 1900s, Tabor was aware that he could not move his family into a house in such close proximity to wealthy whites. Along with friends and family members, one of whom owned a trucking company, they split the house into sections, loaded each section onto trucks, and moved the house to the only area where African Americans were permitted live, the area now known as Oakwood, where they reassembled the house. Members of the Tabor family lived there for decades before finally selling it to white residents.

Navalette was Irvin Tabor's niece and lived almost her entire life in Oakwood. Flipping through old black-and-white photographs and newspaper clippings as we sit on a sofa in the living room of the house her father built, she recounts her extended family's early experiences in the area, calling attention to processes of residential segregation and white flight that led African Americans to become concentrated in a few blocks.

ANDREW: When you came here, how'd you know that you had to live behind West Washington Boulevard and Lincoln? How'd you know that this was the area?

NAVALETTE: This was the only place that they would sell to you. We knew.

ANDREW: Did your family try to buy in other areas?

NAVALETTE: No, we never did. But right here in this area now, my cousin's family, they were the last ones [in the Tabor family] to come out. And my dad moved 'em all in there. He pulled 'em on rollers. There were two or three houses built from the ground up, but the others were brought in, and there were eight altogether. So as the family came out, they all had places to stay anyway. And their kids, later on, had a place to stay. And so when more families were coming in, when the neighbors found out, you know, they resented it—the white neighbors did. And so my dad and them would go over at night, and check 'em out, you know, with guns on 'em and everything. Because they threatened to burn 'em out. Then my youngest uncle, my dad's youngest brother, he bought a house across the street. He bought it from a [white] guy that wanted to get away from us so he sold him the house. You know, that was the property across the street, and now we were spread out all over two, three blocks.

Later in life, when Navalette's son became an adult, having a house on a double lot allowed her to provide land to construct another house behind hers and become a third-generation Venice homeowner, despite the fact that property values were slowly increasing and purchasing additional homes was becoming more difficult. In many cases, the children or grandchildren of original black homeowners eventually purchased or inherited the homes in which they grew up from their parents, grandparents, uncles, and aunts. Over the years, a small number of black families acquired multiple lots, creating a miniature (and in two cases I encountered, not so miniature) real estate empire, owning several properties on their own streets and elsewhere in Oakwood.

The African American population of Venice grew steadily until 1970 (see table 2). Beginning in the 1940s, people came from the South in search of better wages and working conditions, as nearby Hughes Aircraft in Culver City and McDonnell Douglas in Santa Monica opened their factories to black employees. Restrictive covenants on housing, exclusion from stores, restaurants, beaches, and other activities, and racist encounters with residents and LAPD officers in surrounding white neighborhoods continued to limit new black residents' movements.

James Thomas, now in his eighties, who moved to Los Angeles from Hope, Arkansas, in 1936, describes the geographical boundaries around Oakwood when he first arrived. "See, you wasn't accepted across Lincoln. You wasn't accepted too much south of California. And you didn't cross Washington. Never! We just knew we were outside of where we was supposed to be." Lila Riley, in her midsixties, has lived her entire life in Oakwood and recalls that during her childhood, "[t]hen the blacks couldn't go east of Lincoln. Brooks Avenue, they changed the name on the East Side of Lincoln. West we called it 'Brooks' and then on the East, when you cross Lincoln, they called it 'Lake Street.' They didn't want to be associated with poor black people."

Restrictions on mobility were passed down to younger, third- and fourth-generation residents, because of the fear of what lay beyond Oakwood's boundaries. Edward Morris, a third-generation resident in his early forties, expressed his perception about the geographic limitations facing Oakwood inhabitants:

> You walked outside of Oakwood, and they called the police. [Imitating a white man] "We need help. There's a black man in my neighborhood." And then the police come right away and they force you back into your community. [Imitating a police officer] "Boy, what are you doing here? Get your ass back over there!" And if you did go, say past Washington [pointing to what is now Abbot Kinney Boulevard], somehow it got back to my mom and my grandmom, and they didn't play. My neighbor would tell my grandmom, [imitating a woman's voice] "I saw your boy goin' over there." Someone would see you, and then you get home, and you were in some shit now. [Imitating his grandmother's voice] "What were you doing over there? Who told you, you could go there?"

These constraints strengthened the ties between different waves of black migrants who came to Oakwood. Although African Americans in Oakwood never constituted a majority in these two census tracts, they became the largest demographic group and entire streets were exclusively filled with houses owned and apartments rented by black families, giving rise to a culture of public interaction and familiarity. Lakesha Holt, whose parents and grandparents still live in Oakwood, has spent her entire life in the neighborhood. Now in her fifties, she raises her own children and grandchildren as fourth- and fifth-generation residents. She recalls streets that until recently were inhabited predominantly by black residents:

> I knew all of San Juan, I knew all of Broadway, I knew all of Indiana. That would be a real community, because they would watch us. And if anything would happen, Miss Reese would call my parents before I even got home. "I saw your little girl and she was doing this, or this, or that. She's on her way." Or coming from this way, you'd know everybody. Older people . . . sat out on their front porches and they watched you. And they all knew you, because we were a family, we were a community. I remember when I was little, walking to

school, every single house you'd know them. Hi, Miss Carter. Hi, Miss Yates. Hi, Miss McClendon. All the way down the street. Because those old people would be out there just to make sure, and if they saw anything funny they would come out. They'd be like, "You get away from those kids," doing this, that, or the other! "You leave 'em alone! You get away from 'em!" And they would. You didn't take no stuff, because people knew, from one point to the next everybody knew each other.

Spatial constraints produced conditions for a burgeoning culture of institution building, which fostered community ties across generations and economic classes. By 1912, although there were only thirty-some black residents, there were already two African American churches in Oakwood.[6] Fifty years later, the congregation of the First Baptist Church had grown to include over six hundred members.[7] Five black churches have served as gathering places, holding meetings and prayer vigils, supporting grieving families, and hosting celebrations. The churches built bridges among families and enabled many who moved away to sustain their ties to Oakwood. As the only religious institutions in Oakwood, the collective presence of African Americans is especially strong and visible, most notably on Sundays.[8]

Beyond religious institutions, the African American community has a history of assembling nonprofit organizations and small grassroots political groups. Many of these have reinforced the intergenerational transmission of the neighborhood public culture, especially during periods of sharp economic decline when new possibilities for homeownership were less likely. During the '60s and '70s, when Oakwood experienced a severe contraction in employment opportunities that was typical of African American neighborhoods throughout the country,[9] local activists—all long-standing residents, many of them homeowners— searched for new ways to improve the livelihoods of their relatives, friends, and neighbors.

They developed teen centers and after-school programs, job training services for those facing difficulties finding work, and food programs for people in need. Most important, they tapped into public and private resources to help construct fourteen housing projects. After the 1965 Watts Riots, Project Action secured financing for the construction of fourteen buildings of subsidized housing, collectively known as Holiday Venice, that were scattered through the neighborhood (see figure 3). The aim of Project Action was to provide stable subsidized housing for the children

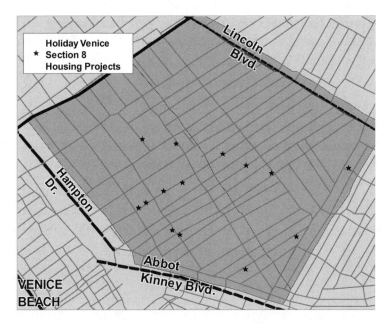

FIGURE 3. Map of the distribution of housing projects in Oakwood.

and grandchildren of African American homeowners and renters who had lived in Oakwood for a long time but were being squeezed out by the changing housing market. During the '70s, when Oakwood was incrementally becoming Latino in its demographic makeup, 98 percent of the residents living in the 176 units in the first eight buildings were African American.[10] According to Bob Castile, an African American resident who was instrumental in obtaining funds and organizing the construction of the buildings in the '70s,

> When we started this project, we started with the intent of looking out for the people that were right in there, which meant that we had to move at high speed to beat the developers to the punch. We got in touch with some influential people and they thought they could make some money out of it too. They came in and helped us to buy up the pieces of property. . . . I knew it was a historical thing to do. . . . We had a group that was handling the management. . . . If we hadn't put those buildings down, it would have been very easy to wipe out the [black] neighborhood. If we followed their suggestion of putting the buildings all right in a row, like a project, if we put them all right there [in one spot], they could have wiped out the rest of it. We managed to get enough sta-

bilization. But the thing that put the big bite on everybody was inflation. The
rents skyrocketed all around: houses that were being rented, apartments, except for the federal buildings. That's the cheapest rent in this whole neighborhood. . . . And they were forty-year mortgages. And we got Section 8 on
them.[11]

Project Action initially owned and managed the buildings; after the
organization fell into receivership,[12] a private developer purchased the
properties. Nonetheless, the new owner was still constrained by the forty-
year mortgage that Project Action had previously secured with the Department of Housing and Urban Development (HUD). Although the
buildings were designated by HUD as Project-Based Section 8 housing,
a government program that provides property owners with stable subsidies while tenants are chosen on the basis of exceptionally low incomes
and special needs, units were initially allocated in ways that circum-
vented the bureaucratic rules by negotiating with a local building manager. The discontinuity in property ownership was countered by the continuation of an informal process through which longtime local residents
obtained housing in Holiday Venice. Shanisse Small, a third-generation
resident in her forties, describes how she got an apartment when she was
eighteen. She had filed a regular application and heard nothing for nine
months.

SHANISSE: My friend Larisa, she called me and was like, "Let's go see if they
    have any apartments. . . . Joe [the manager] said he was going to give me an
    apartment, he gonna give you one too." . . . So we went over there and we
    talked to him. And he was like, "Do you think you're ready for an apart-
    ment? You already had one baby, and I see you're pregnant again." I was like
    "Yeah, and I can't bring no baby into my mom's house again, she gonna kill
    me." He was like, "OK, well I got some apartments coming up and I'll see if
    you're responsible . . . and I'll think about getting you one."
ANDREW: At this time there was no waiting list or anything like that? I mean,
    now it's really hard to get apartments in there and Section 8 has a really long
    waiting list.
SHANISSE: No. At this time the list was moving [snapping her fingers to show the
    rapid pace]. . . . See, then, when these apartments were first built, they were
    built for the community. People that lived in the community got 'em. That's
    how it worked.

The dispersed placement of the buildings gave residents a further sense of control over this one-square-mile area and enabled them to sustain connections with homeowners, many of whom lived on the same blocks as one of the housing projects. This history of organized attachment to Oakwood has allowed African Americans to more easily call meetings and public responses in the face of perceived wrongdoing. Moreover, a shared history of segregation and collective protections has allowed activists to continue to promote Oakwood's public culture as a black neighborhood.

In addition to sustaining the material foundation of neighborhood attachments through housing, African American activists influenced Oakwood's symbolic representation as a black neighborhood by persuading city leaders and affordable housing developers to label spaces to celebrate the memory of community members. Streets and housing complexes are named after the Reese and Tabor families. The sports field at Oakwood Park was renamed in memory of an African American resident who organized the youth football league. When the Venice Library, formerly in Oakwood, moved to another part of Venice, the old public library building was renamed the Vera Davis Center in memory of a respected black activist. The block surrounding the First Baptist Church was renamed Holmes Square, in memory of its longtime pastor who died in 1999. Although the black population has declined sharply, the visibility of institutions and public memorials evokes a historical narrative about the organizational capacity of the African American community.

Symbolism relies on collective practices and rituals to reinforce the local story. Sociologist Randall Collins calls this historical web of public associations "interaction ritual chains." Individuals give rise to community events and public interactions in which they present "solidarity and symbols of group membership" that connect them with local institutions and public spaces over time, generating recurring moments of visible collective identity.[13]

Oakwood Park is the central public space in the neighborhood, and the African American community has had a strong historical presence there. Over the course of decades, the directors of the park have often been African American men or women, and even when they were not, they hired a mostly black staff. Most recently, an African American woman replaced the first Latino director after his very short term ended because of persistent and organized criticism by black activists about his failed leadership. Older African American men have long congregated at the picnic tables on a daily basis to play dominoes. African American activists have organized and held meetings and protests in and around the park. African American children have long used the gym and resources inside the recreation center. Festivals, reunions, barbeques, and other celebrations, sometimes bringing together over a hundred people in this public space, reinforce this visible collective identity.

Nonetheless, socioeconomic changes among Oakwood's black population have altered the modes and meanings of these interaction ritual chains. Historically, Oakwood was a working and middle-class black neighborhood made up skilled laborers in factories (building airplane parts), hospitals (as technicians, nurses, and equipment repairmen), and schools (as assistants, teachers, and custodians). Since the 1960s, it has developed a quite different reputation as "poor" and "dangerous," once labeled by the LAPD as the most crime-ridden area in the Pacific Division. This narrative reverberates well beyond its boundaries. Despite the hesitancy of long-term residents to entertain this label as its defining feature, it is no secret that Oakwood has a history of intense drug distribution and occasional gang violence.

Most residents and law enforcement officials can pinpoint the exact spots where customers can make a drug purchase. A city attorney correctly informed me when I first embarked on this research, "Sit in your car on Seventh and Brooks and you can watch the dealing all day long." Young black men and women spend their days and nights in the spaces directly surrounding the park. A few of the men approach vehicles and passersby holding out a small plastic bag or ball of tinfoil, asking, "What'cha need?"

Visible drug distribution and gang tags on public buildings (see figure 4) bolster the public's connection between "black" and "crime." Drug dealing has been commonplace on the streets of Oakwood for decades,[14] but police tactics have contained most of the drug activities, once carried out on various streets, to the more centralized park setting. The park has always mixed together African Americans with different daily routines, such as seniors playing dominoes, younger men and women in their twenties and thirties socializing, and children and teens playing various games and sports. Now, drug dealing has become mixed into the same physical space. Marcus, a community activist in his early forties, discusses his past experiences as a drug dealer and the multiplicity of types of people who congregate outside of Oakwood Park. He explains

FIGURE 4. Oakwood Recreation Center with Shoreline Crip tag.

how the intermingling between nongang individuals and gang members on the street corner really works:

> It's not just about those people outside there selling drugs. I used to be a drug dealer, and in order to sell drugs you need to have connections and money. Only a small percentage of the people that are out there are selling drugs out there. A lot of what is going on out there is a social activity, and that goes beyond just dealing drugs. This is part of the problem with the perception of the park. My nephew wakes up and goes out to the park in the morning and I know for a fact that my nephew is not slinging drugs. For one, it's my job to know these things, so I know who is and who isn't slinging drugs. And for my nephew and some of the other guys, it's a social activity. Those are their friends out there, and so they go out there every day. There's an element out there, but not all of 'em.

In actuality, the black community remains quite diverse in its orientation toward this public activity. Stratification takes place both between families and within them. Shanisse Small acknowledges a complicated community structure that bridges together African Americans in Oakwood, but she also recognizes clear cultural differences that separate people, even individuals in her own family:

I don't walk away from my friends and I don't deny none of them over there at Oakwood [Park], because half of them are my family members. They're my friends, my loved ones, and I'll hang with them. And I'll go up there and hang there on a Friday night sometimes, or I might go up there on a Saturday. . . . I'm not going to hang 'til the bitter end every day. I drop in, "Hey, how y'all doing and everything?" They're my people and I love my people. . . . But I would love to see a change. I would like to see them change, because a lot of them have a heart and they're smart, and if they could all just come together and get on with it, they can just build this community, the little community that we have left, because they feel like . . . all they got left is that little cor- ner right there. . . . But I don't want my kids and grandkids up there, spending their days out there, all day and night, ya know? So that's where I put my foot down. Don't let me catch you getting involved with that. You want to go to Oakwood [Park]? OK. . . . You go to the teen center and work on your home- work, you go and join the basketball program. If you're over there, you're do- ing something. You're not hanging around outside, trying to be grown, like I don't know what you're doing.

Although many residents make an effort to understand the complex- ities of their families and childhood friendships, many others also work hard to distance themselves and their kids from the detrimental effects of what sociologist Elijah Anderson calls "street" culture.[15] As I stand outside the Oakwood Recreation Center with Monica Jones, a lifelong resident of the neighborhood in her early forties, we take notice of the surrounding activities:

Several black men, approximately twenties to thirties, are hovering on the porch of the recreation center and they're smoking pot. The smell trickles down to where we are standing and Monica looks over at them and shakes her head. She says to me, "I can't stand this anymore. It makes me sick. Why do they have to do it right there? There's kids in there playing. And a lot of 'em, it's their own kids. Is this what they want for their own kids? It just doesn't make any sense. When are we going to get rid of this nonsense and stop putting up with it?" She looks over at the individuals smoking pot, this time shaking her head directly at them, showing absolutely no fear of them. She turns toward me with her back to them. "Some of them don't even live here anymore. They just use our neighborhood for what they can get out of it. They don't give anything back. How can you feel sorry for someone like that?

Now, their kids, that's a different story. Let's focus on the ones inside playing basketball. What chances do they have when that's your father and that's your mother [pointing to one of the men in the distance, standing with a woman who appears to be strung out on something, stumbling across the street and yelling and cursing at someone]. Today they're out here on the street, but tomorrow they'll be incarcerated again. So, what kind of chance do their kids have?"

Even with internal stratification and differentiation among Oakwood's black residents, constraints that historically rendered them invisible from the rest of Venice developed into a lasting culture of collective visibility in Oakwood, a direct contrast to the largely white neighborhoods that have long prevailed along the Los Angeles coast. This neighborhood public culture has helped African Americans obtain resources from the city and the state, and has drawn recognition from politicians at all levels. President George H. W. Bush even visited Oakwood during his presidency to honor a local black resident with a "Point of Light" award for community efforts to prevent gang and drug activities.[16]

Although African Americans were a shrinking minority of the neighborhood's population, during the course of my research I attended over a dozen political forums held by the city's Human Relations Commission, the city council, or the LAPD specifically to address the "problems of the black community." These meetings, which were attended almost exclusively by local African Americans and city officials, made no reference to the fact that Latinos made up a larger proportion of Oakwood's population than African Americans. This phenomenon raises the question of how Latino residents fit into an evolving urban color line that has historically conceptualized race relations in terms of white and black dynamics.

Latinization without Latino Identity

The Latinization of Los Angeles has had an overwhelming influence on the city's public culture. In 2005, Los Angeles elected its first Latino mayor since the nineteenth century. The remnants of a Mexican mural movement appear on walls throughout the city. Businesses operate on the sweat of low-income Latino men and women. Varied Latino-influenced restaurants exist in every community. Vendors from Mexico and Central America distribute fresh produce on countless street corners. Latino gardeners and Latina nannies and housekeepers tend to the homes of L.A.'s white, affluent residents. Public marches draw attention to tens of thousands of underpaid, nonunionized Latino laborers, as well as hundreds of thousands of Latino men, women, and families, to protest proposed federal legislation targeting undocumented immigrants.[17]

This visible Latinization of Los Angeles has not translated into the enactment of collective visibility in Oakwood. During the 1970s, Latinos were moving into Oakwood in such large numbers that they overtook African Americans as the largest proportion of the population. Although their presence became noticeable due to sheer volume, Latinos have not had the same degree of influence on the neighborhood public culture as African Americans. Despite economic and cultural stratification within the black community, they continued to mobilize a collective presence. For individuals of Latin American origins, coming from a wide variety of places and arriving in different phases have contributed to different experiences, alternative networks, and a lack of collective action across this pan-ethnic identity *within* the boundaries of Oakwood.

Some immigrants from Mexico, who arrived prior to the 1960s, developed multigenerational ties to the area and closer relationships with African American families as their children grew up and went to school together. The second phase of Latino population growth, which occurred during the 1960s and '70s, consisted largely of undocumented immigrants from Guadalajara, Jalisco, and Nayarit in Mexico, and San Salvador in El Salvador. When Interstate 10 was extended into Santa Monica in the mid-1960s, Latino and African American residents were uprooted, leading additional families to relocate to Oakwood. Since the 1970s, immigrants from Oaxaca in Southern Mexico have moved into the area. Today, they make up a large segment of Oakwood's Latino population.[18] Over time and across generations, Latinos in Oakwood have remained fragmented rather than coalescing around a common identity, participating in an array of institutions and social activities beyond, rather than within, Oakwood's boundaries.

Early Chicanos that settled in the neighborhood were similar to African Americans in that they developed multigenerational family status. Living in the same houses over time led to very close relationships with black neighbors. Louis Moreno, a third-generation resident now in his early sixties, has lived in Venice since 1957 when he moved in with his grandparents who had bought a house. Several years later, his parents also purchased a nearby home and moved into Oakwood. He explains the close relationships between Chicanos of his generation and their black neighbors:

> You grow up with the kids you saw on the street in your neighborhood. That's why color didn't mean much. For one thing, there were so many blacks on the streets. Just standing around, hanging out. On the corners, outside their houses, at the park, just everywhere. Not like it is now, where there's a few here and there about. They were everywhere. On Westminster where I was living at the time, there wasn't a white family on our street. The whole street, not just our block. Just blacks and Mexicans. And I went to Mark Twain for [middle] school. No white kids in the school. Just blacks and Mexicans. . . . As kids, we looked around and you just fall in hand with those that are closest. In Venice, the blacks and Mexicans lived in the poor area and that's how it was. We were all poor. My parents had jobs, but they were working people. So it wasn't like there was that much difference between us.

In contrast, those who came without papers or overstayed their visas found that their precarious legal positions constrained their relationship to the locality. Immigration officers historically harassed and monitored them, generating a sense of fear about occupying public space. Juan Gutierrez, now in his early sixties, moved from Guadalajara to Los Angeles in the 1960s. Recounting his experience upon arriving to the area, he said, "They hunted for us. They would wait at different places, bus stops, where we worked, and around the neighborhood, just looking for us."

Fear of immigration authorities forced undocumented immigrants to remain discreet in their social and economic activities. People traveled between home and work, not by public transit, but less visibly, walking several miles to jobs in hotels and restaurants in Santa Monica. They often navigated through back roads and alleyways—a central feature of Los Angeles neighborhoods—to stay out of public view (see figure 5). When they did take public transportation, they had to remain alert to their surroundings. Silvia Vargas, in her sixties, originally from Guadalajara, told me that her bus driver would purposely avoid dropping off residents at the bus stops if he spotted immigration officers waiting, because he wanted to give the regular commuters, almost all of whom were Latino, a chance to escape.

Maria Beltran, an undocumented Salvadoran immigrant who lived in

FIGURE 5. A typical Oakwood alleyway.

Venice between the 1970s and 1990s, recalled going on a date to a restaurant about a mile from where she lived. Her fear of being stopped by
immigration officers made her body shake all the way to her destination.
This fear was so palpable for the wave of immigrants arriving in the '60s
and '70s, she explained, that they created alternative forms of entertainment. Instead of going out to parks, restaurants, movies, or public places,
they often held parties in their already crowded apartments.

    Latinos arriving during this time period encountered a neighborhood
with a well-organized, yet increasingly poorer, African American community, which helped to shape their perceptions of racial differences. For
new immigrants, language and other cultural barriers tended to limit social contacts with black people and more established Latino residents.
Despite African Americans' marginalized status in relation to whites,
Latino immigrants tended to view them as "Americans." Sal Beltran,
Maria's thirty-year-old son, grew up in Oakwood and pointed to the difference in African Americans' and Latinos' experiences and perspectives: "Black people were very patriotic in their views," he said. "The African Americans saw themselves as just that. 'We're American. We're

African *Americans.*' And that's how they viewed it first and foremost."
Sal regularly referred to the hostility expressed toward Latinos by African Americans without jobs. He said that they believed that men and women who were not "American citizens" were willing to work for less than minimum wage, thus undercutting African Americans' chances of getting these same jobs.

Latinos moved into a neighborhood that had developed a reputation as dangerous and often perceived African Americans in this light.[19] Many Latino immigrants found themselves in a difficult predicament: either they faced the possibility of encountering law enforcement when taking public transit, or they faced the possibility of being robbed when walking through back alleys. One former resident originally from Guadalajara, Cecilia Aguilar, now in her early sixties, described the fear she and other Latinas felt while walking home from work at hotels in Santa Monica:

> If I walked home from work, I had a long walk. And I was tired, and I had to go through the neighborhood, and every day I thought about if I was going to be attacked, ya know, mugged. They [African Americans] stop you and take your money. It was a frightening feeling. But everyone in my family, all the women, someone was always robbed on the way home.

Angelo Gomez, from Guadalajara, in his seventies, first arrived to Oakwood in the mid-1970s. He recalled,

> When I first moved to here, I would take a short cut when I walk, because I didn't want to cross Seventh Street [historically an area with a high concentration of drug dealers]. There were a lot of criminals there and people got robbed right and left. I remember, I wore a shirt with buttons on them, and I would put my paycheck in my pocket and button it. But I would try to avoid that area. And when I had to go into the area, I would say prayers and bless myself. When I first moved here, friends living in other places, we would tell them to come visit us, and they would say, "No way! You live there? No way."

While long-standing Mexican American families were used to the public culture of African Americans, visibility of black people on the streets exacerbated the level of fear among Latino immigrants. Sal Beltran and Pedro Gonzalez, both second-generation Latinos in their thirties, explained as we sat in a coffee shop that their parents, uncles, and aunts were uncomfortable with the African American street culture, not only because they worried about being mugged but also because of the sheer number of people they observed. They remembered that during their childhood older family members repeatedly used the phrase *muchos negros* to signify their feelings of trepidation about encountering black people in public spaces.

SAL: There wasn't much association [with African Americans] for them [their parents].

PEDRO: A little bit more for us [children of immigrants], because we knew a lot of kids at school.

SAL: *Muchos negros.* [They both laugh].

PEDRO: [Still laughing, he repeats,] *Muchos negros.* We heard that all the time, "*muchos negros.*" Because they felt like black people were everywhere. Ya know, always out there, chillin' and everything.

Latinos in Oakwood did not coalesce socially or unify politically. Those who had been in Oakwood for a longer period of time tended to distance themselves from those who had arrived more recently. They grew up in the neighborhood, and like African Americans, developed multigenerational associations and became Americanized in their values and beliefs. They avoided close ties with new immigrants so as not to draw attention to their cultural identity as different. Louis Moreno remembered with regret how as a teenager he and his friends called the new Latino immigrants "Putos," "Wetbacks," or other derogatory terms that separated them from others in the neighborhood. He stressed the strength of the ties between longtime residents that linked Latinos and African Americans and the fragility of the ties between new Latino immigrants and older "Mexican American" residents:

Anyone that was unfamiliar, whether they were new to the neighborhood or were coming to visit or whatever, they were considered suspect. We knew who lived here, on our streets—black and brown. We knew the familiar faces. So new people were the ones that we took a second look at.

As African American activists worked hard to solve problems through collective efforts, Latinos largely distanced themselves from local political involvement. Only when the stakes were extremely high, involving employment or immigration policy, did Latinos organize politically. Maria Daldivia, a Latina activist during the early '90s, said that she would try to encourage others to participate, but they told her that they were too busy working to attend meetings, and undocumented immigrants did not want to risk public participation because of their citizenship status. Daldivia pointed out that although African American women had a long tradition of grassroots activism in Oakwood, Latina women were hesitant about joining without the support of their husbands.[20] Liliana Vasquez, in her early fifties, moved with her family to Venice from Nayarit, Mexico, when she was five years old. She says that different phases of migration led to different "types of Latinos," which has limited political unity and collective visibility:

> There isn't like a social component to the Latino community here somehow. Or a centrally localized place where people congregate, basically. Not like black people, who have their park and their groups and their leaders. Maybe you go to church, everybody worships, and then maybe they have a little something once in a while. But they [Latinos] don't really rally around issues. Also, another thing is there's different types of Latinos that are here. The newer people, like the Oaxacans. There's a lot of Oaxacans who I have absolutely nothing in common with. And then there's the people that have been here for a long time. Also you have the gang and drug type families and that whole environment too.

Even when Latinos were being evicted from apartment buildings throughout Oakwood, a common occurrence as demand increased, given their lack of political status, they mostly dealt with these issues on an individual basis, uncertain how to advance their group needs. Silvia Vargas, now in her early sixties, shared tales of distress as she became homeless while she looked for another residence, sleeping in her car near Penmar Park and having friends and family members watch after her children for weeks at a time. She eventually settled in South Central where her children had to navigate a tough reality, commuting to Venice High School on a daily basis, practically sneaking back into their South Central neighborhood at night to avoid gang altercations.

Some sought out the assistance of Flora Chavez, a white woman married to a Mexican man who directed a local Community Service Organization (CSO) since 1972.[21] Chavez organized voting registration drives; assisted Latino immigrant families in times of trouble; helped people gain representation in housing struggles when landlords treated them unfairly; fed, clothed, and housed the homeless; and sustained a credit union until she was eighty years old, dispensing more than 680 loans totaling over $2 million to people in need.[22] Having grown up as part of the dominant culture, Chavez learned how to access the resources that immigrants, in particular, were unable to obtain on their own.

This lack of collective action in Oakwood does not mean that Latinos did not participate in public life. Rather, unlike African Americans, they have not established institutions, collective uses of public spaces, and collective rituals and commemorations within the boundaries of Oakwood that make them visible as a unified group. Instead, they have commonly attended churches outside of Oakwood and even outside of Venice. Many members of the Oaxacan community, for instance, attend the St. Anne's Church in nearby Santa Monica (see figure 6). It provides a vibrant public life that includes festivals, ritual celebrations, parties, political meetings, services and resources, but it is located more than four miles away from Oakwood.

Latino residents also commonly use public parks in other parts of Venice, describing the Oakwood Park as an exclusive site for African

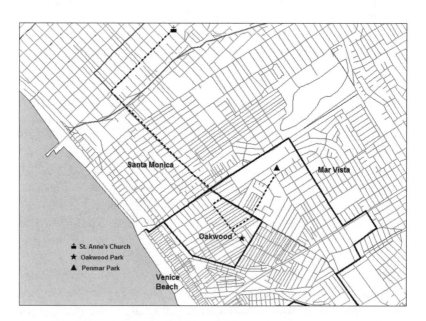

FIGURE 6. Map of Latino residents' routes to a church and a park beyond Oakwood.

American sociality. Carlos Ortega, a second-generation Latino in his late thirties who grew up in Oakwood, said,

> They held the key to the park. The directors were always black, so they had access to the park when they wanted it. We didn't have access to resources, or access to school settings. The idea of having access to spaces, like Oscar De la Torre has a youth center [in Santa Monica], or Jaime Cruz has a place over at Santa Monica College, [they're] people that understood that we need another level of organization at the institutional level, to be able to use it as a resource. That's really what was lacking here. One thing you have to ask yourself is, who uses the recreation center at the Oakwood Park? Who uses the California space [Vera Davis Center]? So even to this day, these people feel very comfortable going in there. But we don't. And in fact, every time when a Latino went in there to use it, they pushed us out. They always found ways to weed us out, by picking fights, by making us look like we were instigators, and by making us look like we were going in there and starting racial tension. And what we took from that was that they were saying, those are our resources, we don't want you freeloading on them. And our parents had no idea that these places existed for the youth. All they knew was that these were places that the blacks hung out. That's the way that they saw it. Because of the relationship we had with them, they would always tell us, "No quiero que va en alli." We don't want you to go there, we don't want you to hang out there.

Feeling "pushed out" or fearing encounters with African Americans at the Oakwood Park led them to find alternative avenues for public participation, regularly attending events and activities in other parks. For example, Penmar Park, located about a mile east of Lincoln Boulevard, has a history of being a Latino site for cultural events, ritual festivities, and celebrations (see figure 6).

These constraints contributed to the collective invisibility of the Latino population in Oakwood by inducing them to adopt a more private lifestyle, impeding the perception of collective life and political unity, and facilitating their participation in institutions and spaces beyond Oakwood's borders. Nonetheless, Oakwood has had historical moments when tensions between African Americans and Latinos became much more visible through devastating violence that brought public recognition to Oakwood as having a hostile racial climate between "black and brown."

Competing gangs long existed in Oakwood, but conflict had a differ-

ent meaning because gun violence was not as rampant. Black-Latino violent conflict became more visible in the 1980s and '90s as the drug trade
and availability of guns escalated. In the '90s, a widely publicized gang
war broke out between the local African American gang, the Shoreline Crips, and two Latino gangs, the Venice 13 (from Oakwood) and
the Culver City Boys (from a nearby community).[23] As the murder rate
multiplied, the LAPD began to label *all* local competitions over space
and *all* local conflicts as "gang-motivated behavior," but those African
Americans and Latinos who had grown up in Venice tended to see it
as "family-motivated behavior."[24] According to Sal, Latinos did have
moments of "unity," but they were reactions to specific situations. He
says,

> Some people who lived around us were so disconnected from this reality they
> didn't understand the historical process that led to that kind of organization.
> They would immediately call and say, there's a fight going on, it's between the
> Mexicans and the Blacks, and then when the cops would come, they didn't
> know our neighborhoods, they didn't know what was going on, and automat-
> ically they would say, we have a gang problem. I remember standing on the
> corner with my dad's cousin. I mean, if you want to label him a gangbanger?
> I remember my aunt comes out of her house late at night, carrying my cousin
> on her shoulder, a very young little boy, and her purse, and someone runs out
> from the alley and snatches her purse. It knocks her down to the floor with my
> nephew on her, while she comes back yelling, oh, some *negro* took my purse.
> My father gets furious, and he gets his rifle, and he calls some of his cousins
> who live in the area, and they all get in the truck, and they go around looking
> for this guy. Organization was at that level.

Regardless of whether the conflict is labeled as gang-motivated behavior or not, mounting violence made the racial-ethnic tensions a public issue. The *Los Angeles Sentinel*, the largest African American newspaper in Southern California, published an article in the midst of the intense conflict labeling Oakwood as "Los Angeles at its worst":

> This is not the Venice you've heard about, where chain saw jugglers and bi-
> kini-clad rollerbladers are just regular members of life's passing parade. . . .
> This is a 1.1-square-mile war zone called Oakwood, a patch of Venice just
> steps from the world-famous boardwalk in which 11 people have been shot
> to death since September. And no one— not police, community groups or

politicians—has any hope things will soon change. . . . Little attention has been paid to the fearsome turf war between Hispanic and black gangs in this drug infested warren of gentrified bungalows and federally subsidized apartment complexes.[25]

This sentiment reverberated throughout Los Angeles news cycles. Although there was little hope in 1994 that the violence would soon end, it slowly subsided several years later after community leaders orchestrated a gang truce and increased police presence led to a new management approach to public space. Today, Oakwood is rarely referred to through a lens of black versus brown conflict, with the exception of moments of extreme gun violence that lead LAPD to barricade the neighborhood. Although Latinos have produced moments of visible organization in Oakwood, they have not experienced the same prolonged periods of collective influence over the neighborhood public culture. For one, the number of Latinos greatly decreased between 2000 and 2010. Secondly, gentrification has increasingly altered not only Oakwood's racial climate but also its socioeconomic composition.

The neighborhood's political configuration has mainly turned to white-black relations, often to the exclusion of Latinos. Since the 1980s, the number of non-Hispanic whites has gradually increased in Oakwood, and during the past decade (2000–2010), white residents became the largest segment of the neighborhood's population. Some have organized in private to challenge the public culture of the African American community. This effort to control the activities of black people in public spaces is strangely parallel to the politics of white-black dynamics that were prevalent in the early twentieth century when African Americans were segregated from the rest of Venice by being confined to Oakwood.

The Color Line Meets the Class Line

Gentrification has become visible in Oakwood due to an increased police presence that has stemmed from newcomers' formal associations with city officials; an accumulating system of symbols that represents affluence and stands in direct contrast to remaining signs of poverty; and the private lifestyles, professional priorities, and segmented cultural practices of newcomers. Despite the fact that gentrification calls attention to class-based tensions, Oakwood's history of segregation has facilitated new proximity of whites and blacks, leading locals to filter the new social and political configurations through a lens of racial differences. The class line and the color line have meshed in Oakwood. African Americans harbor feelings of defensiveness about gentrification, now competing with affluent whites over a territory in which they were once forced to live and where they subsequently developed influential traditions. At the same time, newcomers reinterpret African American collective visibility as collective stigmatization, employing a process of power labeling.

There have been different periods of gentrification in Oakwood. There are those who moved into the neighborhood between the early 1980s and early 1990s and lived through the violent gang war between African Americans and Latinos. These residents, by their own accounts, are middle class. Those who have moved in after the gang war, between the mid-1990s and 2010, tend to be wealthier. They have torn down houses and built new ones from scratch, following the path set by developers who have consistently converted empty lots and older properties into high-class condominiums throughout Oakwood over the last decade.

Beginning in the late '70s, many Venice neighborhoods were changing to include residents with greater levels of wealth. Oakwood, however, was a noticeable exception along the coast. According to Dante Miller, a third-generation black resident in his forties, "White people didn't come here. And police didn't either. We didn't see people like you. White people think that we exaggerate about the police, like the police don't really ignore our neighborhoods. But it's true! We had all sorts of crime and things that we were dealing with, but the police wouldn't come out when we called. We had to take matters into our own hands a lot of the times."

Oakwood's physical proximity to rapidly changing neighborhoods was central to its "discovery" by outsiders. In 1980, the Venice Family Clinic on Rose Avenue, now the largest free medical clinic in the United States, held its first Venice Art Walk. The annual art walk began as a form of payback by artists to the clinic, quickly emerging as a famous Los Angeles event and key source of fund-raising. As the event became more popular, it attracted wealthier whites in droves from other parts of Los Angeles. Making a donation to the clinic allowed them to visit studios of local artists, many of them located in Oakwood, as artists were among the earliest gentrifiers, looking for cheap housing in the area.[26] Although longtime Oakwood residents appreciate the clinic's services, they are more critical of the art walk as the start of gentrification. The invasion of voyeurs and their police escorts manufactured a feeling of safety, a contrast with the past when outsiders were unlikely to enter the neighborhood. Lakesha explains,

> When they started the art walk for the clinic that's when they started coming back, because they started to notice all the property and how cheap it was. They didn't even know it existed before. But they started walking through the community. And high police presence! And they started noticing! Wait, I could get a house for what? That cheap? Are you serious? So close to the beach? They'd take people to jail about a week or two weeks before the art walk was about to begin, and the police would walk people through on the day of the art walk. And we always joke about it, because the art walk changed the community!

As the neighborhood started to change, the gang war traumatized locals of all racial-ethnic backgrounds. Residents became wary of entering the public spaces around their homes. Even during daylight hours, many were afraid to take their trash out to the curb, sit in their yards, and walk around the neighborhood. They awakened to dead bodies on their front yards and bullet holes in their houses, windows, and cars. When discussing this period of gang violence, several white residents I interviewed still asked to remain anonymous, fearing retaliation for their words. One resident remembered waking up to earth-shattering screams of a mother who found her son dead in the street. An antigang activist put bars on his windows to keep people out and chicken wire screens to block gang members from throwing Molotov cocktails (fire bombs) at his home. One man rearranged his house so he and his wife's bed faced the backyard instead of the street, for fear of being hit by stray bullets.

Even members of the Shoreline Crips and Venice 13 reorganized their understandings of public life. Two former gang members, one in his early forties and the other in his midthirties, together describe how they and other gang members arranged to protect the senior members of their community. Jamal Graves, in his thirties declared, "We had to walk our grandmothers to church so they wouldn't get shot at." Dante

Miller says, "You should've seen us. Watching out all the time. We knew our surroundings better than anyone, so we could be ready if someone was gonna ambush us. Out of nowhere, driving by, that could be it. So we had to watch out for ourselves and our families. I lived with my grandmother and my son, so it was more than just someone out to get me. I had innocent people I had to look out for."

A new cultural distinction emerged between direct and indirect organizing. While black and white activists had a similar goal, to see the end of the drug dealing and violence, their political approaches differed. African American activists have historically taken it directly to the street to deal with *problem individuals*. White newcomers, in contrast, have taken their issues to city officials, ignoring particular circumstances of criminal action and making "black" a *problem category*. African American activist Pearl White told a *Los Angeles Times* reporter in the '80s, "Kids, mostly 12 to 16 years old, are selling drugs on the open market. . . . and they are making life miserable for the people who live here. Something has to be done—and we're going to do it. We're not snitches, the police already have enough of those [referring to newcomers]. What we want is for the drug dealing to stop. And it is going to."[27]

In fact, black homeowners have a long tradition of organizing to clean up the neighborhood, but they worked without assistance from police officers and city officials whom they distrusted. Two black residents started the Oakwood Beautification Committee in the 1980s to organize long-term Oakwood homeowners. According to one of the founders, John Wilbanks, "Once word went out . . . white people started calling and wanting to get involved. That hurt us. The whites and the developers just supported this whole conspiracy theory" that new residents, police, and developers were in bed together. At one point, police officers started coming to the meetings and black organizers asked them to leave, because many black residents were critical of the role that police officers played in the process of gentrification.[28]

Myra Washington, in her midseventies, like many longtime residents, was confused about the effects of increased police involvement in Oakwood. Although she saw the potential to eliminate drug dealing and gang activity, she recognized the possibility for targeting Oakwood as a "bad" part of town. "I went to a meeting and that's when they were talking about, 'We're gonna call all this little section Oakwood. And we're gonna have more police than ANY OTHER SECTION in [Venice].' And it sounded good. But, in the back of my mind I'm thinking, 'Is this good or is it going to be bad?' It actually turned out not to be good, because then we developed the reputation that this is the bad section. This is where the bad people live. And to me, I couldn't see dividing it like that. We always just said we lived in Venice. Now, all of a sudden we were Oakwood and Oakwood was a bad place."

The history of gang violence and drug dealing has had a lasting influence in shaping relationships between white newcomers and black oldtimers. The narrative about "curbing danger" was a key tool for newcomers to build bridges to the city bureaucracy, showing a willingness to work with city officials, including members of the LAPD.[29] Steve Nelson, in his late fifties, a white activist who moved to Oakwood in the early '80s, describes the limited role people of color played in their organized neighborhood task force against drug dealing and gang activity:

We had a pretty strong neighborhood watch group, block captains, maybe twenty people that would come to regular meetings at the police station. And of course, there were *some* Latinos and *some* blacks involved but not many. Certainly, it was disproportionate to what the actual population was at the time. And word got out that the police were holding secret meetings. And they were secret, because we would discuss a lot of confidential stuff. We talked about the drug dealing that was going on and who we saw dealing drugs and where they lived and what was going on. And we gave the police a lot of dead bang information that led to the gang injunction.

The city councilwoman of that time, Ruth Galanter, and her chief of staff Mike Bonin, told me in separate interviews that they remembered receiving countless phone calls requesting that they lobby for an injunction against Venice gangs. LAPD and city attorneys define a gang injunction as "a civil suit that seeks a court order declaring the gang's public behavior a nuisance and asking for special rules directed toward its activity."[30] According to Bonin,

We pursued the injunction with [then–Los Angeles mayor] Hahn's help, for the three gangs, V-13, Shoreline Crips, and Culver City Boys. I was in the courtroom because I had been working on it. The deputy city attorney was like, "Everyone is too afraid to get up and speak, and the judge is going to think nobody is in favor of this." And he says, "What do you think?" And I was like, "What the hell." So I got up and talked about the climate and the fear in the neighborhood. About the calls we were getting in the office. I was the sole community witness.

Galanter and Bonin were repeatedly pushed into the middle of Oakwood's political conflicts, forced to make tough decisions about how to intervene in these local crime waves. Replying to statements made by leaders of the Nation of Islam who asserted that the gang injunction was a racist effort to facilitate gentrification in Oakwood, Bonin replied, "Creating safe neighborhoods is not part of a gentrification agenda. . . . It's just basic human rights. . . . I certainly welcome their efforts to help people turn their lives around, but the charges that the injunction is racially motivated are ludicrous."[31]

The gang injunction in Oakwood allowed LAPD officers to build a case against particular individuals believed to have gang affiliations, which filtered the opposition through a racial lens. LAPD Gang Unit officers documented the activities of alleged gang members and brought these allegations to a judge who either supported adding individuals to the gang database or dismissed the allegations if the LAPD did not meet the burden of proof. Individuals who were added to the database were greatly constrained in this geographic area in terms of what they could wear and with whom they could associate in public.

LAPD officials and Los Angeles Neighborhood Prosecutors reinforced in multiple public meetings at the Oakwood Recreation Center that people are placed under the gang injunction due to accrued evidence of misconduct. To determine whether a person is a gang member or not, the California State Anti-Gang Coordinating Committee, an office of the California Attorney General that coordinates intelligence information about gang participation, developed the following set of criteria known as the CalGang System that LAPD officers use as their guideline to gather evidence about a suspected individual:

1) admits gang membership or association; 2) is observed to associate on a regular basis with known gang members; 3) has tattoos indicating gang membership; 4) wears gang clothing and symbols to identify with a specific gang; 5) is in a photograph with known gang members and/or using gang-related hand signs; 6) name is on a gang document, hit list, or gang-related graffiti; 7) is identified as a gang member by a reliable source; 8) arrested in the company of identified gang members or associates; 9) corresponds with known

gang members or writes and/or receives correspondence about gang activities; and 10) writes about gangs (graffiti) on walls, books, paper, etc.[32]

The gang injunction provides official backing to the redefinition of acceptable public association. African American activists believe that the criteria they use are broad enough to include individuals with no gang affiliations. Law enforcement agents placed so many longtime black residents on the list that almost every long-term black resident I came to know in Oakwood has family members on it, which leads them to continue to interpret the injunction as racist. In 2004, about a decade after its implementation, the Los Angeles Human Relations Commission held a series of public meetings about the relationship between the LAPD and the African American community. Locals complained about the functions and ramifications of the injunction, fervently criticizing its inability to deal with onetime gang members who turned their lives around. They also questioned the definition of a gang, arguing that relatives were placed on the injunction without actually participating in criminal activity but simply by affiliating with gang members who were family members or long-term friends.

Nuisance abatement and city code enforcement programs similarly defined acceptable building uses and appearances, which had direct repercussions for long-term black and Latino residents. The city attorney's office used nuisance abatement programs to intertwine criminal residents with their family members. For example, the Safe Neighborhoods Division of the City Attorney's Criminal and Special Litigation Branch brought a suit against a longtime black Oakwood family for purportedly distributing crack cocaine out of their house. In a thirteen-month time span between May 2003 and June 2004, sixteen people were arrested at this property for drug-related crimes, including several members of the family. A superior court judge labeled the home a "public nuisance" through a legally binding order that prohibited four of the adult children from living in or even entering the property. The legal injunction also required the homeowner to pay $140,000 in fines and penalties,[33] forcing family members who had owned the house for decades to sell the property in order to make the payments. The house has since been demolished and replaced by an expensive new condominium.

During the late 1990s, representatives of the Los Angeles code enforcement agencies, Pro-Active Code Enforcement (PACE) and the Systematic Code Enforcement Program (SCEP), walked through the neighborhood looking for housing and apartment structures in need of repair. Long-standing residents and community organizers contend that these city agents targeted low-income and senior citizen homeowners. They allege that residents received tickets for minimal violations, many of which were aesthetic in nature such as chipping paint, broken flower planters, mangled fences, and cracked lightbulbs. These violations forced senior citizen homeowners, some of whom were living on fixed incomes, to pay fines and invest in repairs. Mike Riviera, a community organizer in Oakwood, recounts,

> The whole thing was pitched [by Galanter] as neighborhood revitalization that can be controlled by the people of the community. "Neighborhood revitalization? Does that mean gentrification sneaking in the back door?" "No, it's OK. You guys are going to be at the forefront of these changes. It's going to be revolutionary. You guys are going to own this." And a lot of people got behind this in the beginning, but a lot of local people were looking around at what was happening. Inspectors were coming up and saying, "OK, here's a fine. You have to fix your fence. Here's a ticket, you have to fix it." And if you don't fix it, then they put a lien on you. Then the developers come in, "Well you're in all this hot water. We can help you out of this. We can buy your house from you and get you cleared really easily. No problem. We'll pay you in cash. It will be good for everybody, so you can get out of this mess." Because a lot of folks just didn't have the money. They might have a house, but they didn't have the equity.

Even if political leaders did not intentionally target African Americans, local activists defined nuisance abatement and code enforcement programs as methods of stigmatization. Likewise, they believe developers and real estate agents act similarly. Developers have targeted the fourteen Holiday Venice housing projects as the most concentrated and densely populated signs of poverty and crime in Oakwood. In response to this reputation, the newest building owners sought to circumvent the Section 8 contracts that have sustained their affordability. During the 1970s, ownership of the fourteen buildings was transferred from the nonprofit organization that ran it, Project Action, to a private owner who arbitrated a contract with HUD to maintain Holiday Venice as Project-Based Section 8 housing. However, when the owner of the buildings decided to sell them in the '90s, the new owners—Namco Capital

Group who changed the name of the buildings from "Holiday Venice" to "Breezes Del Mar"—decided in 2001 that they wanted to relinquish the Section 8 contracts by prepaying the HUD mortgage that required the project-based subsidies.[34] If they had succeeded, they could potentially have evicted the low-income tenants living in 246 affordable apartment units, raised the rents to market rate, or even demolished the buildings and petitioned for new zoning, which would have allowed for condo conversions or another form of housing.

African Americans, continuing to confront stigmatizing actions, built a political campaign. Although long-term black homeowners had no economic interest in sustaining the housing projects, many had close ties with residents living in them. The Holiday Venice Tenant Action Committee, along with the assistance of long-standing homeowners and community organizers, protected the buildings by mobilizing more than two hundred people to protest against these changes. The organized struggle was somewhat successful, pressuring HUD to require the new landlord to uphold the contracts until they are due to expire. However, an uncertain future for these low-income apartment structures haunts long-term families and housing activists, as their economic surroundings continue to change.[35]

During the 1990s and early 2000s, a number of African American tenants were forced out by the new management company through allegations of gang affiliations, drug distribution, and violence against security officers hired by management to monitor the buildings, charges that local activists still dispute. In March 2008, LAPD, FBI, and Bureau of Alcohol, Tobacco, Firearms, and Explosives (ATF) officers swarmed into Oakwood between 2:00 and 4:00 a.m. Looking for gang members, they crashed down doors and shattered windows of houses and apartment units occupied by African Americans. They woke people up, some of them senior citizens, who alleged that officers held shotguns against their heads, forcing them out onto the streets in bathrobes and slippers.

These actions had repercussions for Holiday Venice tenants. The management company, unhappy about the destruction to their buildings, evicted several African American residents whose doors were knocked down, in line with a clause in their rental contracts with HUD. One distraught woman stood up at a community meeting and explained that the person the authorities were looking for put down her address but never even lived in the apartment. She had been evicted, and although she had lived in Oakwood for all of her fifty-plus years, she was uncertain about whether she could find another place to live in the neighborhood.

Actions by real estate agents reinforced a common narrative among black residents that their property and housing rights were under attack. Many black homeowners with whom I spoke believe that real estate agents harass and pressure them to sell their properties. Unsolicited postcards and roving real estate agents are commonplace throughout Venice, as real estate brokers are trying to earn a living by capitalizing on this coastal property in high demand. Yet Oakwood's complex racial history leads African Americans to translate aggressive real estate campaigns as active threats to their longevity. Regina Stanton, late eighties, shows me postcards she received in the mail, some with photographs of her house and captions that read "We can sell your home," "We will get you top dollar for your property," or "You won't believe what your investment is worth." She explains,

> God, I get calls, five or six calls every day. I get mail. They say, "Why don't you want to sell? I could offer you this, that, or the other. You can be a millionaire." And I say, "Who the hell wants to be a millionaire?" You know, I say, "I'm not moving. That's up to my kids if they want to sell." I said, "Here I am, almost ninety. I'm not thinking about moving." I said, "Money don't excite me."

Agents knock on their doors, sometimes encountering hostile homeowners, as in this example when I was visiting Myra Washington at her home:

> A man walks up to the door and rings the doorbell. With a raspy voice, Myra opens the door. "Hi. Can I help you?" The white man at the door is young, early thirties, and dressed in beige pants and a blue button-down shirt. "Yeah my name is Jay from Boardwalk Realty. I live in the neighborhood and I sell properties and I'm—" Myra cuts him off. "Don't you think that if I'm going to sell my property I'm competent enough to search someone out who I trust and know?" Jay says, "Yeah, I'm not trying to sell your house. I'm just saying if you're interested, we can get you a good price." Myra becomes more agitated, firmly responding, "Well, I'm not interested. What makes you think I'm interested?" Jay stumbles over his words, "Well, yeah, I'm not—." She cuts him off again, "Well, I'm not interested." With sarcasm, she says,

"Thanks a lot for coming by, though. Have a great day." She shuts the screen door and I can see Jay turn around and walk away. Myra turns back to me, "This happens all the time. It's constant. Phone calls, mailers, people coming to your house. What makes them think that I don't want to live here anymore? It's borderline harassment at this point."

As some families hold onto their properties, other homeowners have benefited from the changing market, selling their properties and retiring to other locations. One black couple I interviewed sold their house and moved to Las Vegas; and another moved to be near family in Louisiana. Moreover, when seniors pass away, they leave their homes to children and grandchildren who commonly sell their properties and split the inheritance between them. Just as African Americans watched white people disappear between the 1940s and 1970s in a process of white flight, those who remain observed a reversal between the mid-1990s and 2010 as more whites moved in. Real estate agents, well aware of these changes, hoped to get in on the most recent wave of gentrification in which new residents have torn down houses, remodeled older ones, or moved into condo conversions, often next door to those with fewer financial resources.

In turn, Oakwood's culture is becoming more private and segmented.[36] Newer residents, typically younger than remaining homeowners, had grown up where privacy was taken for granted as part of their class status. Their professions and leisure activities require them to spend most of the workweek outside of the neighborhood, establishing friendship networks beyond the boundaries of Oakwood. Despite living within feet from others of different backgrounds, their markedly different ways of living in Oakwood lead them to categorize black public activity as gang, drug, and crime related.

Some newcomers erect tall fences around their properties in order to block visual access between public and private spaces (see figure 7). Although many of the fences exceed the legal height limit, the Department of City Planning does not enforce the building code. The separation of public and private is also signified by methods of entering and leaving homes. People pull up in luxury vehicles in a back alley, open electronic gates, enter and close the gates behind them, remaining invisible to their neighbors. Young professionals rent apartments where they relish their private spaces and beach-proximate lifestyles. John Cheney, a white man in his late twenties, works in the film production industry and rents a

FIGURE 7. A fence, approximately seven feet tall, surrounding a house.

small cottage behind a larger house for over $2,000 a month. When I attended a party at his place, the only entranceway was through the gate out front, which was locked:

> Without a phone, my wife and I wait on the street trying to figure out how to get inside this blocked-out world, which escapes any public visibility. As I look around, African American children are running around in the street and teenagers watch them, leaning up against a concrete wall in front of a house, looking out at us as we try to enter our friend's home. John finally lets us in and we walk to the back of the property where about twenty people are standing around barbequing, drinking, listening to music, and talking. Only one other person at the party lives in Venice. Everyone there knows each other from either work or college. At one point in the evening, I ask John about the neighborhood and he knows a little bit about the culture of the street from his landlord, but he says he basically keeps to himself. His landlord advised him to talk to an African American woman who lives down the street if something suspicious happens. She apparently knows everything about the street and ev-

eryone on it. It's not the history, but the proximity to the beach and the secluded lifestyle in his back cottage that drew him to the neighborhood.

Privileging private life, new residents raise concerns about the uses of
public spaces, inverting the meaning of African Americans' public culture, once a celebrated fact of local life, into a sign of danger. For example, in 2005, a few residents continuously called the police about drug
dealing around and inside Oakwood Park. They complained about daily
activities by the picnic tables, alleging that the tables attracted African
Americans to engage in illicit activities. While African American activists refuted these allegations on the grounds that the park was a mixing
ground for a variety of uses, the city councilwoman at that time, Cindy
Miscikowski, ordered the park administration to remove the picnic tables from the area. Recurring protests by local African Americans led
to a lengthy, several-month investigation, and eventually park administrators returned the picnic tables. African American senior men quickly
resumed playing dominoes in this public space, as they had done for
many years before.

Ceremonial events, such as funerals, festivals, barbeques, and reunions, have served as moments of intense African American sociality,
with families and friends joining together in crowds of one hundred or
more on a street or in the park. Sometimes locals associate openly with
LAPD-identified gang members who are relatives or longtime friends,
having grown up together in the neighborhood. Public visibility draws
the attention of new residents who alert the police:

> A funeral for one of the old-timers brought in a lot of people today to pay
> their respects. People gathered on the streets, happy to see one another. What
> began as a funeral turned into an all-day reunion that lasted for many hours,
> and people around the neighborhood, uneasy by the number of black people
> in the streets, repeatedly called the police. Throughout the day, the commu-
> nity gathering slowly transformed into a site of intense police surveillance,
> as LAPD cars continued to drive around in circles and officers monitored
> the streets on foot to make sure things were "under control." Angry about
> the heightened police presence, African Americans participating in the so-
> cial event questioned why they were under the watchful eye of the police, be-
> coming defensive about their right to visit family and friends and celebrate
> the life of a community member.

Residents merge individual characteristics with collective histories and group identities, generating fear among newcomers and defensiveness among old-timers. Power labeling demonstrates how these distinct social positions work in practice. While each side interprets the other as "foreign" to its own accepted ways, only one group has the ability to officially label the other as dangerous. In April 2004, the LAPD temporarily positioned a mobile police station outside of the Oakwood Recreation Center to intimidate drug dealers and alleged gang members, and its presence created a stir on the street with "new versus old" and "white versus black" dynamics.[37] Commonplace public interactions reproduce a local myth in which "white" translates as legitimate homeowners who support increased police control, whereas "black" translates as resisting criminals opposed to police surveillance:

> About twenty or so African Americans, mostly young adults in their twenties and thirties, and young teenagers, fourteen to fifteen years old, are outside the recreation center hanging out. Four police officers in uniform stand together near the police substation, two with dark black shades, waiting with their arms crossed. I follow a white couple walking hand in hand. The officers greet them and then they greet me as well. I stop to talk. I suggest to them that some people think their presence is intimidating. One officer responds by saying that they are not aiming to be intimidating at all. In fact, he feels as though he is protecting people, telling me that the homeowners in the neighborhood are unhappy with drug dealing, graffiti, and gang violence on the streets and they want to get rid of it. By his comments, it becomes clear he means new homeowners. "They pay a lot of money to own homes here," he says, "and they have a right to feel safe in their own neighborhood." As we are standing on the street, a white woman walks by with two dogs. As she approaches them she stops briefly and says, "I'm so happy that you guys are here."
>
> Then the officer walks with me a few hundred feet up the sidewalk and points out a broken car antenna on the street that is snapped into a small handheld size. He picks it up and holds it out to me. "Handmade crack pipe. See the burnt tip?" A black woman and her son walk by us, and the child, no older than seven or eight, waves to the officers. The woman, who appears to be his mother or caretaker, scolds him: "Don't wave to those pigs. They're a bunch of muthafuckers." She walks off cursing and yelling at the officers. The one officer asks me, "Did you see that, did you see her give us the finger and curse at us?" I raise my eyebrows, uncertain how to act in this situation, not wanting to appear too close to the LAPD. Meanwhile, another kid yells out

to the officers, "Suck my cock!" The officer yells back, "Do you even have one?" The kid pulls down his pants to show him. The officer turns to me and asks, "What are we supposed to do about that?"

Population changes in Oakwood amplify the white-private/black-public tensions. Cynthia Dell, an eighty-five-year old African American woman who has lived in Oakwood since 1936, summarizes a popular sentiment among long-term residents about the effects of gentrification on social ties between neighbors:

> When the whites started moving back, they don't like some things. We're two different kinds of people. There are things we like to have, like yard parties and everything. And wherever there's a white family, they build that big high fence, and you just don't know who is in there. . . . They don't want to socialize with nobody, not even the other white people in the neighborhood. They're very private.

Newer white residents, on the other hand, interpret the condemnation of their private culture as hypocritical. Jackson Norris, a two-year homeowner in his early forties, represents this viewpoint:

> Some people think because they're here longer that their way of living is better for the neighborhood. And that's fine, I mean, people have a right to complain that I'm killing the neighborhood, that my fence has ruined their lives, or the size of my house goes against the idea of Venice [laughs]. But that's OK. It's not a mean thing, ya know? They're being protective. There are people they've been here a long time and don't want things to change. But, what's not OK is being hypocritical about it all. Like complaining about the size of my fence, but not about the guys that deal drugs right out there on the corner every day. Right in my face. They don't even try to hide it. That somehow is fine. But I put a fence up and then they act like I committed a crime.

In Oakwood two competing systems of local culture now exist side by side, with Latino culture in the background of these emerging white-black tensions. As African Americans call upon a history of segregation and community building that has sustained their collective life in the face of population decline, newcomers build upon an accumulating culture of privacy, often challenging established uses of public space.

Conclusion

African American segregation, Latino immigration, and white gentrification produced a distinct trajectory of intergroup power struggles over
the control of the neighborhood public culture. In this case, the historical violence of African American segregation gave way to community
organizations, a culture of public sociability, collective actions, and the
labeling of spaces in honor or memory of black residents, which has produced a legible and consistent story line for people to classify Oakwood
as a "black neighborhood." But we should also be wary of this narrative
and overall perceptions of black homogeneity. Sociologists of the black
community have long dispelled the myth of black uniformity by showing
the political rifts, diverse lifestyles, and divergent class and status positions among individuals of African descent.[38] Similarly, Oakwood's African American population actually became more, not less, culturally
and socioeconomically diverse over time.

The history of constraints and opportunities that African Americans
encountered enabled them to construct and reinforce a neighborhood
public culture, while the constraints and opportunities that Latinos encountered undermined the possibility of a pathway to a durable neighborhood representation for them. A history of state surveillance of Latinos
and restricted public resources found in Oakwood have limited Latino
collective visibility and the degree to which people associate this neighborhood with Latinos, despite the fact that they made up the largest proportion of the population for several decades. But we also have to be
careful about buying into a widespread myth about Latino invisibility.
In Los Angeles, Latinos are increasingly gaining a great deal of cultural
visibility, if not consistent political clout and economic influence. Yet the
historical constraints on Latinos in Oakwood made them collectively invisible in this particular place. Nonetheless, they collectively produce a
vibrant public life beyond Oakwood, including in Penmar Park, located
in another section of Venice, and in several churches in Santa Monica.

Latino collective invisibility is distinct from the new private culture of
a recently arriving wealthier class. During the last decade, new residents
have challenged the public culture of the African American community
through a new politics of privacy. This tension brings forth historic scars
of racism that made and sustained Oakwood as a black neighborhood
in the first half of the twentieth century. Now that coastal property is

in higher demand, African American visibility is a source of concern for newer residents. These individuals do not march in public, generate community organizations in Oakwood, or collectively advertise their viewpoints; but they do work behind the scenes, pay attention to public spaces, and lobby city council members, city attorneys, and LAPD officers to respond to disruptions to their quality of life.

While Oakwood is a case where segregation, immigration, and gentrification were localized in a single neighborhood, competing attachments and cultural systems help us to see how political configurations take hold and contribute to an ambiguous and diverse neighborhood public culture. Looking to other cases improves our understanding of the underlying social processes at work in building group identity and sustaining configurations between distinct groups within neighborhoods. The simultaneous expansion of homelessness, social services, and gentrification in the Rose Avenue district has given rise to a distinct set of intergroup tensions and another ambiguous neighborhood public culture.

CHAPTER THREE

People out of Place

After breakfast on a hazy Thursday morning, I take the garbage out to the dumpster behind our eight-unit apartment building. I walk through our back door into a common area enclosed by a solid wooden fence, filled with flimsy plastic furniture. I unlatch the gate on the fence, push it open, and to my surprise almost pound the head of a man sleeping on the sidewalk. Curled up on the other side, he had moved the dumpster away from its original location to manufacture his own personal space free from the public view. I think for a few seconds about whether I should wake him up, ask him to put the dumpster back to its original location, and request that he move out of the way so as not to block the back entrance.

The act of throwing away trash has become more complex in recent weeks. Due to an increase in the number of people picking through our dumpster for bottles and cans and others discarding a range of objects that fill it beyond capacity, often leaving remnants on the ground, our landlord installed a combination lock that now requires me to line up the correct numbers. "It's for the protection of everyone living in the building," he told us. Our landlord is involved in a battle with some of the homeless people living around the neighborhood to control his property, and as a result there is now no way to gain access to the lock and open up the dumpster without asking this homeless man to move. I look at him carefully while considering what to do: he is draped in layers of soiled clothing, wearing two different types of shoes, sleeping atop multiple bags of belongings. I decide to place the garbage bag on the ground against the fence until he moves.

After years of living in this apartment, I had become accustomed to seeing people day and night who live and sleep outside on sidewalks, in

public parks, on the boardwalk and the beach, on abandoned and overgrown housing lots, or in vehicles. Many park their dilapidated buses,
RVs, and cars throughout Venice. The roofs of some vehicles are so
damaged that their owners have covered them with blue plastic tarps.
A few without curtains in their windows expose years of hoarding possessions, drawing dismay from passersby. Decades old and poorly maintained, some of the RVs and school buses emit dark black clouds of exhaust that drift into nearby homes.

Homelessness has become engrained into the daily fabric of this
coastal community. Over a period of years, I learned about the struggles
of people living on the streets: struggles to secure safe sleeping arrangements and protection for their most prized possessions; searches for food,
clothing, alcohol, illicit drugs, or moneymaking prospects; and opportunities to establish camaraderie and a sense of belonging. I also learned
that a small segment of this population is responsible for a large proportion of daily problems. Most homeless people are courteous neighbors
who try to fit in. They nod hello, keep to themselves, and tidy up the areas where they sleep. Facing greater risks than most people with private
residences, they keep a constant lookout on the street for suspicious activity, trying to maintain an overall sense of order.

Some, however, act in erratic and aggressive ways; and others are un-
responsive to their residential surroundings, lacking in neighborhood civility. In the case of my apartment building, a few used the space where I
found the man sleeping for their own personal pursuits, which neighbors
deemed not only a nuisance but also a health and safety hazard. Besides
sleeping in this space, individuals defecated and urinated in it; smoked
crack, methamphetamines, and marijuana; and engaged in sexual activity. One neighbor, a quiet woman in her fifties, went outside in the early
morning to confront a man defecating in the space and asked him to
move elsewhere. As the hours of public restroom operation throughout
Venice are highly restricted, the man was limited in where he could go.
He reacted with anger. I heard yelling and went outside. The homeless
man, pulling up his pants, was humiliated by being caught off guard in
the midst of conducting a private act in public space. Taken aback by
his harsh reaction but ready with her cell phone in hand, my neighbor
called the police to report the incident. By the time the officer arrived,
the man had already left, but not before screaming, "Fuck you, you fuck-
ing whore!"

This scenario represents the collision of poverty and gentrification and the disruptions it can pose for housed residents. The meaning of homelessness, once recognized as an alternative lifestyle, has transformed in Venice into a quality of life problem. During the three decades following World War II, the boundary between housed and homeless was commonly blurred. Housed residents, mostly working-class and poor renters, tolerated and even took part in Venice's ephemeral culture that attracted beatniks, hippies, and artists. However, since the late 1970s, five significant changes redefined the homeless situation: (1) the number and types of people living on the streets increased; (2) influential nonprofit social service agencies prospered; (3) the Venice Boardwalk became one of the most popular attractions in Los Angeles, generating a range of informal survival opportunities for the most destitute; (4) the influx of upper-middle- and upper-class residents distanced Venice's housed population from its historic bohemian counterculture; and (5) law enforcement increasingly incorporated "broken windows" and "nuisance abatement" strategies.

Due to the failures of federal, state, and city governments to create sustainable solutions for curbing chronic poverty and homelessness, the daily burden has become localized in specific neighborhoods. In Los Angeles, it falls on social service agencies and law enforcement officials to manage the problem; it requires housed residents to adjust their lives to regular encounters with people living on the streets; and it pushes many of the chronically homeless, facing recurring constraints that limit their prospects of escaping this predicament, to embrace daily survival tactics particular to the locale.[1]

Gentrification and homelessness have converged along the C-shaped corridor that runs from Venice Beach to Lincoln Boulevard along Rose Avenue (see figure 1), giving rise to competing systems of neighborhood attachment. Many housed residents have worked hard to save money in order to purchase or rent property in Venice. They believe that when people own homes and businesses and, to a somewhat lesser extent, when they rent apartments, they make financial and emotional commitments to a location that grants them the right to define who and what belongs in surrounding public spaces. They encounter individuals around their homes and stores who have not showered; who defecate and urinate on sidewalks and in alleyways; who filter through trash for food and recyclables; and who do not own or rent property or pay taxes.

According to anthropologist Mary Douglas, when certain objects or behaviors do not fit precisely into a local classification system, people la-

bel them as "pollution" or "matter out of place." In a gentrifying neighborhood, the homeless stand out as inconsistent with taken-for-granted
residential norms as "people out of place."[2] At the same time, homeless
people have established entrenched relationships to the neighborhood.
Stabilizing mechanisms reinforce their collective attachments, attracting
new cohorts of people living on the streets, facilitating adaptive survival
techniques, and reproducing the identity of Venice as a "home for the
homeless."

A Rolling Stone That Gathers No Moss

Venice residents are accustomed to the signs of homeless destitution:
panhandling; picking through trash for cans and bottles; tattered and
soiled clothing; sleeping on park benches, sidewalks, and in back alleys;
and the worst off smelling like a mix of musty body odor, cigarettes, and
sea-salt air. Yet the social category of homelessness is made more complex by Venice's historical identity as bohemian. Individuals who slept
outside were not always stigmatized as homeless, a label that points to
the forced constraints of poverty. Rather, it was once a sign of freedom
that came with a life on the road without being tied down to a specific
place.

Beat writer Lawrence Lipton wrote that Venice attracted "the rebellious, the nonconformist, the bohemian, [and] the deviant among the
youth."[3] People identified Venice with its cheap rents, empty lots, wild
parties, artistic crowds, radical politics, racial and ethnic diversity, and
high-crime rates. Long-term residents affiliated with these bohemian
ways recall a different relationship between property and neighborhood
belonging than that found in the current setting. Bill, a longtime resident in his sixties, describes it as a culture of temporary attachments. He
says, "Venice has a reputation of being transient, and they used to say
that they came here to get their heads together and then they'd go get a
job." Another long-term resident, Stan, moved to Venice in the 1960s before it had a "capitalist feel," when "the demand for property was much
lower." Other long-standing residents repeatedly tell stories, not simply
of affordable rents, but also of landlords who forgot to collect rent altogether. There were months when people lived rent-free in a house or an
apartment in Venice.

In this characteristic bohemia, homelessness was, to quote an old proverb, "a rolling stone that gathers no moss." Homeless people were travelers, individuals passing through on route to somewhere else, and the housed and homeless shared a lifestyle. "It was more laid back," says Jonas, an old-time homeless man in his midsixties who initially lived on the streets and now resides in an RV. First arriving in Venice during the late 1960s, he explains, "Nobody was worried about whether you were sleeping in your car, or if you were traveling in your car. There wasn't anybody worrying about whether you had holes in your pants and a backpack." People who lived in Venice during that period recall "transients" sleeping on the beach, establishing camp on empty residential lots, and living in vehicles. Darla, a third-generation resident in her early sixties, says,

> People would come here because they knew it was OK. It was a stop that people knew about. Still people come here! It still has that reputation. You see hippie buses coming in here all the time, and you go, "Oh, there's a new hippie bus. I haven't seen that one before." But now they get run out and they leave. It's not like it used to be, where everyone accepted it. It was accepted because it was an alternate lifestyle, not because they were homeless. I don't remember hearing that [term], because there were a lot less people that were homeless through poverty and disabilities and not having health care. It was an alternate lifestyle.

The tendency of residents to identify with countercultural trends made them willing to provide material resources that helped people survive without a stable residence. They saw themselves as generational brethren who adopted the same ideology about community and economic simplicity. During the 1960s and '70s, many lived on countless empty lots throughout Venice, especially in the Canals neighborhood, the center of Venice's unconventionality during that era. A major development boom on the canals eventually pushed them out to the Venice Boardwalk and Rose Avenue. Those who adopted transient ways often found a connection with housed countercultural residents who provided them with a continuing affiliation. Even if they left for a period of time, they could come back and resume their lives in the local environment. Dominick first arrived in Venice in the mid-1970s, and although he eventually became a renter in the 1980s, for almost a decade he would occasionally leave and then return months later. He once lived in a school bus on the streets of Venice and relied on the good will of a local homeowner:

Jeff was what we called the pad connection. He was kind to us. A friend of mine knew him and we'd stop over, and we'd get some grub, clean up, barbeque, and that sort of thing. We had a school bus and we were fixing it up so we could sell it and so we stayed on the bus. And he let us use his electricity and helped us out with food and water and whatever. And we'd leave, hitchhike somewhere, get some change in life, some perspective, but then we'd come back to Venice. And Jeff's pad was what I knew, so I'd go back there. And he didn't really know me from anybody. I was just a friend of a friend. So then when I didn't have the bus anymore, then we were on foot, and I had nowhere to go. And I was by myself, so I just ended up going back to Jeff's pad and he let me sleep on the side under a tree. I mean he let this cat sleep out there too, so it wasn't that big of a deal. But things were looser back then.

As the demographic composition of the housed population shifted during the late 1970s into the '80s, newer residents were concerned, but not necessarily alarmed, about people living on the streets, in vehicles, or on empty lots. Sally, in her early sixties, has been a homeowner since the early '80s. She remembers when she first arrived that people were living in their vehicles in front of her house, but residents did not collectively view it as a problem. "I know I wasn't exactly thrilled about it, but it was kind of just the way it was. You go outside and it was like, 'Why is this guy sitting in his van watching me?' And then you realize, 'Oh, he lives in there.' It took some getting used to, I guess, but no one did anything about it." The continuing changes in the residential population and the simultaneous growth of the homeless population spurred a further transition from collective passivity about "strangers on the street" into a new collective classification of the homeless as "people out of place."

Stigmatizing the Homeless

The situation of Rose Avenue is distinct from that in Oakwood in several ways. First, in Oakwood, African Americans have long-standing property ties that predate white gentrifiers, whereas in the neighborhood of Rose Avenue, gentrification and homelessness expanded at the same time. Secondly, the homeless are defined by their lack of property. African Americans ultimately sustained a public culture in a way that transcended exclusive reliance on property relations, but their collective attachments were initially rooted in organized efforts to maintain stable

housing. Although homelessness threatens the prospects of gentrification in some direct ways, lack of property equates to lack of legitimacy to
make authoritative claims over territory. Third, African Americans have
a different relationship between public and private space than most white
newcomers, but homeless social life is quintessentially public. Unless people figure out a way to resolve the foundations of this widespread urban
problem or figure out a way to move the collective stability of homelessness in Venice to another section of Los Angeles, street life will continue.

Fourth, stigmatization of African Americans and the homeless operates differently. Gentrification has introduced middle-class conventions
into both neighborhoods, but the stigmatization of African Americans
is subtler, because even the most adamant antigang activists deplore
explicitly racist labels. Simply stated: it is more acceptable to hate the
homeless, who produce an ongoing daily nuisance that makes them perceived as less than human.[4] Residents and city officials draw upon two
methods to stigmatize the homeless: cultural repertoires and discontinuity techniques. Cultural repertoires are preexisting expressions that lend
residents a language for reinforcing status positions in specific times and
places.[5] Moral conventions, aesthetic repulsions, public health concerns,
safety anxieties, and property relations are five prominent cultural repertoires used to define homelessness as a neighborhood problem.

Residents view a wide variety of homeless behaviors as morally rep-
rehensible, finding it appalling that people urinate and defecate in public, throw garbage on the ground, establish encampments, park rundown vehicles on their streets, and pick through their trash as a way
to earn money. Claire, a woman in her midfifties, complains about the
"recyclers" rummaging through her trash and leaving remnants on the
ground. In a neighborhood meeting of approximately twenty-five people, she says, "It's creating a huge problem, because I have to clean it up
every day. The people that do this for a living are not functional. Diving
into trash to make a living is just not a functional way to live."

Social services are also defined in similar terms. The St. Joseph Center is seen as attracting the homeless to the Rose Avenue neighborhood,
but not fulfilling the task of solving the homeless problem. Mira, a white
resident in her eighties, maintains, "My personal position is that if we are
going to feed the homeless and try to make a home for them in Venice,
then we have to provide beds for them. If you can't do that, it's cruel for
everybody involved." Residents argue that social services should adopt a
moral imperative to achieve housing rather than enabling the homeless

to thrive on the streets of a residential neighborhood. James, a resident in his early fifties, says in a public meeting,

> We want compassion. Does St. Joseph's get people into housing? Do they get people out of homelessness? No. How is that compassionate? They get homeless to live on St. Joseph's, to become reliant on them. St. Joseph's does a great job if you have a problem with the homeless in your alley or in your area. They're great. Call them and they help out. But they don't solve the problem. They make it worse because they attract the homeless. If you build services, people come to them from near and far. If you build it, they will come.

Seeing homeless people who linger around on streets near their homes after making use of local services leads people to label homelessness as an objectionable lifestyle. When residents look out on to the streets, they cannot see the biographical and social-historical conditions that produced this predicament. Instead, it seems as if individuals are idly hanging out and avoiding personal responsibility. Michael, a homeowner in his fifties who moved to Venice in the 1980s, says,

> I'd love it if I saw poor people getting help. But all I saw was St. Joseph's burning up ten to thirteen million dollars a year for parading people up and down the street on Rose Avenue. What I've learned about the homeless over the years is that most of them are so dysfunctional; they're too lazy to do crimes. It's like, "Hey man let's get together and hold up a liquor store." "Uh. No man, I'd have to get up at 11." It's like, "Here we are, let's go down to the beach. We'll make some money, get some coffee, get a croissant, and look at the girls." And it's like what everybody else wants to do, except they have to go to work. Basically, the question is, do you want to live in a place that is run for the convenience, and again, I hate using the word bums, but let's call 'em slackers? I mean they won't even work in the coffeehouse. George Carlin once said, if we're put here to serve others, what were the others put here for? It's like, do we have to maintain Venice for a bunch of people who want to go to garage sales on Sunday and sell what they got at the garage sale at Venice Beach and live in their van in between? You start letting people live in their vans, the problem is that you'll have people coming from all over to live in that place. Step right up and bring your van.

Residents also define the public presence of homelessness as aesthetically unpleasing. They dislike looking out their windows and seeing people standing around outside; they are troubled by the looks and smells of homeless people whom they encounter; and they despise the mess that some homeless people create by searching through trash cans or leaving garbage remains on the ground. Charles, a resident of two years in his early forties, discusses his and his wife's central reason for attending a meeting about overnight parking districts that, if passed, would require residents to purchase a permit to park on the street during restricted hours and force homeless people living in their vehicles to move elsewhere: "We paid over a million dollars for our house and I look out my window and there's a guy in his van standing out front. He's *always* there! He can see us and watch us all day long and it's absolutely ridiculous. We close our shades in the middle of the day when we should be having our windows wide open."

As I walk around the Rose Avenue area with Evan, in his midforties, he points out things that are aesthetically pleasing and unpleasing to him:

> "Look at that," pointing out a pile of trash in between two RVs. "Nobody cleans it up. It just sits there." We approach a building under construction, which for Evan is a sign of the direction in which the neighborhood should be moving. "That's a new development right there. It's gonna be nice. I think they're asking 1.5 million. I bought my place for much less," smiling as if he got away with something. We approach a section of the street where there are twelve vans and RVs in a row. He says, "I personally don't see this type of stuff lasting much longer. Anybody that lives around here and says they're not bothered, they're just straight up lying." He stops to inspect a beat-up maroon van with a dented fender and a yellow and brown stripe along the side. "This one I really hate. He has no care for the neighborhood at all. His van is filled with crap. Look at this." He points out the amount of material objects piled up in the van: clothes, books, papers, and bulging plastic bags. "Have you ever seen anything like that? Can you smell it?" I nod that I smell the musty odor emanating from the van.

Residents often refer to the homeless through a filter of public health concerns. People believe that human defecation and urination are dangerous to their own personal well-being and the well-being of their children.[6] Thomas, a resident in his early fifties, says, "It's really a public health issue. I have to clean up shit on my sidewalk every day. Not dog shit. Human feces. I go out there with a newspaper and a plastic bag and clean it up." Laura, a woman in her late forties, asks, "How many [RVs] are there? Fifteen? Twenty? It's a dumping station. Is this healthy for the neighborhood: drugs, garbage, prostitution, dumping sewage on the street? Would you let your kids play outside and run around there?"[7] In addition, the definition of the homeless as "sick" is central to the stigmatizing dialogue about public health. Carl, a forty-eight-year-old homeowner who has lived near the boardwalk for fifteen years, says as we walk around the neighborhood,

> "I've seen some people out here for years, and they used to act normal, or more normal." Pointing to a homeless man, whose pants are soiled and who is adamantly arguing with himself, he says, "I remember when Gene first came here, eight, ten years ago. He wasn't crazy. Not like that. He was always off a little bit, but you could carry on a good conversation with him. But you can't now. You can't even try. Life out here makes you crazier. I've seen it. He needs medication, he's schizophrenic, I think. I mean, without that how can he get a normal life?"

Another common way of talking about the "homeless problem" is through the lens of personal security. Those who adopt this viewpoint argue that their opposition to homelessness and social services is based on concrete behavioral concerns and unpleasant interactions that can be startling and disruptive to individuals' sense of comfort in their own neighborhoods. Residents describe being followed, harassed, and even attacked by homeless men and women living on the streets. As a resident, I have experienced such behaviors on a number of occasions.

Los Angeles street life is distinct from that found in New York, a city known for its steady flow of pedestrian traffic. On most residential streets there is little public interaction and at night it completely comes to a halt, making it possible for people to navigate their way with no one else around them except those who sleep outside. As I walk with Lisa, a woman in her early thirties, she says, "See that woman in the red car?" pointing to a woman whom I have encountered before who has been there for a few years. "She terrifies me." When I ask her why, she replies, "When I walk home at night [after work], she's always there and she'll like curse at me and yell at me, like 'You fuckin' bitch, with your long hair. I'll get you, you stupid bitch.' I try to stay away from her even during the day, because it's terrifying."

Residents complain that homeless people follow them, a practice I have also experienced on a number of occasions. I draw the following example from my field notes. I am walking at a rapid pace with Dana, a woman in her midthirties, and a homeless man approximately in his late thirties to early forties walks quickly behind us:

> I turn around and ask him to stop. Instead, he continues walking faster, getting much closer to Dana and me and trying to walk in between us, laughing and making hissing noises. I ask him again to slow down and lay off. He gets angry and says assertively, "What's your problem?" I say, "I don't have a problem, I just want you to stop following us." He responds, his eyes becoming wider, "I really like you guys and want to walk with you!" He then starts laughing hysterically and continues to walk at our pace. I take my cell phone out and threaten to call the police. Only then does he slow down and back off.

Sometimes, people lose control of the situation and face moments of direct danger. The homeless people living on the streets who have severe mental disorders can act in erratic, threatening, and even violent ways. May, thirty-one, who manages a store, told me that she and other employees in the area regularly have to deal with the homeless as part of their duties. She and her coworkers are sympathetic, even helping a few by paying them to do odd jobs such as carrying boxes and sweeping, but sometimes people's behaviors become uncontrollable and they feel that they need to call for help. She recounts an example:

> There is a light-skinned black guy with pretty blue eyes. Everyone knows him because of his eyes and he's there all the time. He stands on Main Street. His eyes are pretty but scary, ya know? He doesn't smile. He's in his own world. If you're close enough to hear him, he talks to himself, but it's all nonsense. Like alpha, mega, saga, bugga. He stands so close to the buildings, leans on the buildings, in between our gates. On Saturday he acted up and we called the police. A pigeon was flying by, he hit it and it went into another store. And then on Sunday, he acted up again, talking really loud and it's a small sidewalk, and it's right in front of our store. And he was really acting up. And it makes customers not want to come in, and he wasn't just yelling, it's his actions too. He was moving around and flailing his arms and pacing. So we called the police and the cops came and we just heard him yelling, "Why do I have to accept things! I don't want to accept things!" So it sounded like he was mad at someone for giving him something, like food or something. When he just stands there and doesn't say anything, it's fine. It's when he talks re-

ally loud and starts moving around and making gestures towards people. Because that scares people.

At a public meeting, Marco raises concerns about the movement of some of St. Joseph Center's homeless services to Lincoln and Rose, closer to his house, because of violence he once suffered at the hands of a homeless man, which scarred him physically and emotionally. "I was a victim of a bad crime by a homeless person," he says. "I was beaten very badly unconscious. Ever since then, I've been afraid of the homeless. I recognize that they need help and mental health care, but I'm scared of them and I absolutely hate it when they end up on my lawn in front of my house."

Property relations are part of a cultural repertoire to explicitly define control over public space. People believe that homeless people are without rights to civic space, because they fail to provide a stable tax base and therefore lack a "stake" in the community. Attempting to install overnight parking districts exemplifies this trend. At a series of meetings sponsored by the Venice Neighborhood Council, committee members explained to residents how to influence the political process in order to implement preferential parking districts. Unable legally to specify the homeless population as the target, these meetings were framed in terms of "parking problems." Nonetheless, the audience saw through the political charade and repeatedly turned the meetings into a forum on ridding Venice of homelessness. These observations were made during one of the initial overnight parking district meetings in 2007:

Dr. John, a longtime homeless resident in his sixties, protests against the proposed restrictions. "This is an attack on homeless people! I've been in this neighborhood for thirty years, and this is an attack!" The committee members sitting in the front of the room around a small table respond by claiming that they are not dealing with the homeless problem. "This is not what the meeting is about," one says. "The meeting is about parking, not homelessness. This committee is *only* about parking. That's all that is on our agenda. Someone comes home at night and can't park and it's a problem when you can't park in front of your own home." Several homeless people in the audience interrupt the flow of the meeting by proclaiming their dissatisfaction. With each interruption, the committee reintroduces the idea that the meeting is NOT focused on homelessness. Yet homeowners sitting in the audience raise questions that juxtapose the committee's political rhetoric with homeowner concerns. One man suggests that his friend who owns a restaurant near the boardwalk should attend these meetings because "he's been really active in trying to get rid of motor homes." A woman, in her midthirties, asks, "Can we have a clarification on what the law is for sleeping in the neighborhood? It's not just motor homes that are the problem. We need to get rid of them too." Another man, midforties, argues, "We're not paying all this money to live here among the homeless and the poor." A woman, midfifties, says, "The problem is really where all the campers park together, and it's like they own the streets out there. Those streets need the most attention." Rebecca, who has lived in an RV in Venice for over a decade, is now in tears. She says, "This just tears my heart out. You're essentially kicking me out of my neighborhood, taking my community away. You want to make Venice a closed space." One of the residents sitting in the back of the room yells out, "How do you contribute to the neighborhood anyway? Do you even pay taxes?"

These cultural repertoires call attention to a specific definition of residential quality of life. Residents fixate on their own individual rights to public safety and moral order: rights granted by an ability to pay for exclusive access to a specific place. The reverse is true for the homeless. Without paying rent, individuals are targeted as problematic. The stigmatization of the homeless blends together with political and law enforcement strategies in a mutually reinforcing relationship. What people commonly describe as "criminalization" is part of a series of discontinuity techniques.[8]

Discontinuity Techniques

Stigmatization repertoires interpenetrate official law enforcement priorities. Politicians designate spaces to facilitate relationships between business owners, residents, and officials, operating like customer service forums that move cultural repertoires to action. In such political arenas, they pass on approaches for disrupting homeless continuity in their neighborhoods. *Discontinuity techniques* are the methods used to create uncertainty in the daily lives of the homeless.

In the early 1990s, the city of Los Angeles instituted Community-Police Advisory Boards (C-PABs) for residents to come together with law enforcement officials to learn how to influence the uses of public spaces around their homes. I attended various meetings of the Pacific

Division's C-PAB Homeless Outreach Committee, a deceptive label in that the group never once discussed methods for reaching out to people living on the streets, but rather focused on housed residents' problems with homelessness. Housed residents of Venice's Rose Avenue neighborhood, representatives of social service agencies, and law enforcement officials attended the meetings moderated by a community resource specialist from the Citywide Nuisance Abatement Program.[9] Attendees detailed incidents, one at a time.

- Following a comment from a resident who described "troublemakers at the same intersection of Hampton and Rose every morning," a police officer responds that residents must take the time to report it. Regarding issues such as defecation on sidewalks or yards, public intoxication, and sleeping in vehicles, the officer says, "You have to stand up and say, 'Yes I saw the person doing that.' Most people are not willing to take time to do it." The officer continues, "You have to see it firsthand, file a claim, take down license plates, take pictures, and report it."
- Several people complain about homeless "vagrants" in their back alleys. An officer reports that she told people to bring trash cans inside from alleys. She says, "They are a problem because narcotics users hide their drug using behind them. They pretend that they are sifting through garbage; meanwhile they are using drugs back there." She also reports that if you're concerned about people going through your garbage and you have a dumpster, "You should think about putting a lock on it."
- The woman running the meeting discusses how the city deals with "public encampments," groups of people making a home in public space. She says the street inspector comes out and starts a paper trail. She describes the details of one scenario in which it took three months to "clean up" an encampment in a local parking lot. She claims there is a mayoral directive to get rid of public encampments. If these encampments are on public property they can be dealt with, and she informs them of phone numbers to get the process started.
- The police talk about how they now pick up trash after the homeless because the city is too slow to respond. They say that in order to deal with people parked in a certain area for too long or those illegally making all the mess, they are putting stickers on the cars as a scare tactic. She then calls for residents to get involved: "If you see someone who should be getting an 85.02 [citation] and you want to deal with it, contact your senior lead officer who will come out and put on the sticker."

In these types of political spaces, people learn the formal routes through which to get LAPD and other city officials involved in neighborhood problems, passing on techniques that disrupt homeless attachments. Discontinuity techniques become a way to challenge daily routines. Landlords and business owners increasingly put combination locks on their dumpsters to restrict their uses to tenants and limit homeless people scrounging for bottles and cans. City leaders have followed suit and installed new enclosed bottle and can recycling containers on the Venice Boardwalk to halt the informal recycling business that has been a central homeless survival skill. Business owners on the corner of Rose and Lincoln hired their own security force to monitor homeless people parking vans and RVs in their parking lot. Upon closing, businesses on the boardwalk now put up overnight gates several feet in front of their entrances in order to barricade the possibility of sleeping, soiling, or vandalizing these spaces (see figure 8). The city locks the doors of the boardwalk's public restrooms after official hours to halt drug use, prostitution, and vandalism by the homeless. An employee in the nuisance abatement program tells me how city officials are "creative with the use

FIGURE 8. Gates such as these are readily installed in front of boardwalk businesses.

of sprinklers," turning them on at odd hours to force people who have become attached to a specific public area to move away.

Discontinuity techniques keep the homeless on the move, so individuals become greatly constrained in their most basic actions. For example, finding a restroom after 10:00 p.m. is complicated by the fact that businesses will not allow the homeless inside and public restrooms shut down. Summer, a homeless woman in her late fifties, discusses the rise of new deterrent practices that target the homeless:

> They won't open the bathrooms on the beach at night. They used to leave one open at night, but that was because the people for Parks and Rec that were cleaning them decided to do that, not because they were supposed to. Then they [residents/law enforcement] get mad because people are peeing and defecating outside of it. Well, they're not allowed to pee or defecate inside of it. By ten o'clock at night, besides Ralph's [a supermarket on Lincoln Boulevard] and some stores that stay open late or some bars and restaurants, there are no bathrooms. So now, homeless people, a lot of them, they don't want them to come into the bars and restaurants. They're for customers only and if you don't have the money to buy something, then you're not a customer. So it's like, you have Ralph's where you can pay a quarter to use their bathroom. But you gotta walk all the way over to Lincoln [a mile from the corner of Rose and Ocean Front Walk]. You have over here the Washateria on Fourth Street [and Rose Avenue] until eight or nine, when they close. . . . So, there's not a lot of options if you're homeless and they're becoming less.

While residents' and businesses' "private" actions serve as a roadblock in the homeless daily round, most of the management falls on law enforcement officers. Changes in law enforcement priorities since the 1980s promoted criminalization strategies across the United States. The ultimate discontinuity technique, they provide the appearance of private-property protection but ultimately produce a recurring cycle of neighborhood conflict without resolution. Focusing on minor infractions to address immediate situations, advocates conjecture that this strategy creates safer neighborhoods by finding more serious offenders among those receiving citations and being arrested.

Former LAPD chief (also former NYPD commissioner) William J. Bratton, perhaps the most famous "broken windows" advocate in law enforcement circles, argued that these police strategies do not target homelessness.[10] Referring to the homeless situation in downtown L.A., Bratton said that police officers focus on "behaviors" rather than "populations," dealing with criminal and harmful practices that negatively affect residents and businesses. He explained his view to a *Los Angeles Times* reporter: "What we focus on is behavior. If the behavior is aberrant, in the sense that it breaks the law, then there are city ordinances. . . . You arrest them, prosecute them. Put them in jail. And if they do it again, you arrest them, prosecute them, put them in jail. It's that simple."[11]

While this logic may seem simple, the creation of ordinances and the practices of enforcing them are actually much more complicated. Many city ordinances, whether or not they were specifically created with homelessness in mind, disproportionately manage the homeless population. City legislators readily implement new regulations that prohibit certain types of behaviors in public spaces and then law enforcement officers pick and choose on what days and at what times to focus on violations of the law, explicitly managing certain populations. The following ordinances classified in the Los Angeles Municipal Code specifically affect the homeless:

- Section 41.18: No person shall stand in or upon any street, sidewalk or other public way open for pedestrian travel or otherwise occupy any portion thereof in such a manner as to annoy or molest any pedestrian thereon or so as to obstruct or unreasonably interfere with the free passage of pedestrians.
- Section 80.54: The Council may establish, by resolution, Overnight Parking Districts with appropriate boundaries and authorize parking restrictions to be in effect on the streets thereof between 2 a.m. and 6 a.m. The resolution establishing an Overnight Parking District shall state the maximum number and type of Overnight Parking Permits that may be issued to any one dwelling. The resolution shall also establish the fee charged for each type of Overnight Parking Permit.
- Section 85.02: No person shall use a vehicle parked or standing upon any City street or upon any parking lot owned by the City of Los Angeles and under the control of the City of Los Angeles or under control of the Los Angeles County Department of Beaches and Harbors, as living quarters either overnight, day-by-day, or otherwise.
- Section 63.44: Except as otherwise provided in this section or as authorized by the Board, no person shall camp on or use for overnight sleeping purposes any beach, or bring a housetrailer, camper or similar vehicle onto any beach.[12]

Prohibiting specific actions, handing out tickets, and then conducting homeless sweeps in response to accumulating tickets are discontinuity techniques filtered through criminalization strategies. Homeless people, by the basic logic of their existence, live outside without shelter, which gives rise to a host of daily challenges. Certain behaviors that are permitted within a private residence are forbidden when conducted outside. In the following example, Jamie, in his midfifties, is participating in leisure activities that are similar to many people I know in Venice. The difference is that Jamie has no shelter to prevent his behavior from being visible, forcing him to live in a state of anxiety in his relations to the police.

Sitting on the lawn, directly adjacent to the boardwalk, Jamie drinks a warm can of beer. He pulls out a "dugout" and a "bat"—a wooden container that stores marijuana on one side and a metal pipe that resembles a cigarette in shape and color on the other side. He bangs it on the chair to loosen the particles stuck inside, twists the bat into the dugout, holds it up to his mouth, lights it and inhales, blowing out the smoke. A police officer drives by and Jamie puts the beer on the ground and his smoking contraption under his chair to keep them both out of plain sight, leading him to call attention to some of the ordinances that impact the homeless:

> It's a catch-22. You can't escape it. You're playing a game with the police force. It's legal if you're over twenty-one to go to the liquor store and buy a beer. It's not legal to drink it on the street. If a cop comes by and gives you a ticket for an open container, he'll say, "You can't have an open container in public. You should be at home, drinking it at home." So if you're homeless, where do you drink it? You're homeless! The camping rule is another one. See this sign over here: "No Camping or Lodging." Well, no matter where a homeless person goes, the minute he sits down he's camping. By law, that's the way it is. I'm sitting down. My stuff is here. My bed is made on the other side of this [concrete partition that sets apart the boardwalk and the parking lot]. I'm camping. It's illegal to sleep in public now. What kind of message is that? Do the police want you to take a bunch of drugs to keep you awake? That's breaking another law. Everything a homeless person does, I mean 99 percent of it is against the law. These are minor things. But still, the microscope is on you.

Steve, early sixties, has been homeless in Venice for over a decade. He reinforces Jamie's point, calling attention to a new ordinance to restrict

smoking cigarettes by the pagodas—the shaded seating structures on the
Venice Boardwalk—where a lot of homeless people congregate:

> The general system here is you give everyone tickets that you can, at any
> chance you can. Like they put up signs that say, "No Smoking in the Pago-
> das." That way, whatever you're lighting, it's illegal. If they can't get you for
> smoking grass, then they'll get you for smoking cigarettes. And the thing is,
> they have an excuse to check you now! See before, they couldn't say, what are
> you smoking? Now whatever it is, they say, "We saw you smoking, what were
> you smoking?" So it's a cover for them doing anything else they don't want
> you to be doing. They can say you're smoking and let's see if you got ciga-
> rettes on you. Oh, OK. You have a kit and heroin too, and now they have just
> cause and you're in really serious trouble.

Officers issue tickets to homeless individuals for a variety of minor
offences that accumulate over time, creating a host of problems for individuals in the long run. Homeless people are unable, financially, practically, or psychologically, to deal with their citations. They cannot afford
to pay the fines; they often have no reliable transportation to get them to
the courthouse to plead their cases; or they do not care about or understand the possibilities that there may be serious penalties as a result. In
this example, I am sitting at the Rose Avenue/Boardwalk intersection
talking with a group of people when two homeless men get entangled
with two LAPD officers:

> One officer walks over to a group of homeless people sitting at the pagoda
> and grabs a bottle of beer out of one of their hands. The officer dumps his
> beer out on the concrete, making a statement to the rest of the people sitting
> around. His partner, somewhat annoyed, tells him to dump the rest of the
> open containers into the grass rather than the concrete. He walks over and
> does it. Across from the pagoda is a bar where dozens of people legally drink
> beer outside at the tables, blocked off by a rope fence, an irony that does not
> escape the homeless guy getting a ticket. "You gonna write me up for this
> shit, when you got people getting drunk right there? This is some crazy-ass
> world!" The officer orders him to keep his mouth shut, and the man replies
> very loudly so everybody can here, "Man I don't gotta listen to you!" Another
> homeless man close by has a shopping cart filled with cans. Having one of
> these carts is apparently illegal and the other officer calls him over and starts
> writing him up a citation. The homeless man then takes the citation from the

officer and rips it up and throws it on the ground. The police officers roll their eyes and shake their heads, as if they don't know how to deal with it, finally just walking away. When the police officers leave, I ask the man about why he ripped up the ticket and whether or not he'll pay his fine. With slurred speech, he yells at me, "I don't give a fuck about that! How am I gonna pay that ticket? I don't got no job. See that basket?" pointing to a shopping cart full of bottles. "That's my job and it don't go into my savings account." Everyone around laughs. "So fuck 'em. Fuck 'em all! They'll get me when they get me. And then they'll get me again another time. It don't matter, cause I'm comin' back. Ain't nobody gonna keep me locked up for that!"

The dozens of homeless people whom I have talked with over the years have accumulated citations for a plethora of offences, ranging from minor to more serious. Some of the minor offences include: smoking cigarettes near the pagodas, public drunkenness, open containers of alcohol, jaywalking, blocking the sidewalk, possession of a shopping cart, sleeping in a prohibited place or sleeping at a restricted time (e.g., sleeping on the beach after it closes at midnight), or having an unlicensed (or untagged) dog.[13]

On some occasions, people take time to organize a ride to the courthouse, only to find out upon arrival that the court has no record of the citation because the officers never submitted any paperwork, merely using a ticket as a scare tactic and technique to disrupt their everyday lives. For example, Jake and Stella, a homeless couple in their early sixties, were ticketed for displaying and selling objects on the boardwalk in a prohibited space. I went with them to the Airport Courthouse of the Los Angeles Superior Court. When we finally found the room in which they had to register, the court official told them they had no record of their citation on file. Talking to others confirmed to me that this practice is commonplace.

Unlike driving citations, which produce a huge amount of revenue for cities and states, tickets to the homeless have a different function. Most of the homeless never show up to their hearings, and they rarely pay fines. The judge then issues a warrant for their arrest, and warrants accumulate. But warrants are not about demanding payment or permanently jailing the homeless. They make it easier for LAPD officers to conduct "homeless sweeps," which move them out of a neighborhood for a period of time, simply giving the appearance of a solution. For example, after a barrage of complaints from residents and business owners about the rising number of "vagrants" on the boardwalk, a sweep in February 2010 led to almost fifty arrests of homeless people for warrants and felony violations,[14] making a loud statement about who belongs in this neighborhood. As they have done many times before, officers moved up and down the boardwalk early in the morning, arresting dozens of homeless people. Jesse, a homeless man in his early sixties, has witnessed and been subjected to countless sweeps in his twelve years living in the vicinity. He discusses the process of receiving tickets, accumulating warrants, and becoming subjected to a homeless sweep:

> I've gotten like five or six tickets, but they've all been for dopey things like being in the wrong place at the wrong time. Like one I got, blocking the sidewalk at 4:50 in the morning. Like there's hordes of people that are trying to get past me at 4:00 in the morning. See those are things when you get to court they look at it, and they say, "They gave you a ticket for what?" Then you tell them, and the judge goes, "That's stupid! Dismissed!" And he tears it up. But if you don't show up, that goes into the register, and it says "failure to appear." And "failure to appear" is worse than the ticket. So then, what they do is they wait until your warrants pile up. [He points to surrounding people who are smoking marijuana and passing around a giant bottle of whisky out in the open.] Cause none of these people go to court: they're too fucked up! And then when the warrants pile up, when a holiday comes along, they do a sweep. They go down the beach checking everybody's warrants, and anybody with a warrant gets taken in, and off you go. What they want is for you to have five or six warrants, so that they have a decent reason for you to go to jail for the Fourth of July weekend. Because if they bust you on late enough Thursday or Friday, you're in jail 'til the next court session, which is Monday or Tuesday. So you're there for the whole weekend, and then when you get to court, it's time served and you're back out on the street again, but you weren't out here in Venice making it ugly for the tourists.

Many homeless men and women fall prey to this process, ending up in city jail at least once. Even when they do not go to jail, homeless sweeps disrupt the organizational capacity of a homeless individual. They make the homeless feel uncomfortable in the neighborhood by setting them back months in terms of acquiring important material objects. Sweeps force people to leave behind possessions that have sentimental value (e.g., family photographs), important practical and personal necessities (e.g., prescription medication, blankets, clothing), or items that have taken time and effort for individuals to accrue (e.g., musical instruments, radios, computers). These actions strengthen the label of "people out of place," disrupting the components of their lives that facilitate continuity in a place over time. Arnold, early seventies, who has been homeless in Venice for over thirty-five years, discusses the impact of homeless sweeps on those living on the streets:

> They come out at three o'clock in the morning. Guys will be sleeping near the wall, and they'll tell 'em, you got five minutes to get outta here. By the time the guy gets up—you know five minutes isn't a lot. He can't wake up that fast, 'cause his body's shot. Either stiff from sleeping on the ground, or he'll be all drunk and doped up. Or they're on meds, and they get up and take their medicine to keep them from going crazy. And they tell 'em, if you're not outta here, you're under arrest. And they take all their shit that they got. The guy don't even got time to take his shit with him, to get it all together. So they just leave it out there. And they do it in the middle of the night to catch 'em off guard. They have the beach trucks with 'em and they pile that shit in and they either throw it in the alley or they take it all the way out of there. One time they threw it by [then-councilwoman] Miscikowski's office in Westchester, right in the dumpsters back there.

I talked with Charlie, a homeless man in his late fifties, a few days after he was a victim of a homeless sweep, at which time his computer was taken because he was coerced by police officers to move more rapidly before he could gather his belongings:

> They chased me off the spot. It was the third computer I'd gotten. And this was the one I saved for. I worked my butt off for another company down the street, fifteen bucks a day, working like six hours, hauling candles back and forth. And finally, after maybe like eight or nine months of doing that, I got enough money to get a computer off eBay. I paid about two hundred eighty dollars for it. The cops did a sweep, chased everybody away from their stuff, told us it'd be there when we came back in the morning. Loaded it all into trucks and threw it away. They took the trucks up to some alley on Lincoln and dumped it all off. I had it in a leather knapsack with a chain on it. I had this twisted wire with the loops in the end, wrapped around the whole thing, and that was chained to the structure down there where the bicycles are, at the end of the parking lot. I was in the space between it and the wall behind it. I heard the cops, they woke me up. I managed to get my bedroll and sleeping

shit all packed up and the last thing to go was that, and it was on a combination lock. And the cop was badgering me so much, and saying, it will be here
in the morning. And it was locked up so I expected it to be there in the morning. But on the way out, I saw the lady cops cutting the chains off the children's bicycles. And they have these big bolt cutters, and I was like "Oh shit!"
When I went back in the morning, I found the mouse pad that I put between
the closed halves of the laptop, which meant that the cops not only cut the
thing loose, but they cut it open. They had to cut the lock off the bag, open
the bag, open the laptop, take the mouse pad out.

Charlie's experience demonstrates the complex ecology that moti-
vates a cycle of uncertainty. The boardwalk provides Charlie with an opportunity to earn money and purchase a computer, and he has free access to public institutions, such as the Venice Library and the Vera Davis
Center, where he can plug in his computer to keep it running. Stigmatizing the homeless through cultural repertoires and discontinuity techniques marks them as "people out of place." Yet it occurs at the same
time that Venice remains a "home for the homeless."

A Home for the Homeless

Despite the barrage of discontinuity techniques, several features of local
neighborhood life enable the homeless to establish durable ties. *Informal survival resources* contribute food, clothing, economic opportunities, and local knowledge to the homeless. *Countercultural associations*
mix together housed and homeless residents and facilitate a sense of belonging through a variety of cultural events and left-wing political actions. *Formal service agencies* from certified and well-funded institutions
have emerged on Rose Avenue and Lincoln Boulevard. They develop
consistent programs for food distribution, mental health care, job training, and other opportunities. At the same time that there are city ordinances used to stigmatize the homeless, there are *governmental protections* that demonstrate the multisided character of the state. Venice's
location in the California Coastal Zone safeguards public access to the
beach, which has secured connections for those living in their vehicles
west of Lincoln Boulevard. Together, these local mechanisms generate
conditions that continue to attract homeless men and women to Venice,

sustain them over a period of time, and give rise to a social geography of homeless clustering.

Practical characteristics of the local area often serve the interests of the homeless. I call these informal survival resources, because they are not organized or sanctioned by any central agency. People learn about them through participation within a given locale. For example, some people transcend their homeless status through routine associations with housed residents. Being in a neighborhood for a long period of time or developing a local function on a residential block facilitates acceptance from housed residents. Karen, now sixty-one, has lived on and off in Venice since the late 1980s. After leaving Los Angeles for several years, she returned to Venice in 2004 and purchased a used RV. Karen shows me inside her RV and walks me around the area immediately outside it, discussing how she inserted herself as a stable neighbor in this specific location:

We walk over to where her RV is parked and she says, "This is my office. I just call it my office because technically you're not supposed to sleep in it." Karen tells me she has parked it in the same spot for over a year and only moves it during restricted times, such as street cleaning days. When she first parked there, a group of homeless had left a huge mess on the sidewalk and she cleaned it up, filling up two large garbage bags. She continued to keep the small block clean, and over time, in place of the trash, she created a small colorful garden in a vacant plot of land. She also took action to deal with feral cats running rampant around and underneath nearby properties, trapping them, getting them spayed, and taking care of them. She became very close with one of the neighbors who helped her with that process. In addition, she was responsible for moving a crack dealer who was sleeping on the corner, blocking it off so he could not move back into the location. Her efforts to clean up the neighborhood were noticed by a few people living in the adjacent apartment complex and residents started to look out for her, treating her as a respected neighbor. On one evening, she told me that a boarder paying rent to stay in her RV was verbally harassing her. She says, "I wanted him to leave, but he wouldn't leave. And I guess our voices got so loud, that [a neighbor] heard us, because we were right outside. And she ran down and she said, 'Karen, are you alright?' And then I said, 'No actually, blablabla.' And she got rid of him. I mean she came out and she laid into him. She verbally whipped him and got him out."

Karen is skilled at building social networks in the neighborhood. One of her friends lives in a nearby house and has provided her with a key to allow her access. During the course of our first interview, we walk over, she lets us into the house, makes us tea, and we sit down and discuss her life as a homeless person in Venice, conducting the interview in the private backyard of a single-family residence.

It is not necessary for every housed resident on the block to accept the homeless in order for homeless individuals to feel as though they belong. When a resident reaches out to a person on the streets, it affects their perception of the location as safe and comfortable. Chelsea, early fifties, discusses her attachment of several years to a specific block:

> There's a couple down there, with the green house. They bring me food, like soup or raviolis or some hot meals. And these people help out with money sometimes. And these other people down the alley, they give me money and food sometimes. And it's not even that. Even if they don't give me nothing, I don't care, as long as they say hi, that makes me feel good. It makes me feel like I'm part of here. They treat me just like they would to anybody else. I've been introduced to family members, and they show me their babies. They tell me about their families and that's real nice.

Despite a trend toward stigmatizing and criminalizing the homeless, Chelsea's story is quite common. Individuals develop meaningful social relationships that bind them to a part of a neighborhood over time. For those with few material possessions and a life without the comforts of a private home, association with and kindness from specific housed residents makes them feel as if they belong and have status in the neighborhood. In some cases, informal ties sustain their social integration by keeping them from falling further outside of communication networks. Homeless people often lose track of their own families and friends, but sometimes the local place makes it possible to track down those without an address or a telephone. Finding a homeless person often becomes a trick of local knowledge, as I learned from my own experiences:

> Carl is an electrician by trade who sometimes hooks up with friends and works on construction projects. He has a job in Oxnard coming up in the next week and he'll spend a few days there, make a little bit of money, and then return to the streets and beaches of Venice, where he has been living, on and off, since 1984. We agree to meet up when he returns so I can spend the day

with him and witness his life in action. I ask how to get in touch with him. He tells me of a local bike rental shop near the boardwalk. I should walk to the back of the bike store and his friend Ron, who is also homeless, will be there. Ron doesn't work there, but he spends his days in the back of the store with the owner, listening to the radio and watching a portable television. I should tell Ron that I'm a friend of Carl's and he'll know where to find him and whether or not he has yet returned from Oxnard.

The popular boardwalk also provides a range of informal prospects through vending, day laboring, panhandling, drug dealing, finding items in dumpsters or discarded on the sides of streets for trash collection and then selling them, and stealing objects and distributing them, most significantly bicycles, electronics, paint supplies, and clothing. The boardwalk also serves as a constant source of food. I hear repeatedly among the homeless that "it's impossible to go hungry in Venice." People rarely need to spend their earned money on food. Film crews on site for days and sometimes weeks at a time leave dozens of untouched catered trays; individuals and religious groups walk along the boardwalk and distribute bagged lunches and snacks; and grassroots activists and other neighborhood groups, such as the Hare Krishnas and Food Not Bombs, serve regular meals.

Moreover, a number of long-term homeless men and women are experts at acquiring supplies, often based on established informal connections, and they then distribute these supplies to others on the street. Jonas has been homeless in Venice for almost four decades and knows a wide variety of residents and business owners from whom he obtains food, clothing, and other supplies. He regularly shows up on the boardwalk with coolers and bags full of fresh food, ranging from breads and pastries to fruits, vegetables, and even different cuts of beef and chicken, which homeless friends will barbeque in the parking lot. He occasionally acquires shoes, clothing, and blankets. Because of his local reputation, homeless people know to come to him if they are hungry or if they need a particular article of clothing. He passes on decades of street knowledge to other homeless men and women living near Rose Avenue and the beach, especially younger men and women, leading them in a direction of self-sustainability. While not part of any organization, Jonas is a key resource for dozens of homeless people living in the vicinity.

The formation of local countercultural associations mixes together housed residents and the homeless through cultural events and political actions. Most of the countercultural housed residents are now in their sixties, uniting with self-defined "gypsies" and "hippies" of the same age who live in RVs, school buses, vans, and cars. This continuing relationship is comparable to the 1960s-era travelers detailed above, although many of the homeless have lived on the streets for decades because of difficult economic, social, psychological, or other health-related circumstances, making the homeless/bohemian distinction very tricky.[15]

Many of the mobile homeless park their RVs or vans on the streets intersecting Rose Avenue, and those without vehicles find a place to sleep on or near Venice Beach. They often make their way to the boardwalk, especially in the summer when it is most crowded, to display and sell handmade arts and crafts or play music, blending into the boardwalk's economic spectacle. They secure social ties with housed residents through the organization of common interests, arranging a wide array of festivities, parties, poetry readings, and artistic and musical events. In figure 9, housed and homeless gather at a Summer Solstice Party at the Sponto Gallery (formerly the famed Venice West Café), which, before closing, was located a few feet from the northern end of the Venice Boardwalk close to Rose Avenue. Homeless poets, musicians, and activists join longtime residents in a free celebration with food, music, poetry, and art. With no entry fee, it attracts more homeless people and blurs the distinction between bohemianism and homelessness.

FIGURE 9. Sponto Gallery integrates homeless and countercultural groups.

Political action also unifies the housed and the homeless. Long-term left-wing activists in Venice, losing their clout due to an expanding mass of gentrifiers, draw upon the homeless population to boost their political stature. When members of the Peace and Freedom Party held a majority on the Venice Neighborhood Council in the early 2000s, homeless men and women joined long-standing countercultural residents in the Poverty and Homelessness Subcommittee of the Venice Neighborhood Council to seek protections for people living on the street. They also appointed a longtime homeless musician and artist to become the Boardwalk Subcommittee Chairman, an act perceived as controversial by many housed residents because of the divisiveness of the homeless issue. In fact, the place of homelessness in the city-funded neighborhood council has caused a great deal of turmoil. It has led to major conflicts in this organization and several threats of decertification by city officials. Tired of the conflicts, many of the countercultural activists pursued alternative political venues. Homeless men and women assisted them in reinstituting the Venice Town Council in order to oppose the city's attempts to implement overnight parking districts.

Formal service agencies stem from a more limited point of departure: certified institutions such as nonprofit organizations, community-based organizations, and religious institutions extend assistance to the homeless and provide a variety of offerings. They officially document their services, accumulating evidence of action for their financial donors, who are some of the wealthiest private corporations and federal and state granting agencies. They also require their clients to sign up and undergo a strict regimen in order to continue receiving services, requirements that are difficult for many of the homeless to fulfill.

Several well-funded organizations transformed their aims to meet the needs of the growing homeless population. The St. Joseph Center and the Venice Family Clinic, both located on Rose Avenue, are the most resource-rich among them. These agencies took form during the 1970s in order to assist financially struggling renters living in the area. Throughout the '80s and '90s, as the homeless population grew, these providers expanded their role in managing homelessness, adding new programs to specifically address homeless problems, which also brought greater recognition from the city, state, and private granting foundations.

Formal resources in downtown skid row intertwine with its symbolic identity because of the sheer volume of services, creating a recurring pattern of supply and demand among the homeless. Even if Venice's home-

FIGURE 10. Cluster of RVs near Rose Avenue.

less are not initially attracted to local social service agencies in the same way as they are in downtown L.A., most learn about the local resources from others and take advantage of them at some point in time. As a result, many cluster in surrounding blocks, sleeping in the area, hanging out on the northern end of the boardwalk, or parking their vehicles either on Rose Avenue or on many of the streets that intersect Rose Avenue, as shown in figure 10. Often equating it to downtown skid row, local residents and business owners have come to label the area as "Skid Rose."

St. Joseph Center and the Venice Family Clinic are central to the everyday survival of a large segment of the homeless population. These agencies are controversial in a very similar way as law enforcement agencies. Like law enforcement, they are middle managers and offer no resolution to the neighborhood's homeless issues, operating on the opposite end of the conflict by sustaining a wide range of services amidst residential life. They also have a great deal of financial security that makes competing with them comparable to challenging a very wealthy neighbor. The Venice Family Clinic has almost $18 million in total assets. The largest free clinic in the country with seven locations, its headquarters and original location are located on Rose Avenue. The clinic serves 23,500 patients, 16 percent of whom are homeless. As part of its homeless outreach, it also offers a "street medicine" program where health care providers make weekly visits to areas of high homeless concentration and offer medical care and advice. Likewise, the St. Joseph Center has revenue from thrift shops, fund-raising, and grants and other contributions that totals close to $12 million. It helps well over two thousand homeless people on a yearly basis. It has a café lunch program where homeless make reservations; it provides showers, laundry, phone and mail services; its staff helps with shelter placement, mental health treatment, and government aid applications, and offers the homeless a case manager in situations where people are ready to commit to long-term change.

Governmental protections play a fundamental role in configuring the composition of the homeless population in Venice. Because the city, state, and federal governments rely on nonprofit organizations like those on Rose Avenue, service providers have strong political connections, receiving large state and federal grants and constant kudos from politicians for their work. City politicians are also forced into an odd middle position. City council members want to secure residential safety for constituents, strongly supporting LAPD and their efforts to alleviate quality of life concerns; but at the same time they realize that social services are taking on necessary responsibilities that once fell to government agencies. Thus, they often support the expansion of services at the same time that they support increased police protection.

Moreover, multiple arms of the state compete over the control of coastal access. The lack of a legal infrastructure for parking makes Venice stand out from surrounding coastal areas as an open site for those who live in their vehicles on the streets of Los Angeles. Many coastal communities have already instituted limits, in certain cases without going through the coastal commission's exemption processes. Yet chronic mobile homelessness has swelled in Venice due to a lack of legal restrictions for overnight parking. The Los Angeles City Council has placed limitations on streets east of Lincoln Boulevard in Venice. West of Lincoln Boulevard, however, is part of the state-designated Coastal Zone under the jurisdiction of the California Coastal Commission. Although nearby Santa Monica, Marina del Rey, and Pacific Palisades, also located in the Coastal Zone, successfully instituted preferential parking districts, the state coastal commissioners maintain that parking restrictions in Venice conflict with the commission's edict that everyone should have access to the coast. While local city council members and congressmen support parking regulations, the coastal commission has overturned two of their attempts to implement them. Ian Lovett (2009) writes in the *Free Venice Beachhead*,

> On June 11, the California Coastal Commission voted 9–1 . . . to reject a proposal to institute Overnight Parking Districts in Venice between the hours of 2–6 am. The vote came at the end of a five-hour public hearing, which featured testimony from the LAPD, City Councilman Bill Rosendahl, and hundreds of Venice residents. At the end of the public testimony, Commissioner Mary Shallenberger said, "As an individual, I find it heart-wrenching, but unfortunately as a commissioner I have to look only through the lens of coastal protection. . . . We're being asked to balance between the homeless and the parking needs of residents, and that's not our job." She then proposed a "No" vote to reject the proposal, explaining that the plan would render the beach "exclusively for Venice residents between the hours of . . . 2–6 am, and that is not consistent with the coastal act."

The simultaneous pattern of stabilizing mechanisms and discontinuity techniques, neither of which resolves homelessness, pins the homeless in a position of constant uncertainty. As a result, individuals on the streets become experts at spatial adaptation, intimately learning how to use the environment to their daily advantages. They develop a subtle local knowledge about the area: a set of methods to protect themselves from LAPD interventions, residential stigmatization, and violence and antagonism from other homeless people.[16]

Spatial Adaptations

Spatial adaptations stem from a special type of street knowledge available to the homeless about how to use the local environment to procure safety. The homeless face a plethora of dangers living in public space. Theft, drug abuse, violence, stigmatization, and criminalization plague their worlds. Sustaining themselves on the street requires people to learn a series of skills particular to a given locale to ease the harsh conditions and protect their bodies and belongings. Although residents persistently complain about social services, Venice actually has few; shelters, which provide the most immediate source of security, do not exist in the area.[17] As a result, the chronically homeless create physical and social boundaries between themselves and others to foster a sense of privacy in public space.

It is true that under certain conditions, the designs of the built environment disrupt homeless attachments, a common thesis attributed to Mike Davis ([1990] 1992) and William H. Whyte (1988). But a closer examination on the ground shows how people employ spatial adaptations to adjust the built environment to their own needs. Physical boundaries, for instance, are the alcoves in the spatial landscape, areas distanced from human contact, and spaces surrounded by concrete partitions, fences, or shrubbery. These become hideaways that enable independence and privacy against environmental and social elements.

I first learned about these physical boundaries from Aldo, a long-term homeless man in his midsixties. One evening after attending a community meeting, Aldo asks me to give him a ride home. My immediate thought response is, "How do I drive a homeless person home? Where should I go?" Once in the car, Aldo directs me to Speedway, an alleyway located one block inland from the boardwalk. He then points out the place where he has been sleeping for several months. We approach a space behind an apartment building, surrounded by two brick walls, with two large dumpsters blocking off the alleyway, and a concrete wall separating the parking lot and the boardwalk. Before he exits my car, I ask Aldo how he found this space, to which he replies:

> It's just a matter of finding spots that you're not gonna get noticed. You feel like a fugitive in a science fiction movie sometimes, where you're up against the guys in the white outfits—that's what the police are. And as far as it goes, unless you know they're not, assume everyone else is hostile. If you find out they're not hostile, it's usually when they open the back door or see you sleeping near their garage or something and they leave you a blanket, and then you're like, "OK this is an OK space."

The homeless use these spaces to construct encampments and to store belongings, often returning over a period of time (see figure 11). Sometimes they retrieve used mattresses, sleeping bags, or blankets, and a few even have tents. On another occasion, I plan to meet Anthony,

FIGURE 11. Homeless encampment between wall and shrubs out of direct public view.

midforties, who at the time of this encounter has been homeless for over four years, the last six months of which were spent in Venice:

> As the weather is getting colder, Anthony says that life outside becomes a bit more difficult, because he only has a thin blanket to cover himself when he sleeps. I tell him that my friend has a sleeping bag that she no longer wants and that I could get it and bring it to him tomorrow. I ask him where he'll be and he walks over to the other side of the boardwalk and shows me a nook in between two buildings. A layer of cardboard fans out across the space and blocks it off from the boardwalk pedestrian traffic. As I approach, it appears like a small hut sandwiched between two buildings. He calls it his "sleeping spot." Behind the cardboard, invisible to the public eye, are multiple bags filled with material belongings and piles of crates and cardboard boxes. He tells me that if he's not around, I can place the sleeping bag behind the crates and he'll get it.

RVs, and to a lesser extent other vehicles, such as cars, old school buses, and vans, also become high-status resources among the homeless to construct physical boundaries. They offer some of the conveniences of a private residence; most significantly, they instantly impose impenetrable barriers between public and private. Although RVs give the appearance of mobility, many of them are semipermanent; people only move them when necessary, operating instead like a small cottage docked in public space. Rebecca, in her early sixties, has been homeless in Venice on and off for close to thirty years, but has only lived in an RV for the last ten. She discusses both the constraints and freedoms:

> Living in an RV is the closest I've had to living in my own home, since I left home being a kid. Because when you live in apartments, it's theirs, ya know? You think it's yours, but it's really not [laughing]. And they're constantly reminding you. In an RV, it's yours. You can paint the ceiling if you want. Like I got seagulls painted all across my ceiling, and a sunset and seagulls flying all across. It's mine. Although, you're still stuck with that [sleeping in RVs] not being legal, because you're not supposed to sleep in it. But for the last three years they've been letting me get away with that. Maybe three years ago, two or three years ago, they tried to do a crackdown. They had us all freaked out. . . . They got rid of some people. And then we found our spot [after trying other spaces where they were hassled], and they never bother us ever.

There is a network related to the mobile homeless world. People buy and sell aging and damaged mobile homes from others on the street. In some circumstances, the same vehicles remain in Venice under different ownership for long periods of time. For example, when Karen moved back to Venice in the early 2000s, she went looking to buy an RV. When she first moved back, she was living in a van in a friend's driveway. Vincent, a homeless friend who had been living on the streets of Venice for decades, helped her find her own RV. Due to his extended time in the community, Vincent was connected to countless people, and one of his homeless connections was planning to move away, opening up the opportunity for Karen to purchase his RV.

People living on the streets without any shelter sometimes find it in another person's vehicle. Many larger RVs have partitions on the inside that separate the total space into rooms and people rent them out for days and weeks at a time, negotiating charges with their boarders. Karen has rented out part of her RV to several different people at different times, to make a little bit of extra money. RVs become safe havens for transients looking to restart their lives, people in between apartments, those trying to avoid some form of danger, or those who are escaping the weather for a short period. She discusses the renting process:

> I met this guy. His name was Joey. He's about early forties. And he was a designing engineer, like doing computer design, really technical stuff. But he had gotten down. He was in the dot-com bubble. But when it burst, he must have been one of the ones who fell. And he ended up on the streets in Venice. And he ended up smoking crack. He was used to earning a hundred dollars an hour and now he was living on unemployment. So he was living in a VW van, but it wasn't running. And eventually what happened was that he was looking for a place to stay. And I said "OK, we'll try it out." I charged him five dollars a night. And he'd pay me his five dollars. And this is a typical homeless scenario. Anybody who's got a vehicle, there's always someone else out there that wants to rent. It's done all the time.

In addition to physical boundaries, others manufacture a sense of security through group associations, forming social boundaries. Constructing social boundaries also relies on local knowledge about where to set up group concentrations. Locations such as well-lit sidewalks under building overpasses, street segments with only commercial (and no residential) buildings, and more isolated corners of city parks and city property can become prime locations for social clustering.

Although living in a vehicle provides increased security, the position of the vehicle directly on the street also generates certain dangers, due to heightened opposition about overnight parking. Many of the homeless in Venice claim that groups of housed residents bang on the sides of vehicles late at night or leave threatening notices on their windshields, and even destroy property. Some have shown me broken windshield wipers, cracked mirrors, shattered windows, and slashed tires, which they attribute to hostile housed residents. In addition, due to regular complaints to the LAPD, officers are often on the scene scrutinizing the circumstances of the rows of RVs. Because sleeping in a vehicle is technically illegal, the mobile homeless must play a game with the LAPD, in which they pretend they are not at home. Most mobile homeless cluster together on the same streets, such as along Rose Avenue, generating a greater sense of security and community.

For those further down in the status system, who are without a vehicle, group associations help establish social boundaries based on the number of people involved and the overwhelming presence of their material belongings, which together siphon off an area as a temporary home. During the summer of 2007, a group of about fifteen homeless people in their twenties were regularly sleeping outside of a boardwalk food stall called Big Daddy's for a period of months, and the collection of sleeping bags, tents, baskets, carts, and suitcases created a clear-cut social separation from their surroundings during the hours between 8:00 p.m. and 8:00 a.m. when the group dispersed. I ask Jacob, a local homeless artist in his late twenties about it:

> Down by Big Daddy's is a safe harbor for a lot of the artists and other people that are in transit, between homes and what not. It's safe. It's out in the open. There's good lighting there. So the police do patrol the area and it's kind of safe. Everything is so risky and very dangerous out here that you try to pick your battles very carefully. There's a lot of people that are using serious speed or drugs that create a lot of anger, because the speed causes people to react very angrily. Especially if you're homeless and dirty and hungry. All you spend your money on is the drug and they see people out here as the opportunities to feed their addictions, whether it's money or drugs. The thing that amazes me most is the homeless preying on the homeless. It happens all the time. So we do that [sleep in groups] for safety, but it's also convenient, because we work on the beach right here, that's like 150 feet away. I carry all my art with me so I keep it with me at all times, because the storage units are so far away that transporting it is very dangerous. Like more than ten times, I've had stuff fall off the cart trying to get it up there going on Rose Avenue to the nearest storage unit available. I keep it with me and as long as it's not going to rain; well even at Big Daddy's it's a good shelter for rain as well.

Such secure spaces, however, only serve as protection from other homeless people. Several weeks after this conversation, business owners decided to install gates out front of the area after business hours ended. Upon closing, they blocked off this sleeping location, which forced this group of young homeless men and women to relocate to another area. The group decided to sleep on the beach closer to the Venice Pier. After several weeks, LAPD officers decided to enforce the ordinance that restricts people from accessing the beach after midnight, which required that the group break up into smaller segments and find multiple places around the neighborhood, independent of one another. This Russian doll scenario, breaking apart homeless clusters into smaller and smaller divisions, once again calls attention to the local knowledge of spatial adaptations.

After this series of disruptions, Jacob walks me over to his sleeping location, several blocks inland from the boardwalk. "It's much safer up here," he says. "I don't need a big group. I only have to worry about the cops." Instead of developing a social boundary with a group, Jacob found an alcove on a mostly commercial street, in a corner where a fence meets a building wall, blocking the view. The idea that sleeping several blocks inland is safer and more steady than the boardwalk in terms of avoiding recurring disruptions is common among the homeless, who must tactically walk a fine line between avoiding the random and violent behavior that stems from a constant pattern of drug use and transience at Venice Beach, and avoiding the strategic eyes of LAPD officers who at any moment can call attention to and confront the minutiae of homeless behaviors.

Conclusion

The relationship between homelessness and neighborhood life is wrought with uncertainties at every turn. Homeless individuals are positioned in the middle of a local ecology of support and ongoing discontinuity techniques. A wide variety of resources helps to sustain Venice as a "home for the homeless," but at the same time law enforcement and political practices seek to uproot them from specific locations as "people out of place." Thrust in the middle of these competing tendencies, the homeless remain in Venice but face recurring prospects of stigmatization in daily life, police citations and arrests, loss of material belongings, and additional dangers posed by other homeless men and women. This position of uncertainty necessitates that they intimately learn how to adapt to the local landscape.

Housed residents are similarly thrust into a complex situation. They are not uniformly opposed to the homeless in the way that many critics of gentrification assert. Some housed residents, especially those affiliated with Venice's historic counterculture, are empathetic to the plight of the homeless and provide meals and occasional money to specific homeless individuals that live on their blocks. Those who stand opposed to the homeless and take part in this stigmatization process face real constraints and dangers. These constraints lead them to establish greater social distance in the face of physical proximity. Although they may understand in principle that the homeless are a group with internal variations, they also learn to filter their interpretations of homelessness through a series of cultural repertoires that stigmatize the homeless as a general social category and seek to solve recurring problems through official political avenues.

Cultural repertoires become intertwined with official political and law enforcement priorities. But even among political, legislative, and law enforcement positions there is no uniform stance about homelessness. City council members are caught in the middle of competing tendencies. They empathize with homeless individuals, support the need for more social services, and simultaneously seek greater protections for housed constituents who want to move the homeless from their neighborhoods. LAPD officers are called upon to manage this large-scale problem, but they lack the ability or resources to solve homelessness. They simply manage its day-to-day existence, using the law enforcement tools of their trade and encountering inconsistent advice from legislators, judges, city attorneys, and their own superiors.

To further complicate matters, different arms of the state clash in their approaches to homelessness. City council members pass new ordinances that provide police officers with additional tools to manage daily infractions. Agencies of the state and federal government reward funds to social service providers who help to support the homeless. Judges often uphold constitutional rights of individuals to access public spaces without harassment, which have protected men and women who sleep outside. Moreover, the California Coastal Commission enforces its own mandate to protect equal access to the coast, overturning many prior city council attempts to restrict opportunities for people sleeping in their vehicles.

The inherent contradiction between the stigmatization and stabilization of the homeless maintains Rose Avenue's label as "diverse" and "gritty." The ambiguous neighborhood public culture stands in direct contrast to the Venice Canals, where a coherent identity as a "scenic neighborhood" has taken root at the exclusion of once alternative possibilities. How did the Venice Canals materialize as a prototypical wealthy Los Angeles enclave when in fact just several decades earlier it was home to the unconventional, a neighborhood where hippies and bikers existed in a symbiotic relationship with perfectly "tragic" surroundings of cracked sidewalks caving into stagnant and foul-smelling waterways?

CHAPTER FOUR

Scenic Neighborhood

Whenever friends and family visit Los Angeles, I take them to the picturesque Venice Canals. We meander up and down a maze of sidewalks, where evenly manicured shrubs separate the footpaths from the sparkling waterways. Arched wooden footbridges allow us to cross over each of the six channels to catch a better view of remodeled and colorfully painted California bungalows, bright and open three-story homes, and a few much larger gingerbread-looking houses with undulating rooftops. Manicured lawns and thriving gardens are set below huge picture windows through which we look at airy architectural designs with open kitchens and high ceilings. The songs of various bird species are heard from every corner of this otherwise quiet neighborhood, where walkways and waterways, rather than roadways, serve as the most visible mode of travel. A slow-moving current quietly slaps the concrete walls; together with a faint salt and algae smell, it evokes a quaint seaside feeling.

The neighborhood blends together these different pieces into a holistic portrait, as if it is a scene to be looked at. Yet achieving this delicate balance of visible cues that have come to represent a coherent upscale lifestyle required the elimination of competing symbolic codes. If we took the same tour forty years earlier, we would have experienced a much different setting. The Canals had a distinct set of emblematic features that shaped its reputation as "unconventional." Broken-down sidewalks were caving into stagnant and slimy waterways; rickety wooden bungalows that were only a few hundred square feet were crowded with tenants; empty lots could be found all over the place, some made into small vest-pocket parks for the children to play in; dogs and ducks ran wild through the canals; jobless hippies lived rent-free in many of the neighborhood's open spaces; renters employed informal methods of sur-

vival that ranged from selling drugs to art to jewelry to fresh produce out
of their homes and garages; and art, music, and the politicization of identity infused everyday interactions.

This chapter examines the shifting political configurations that transformed the public culture of the Canals from an unconventional countercultural haven into a scenic upscale neighborhood. The six canals that
remain today were initially part of Abbot Kinney's grand design to rep-
licate Venice, Italy. Yet most of the waterways were filled in during the
1920s to make room for the automobile. Those that remained fell into
disrepair along with the rest of Venice. Three decades later, speculators started to rebuild and restore the coast, and as part of their strategic
plan, they wanted to make the waterways navigable by larger boats and
connect them to the brand new Marina del Rey, where people could then
sail out into the Pacific Ocean. For over twenty years, countercultural
renters fought off the influence of speculators.

The in-migration of the middle class into the Venice Canals during
the 1970s introduced a new set of visible cues that stood out as distinct
from the countercultural renters of the neighborhood. Some members
of the middle class sought out proximity to this unique bohemian lifestyle while others simply wanted to purchase an inexpensive house by
the beach. Yet taking part in the process of neighborhood change, they
displaced the possibility of a continuing countercultural resistance. They
took part in a new political dispute with speculative developers that
changed the types of political conversations about the future of the Canals neighborhood. While the countercultural residents were engaged in
a battle to completely hold off physical renovations of the infrastructure
and preserve a stable renter class, the property-owning middle class and
the speculators changed the debate about the aesthetic character of the
environment. The conflict was no longer about whether the restoration
should take place; it was about how it would happen and what it would
look like.

The reinvention of the Canals as a "scenic neighborhood" was typical of Southern California's postmodern urban planning. Just as Kinney's Venice of America was an imitation of the romantic Italian original, the effort to remodel the Canals was an imitation of Kinney's Los
Angeles original. While speculators sought out ways to link the existing
waterways to Marina del Rey and promote a more upscale locale, the
middle class fought to make the Canals into a "historic neighborhood"
by inventing a new meaning of history that never before existed out of

remaining physical fragments. They conceived of a new idea of a charming, scenic neighborhood by advocating for lot size restrictions, limitations on housing development, and wildlife preservation, believing that it somehow accurately reflected the original intentions of Abbot Kinney.

The relationships between middle-class property owners and speculators led to new political compromises and a significantly modified plan with shallow waterways, restrictive building codes, and no connection to Marina del Rey. Nevertheless, after thirty-two years of battles over how to build a scenic neighborhood and fifty-one years after the city initially closed down the sidewalks to public access, the restoration finally took place. A neighborhood homology between groups, symbols, and space came to represent a coherent upscale public culture. The middle-class private culture and work ethic became intertwined with the architectural ingenuity of a more luxurious class who have continued to view restrictive building codes as a design challenge that forces them to adopt cutting-edge methods that maximize space and amenities. After the renovations, the newest residents were even wealthier than previous ones, as property values multiplied. Despite profound economic differences between the middle and upper classes, successive waves of homeowners shared similar cultural conventions, erased the major class conflict of the past, and contributed to building a well-manicured scenic neighborhood.

An Unconventional Neighborhood

When visitors walk along the canals, avoiding the quacking mallards that waddle beside them on the sidewalks, it is impossible to imagine the countercultural haven that existed several decades ago. The environment is quaint and quiet: couples stroll hand in hand, neighbors work in their gardens, and families sit outside enjoying the breeze rolling in from the Pacific Ocean. Yet the 1960s milieu gave off completely different symbolic cues that were supported by a ramshackle infrastructure, outsiders' perceptions of danger and disorganization, and a countercultural moral code.

The infrastructural conditions were key to the Canals' collective representation as a countercultural haven appealing to hippies, artists, and bikers. The look and feel of the area that attracted them averted a massive and instantaneous middle- and upper-class overhaul that was characteristic of the brand new marina development directly to the south. The Canals were a relatively secluded neighborhood with only one car lane passing through it, which limited spontaneous discovery. In the 1940s, the city closed off the sidewalks to the public because they had caved into the waterways (see figure 12). Two decades later, these conditions still existed along with rickety, paint-peeling footbridges and small bungalows. People who knew of the Canals often referred to the area as a "swamp"; the water was at times so stagnant, shallow, and filled

FIGURE 12. Canal sidewalks prior to redevelopment. Photograph by Darryl DuFay.

with algae that it appeared less like a series of man-made waterways and more like a slimy, mud-filled marsh. Jacob, in his midfifties, who moved in with his girlfriend in the 1970s, describes the conditions at that time:

> Where we lived on Linnie Canal was like a wild riverbank. All of the sidewalks had broken away. It was just muddy flats. You couldn't access it on one side and it had grown over on the other side. So the couple of years we lived there, not one person ever passed in front of our house. It wasn't pedestrian friendly at all. You had to walk over craggly, jagged, broken slabs of cement to get around and most people just didn't know this was here. Before I moved in, I lived [in another Venice neighborhood] for a year and a half before I realized that it was back here. It was a hidden kind of place.

The Canals were the most extreme locale in a beach town already recognized as unconventional. Outsiders and hopeful speculators interpreted the conditions as dirty and unkempt. Jack Smith of the *Los Angeles Times* described the Canals in 1961:

> Today [the Canals] are no more than unsightly troughs, littered with cans, bottles, tires and dead fish. Their sluggish waters generate unpleasant odors. Recently a gas boiling up from the Grand Canal [the western-most waterway and the source of fresh ocean water into the canals] . . . peeled the paint from nearby homes. . . . The canals and their adjoining sidewalks have been legally out of bounds since 1942, when they were withdrawn from public use. They are posted now with no-trespassing signs. Adding to the general deterioration have been the oil fields in the canal area. Brine produced by this industry's operations has backed into the canals, compounding the odor problem.

This description was not just newspaper hyperbole. The journalistic impression speaks to a middle-class aesthetic code about what was wrong with the area. A clear pattern is evident among current residents who describe their initial perceptions of the Canals years or even decades before they even considered moving in. In the 1960s and early '70s, they recall a dangerous and rundown place that they would *never live in*. Marissa, in her late fifties, who eventually moved into the neighborhood in the late '70s, remembers visiting in the '60s, "I remember driving over the canals and looking down at them. They were broken down. And every house was a cottage and there were empty lots, and motorcycles, and at that time I thought it was dangerous. I certainly didn't come down here and hang out."

Jacob, a UCLA student during the early '70s, wanted to live near the beach within relative proximity to his college campus. He ended up choosing Marina del Rey before moving to Venice and eventually into the Canals. He says, "Actually one night we came here to look at an apartment and it was nighttime, and I'll tell ya, the place was so scary, that I thought, 'Ya know, this place isn't for me.' So I left and didn't even come back to look around for at least six months."

Marvin, in his early sixties, a current resident who moved into his multimillion-dollar Canal house in the early 2000s after he sold his 5,500-square-foot home in a wealthy L.A. hills community, discusses his first and only visit to the Canals before relocating there four decades later: "The first time I knew about the Canals was some time in the mid-[19]60s. We were invited to a party here. It was at night. I couldn't find a place to park. I couldn't find the address. There weren't any sidewalks. My wife and I said to each other after the party, 'Let's get out of here and we're never coming back here, that's for sure. This place is really a wreck.' We never thought about it again [for the next forty years]."

This perception of the Canals as an area to avoid was commonplace during this period. In fact, one-third of the neighborhood's parcels were vacant, a symbol of high supply and low demand, a sharp contrast to today's fully occupied environment where property values have largely withstood the most recent economic slump of the 2000s. Yet the very symbolic codes that either repelled people with money or made them want to "invest and restore" the environment—the ramshackle infrastructure, cheaply constructed, wood-frame bungalows, and abandoned lots—were central to a specific subset of the population who cultivated a lifestyle and identity that benefited from the surroundings.

A rundown environment meant cheap rent, so residents did not have to hold down steady, full-time jobs. These conditions were amenable to the local germination of a more widespread countercultural moral code that was sweeping through the nation in the '60s. Young men and women with predominantly middle-class upbringings renounced their previous existences for a simpler and more communal lifestyle. This self-imposed poverty was distinct from the poverty stemming from chronic homelessness or forced segregation and isolation in Oakwood. In this instance, it was about the freedom to make a clear break from the past, collectively constructing cultural commonality rather than having categories imposed upon you.[1] According to Mark, now in his early sixties, who moved into the Canals in 1968,

> It was a secluded place and that allowed a subculture to grow. My friends from Hollywood [where he grew up as a middle-class kid] thought I was crazy for living here. It smelled and it was dangerous. There were biker gangs, like Satan's Slaves. They would literally come into my friend's house and take over. They'd eat what was in his refrigerator, put their arms around his girlfriend. They were violent—we would walk around trying to avoid them. So people didn't really want to live here. It was dirty, dangerous, and it was drug-infested. But there were also a lot of young people who had common interests in music, art, fashion, and politics. There was a lot of partying and a lot of hanging out. And not caring about money was the main thing. People just got by and survived because the rents were inexpensive. They didn't have to get a regular job. If you needed cash, you just did what you needed to get by. Some people sold drugs, or I should say a lot of people sold drugs [laughing]. I remember one guy sold vegetables out of his garden. I sold things out of my garage and that became a weekly thing. Every Saturday, I sold clothing, antiques, and other things out of my garage. And these hippie girls would come in and buy things.

The self-imposed poverty directly contrasted with the American middle-class, suburban dream that everyone should have a private house and a backyard.[2] The inexpensive neighborhood allowed people to avoid the established conventions of single-family dwellings, constrained gender divisions, and career ambitions. Gina describes her experience moving into the Canals in the early '70s as an escape from suburban gender norms. In her new neighborhood, equality ruled the day, angst about making a profit was commonplace, shared political consciousness was paramount, and acceptance of visitors and strangers was the norm.

> I was trapped in a sense in the Valley, in a kind of traditional marriage, in a traditional setting, and I really wanted to get out of it. And Venice was a great place to come for that. So I ended up in Venice in 1970, and I was separated from my husband. For the first time women were exerting themselves as independent people. So I remember walking in the Canals and there were topless women working in the garden, and I was like, "Oh wow, this is *not* the valley." And just down my street, were these great women artists, filmmakers, musicians, and music organizers. There was so much happening. The first all

women's band, Lizzie Tisch, would play on an open lot, and if you were working on something and you wanted to talk to somebody you just walked down
the street and there would be another painter. You would sit out there and everybody would smoke grass. And they would look at people's work and talk
about it. It was just a lovely sense of belonging. And lots of young people, and
most of the people were vegetarians. There was a common consciousness. It
was the hippie canal. There were hippies living in buses, using my water fountain to bathe in the morning. There were lots of dogs and creatures. It was
open and very free. . . . And a lot of people didn't do the day-to-day jobs. Because it wasn't like everybody was working eight to five. That was *the man's*
thing to do. People were home and they were poor, and it was actually pref-
erable. You were suspect if you weren't poor. People who came around and
were making a lot of money, we didn't trust them.

The '60s counterculture became intertwined with the place itself. Locals held communal meals and took in temporary boarders to help ease
their rental obligations, sometimes packing over a dozen people into
a one- or two-room house, as opposed to adopting the logic of single-
family dwellings and private space. People spent their free time outside
with others and grew gardens with fresh vegetables, in contrast to living secluded from neighbors and shopping at supermarkets. Neighbors
got together and fought to keep city-owned lots vacant, empty, and overgrown, rather than seeking to manicure and develop them. They took
over certain lots without city authorization and created small parks for
children rather than following city guidelines. They perceived visitors as
"interesting" and included them into everyday life rather than perceiving them as "dangerous," a response typical of suburban privatization.
And they held protests against the war in Vietnam, inequality, development, and the impending canal restoration, rather than sitting back and
falling prey to urban renewal programs.

The local counterculture started as an opposition to a generalized
other, an avoidance of the "mainstream." But within the neighborhood,
the counterculture took on a more concrete form as people positioned
themselves against specific "others." The unconventional neighborhood
was interpreted in quite distinct ways depending on one's social location in the trajectory of change. On one hand, groups of new homeowners and investors had specific ideas about what the Canals neighborhood
could and should become, viewing the area's unconventional status as
wasted potential. On the other hand, many of the local renters passion-

ately believed in unconventionality as a way of life, fighting to strengthen and secure its attachment with the locale, therefore interpreting home-owners and investors as outsiders.

Failed Attempt to "Clean Up" the Canals

As countercultural renters established a new reputation in the Canals, there was also a constant undercurrent that sought to change the neigh-borhood's look and feel. The political struggle between countercultural renters and speculators wanting to renovate the neighborhood emerged through the filter of a class conflict. Central to this battle was the rise of competing organizations that personified socioeconomic distinctions. People challenged the current representation of the "unconventional Ca-nals" through two central avenues: a new restoration proposal and var-ious types of cleanup campaigns. These collective approaches linked a specific subset of the population with city leaders and created official definitions of proper and improper representations of the neighborhood.

For well over a decade, challenges to the local counterculture streng-thened its visibility, as renters transformed their collective lifestyle into a more strategic neighborhood movement. Two types of organizing were central to sustaining the representation of the Canals as an unconven-tional place in response to new interventions: organizing to oppose the restoration project along class lines; and organizing protests over the free uses of public spaces to protect the open culture as consistent with their established bohemian lifestyle.

With the planning and construction of Marina del Rey, talks be-gan about how to revitalize the waterways. In 1961, a group of property owners—only a few had already constructed new houses, but a number of people had purchased one or more lots in hopes of gaining an edge in the transition—formed the Venice Canals Improvement Association to propose a special assessment district in which private citizens would fi-nance a large portion of the restoration by taking a higher rate on prop-erty taxes. At this time, owner-occupied properties were the minority in the neighborhood. One-third of Canal parcels were without structures; the city, which owned over one hundred lots, was the largest property owner in the neighborhood; and the majority of residents rented small cottages.[3]

The city, as one of the Canals' key landholders, did not need much

convincing from energized property owners. Envious of the Los Angeles County's ongoing efforts to create a small boat harbor that would
eventually become the successful Marina del Rey, then-mayor Norris Poulson and the city councilman for the district that housed Venice,
Karl Rundberg, immediately entertained the possibility of creating their
own residential enclave that would connect with the marina. The goal
was not to compete with the marina development with high-rise, high-
density structures for middle-class professionals, but instead to maintain the residential, low-density character of the Canals as a way of com-
plementing the harbor to the south. As the planning moved forward in
the following years, the new mayor, Sam Yorty, and the new city councilman, L. E. Timberlake, were just as enthusiastic. According to Howard Chappell, vice president of the Los Angeles Board of Public Works
in the mid-1960s, the city wanted to create a residential enclave where
"middle income people will enjoy the pleasures normally reserved for
the very wealthy."[4]

The proposal included dramatic changes to the environment that
would instantly overhaul the identity of the neighborhood: deepening the canals from six to eleven feet to make them navigable by private boats; widening the canals from fifty to seventy feet to create more
room for boats to dock in front of houses; dredging the waterways in order to clean out the grimy canal floors; new sidewalks lined with gal-
vanized handrails to surround the waterways, promoting a safer and
sturdier environment; vertical concrete walls to replace the organically
sloping and muddy banks; construction of a bridge at Washington Street
(now renamed as Washington Boulevard) that would allow traffic over
the Grand Canal and make headroom for boats passing from the canals
into the marina and out into the Pacific Ocean; and four new bridges on
Dell Avenue—the only car-accessible roadway through the canals—to
pass over the four east-west waterways.[5]

This plan immediately faced a number of problems ranging from its
costs to difficulties inherent in its ecology and engineering. The most
consistent thorn in the city's side, however, was the organized opposition
by renters about restrictions to participating in the planning process, the
fairness of imposing an assessment tax on property owners who contested the construction but would be forced to finance it through higher
property taxes, and the legitimacy of homeowners financially benefiting
from any city investment. The delays were costly. The plans for a special assessment district started in 1961 at $3.85 million;[6] by 1965, it had

become a $9.5 million tax assessment district;[7] by 1967, it increased to $17 million;[8] by 1969, to $18.5 million;[9] and by 1971, a $24.6 million tax assessment district was proposed.[10] Adjusting the prices for inflation, the cost of the proposed plan increased by almost five times in less than a decade.

With escalating costs, the conflict was no longer simply about the aesthetics and function of the waterways. Property owners would have to make a serious investment and were concerned about who should be included in the decision-making processes. Organized property owners were adamant that renters not have a voice in the process. City council members agreed. They claimed that it would be unfair for renters, with no financial obligations in the assessment district, to have an equal say. At the same time, the Peace and Freedom Party's Free Venice movement was in its early stages, initiating a fight against development, economic invasion, and city-instigated code enforcement programs, especially in areas closest to the beach. With the canal restoration plan under way, the movement quickly turned into a neighborhood class conflict.

Rather than new speculative challenges removing the countercultural association with the neighborhood, they prompted local activists to organize. The Free Venice movement gave rise to the Canal Emergency Action Committee, the Save the Canals Committee, and a host of other Canal associations. Members of the Save the Canals Committee adopted a philosophy of stalling. They believed that postponing the renovations would dramatically increase costs and make it impossible for the city and speculators to move forward. According to one of the key activists, Rick Davidson, opposing the "Canal Project was relatively simple; delay, delay, delay. Time would cost the city the project."[11]

The Save the Canals Committee was a major force of resistance with the capacity to round up dozens and even hundreds of people on short notice. Davidson describes the power of the movement to draw on a readily available countercultural population:

If I or John Haag, Bob Wells, Jane Gordon, Steve Clare, Judy Goldberg, Ron Guenther, Mary Jane, John Heller, or many others were to walk to the center of the Canal Community . . . and begin ringing a bell and shouting, "Free Venice, Free Venice—everyone come," in no time people would pour out of their homes, garages, yards, alleys. . . . Now when they arrive at the vacant lot . . . they see me (or any of those others mentioned above) standing on a soapbox. I use soapbox because it's politically poetic; more than likely it

would be an old beer case. Anyway, there I am, or one of the others, still ringing this goddamn bell as I explain that we need everyone's support; there's a
bulldozer ready to knock down the little house at Howland Ct. and Eastern
Canal. Before I finish the "Come on, we need your help," . . . the Canal Community is off and running with me trying hard to catch up.[12]

Because of the vibrant community already in place, activists easily
rounded up hundreds of people to travel to L.A. City Council hearings
to voice their concerns about the renovations. One instance in particular stands out as a turning point in the movement. Although renters
made up a more substantial majority of residents in the neighborhood,
at one council meeting in March 1969, two LAPD officers manning the
door outside of city hall forbade them to come inside, only permitting
property owners to participate in the meeting. This restriction on renters gave the Save the Canals Committee leverage to challenge and stall
the proposal.

With the help of attorneys from the Western Center on Law and Poverty, they argued in California State Superior Court that (1) the city council must allow "all interested people to speak at the hearings, whether
they own property in the project or not"; (2) that the Supreme Court
had already ruled that "rights cannot be conditioned on wealth and ownership of real property"; and (3) that although the city referred to the
project as a special assessment district, it was actually part of the city's
"redevelopment project," which required open hearings and a comprehensive relocation plan for displaced residents.[13] The established countercultural lifestyle—built upon a choice to live without a job and in poor
conditions—gained official recognition as a class conflict between renters and owners.

The struggle over the renovation continued for years. By the early
1970s, lawsuits were coming from every feasible direction and caused
major delays on the construction. Howard Hughes Tool Company, which
owned thirty-four lots along the canals, sued the city over the $1 mil-
lion assessment facing the company, arguing that the project was unwar-
ranted and unfairly benefited homeowners; a class action suit sought an
additional $250,000 for 750 renters who would be displaced; and the city
countersued with the backing of 150 property owners, claiming it was an
improvement project with a tax assessment district rather than a city-
led redevelopment program.[14] By 1973, city leaders officially dropped
the original plans. Frustrated, they spent over $1 million to survey the

local population about how to move forward, and as a consequence of the survey, faced new prospects of seven plans put forth by different local groups.[15]

An active group of property owners and city leaders were unified in their renewal strategy for the Canals neighborhood and shared an interpretative framework about the meaning of "improvement." Speculators and city officials established complementary cleanup campaigns, as class dynamics emerged through an official definition of aesthetic preferences about what waterway design counts as appealing and about what types of people should be visible in the neighborhood's public spaces.

The Los Angeles Board of Public Works initiated a cleanup program in the early '60s. Comparable strategies, sometimes organized by the city and other times by local property-owning groups, occurred on and off for the next two decades. The initial campaign focused on illegal dumping on vacant lots, established a lot-cleaning crew to get rid of debris, posted "No Dumping" signs throughout the Canals, and called in law enforcement officials to target violators who dumped on these vacant spaces.[16] These programs continued for decades (see figure 13). Mary

FIGURE 13. Canal cleanup campaign on empty lot. Photograph by Mike Sergieff. Herald Examiner Collection. Copyright Los Angeles Public Library.

Lou Johnson, a Save the Canals activist during the '70s, discusses another cleanup campaign in later years:

> The cleanup campaigns were so incredible. It was a real military operation. When I was first aware of [one in the '70s], I hadn't seen any of the flyers. It was like a blow horn. [In a loud voice], "Alright now, Canal residents, get out of bed, we're gonna clean up these canals today." I said, "Oh god, I don't believe this." They came through here like a dose of salts. They were sweeping the dirt. If they saw it as trash, then it was trash. There was no, "One person's trash is another person's treasure." There was a big old fallen log in the canals that people liked to sit on and feed the ducks. Forget it. That was dirt. The old sofa that people sat on. They came through and they cleaned it up. There was just a cloud of dust. One guy came down, and said, "Hey, what's wrong with clean up?" I said, "Well as long as I've lived down here, whenever people start talking about cleaning up the Canals, they really meant that they were cleaning up the people." And he said, "Well I might as well be honest with you, there are a few people I'd like to clean up."[17]

In fact, some did attempt to "clean up" the people. Another method of cleaning up the neighborhood was to target so-called transients living on abandoned lots. The established countercultural renters integrated and celebrated the free-roaming, music-devoted, animal-loving hippies. In fact, locals commonly tell stories about how the Canals had more hippies, dogs, and ducks roaming around than residents paying rents or mortgages. Because of their communal lifestyle but lack of official residences, they camped outside on empty spaces and were constantly walking around, hanging out in empty lots or parks, and by virtue of their public presence, shaping the public culture of the neighborhood as the "hippie canal."

By the early '70s, many property owners, who still had not moved into the neighborhood, were frustrated about the established counterculture that contributed to the failed restoration projects. Just like the homeless, the transient hippies were defined as "people out of place." Members of the Venice Improvement Association and the Venice-Marina Chamber of Commerce called in the police to deal with them, reporting "100 to 300 people . . . currently living on private property in the canals area." They complained that individuals were camping out and that vehicles were illegally parked, for example, targeting fourteen people living in a large YMCA bus who connected "wires into a house across the street to get electricity."[18]

Tim, in his late fifties, who moved into the Canals during the early 1970s, remembers the hippie culture as a nuisance. This incoming home-owner was bothered by their overzealous communal mentality and their public presentation, and maybe most significantly, by their extremely different understandings of private property. He said, "There was a park directly behind where my old house was and people lived there. There was petty theft, robbery, they broke into people's houses. And they would take food, sit down and watch television, take a shower, use the bathroom. And that freaked out my wife. She was like, 'Oh they used my towels. Ohhh!' These people were filthy."

The city went after the counterculture by any legal means possible, targeting the public uses of vacant lots and rundown conditions of neighborhood bungalows. Starting in 1968, locals constructed parks on empty lots with their own resources, building wooden sidewalks and inserting telephone poles on which children could climb. The city repeatedly tore down these parks, one after another for several years, due to "safety concerns," an irony that did not escape residents who lived in a neighborhood with cracked and jagged sidewalks falling into the waterways. Collective resistance to these actions reinforced the public visibility of the countercultural identity. After the city bulldozed five successive parks, activists applied for permits to build yet another one, but they were once again denied. They built it anyway and when the city intervened, residents united in opposition. Mary Lou Johnson describes how they managed to establish a park in the face of these challenges, dramatically protesting in front of the media and exposing their local culture to the masses: "The city came out and said they couldn't have the playground because it wasn't safe. And in full view of television [cameras], proceeded to bulldoze the whole thing down. . . . It hadn't cost them a penny to have the playground built, but cost two to three thousand dollars to bulldoze it down. And people chained themselves to the wooden boardwalk and the railing. And then the city said, 'OK, you can have this other lot for your playground. The one on Dell.'"

As the city targeted the public culture by tearing down vest-pocket parks, they also implemented code enforcement programs and demolished rundown properties. Local activists united to refurbish buildings scheduled for demolition. One in particular became the Venice Canals Community House, which operated as a stabilizing agent not only for oppositional political actions but also for their collective lifestyle and public identity. According to longtime local Maryjane, after the city "code forced" the owner to demolish the property in 1969, activists persuaded the owner to allow them to fix it up and use it for the community. She writes in her memoir,

> It became a headquarters for activism, for cultural and media events. Music was constant, but not interfering with daily life. . . . We offered homeless shelter and feedings. We had "Hot Lines": rape, battered women [and] children, tenants rights, legal aid, emergency medical care referrals, human-civil rights, gay-lesbian rights, help with police violations, bail funds. It was a meeting site. . . . We built our third park here, with a play area, and with our vegetable gardens. . . . So people were there day and night. It became center to Free Venice, Free Venice Organizing Committee, Free Venice Survival, and Save the Canals.[19]

A series of annual Canal Festivals that took place from 1969 to 1976 broadcast the bohemian identity, thrusting this shabby, secluded, unconventional enclave into a public attraction. The countercultural identity emerged as something for the public to see, a stylized and artistically savvy form of cultural rebellion. The festival began as a direct response to the early restoration proposal, with the Canal Festival Committee sending out flyers that called for the public to "demonstrate their solidarity with the Venice community's efforts of self-determination."[20] By 1973, the festival had grown into a famous Los Angeles event, advertising in the *Los Angeles Times* and attracting ten thousand people into the neighborhood. It showcased hundreds of art exhibits, including ceramics, sculpture, jewelry design, leather working, clothing, paintings, drawings, and films, as well as performances by mimes, belly dancers, and gymnasts. It had three musical stages, one for classical music, another for rock and jazz, and a third for folk, country, and blues. The festivals, like the more frequent and equally wild Canal parties, were public spectacles that took place on porches, inside people's houses, on vacant lots and in open spaces, as well as on floating barges. They crystallized the politics, culture, and arts that had existed on a daily basis over the previous two decades.

Although property owners, investors, and city officials made major efforts to eradicate the countercultural identity and re-create a new set of material and symbolic ties on the Venice Canals, by the mid-1970s it was clear that the countercultural residents had stalled the project and sustained their visible bohemianism. At the same time, however, a new cohort of middle-class residents slowly seeped into the area. Unlike the speculative class, they did not try to instantly reinvent the identity of the Canals, but their actions unintentionally contributed to a more conventional locale.

The Middle Position

By the mid-1970s, Marina del Rey was over a decade old, the oil derricks on the adjacent Venice Beach were cleared away, and the reputation of the Canals was slowly shifting from being known as a disorganized, dangerous, and unconventional neighborhood into what the *Los Angeles Times* described in 1975 as a "slum without misery." The Venice Canals were still "neglected and falling apart," but people no longer viewed the neighborhood as frightening. Instead, this "extraordinary slum" had become a place that "beckons the visitor to linger and wander a while."[21] This shift in neighborhood reputation was due to an influx of newcomers who occupied the middle position between the countercultural renters and the speculative class.[22]

The middle position, maybe more than any other, constitutes a world of unintended consequences, in which people move into a neighborhood with little or even no awareness about how they might influence its future.[23] The timing in which people arrive to a neighborhood matters in shaping their connections to the environment and associations with others, creating what sociologists refer to as a "cohort effect."[24] All neighborhood transformations involve the reconfiguration of cohorts over time. As history evolves, the cohort that occupies the middle position between more established residents and those who follow them into a neighborhood can shift the power dynamics and reshape the neighborhood public culture. We cannot simply base our understanding about how newcomers influence a neighborhood by looking at their intentions. In some cases, the reconfiguration of cohorts over time creates complementary, if not strategically organized, positions: it gives rise to a neighborhood homology between groups, symbols, and spaces, and makes a neighborhood public culture more exclusive.

The mid-1970s through the early 1980s were significant years in the history of revitalizing the Canals neighborhood, but not because the waterways were actually rebuilt. The restoration did not take place until 1993. It was significant because a middle-class invasion slowly altered the neighborhood public culture and moved countercultural renters to a position further outside of the debates about the future. The transition eventually allowed middle-class residents—both homeowners and new renters—to reinvent themselves as the old-timers in later years. Individuals with recognizably distinct lifestyles made their homes in the Canals section, occupying a middle position between the countercultural residents and those seeking to "clean up" the neighborhood.

Without investment in the previous struggles and without foresight into what would follow, middle-class residents played a key role in shifting the political discussions away from the countercultural opposition, which turned out to be a crucial stage in reshaping the neighborhood. There were several components that established the middle position: a willingness to live near and even appreciate others labeled as unconventional despite one's own conventionality; new economic and cultural symbols and practices that distinguished newcomers from previous residents; and justifications about their form of gentrification by distinguishing between those who sought to live in the neighborhood and those who were merely speculators.

Many who moved into the Canals during this period did so because it was an inexpensive location near the beach, which made them willing to put up with people they identified as more unconventional. Jason was one of a number of new creative professionals who had the skills to fix up his houses. Some creative professionals were renters, who repaired, renovated, and redesigned cottages, producing new conditions for middle-class and upper-income investors, comparable to Soho artists who renovated loft spaces.[25] Others like Jason were able to purchase properties and renovate them at the same time, changing the look of the neighborhood but also benefiting financially as the neighborhood continued to change. He describes his entrée into the Canals as an architect in the beginning of his career:

> When we came in, a number of other people also came in who were artists, writers, and filmmakers. It was a great time and a very vibrant community. Everybody just left everybody alone. We were the young adventurous ones and we basically came in and sort of tamed the neighborhood. There were a lot of abandoned houses and we're talking about a bunch of people who moved in, didn't have a lot of money, but had a lot of energy and were able to fix the places up for themselves. I mean I bought my first house for forty-two thousand dollars [or what would equate to $170,229 in 2010].

Not everyone moving in had the same skill set. A number of middle-class people bought homes because they wanted to live near the beach. The changing Canal environment fit their budgets. Because acquiring a loan was difficult for first-time home buyers in the Canals during this period, having access to other resources helped them to make their down payments. Janice and Phil, both college graduates and young professionals during their initial venture in the early '70s, discuss their interest in the neighborhood:

> We had friends who bought a little fixer-upper, and we wanted to live on the water, and we couldn't afford being on the oceanfront. Even then, we were in our twenties, so there was no way. So we ended up here, because it was affordable for us at the time. And we were a little too conventional to buy a fixer-upper, because we didn't have any skills. We saw this place, which was the ultimate '60s duplex. We changed the look, but it was very '60s. Plus we were attracted to the idea of having [an additional floor to rent] and so we were excited. We couldn't get a loan until almost the very end of our escrow because the area was redlined. They weren't doing loans. There was this big deepwater project and the lenders weren't sure if it was going to go through or not. So we had to get Phil's parents to cosign and more of a down payment from his grandmother.

Some liked the idea of being near the bohemian culture. They felt like outsiders in their own suburban milieus, but they had the resources as members of the professional class to buy into a place that they deemed more adventurous. They did not adopt the bohemian ways, but they wanted to be near something edgy. They moved in and stood outside of the culture as observers. Sherry, now in her late sixties, was attracted to the counterculture by the beach, but her professional middle-class existence and the sale of her previous home in the Valley provided resources to acquire three properties at a time when homes were very affordable for those in her position:

> I was attracted to the bohemian culture, but it also seemed kind of menacing to me, because I'm very middle class. I need a certain security and stability and predictability in my life. These young artists were going against society to such an extent, in a risky kind of way. And I lived in the Valley and I didn't like it there and I always had this longing to live by the beach. And I was spending one Sunday on the boardwalk with a friend and afterwards, she

went to her car and I kept walking, and I walked into a realtor's office. I met this young hotshot realtor who just graduated from USC and he began showing me real estate in Venice. He showed me three parcels, and I bought all three that year, including my house. And they were all kind of dumps, but they were within my reach financially.

As middle-class homeowners slowly replaced countercultural renters, those who remained were those who purchased a house. They figured out that to facilitate longer attachments, they had to adopt some middle-class conventions. Gina, the artist who initially moved into the Canals during the '70s as a renter, moved out a few years later, purchased a house elsewhere, built up equity, and then eventually moved back into the neighborhood:

> I didn't buy a house on the canals until the '80s. I got run out of two or three [rented] houses by owners [in the '70s]. I would fix them up and then they would move me out. Finally I moved to Topanga and I was able to acquire enough equity to come back and buy a house, still before the restoration happened. At that time the Canals were relatively affordable. I bought a little funky house and rebuilt it.

There were clear distinctions between the new middle class and the established counterculture. First, most of the former were homeowners. By purchasing properties that already existed, as opposed to the more speculative buyers who purchased empty lots and fantasized about the construction of their "dream houses," they forced out renters who were previously living there. Janice and Phil discuss the transition when they moved into their duplex.

JANICE: When we moved in we were the yuppies. We were the people that were coming in and ruining the neighborhood. We were buying places.

PHIL: A lot of these were rentals. Both of these [in their duplex] were rentals. And it started to push the prices up. And then people can't afford it and they resent the fact that they can't afford to live where they have lived for x number of years.

JANICE: And our friends who bought their house paid a little under twenty thousand dollars [approximately $80,000 when adjusted for inflation to 2010 dollars] for that place. There was a renter in there, and when they bought it, they moved out the renter. The renters were losing their places to live.

In addition, the newcomers held different orientations to work, established more private, home-based and family-oriented lifestyles, and produced clear symbolic indicators that separated them from the countercultural old-timers, such as having new cars, bicycles, and houses with freshly manicured landscapes. Sherry points out that although she liked living near the countercultural residents, she had a different orientation to work, finances, and her surroundings:

> I have a very strong work ethic, and I think that work is important, and I think that having a regular job is important, and I think that having a predictable source of income is important. A lot of them were artists and they were renting, and they didn't seem to mind the kind of living by the wits. My work ethic is very strong and with it comes a lot of other values. I like a certain order in my life and when I first moved in, I kept to myself. I went to work and I had work friends and work was very satisfying, but at home I was more private.

Some people who moved in had more expensive luxuries, representing a different standard of living. Don and Patti, in an interview conducted in the late '70s, describe how distinctive practices of hard work, leisure activities, and home improvements operated as a new kind of urban existence that separated them from both the typical suburbanites of their socioeconomic status as well as the countercultural old-timers. They refer to these social and economic differences as "natural" oppositions.[26]

DON: I remember one of the old-timers coming over and looking at my house and saying that it was a capitalistic house that sucks up water and blocks off the air. People just totally made the determination that we should be stratified. If you whip into the Canals in your Mercedes and someone else is trying to figure out where to get their car payment from, there's a natural inborn resentment, just like there's a natural inborn resentment that I may have to others that can just let their hair down and take it easy, flopping around all day long or not care about where their car payments will come from.

PATTI: In order to live the way that we live, we have to work real hard. And so we spend a lot of time on our home, making improvements. My husband made all of these shelves. We've done all the landscaping on the house. We're always improving the house and each season we put in new flowers. And like today it was a perfect day and we got in our little boat and we went around the

canals. And we'll maybe row to Baja Cantina and get something to eat. And
we were saying today how funny it is that we could never live in suburbia.

Even as the middle-class newcomers slowly altered the look and feel
of the Canals, they defined their invasion as more "pure" than the gentrification of more speculative owners who were simultaneously buying
up abandoned lots and building homes from scratch. Those in the middle position often fail to see the role they are playing in brokering relationships with more upscale newcomers in a dramatic class transformation. In this case, they believed that their connections to the small-scale
housing and appreciation of the organic environment allowed them to
distinguish their own "intent to live" versus others "intent to profit."
Don summarized this perspective when he said, "It's one thing if people
move in with the idea of being carpetbaggers, and another thing if they
move in with the intent to live."

Despite their role in shaping change, newcomers believed they carried on some of the traditions of the past. A few actually had direct lin-
eage. As mentioned, Gina had connections to the bohemian past as a
renter, artist, and political activist involved in many of the local movements of the early '70s. Other middle-class professionals were renters
and able to afford the increasing rental prices, but they feared that speculation would affect them as it had previous renters. A few middle-class
homeowners purposely positioned themselves in relation to the past by
renting out properties for way below the market rate. Sherry owns three
properties and prides herself on her "socialist" ideal. She says, "I charge
ridiculously low rents, way below the market rate. I don't really need to
rent it for more, because I live rather comfortably with very low rents. So
this idea that you need to maximize your capital, I mean smart people,
smart investors do maximize their capital investment, but you can still
live well and not do that. It's kind of a socialist idea of mine."

Middle-class residents developed their own local norms and customs,
had their own aesthetic preferences, and gave off their own symbolic
cues. Even though they played a major role in reshaping the Canals'
everyday culture, they were also very protective of its particular reputation and character. As the neighborhood continued to change and development rapidly picked up between the 1970s and '80s, a new political
configuration was born. Those in the middle position became the protectors of an invented history about the quaintness of the Canals.

The Politics of Quaintness

A number of conditions in the Canals were inviting to another round of speculators: its coastal location, the possibility of renovated waterways, and its proximity to the marina. As a result, between 1976 and 1984, developers and speculators constructed 110 new residences. Developer Alex Mlikotin led the charge, erecting 39 new houses in this time period. The new properties cost well beyond what previous countercultural renters could afford. The newest constructions in the '80s also increasingly stood outside of the price ranges of middle-class homeowners who purchased their properties in the '70s for much lower prices, often in the $40,000 range, or after adjusting for inflation, what would be about $120,000 to $220,000 in 2010. By 1984, home prices increased, ranging from $260,000 to $425,000 [or in 2010 dollars, $546,000 to $892,000], attractive to upper-middle-class and upper-class professionals.[27]

For the first time, the proportion of occupant-owners to renters reversed, a monumental transition that meant that middle-class and upper-middle-class residents made up the majority of the neighborhood. Moreover, the housing boom led to constant construction that altered the neighborhood's appearance. The abundant number of empty lots that once created a parklike setting faded, and the free-roaming hippies who occupied the empty spaces were forced to find other places to go. A segment of the hippie culture blended together with the homeless population, creating a complicated configuration between the housed and the homeless in the areas surrounding the Venice Boardwalk and the Rose Avenue neighborhood. According to a 1984 interview with Mlikotin, "There are no flower children here now. . . . For the first time since I bought my first piece of property in the canals [in 1974], there are more owner-occupiers than tenants. That is one of the main reasons for the drive to make improvements. Let's face it, the canals look crummy."[28]

The middle position shifted the environment from a countercultural haven into a conventional middle-class milieu. It also reconfigured local politics between those in the middle position and newcomers with greater financial assets. This shift to a middle/upper-class opposition produced a new bourgeois politics of quaintness that reinvented the overall meaning of living in the Canals. I use the term *quaintness* because it evokes an image of old-fashioned charm. The type of activism that emerged was not about protecting renters, stopping development, halting the waterway restorations, or keeping vacant lots free and clear for roaming travelers and public festivities. These were all characteristics of the previous countercultural class resistance that sought to protect "the people" and specific definitions of "the public." Those in the middle position were not trying to keep the neighborhood poor and open to anyone. Instead, they invented a new meaning of historical stability and pushed aside the interests of the poorest residents, ultimately benefiting all property owners in the long run, even if individual homeowners did not initially intend these outcomes. The politics of quaintness was about protecting housing size, preserving open-space requirements on private residences, and maintaining a certain aesthetic look of the public waterways and sidewalks.

Just as organizations defined the local political battles of the previous era, new organizations formed in the mid-1970s. Middle-class homeowners established the Venice Canal Resident Homeowner's Association. Another group of property owners, consisting of developers and speculative homeowners seeking to construct their dream retirement houses in the Canals, carried on the traditions of the Venice Improvement Association and formed the Resident and Non-Resident Property Owners Association, renamed the Venice Canal Association (VCA) in 1976. The Venice Town Council carried on the countercultural traditions of the Save the Canals Committee. Janice and Phil discuss this new political configuration between homeowners, speculators, and countercultural renters.

JANICE: There were speculators who came in here to buy and build. And suddenly it was like, "Oh my god, people are tearing down the old stuff." Developers and builders were buying up empty lots, knocking down old structures if lots even had a structure, and built new structures and then sold them to people.

PHIL: At first they were mostly building on the vacant lots because that was easier.

JANICE: But they were building much bigger houses than what was here and suddenly you've got this big thing looming next to you and people were upset about it. So we formed the Venice Canals Resident Homeowners Association. We started an organization because we were concerned about the development. And you had to live here to be a member of our group. We didn't want the developers. We weren't a property owners' association. So the corresponding group that came up later was the Venice Canals Property Owners' Association, which largely consisted of people who wanted to build on the Canals. They wanted to build as big as they possibly could. We were the twenties, early thirties people that were buying our first homes and they were older. They already owned homes, and this was going to be their retirement home. And their big argument was that we were a bunch of communists. We were restricting it.

PHIL: At that point in time we were sort of the middle ground. There were still remnants of the hippies in the Venice Town Council. They wanted no development whatsoever. We felt like we were the compromise group. We were trying to find a balance between the two and we came up with a whole set of guidelines that we felt would protect the air space around the smaller cottages.

The first major debate in this new political configuration was about the size of housing. Newcomers and speculative builders proposed projects that many of the middle-class homeowners considered out of scale for the neighborhood. Official minutes from the California Coastal Commission meetings of 1975 and 1976 demonstrate the new political configuration in practice. The countercultural activists, represented by the Venice Town Council, argued that the coastal commission should allow no new houses and that the vacant lots should remain empty. Appeals by the Venice Canals Resident Homeowners Association argued that the coastal commission should restrict the size of the housing; pay special attention to "out of scale" development, such as a proposed project to build nineteen contiguous townhouses without any space between them; and closely monitor the more than one hundred vacant lots in the neighborhood that were prime for future development. Those from the VCA argued that their proposed constructions were only about two hundred to three hundred square feet larger than houses that the coastal commission already permitted; architectural diversity was imperative for the revitalization of the neighborhood; and size restrictions would hinder architectural creativity.[29]

The Venice Town Council position was completely shut out of the discussion and ruled too radical. The Venice Canals Resident Homeowners Association took over the "established" position with great success in a new politics of quaintness. The coastal commission agreed that the development of contiguous buildings was out of character for the area and instituted new guidelines on development, including a twenty-five-foot height limit and a square footage requirement initially less than two

thousand square feet per lot. Builders continuously challenged these limitations, however. One developer, Sherman Grinberg, argued that any
house with less than two thousand square feet of living space "is building the blight of tomorrow today."[30]

As a speculator, Albert purchased his first property in the Canals
in the 1970s, contracting for a builder to construct a house on a vacant lot. At the time, he thought the neighborhood would one day be
a great retirement location; he did not move in until the early 2000s.
He said, "They wanted to keep it cutesy, and all of the houses little and
sweet. They didn't want the big houses, because that meant people with
more money. Cute little houses meant that people from Beverly Hills
weren't moving in, because they want 3,500 and 4,000 square feet. But
it gradually became more fashionable, and people chipped away at the
regulations."

The middle class and the speculators ultimately reached a compromise through the L.A. Department of City Planning and the California
Coastal Commission, demonstrating a movement of local politics away
from the left-wing radicalism of the previous years. Instead of a twenty-
five-foot height limit, the L.A. Department of City Planning ultimately
established a thirty-foot height limit, still much less than the forty-five-
foot height limit in surrounding neighborhoods. They also implemented
a novel ten- to fifteen-foot setback on the second story so new houses
were more open on the top level, allowing light to shine through without
looming over the smaller cottages. This setback requirement, producing a more quaint housing style for larger dwellings, was clearly distinct
from the patterns of construction on the southern end of Venice Beach,
directly next to the marina, where bulky, block-like, three-story structures overlooked the ocean. Lastly, they required builders on the Canals
to incorporate open spaces. Three-foot side yards eliminated the possibility of contiguous buildings; and nine-foot backyards and an additional
10 percent of the lot area remaining open forced owners who complied
with the mandate (some did not) to make room for a yard and sustain
nesting spots for the duck population that many middle-class homeowners viewed as central to the neighborhood's public culture.

Another element of the politics of quaintness involved the look of the
impending restorations of the waterways, sidewalks, and footbridges.
With the countercultural movement pushed further and further outside
of the political configuration, the debate was not about whether or not a
restoration *should* take place. Instead, the conflict turned to *how* they

would accomplish this feat that was twenty years in the making. Those in the middle position advocated a structure that they believed resembled the historic character of the canals; while those on the other side of the debate argued for a more modern and elaborate façade.

The notion of connecting the waterways to the marina faded away and was deemed too complicated and costly. Yet property owners and builders still petitioned for the city to organize a new shallow water restoration project to fix up the canals and sidewalks. The debates picked up in the early '80s with a more modest set of proposals. Los Angeles city councilwoman Pat Russell strongly supported the VCA's plan. Russell said, "The canals have strongly needed improvements for some time, certainly in the 15 years I have been here. There is no more validity to say let's not clean up the sidewalks in the canals than there is in other areas of the city."[31]

The middle-class homeowners who altered the neighborhood's public culture now positioned themselves as official protectors of its history. They remade themselves into the "old-timers" by inventing a version of the past that had nothing to do with the types of people who lived on the canals and everything to do with how they looked. For example, in 1982, a group of residents succeeded in getting the Canals neighborhood placed on the National Register of Historic Places, an interesting designation that only focused on the waterways, had absolutely no effect on housing size or types of construction, offered no security for renters, and lacked any affordability provision for new owners. It was a mere status marker that stated that the Canals were historically significant as an engineering matter. These preservationists used the past as a cultural tool in their political opposition. Tom Moran, a journalist, bought a house in the neighborhood in the mid-1970s and was active in the movement to gain historical status. He told a *Times* reporter, "The city's plan would substantially change the character of the canals from a unique Venetian system into a concrete bathtub or a mini-marina. . . . They've chosen a design that cleans up the canals but does little to preserve their historic significance."[32] For instance, instead of vertical concrete walls, the protectionists wanted to maintain organic, sloping edges.[33]

Their concerns about historic status initially held very little weight with the council office, as the VCA submitted petitions with signatures from almost 75 percent of property owners. After two decades of battles, with such a substantial majority of owners willing to pay for the renovations, it looked as if the restoration would finally come to pass. In

1986, the city council supported a plan to move forward. They approved a $3.3 million proposal to dredge the waterways; add vertical, concrete retaining walls; install new sidewalks; construct boat ramps for small vessels; engineer storm drains; and plant new shrubbery. Homeowners would finance the bulk of the project, paying $2.8 million through a special assessment district, adding up to approximately $7,000 per resident living on 370 canal lots over a ten-year period. The city agreed to fund the remaining $540,000 for improved pedestrian bridges and a tidal flushing gate that automatically opened and closed to filter fresh seawater into the canals.[34]

All that remained was for the California Coastal Commission to agree with the city council. In 1987, the California Coastal Commission halted the project based on its environmental impact. In addition, Ruth Galanter defeated incumbent councilwoman Russell in the race for the Los Angeles City Council seat in the district that included Venice. Russell had been working with the VCA for over fifteen years, but Galanter, an urban planner by trade, was also a longtime coastal activist and former state coastal commissioner. Her sympathies rested with middle-class homeowners and environmentalists, forcing another round of negotiations and compromises between middle-class homeowners and speculators.

Galanter was a particularly strong proponent of environmental protections. She supported the views of the California Coastal Conservancy, which labeled the waterways as part of a protected wetland that required wildlife preservation. Instead of vertical concrete bulkheads, they called for sloped walls made of an alternative substance to help a variety of plant and animal species thrive. The VCA strongly opposed this plan on aesthetic grounds. It took another two years for them to find a compromise material that was also aesthetically pleasing. Galanter summarizes the turn of events:

> I called the coastal conservancy and said give me an example of how we can do sloping walls that will meet all the criteria. They gave me a proposal and they came down and presented and the Canals residents hated it. It was a product called ArmorFlex, which is like cinder blocks but you plant in between and plants grow over and you don't even see the concrete. But when you need to replace one, you just lift it out and put in another. Well, they hated it. They thought they were ugly. As long as we agreed on what the problem was—we needed to have canal walls that supported vegetation—I said, "If you have a better solution, I'd like to hear it." They found one. It cost a bit

more, it was a little less efficient, but if we can solve it, it was worth the difference. We agreed, went to the city, went to the coastal commission with a revised plan. They got restored with the assessment district and the sidewalks
were officially opened to the public fifty-one years after they were officially
closed.

In 1991, the California Coastal Commission approved a $6 million
plan to renovate the Canals, which included: 55-degree, sloped Löffel
block walls as opposed to the initially proposed 20-degree Armor-
Flex block walls; dredging of the canals; installation of automatic tidal
gates and a flushing system; construction of new sidewalks; refurbished
wooden foot bridges over the canals; and boat ramps and duck ramps,
the latter to help the ducks maneuver out of the water.[35]

The restoration began at the end of February 1992 and was completed
in October 1993, despite a lingering politics over environmental issues.
A major "duck war" broke out during the restoration. The resident duck
population was dying during the dredging of the waterways. One side,
believing that the deaths stemmed from the disruptions of the habitat,
did everything in its power to save the ducks, siphoning them into vans
and taking them to alternative locations. The other side feared the ducks
carried a dangerous virus; some residents even went around smashing
duck eggs to make sure they did not procreate. An additional battle occurred after the restoration was completed. Leaders of the VCA refused
to allow renter participation on the board, even though at this point most
renters were middle- and upper-class residents paying hefty rents, rather
than members of the counterculture, and they made such a small minority of the overall population. Those opposed to the VCA formed a new,
more inclusive organization called the Voice of the Canals (VOC).

Despite lingering political differences, the middle class and the upper class, and renters and homeowners, upheld enough complementary
pieces that the politics of quaintness transformed the neighborhood into
a scenic locale. A completely renovated environment led to soaring housing and rental prices. Wealthier people moved in with little interest or
knowledge of the history of these symbolic battles, and in another ironic
turn of events, key members of the VCA began protesting the larger size
of houses built for and by "newcomers." The VCA members, once the
newcomers fighting for their own larger homes, lived in houses that were
now smaller than some of the new structures, demonstrating an ongoing
evolution in neighborhood positions. In the new scenic neighborhood,

FIGURE 14. Scenic Venice Canals in 2006.

the established middle- and upper-middle-class homeowners emerged as the relative urban poor. When the poorest residents share the everyday conventions of the wealthiest newcomers, including a stable professional life and long work hours, a more private lifestyle, and the possession of million-dollar houses, the transition brings about a neighborhood homology between groups, styles, and space (see figure 14).

A New Scenic Neighborhood

When thinking about the creation of exclusive borders in such high-class places as Bel Air, couched in between Beverly Hills and Holmby Hills, it is easy to envision how they collectively maintain clear-cut and exclusive barriers as part of the "Platinum Triangle," one of the wealthiest sections of the United States. Twenty-four-hour surveillance, private security forces, and high walls and shrubbery surrounding individual mansions exaggerate what is evidently a luxurious residential setting. How do neighborhood borders work in a place like the Canals, when highly visible forms of racial, ethnic, and socioeconomic diversity are found just blocks away?

Neighborhood residents have established no uniform privatization plan; houses are only three feet apart, making it impossible to hide from neighbors; cutting-edge architecture, public waterways, and historic status attract busloads of tourists; and multiple entry points enable beachgoing visitors to stroll along the recently refurbished sidewalks. Once a center of unconventionality, the quaint "Gold Coast" embraces a new reputation through a visible code that includes: new signs of wealth, unifying community events, and clear indications between the inside and the outside of the neighborhood.

The relationship between property and wealth is apparent in the Canals, as prices rose beyond what the middle class could afford. By 1991, lots were selling for $400,000 (or what would be $640,399 in 2010 dollars).[36] According to a local real estate listing, the sale prices of three-bedroom houses in 1997 ranged from $600,000 to $1 million (or what would amount to between $815,162 to $1,358,604 in 2010 dollars). In 2009, three-bedroom houses with comparable square footage sold for prices between $2 million and $3 million.[37] Although renters now make up the minority, rental prices also dramatically changed during this period. One owner who rented out a two-bedroom floor in her duplex in the early 1990s charged $1,500 per month; she now rents the same space without having modernized it for over $4,000 a month. Those renting out entire houses offer amenities that signify upscale design and ask much more. A three-bedroom, three-and-a-half- bathroom house with a chef's kitchen including a "4 burner Wolf range plus grill" as well as "Hardwood floors, French doors, 2 fireplaces, spa tub, 3 balconies, roof top sundeck, lush gardens [and the use] of boat included," was on the rental market for close to $9,000 a month in June 2010.[38]

The changing levels of wealth are not simply about home and rental prices. The Canals now attract a different type of resident altogether. Not only do people purchase multiple multimillion-dollar properties, but also how they purchase and interpret these properties has changed since the 1970s and '80s. For example, some of the residents in the middle position who arrived in the mid-1970s, almost two decades before the restoration, slowly pieced together a small collection of houses, most of which were well under $100,000 at the time. The timing of their purchases allowed them to earn substantial returns on their investment. These individuals tend to reside in one of the houses; some renovated or rebuilt a completely new structure for their own personal residence and continue to rent out the others.

Newcomers to the Canals are a different lot. They purchase multiple adjacent properties, not scattered parcels, spending millions to build the Canal version of the Los Angeles housing compound—the *quaint Canals compound*. A Hollywood writer bought an adjacent house because he and his wife had a baby and he needed a quiet place to write. A woman owns two houses next to each other and uses the second, a smaller cottage, as her exercise studio. One couple purchased the next-door lot and strategically kept it vacant to use as a lush garden. Another couple purchased a smaller cottage next door to their larger house when it became available in order to protect the ambience of their main residence.

The logic for buying the adjacent property is not simply investment: it maintains privacy, allows individuals to control the uses of neighboring spaces, and provides extra room for the upscale leisurely beach-town lifestyle, such as relaxing in the yard, gardening, throwing lavish parties and friendly get-togethers, or adding extra rooms for visitors. Altogether, it represents a new sign of privilege. Marvin, for example, moved in during the early 2000s. When the next-door property went on the market, he and his wife purchased it. He explains, "If they sold it to someone else, the cost of the property was going to demand that the cottage [on the lot] get knocked down in order to get more value out of it and build something appropriate to the land. It would have destroyed the garden, the ambience of the house, the view, the natural lighting in the house. It would have destroyed everything. We just had no choice. We had to do it and we never regretted it for a day."

The quaint compound is not about building up, but instead about building out. Many locals are enamored with the historic small-scale housing style. The refurbished California bungalow is one of the preeminent signs of the quaint Gold Coast. Actors Orson Bean and Alley Mills, for example, have appeared in multiple newspapers and magazines showcasing their compound of four bungalows in a row, as documented by Ryon (1999) in this *Los Angeles Times* piece:

> For years, [Bean] had noticed that the kitchen is where everybody hangs out when there is a party, and Bean has always liked a good party. And, so, soon after he married actress Alley Mills, they built a kitchen large enough for a grand piano—large enough, in fact, to be a house. That's because before the kitchen became a kitchen, it was a house. With two bedrooms, a dining room,

kitchen and living room in 1,200 square feet, it was the smaller of two Venice houses that Bean owned before he and Mills were married in 1993. . . . About the same time, the newlyweds connected his two Venice houses with a glass walkway and gutted the smaller house, turning it into one room: the kitchen, with a stove and a refrigerator at one end, a couple of couches and the grand piano at the other. The small kitchen in the 2,400-square-foot house next door became an entry hall. "Now Alley plays show tunes every night, and I sing," Bean said. And they don't have to worry about bothering the neighbors, because, as Bean put it, "we are the neighbors." . . . After they were married, Mills bought two more houses. So now the couple has a compound of four homes, built side by side during the 1920s. "We love the little old cottages on the canals," he said.

The quaint compound and new colorful and open designs by innovative architects are symbiotic housing styles that reinforce the neighborhood's charm. Some of the most interesting architects work within the confines of the restrictive planning code, designing homes that are larger than the classic cottage but still mesh with the surroundings. Renowned architects Mark Mack, Glen Irani, and Whitney Sander, for instance, adapt modern spaces to fit in with the overall aesthetic character and planning requirements of the area. Their designs are bright, full of wall-length windows for natural lighting, opening directly into the surroundings, and employing environmentally friendly materials. One Irani house uses concrete flooring that together with ample windows creates an energy-efficient structure. The *Los Angeles Times* describes it as follows: "A three-story structure with a front wall that is almost entirely glass. Large windows, doors and panels slide, swing or pivot to invite in natural light, fresh air and a view of the water. In the west-facing bedroom on the top floor, light streams in through clerestory windows, which Irani calls 'my natural alarm clock.' The rest of the day, shadows shrink and grow to reflect the passing hours."[39]

Over the years, some have built much larger dwellings after being granted variances from the city that have allowed them to add extra height and extra square footage. But the variances only sanction modest additions. A few, however, have completely ignored the planning codes, interconnecting adjacent houses or knocking down buildings on two or more lots to erect mansions that cross over multiple parcels. The planning department lacks the resources to regulate these unauthorized actions.

Canal compounds, architectural innovations, and canal mansions are multimillion-dollar investments, as the neighborhood has developed a more exclusive stature as home to well-known architects, Hollywood writers, producers, directors, established music and business executives, doctors and lawyers, and a few actors (although the lack of neighbor-privacy thwarts the most recognizable from moving in). For some, the Canals are merely a second or third neighborhood; they spend the majority of their time in other places and leave their waterfront home empty for much of the year. People of this income bracket spend their money in a way that differentiates them from the middle- and upper-middle-class residents of previous decades. Janice contrasts her own middle-class lifestyle with the newer upper-income homeowners who renovate their houses on a regular basis:

> We have so much building going on down here. Not just new houses. Tearing down, or completely gutting, or completely remodeling a house that's ten years old. You don't see that in middle-class neighborhoods. People remodel once and that's about it. And then you're done for the next ten years. You do the kitchen and it stays that way and that's it. But we've been through four complete remodels on that side, a couple more on this side, and these are all from the same owners. Another one right there [across the canal] was a brand new house. Just built. And when the new guy moved in, he didn't like it, and completely revamped it into a Spanish Terracotta. Who does that? A whole house transformation in a brand new house? Who has that kind of money?

The Canals have passed through successive stages as an unconventional neighborhood, a slum without misery, a middle-class milieu, and a quaint Gold Coast, providing new symbolic cues that help the public make sense of its identity. While wealth is visibly apparent, it is equally striking how a neighborhood surrounded by such diverse settings almost completely eliminated lower-income rentals and poor residents. This dramatic shift and the neighborhood's visible contrast with its surroundings make it easier for locals to keep track of "outsiders." The past relationship between the inside and outside was built upon a philosophy of openness. Whether all residents liked it or not (and clearly there were groups who did not) vacant spaces and hippie transients dominated the public culture and blurred the boundary between "insider" and "outsider." Now that the neighborhood is a more exclusive mix of upper-middle and upper-income residents, they can control the relationship between those who belong and those who do not.

Residents collectively construct insider status by taking over public spaces for festivities and beautification campaigns, which present a new type of peaceful and cordial environment. The VCA and the VOC, at this point quality of life "homeowner" associations (although the VOC allows renters to participate), organize local events. These planned occasions are different from the politicized festivals of the late 1960s and early '70s that started as opposition to development and were open to anyone, publicly advertising and inviting thousands of people into the countercultural haven. The new community events operate less as public festivals for ten thousand people and more as private stylized territorial performances for Canal families and friends, the attendance numbering closer to one hundred.

The VOC organizes a holiday party and bridge lighting, where about one hundred people turn out to drink hot spiced cider, mulled wine, and Mexican hot chocolate while listening to folk music and using the event to raise money for the Venice Community Housing Corporation on Rose Avenue. The VCA organizes a yearly Holiday Boat Parade around the same time. Crowds of residents and friends line the sidewalks and watch as boats glide down the waterways. People decorate their homes and vessels with Christmas lights, and they perform skits dressed in costumes as they drift along and sing. Prizes are given for the best-dressed homes and bridges. In the summer, they arrange free "row in" movie nights, where people float in their canoes, kayaks, and paddleboats while watching a movie outside with their neighbors. They also plan the Downwind Regatta, in which residents come up with innovative ways to sail wind-powered boats down the Linnie Canal, the winners receiving trophies.

These events present a stylized, rather than politicized, public culture built upon leisure, neighborliness, relaxation, and family fun. There is no struggle involved, no open conflict between opposing sides, no overwhelming changes to argue about, and no celebration of a subversive lifestyle. In fact, the VOC and the VCA are basically twin organizations at this point, as rising rents mitigate class differences. New homeowners readily join both with only a vague awareness of the decades-old battles, sometimes hearing stories from their neighbors. Members with longer memories harbor some resentment toward the other side, claiming that the "laid back" and "more rebellious" group still throws better parties than the "tight-asses" who devote more time to beautification and planning. Still, for most new residents, these distinct organizations basically serve the same function.

The restored waterways, sidewalks, and footbridges are almost two decades old, and the refurbished surroundings are fully integrated into everyday life much like the organic surroundings were for the counter-cultural residents of the previous era. They are now part of the over-all functional and symbolic scene and people move in with an appreci-ation of its quaint character, rather than being determined to fix it up. The conflicts that remain are more trivial, not about belonging but about beautification measures. Albert, who moved in during the early 2000s, talks about the small beautification touches that keep the Canals atmo-sphere visibly charming:

> I belong to both associations. But generally speaking, everything now is pretty much agreed upon. Now it's just little odds and ends, like what kind of plants to plant. We have various little projects, like the landscaping project at the entrance of the canals and we had a vote about what kind of trees were going to go in there, and now we're doing the same thing at the city lot down the way by Twenty-Fourth Avenue. We had crosswalks put in.

The neighborhood public culture stems from complementary pieces coming together: architectural designs, private lifestyles, natural wild-life, wooden footbridges over serene waterways, and relaxed neighbor-hood events. Together, these elements crystallize as a boundary that easily distinguishes between insiders and outsiders, although not all outsiders are perceived as dangerous. Appreciative tourists are gener-ally accepted. In fact, many residents like that certain outsiders value the fruits of their labor. Those who visit the Canals are different from the masses on the highly commercialized Venice Boardwalk, where in-dividuals from a wide range of racial, ethnic, and socioeconomic back-grounds face countless options for fitting in, creating and maintaining a nonconformist milieu. On the residential Canals, the options for fitting in are much more limited. Tour buses stop on a bridge on Dell Avenue. People walk out and take photographs of the scenic surroundings. They wander like schoolchildren in a single file line down the maze of narrow sidewalks, with a sense of appreciation and awe of the quiet man-made "natural" wetland. Couples meander, holding hands amidst the romantic setting. They gawk at the architectural styles, stopping to offer personal criticisms of colors and designs, guessing how much each one costs, and longing to live in their favorite houses. This public culture is part of the everyday order.

Yet the contemporary order also obstructs unconventional behaviors. Since 1997, residents have hired a private bike patrol and security-service operation. According to one of the organizers of the program, only about one-third of the residents fund the patrol, but they hope that more residents will eventually contribute. Residents pay $32 a month and the patrol works about eight to ten hours a day, seven days a week—not yet the twenty-four-hour surveillance system found in L.A.'s highest-class neighborhoods, but a clear sign of a place that is moving in the direction of exclusivity. The visibility of the community patrol thwarts "crimes of opportunity," the most common types of offences in this neighborhood where criminals see an easy target, such as stealing a bicycle out of an open garage.

The physical structure of the neighborhood also makes foreign behaviors more visible. The ordered construction of houses only three feet apart and directly facing neighbors across the waterways in the front and across the alleyways in the back facilitates surveillance. Devon, in her late fifties, explains,

> If somebody is gonna break in they're only gonna take what they can carry. And they have to haul it a long way. You're not going to haul a sixty-inch flat screen down the alley. It's crimes of opportunity, people leave their windows open or somebody breaks into a car if the car's not locked. And they can only really steal small things. It's too difficult down here. You can't be that unobtrusive.

Because of its design and upscale character, the Canals have a number of advantages when dealing with the homeless issue that afflicts other parts of Venice in a more significant way. The limited number of public parking spots in the neighborhood restricts visitor overnight parking, one of the key stabilizing mechanisms for the homeless along Rose Avenue. Private residents get away with transforming the only available public parking, located in back alleys and along Dell Avenue, into private driveways; many even put up their own signs warning visitors that parking in this "private space" may result in their car being towed. Vacant lots and open space have been eliminated, with the exception of one remaining city-owned vest-pocket park with limited and monitored hours of operation. Homeless individuals who do stay in the park or around the perimeter of the neighborhood encounter constant inquiries from residents, private security, and LAPD and quickly decide that staying there is not worth the hassle when they can easily sustain themselves in other parts of Venice. According to Sharon,

> [Homeless people] used to hang out at the park. That was a big thing. And they passed some rules that you couldn't stay in the park at night and they used to be at another spot, and then the police came in. And the security do a good job as well, making sure that people aren't up to no good. We really just don't have a problem with the homeless here.

The neighborhood homology makes it easy to identify anything outside of the norm, which also includes the very few remaining homeowners who do not put in the time, effort, and resources to maintain the appropriate aesthetic milieu. Marvin discusses one such circumstance:

> The woman who owned that house for some reason moved out. It's one of the original Canal houses. It's very old and very small. The house was deteriorating and she didn't have the inclination to fix it. And she moved out and then there were squatters in the house and one of the neighbors said that some of them were confrontational. I would see these guys sometimes coming down the alley, when I walked the dog at eleven or twelve o'clock at night. And they'd be riding a bicycle and he'd have another bicycle that he's got by the handlebar. And I'd see another guy with pit bulls coming in and out. It was a real mess and the police raided the house early in the morning. They had these big assault rifles and helmets, and face masks, and bulletproof vests, and it was like they had the house surrounded. . . . They took out of there something over forty really nice bicycles. It was a bicycle chop shop. The police came with these big vans and pickup trucks, loaded up the bikes and took them away. And then, the police, the city somehow got into this thing where they said that the house was uninhabitable. They put up a sign that said that nobody could go in or out of the house. It was a health hazard. Don't go in the house.

These examples speak to a new material and symbolic order that has settled into place along the Canals. This latest form of stability as a scenic neighborhood, an increasingly upscale and homogeneous locale, isolates outsiders and calls attention to any form of unconventionality, a clear contrast from its more heterogeneous past. The Venice Canals have become a place where complementary interests and actions have hardened into a coherent border between the inside and the outside.

Shifting Positions and the Rise of a Scenic Neighborhood

This chapter highlighted how shifting political configurations, based upon changing classifications of old-timers and newcomers and the invention of a quaint Canals history that never actually existed, facilitated the rise of a scenic neighborhood. Countercultural renters were influential in shaping the public culture in the 1960s and '70s, but as the neighborhood's composition shifted, their presence and collective identity faded. Those in the middle position did not intend to turn the Canals into a scenic locale, but they made it easier for speculative developers and upper-middle-class property owners to invert the homeowner/renter ratio. Because the middle class shared some of the same sentiments as the counterculture, opposing a modern restoration and major development projects, one might label them as preservationists. But by virtue of their social position and cultural conventions that complemented the upper-middle class, they also unintentionally influenced the trajectory of neighborhood change.

As wealthier property owners moved in, the political configuration between the middle class and the upper class shifted the discussions toward the center. Organized countercultural resistance to the Canals restoration no longer held a place at the table, and compromises were made between two gentrifying classes. Although residents in the middle position transformed themselves into the "old-timers," the new political configuration also increased the appearance of homogeneity through a new neighborhood homology between groups, styles, and space and gave way to the invention of a scenic neighborhood. Unlike Oakwood or Rose Avenue, the new configuration was made up of complementary elements rather than competing symbolic codes. Residents of opposing sides built a new form of stability out of the politics of quaintness. Both sides were almost exclusively made up of white property owners, a clear contrast to the black-Latino-white configuration that has sustained Oakwood's durable identity as diverse, and to the enduring homeless-housed configuration along Rose Avenue in which two forms of stability are in constant conflict over the uses of public spaces.

These cases shed light on the politics of urban change in three residential neighborhoods. Two of them have sustained identities as ambiguous and diverse, while the Venice Canals have established and reinforced a coherent boundary as an exclusive scenic neighborhood. How do the tensions between diversity and exclusivity operate in commercial neighborhoods? The next two chapters tackle these processes in two places that have commercialized Venice's historic bohemianism: the Venice Boardwalk and Abbot Kinney Boulevard.

CHAPTER FIVE

Bohemian Theme Park

On a Sunday afternoon, a group of musicians consisting of five conga drummers, two guitarists, a bassist, and a saxophonist plays a mix of Afro-Caribbean, jazz, and blues. The songs have no beginning, middle, or end; as in an extended jam session, the tunes flow into one another. Jonas, a sixty-two-year old homeless African American man and long-time artist, musician, and activist on the Venice Boardwalk, coordinates the performance at the same time that he bangs on his drum and improvises an unscripted sermon about freedom. A group of homeless men and women stand just behind the drummers. Jasmine, in her late fifties, endlessly twirls around in circles with her eyes closed, her stringy, gray-accented blond hair flinging outward. Slim, a lanky white man in his early sixties, shakes a tambourine, as an exuberant smile pierces through his bushy white beard. Others of different ages and racial and ethnic backgrounds—young, middle-aged, and elderly; white, Latino, and black—sit on a concrete wall and bob their heads to the rhythm. Tourists crowd around. Some take photographs and dance, as others study the scene.

After almost an hour, a police officer in an SUV approaches on the beach. He aligns his vehicle with the performers and monitors their actions from about one hundred yards away. The vehicle slowly creeps toward the boardwalk, perfectly synchronized with four other SUVs that suddenly appear from around the corner. More than ten police officers surround the group. The officer in charge, a towering, solid white man in uniform, approaches Jonas and orders him to stop performing. He writes him a ticket for playing music without a permit, a new requirement under a revised city ordinance. Jonas inspects the ticket and responds, "Playing music is a crime? I don't know how y'all get away with this."

The crowd shuffles closer, collectively chanting, "Let them play! Let them play!" The officer steps toward Jonas to tune out the crowd and reasons with him. "You can't keep playing here if you don't follow the rules. You can get a permit and play in an assigned space, but you can't play here without a permit." Jonas responds, "I don't gotta get a permit to play music. This is first amendment. How you gonna stop it when the boardwalk is for free speech?" The officer points to a translucent plastic canister filled with dollar bills in the middle of the musicians. He asks, "Did you collect any money?" Jonas answers, "We don't collect money. Our friends give donations. But we don't *collect it*. They just do as they see fit."

The officer rebuts a little bit more forcefully this time, "Do you really want us to arrest you? That's what's gonna happen if this continues." Jonas asks, "Arrest me? For what? I'm a disabled veteran. I served this country. Now you gonna arrest me?" The officer does not answer, but pleads, "I can set my watch to the complaints. The second you start playing, the phone calls start coming in. You have to follow the new ordinance" that includes a prohibition on music that can be heard from beyond fifty feet. The musicians, upset that their session is disrupted, talk among themselves and reluctantly agree to stop for the day. The lead officer, temporarily satisfied with the outcome, warns, "I'm gonna come back later, and I don't want to see you playing." He disbands his unit, which disappears just as quickly as it had arrived.

Jonas is left holding a ticket and the crowd is noticeably confused about the circumstances of the police intervention. Charlie, one of the drummers, overhears someone in the crowd asking, "What did he do wrong?" He defends the group, "We didn't do nothin' wrong! We're just playing music. See this guy right here?" pointing to Jonas. This guy's been doing this right here for over twenty years and now they want to get rid of him. They're tired of freedom at Venice Beach!" The crowd gradually disperses. Musicians, activists, and homeless men and women waiting in line for a meal served within feet from the performance remain behind.

A Town Hall meeting a few nights later addresses the implementation of the new regulations on the Free Speech Zone, the one-and-half-mile stretch of the beachside of the boardwalk where people encounter an eclectic mix of countercultural activism, the arts, and economic activities. Longtime homeless activists distribute food and information. A Latino folk singer plays 1960s favorites. Young sculptors from Mexico City sell hemp jewelry and ceramic skulls. Oaxacan men and women accompanied by their children sell the same mass-produced figurines up and down the boardwalk. Asian artists demonstrate their skilled calligraphy. African American painters sell large portraits of jazz musicians. Many more of diverse backgrounds sell an even wider variety of products that incorporate some element of self-proclaimed "free expression," including paintings, jewelry, woodwork, ceramics, bumper stickers, or clothing, all with religious, ethnic, or politically encoded messages.

Councilman Bill Rosendahl convenes the meeting, which begins with a collective prayer that includes a drum session by some of the boardwalk performers. Recently elected, the councilman wants to hear from multiple sides about the controversial regulations that were imposed before he took office. Jon, a white man in his late thirties, introduces himself as a four-month renter residing in an apartment near the boardwalk. He addresses the councilman and the audience of about seventy-five people. "Week after week we are subject to excessive noise. Performers manipulate their audiences into making more noise and screaming. They tell jokes with obscenities and racial and sexual orientation epithets that are quite offensive. They are creating a huge crowd in front of where I live to the point where it's a safety hazard. Residents are held hostage by the performers. They are disrespectful and don't care about working with the community. What we want here is a better quality of life." Louis, an African American performer in his late fifties, has lived in Venice for several decades, both on the streets and in different dwellings. He calls out, "How can you even speak about this? You've been here four months. This has always been a place where people can come and be free. After four months, how'd you become an authority?"

People at the meeting complain about more than quality of life. Some point to the differential effects of economic competition between so-called legitimate and illegitimate interests, reminiscent of Duneier's (1999) description of "space wars" between the homeless vendors and nearby businesses in New York's West Village. At the meeting, a developer gripes about not being able to rent apartments in his new building because of noisy performances. A property owner who rents out space to retailers criticizes the unfair competition facing his tenants, many of them Korean immigrants who work "eighty hours a week to give their families a better life." A Korean woman who has owned a T-shirt store on the boardwalk for over a decade speaks out on behalf of some of the rent-paying boardwalk businesses, especially a group of Korean merchants who sit beside her. In a rare public presentation of opposition, as the interests of Korean merchants are usually represented by white property owners who rent spaces to them, she says, "We support the artists [selling paintings in public space], but we need to have an ordinance. Some people want to make it into a business and it is not fair. They sell the same products [in public space] as we do [in rented space]. They don't sell art. It's a business. We pay our rent and our taxes and it is hard to compete with free space."

As she speaks, a small group of the boardwalk's Free Speech Zone vendors standing together in the back of the room—two black men and two white men—pull apart their eyes to appear slanted, mocking the Korean woman. One of the African American men insults her, "We pay taxes, no make egg roll." An outburst of laughter follows. Corina, a white homeowner in her early forties, is outraged by their reaction to the Korean business owners. She criticizes their disrespectful behavior as "racist." A white female jewelry vendor calls out to the Korean merchants who sit together in a row, "I used to shop at your stores for gifts and everything, but not anymore! Who do you think is next when they get rid of us? You think you'll be able to afford the rent when they make this into Third Street Promenade [a more upscale commercial pedestrian street in bordering Santa Monica] and all the fancy stores come in? You're next!"

Additional complaints come from activists supporting the Free Speech Zone. Many dislike the city's new lottery method for divvying up spaces, replacing the informal first-come, first-serve system that existed for decades. A white peace activist in her sixties distributes political information on the boardwalk. She criticizes the city as "experimenting with our lives." An African American in his midforties sells incense, now a restricted product under the new ordinance. He says, "We have families to support too and you're taking away our livelihoods." Jonas and a number of other self-professed "longtime boardwalk activists" complain about "selective enforcement," as the Department of Parks and Recreation and LAPD officers target those who refuse to purchase a permit rather than addressing those breaking the law by selling commercial products.

During the last three decades, countercultural activists, artists and performers, homeless men and women, immigrant entrepreneurs, gentrifiers, developers, and city officials from a variety of departments have become entangled in the boardwalk's ecological structure. Locally learned and enacted economic, cultural, and political adaptations serve

FIGURE 15. Venice Boardwalk scene. "Free expression" vendors lined up on the beach side, to the left of the photograph, opposite rent-paying businesses to the right.

as a guiding logic of immersion and attachment to Venice Beach, positioning "formal" inland ties against "informal" beachside ties. Formal neighborhood connections through rent and property ownership give rise to a local classification of the Free Speech Zone as a unique urban problem; yet informal economic, political, and cultural connections to the public space reproduce a territorial association that is difficult to disrupt (see figure 15).

Los Angeles City Council members, LAPD officers, city attorneys, and officials from the Los Angeles Department of Parks and Recreation are regularly called upon to mediate between the two competing sides, much like they have in Oakwood, Rose Avenue, and the Canals.[1] Over a period of three decades, they have implemented ever more stringent regulations over informal economic uses of this famous public space, further cementing distinctions between formal and informal attachments as "order" and "disorder." Here, as on Rose Avenue, after devoting ample time and resources to this problem, they continuously fail to accomplish regulatory goals, unable to grasp the complicated social, economic, and political conditions that underlie the rise of these local quality of life concerns.

Rebirth of a Popular Attraction

Sociologists and cultural critics often argue that mass culture has detrimental effects, because marketing firms and corporate economic investors adapt trends and objects to reach a larger and larger public without consideration of local culture. Musical forms are often thought of
in such terms. Record producers catch wind of a popular local subculture, such as the birth of hip-hop in the South Bronx, slowly take control of the style, and filter it through market practices that distribute it
to ever-wider audiences. This movement from subculture to popular culture, from local autonomy to profit-making mechanism, is described as
having a homogenizing effect that eradicates connections to its original
and more authentic producers.

Studies of gentrification and more specifically commercialization of
neighborhoods and cities often evoke similar notions about mass culture and markets. Critics argue that places shift from having an authentic local culture that is attractive to artists, musicians, mom and pop
stores, small-time landlords, and lower-income populations into more
homogeneous places controlled by corporate landlords and greedy businesses. Wealthier interests filter in new resources, make popular amenities available to upper-middle and upper classes, and displace the subcultures that initially put these places on the map. Adopting the logic
that transforming neighborhoods and spaces involves a perfect market
process, they argue that everywhere looks and feels the same, witnessed
by the replication of urban designs and corporate chains.[2]

Not all mass cultural attractions follow the same commercial channels, however. This section describes how the relationship between five
historical events transformed the local social and economic conditions
and facilitated the rediscovery of the boardwalk by the masses. The process of transformation involved the configuration of local neighborhood
circumstances with broader regional changes, ultimately turning the
boardwalk into a highly commercialized yet complex multiuse environment filled with racial, ethnic, and socioeconomic diversity. The following conditions accumulated and set the foundation for the shift from the
boardwalk as a bohemian enclave into a bohemian theme park for the
masses: (1) the creation of a rundown building infrastructure abutting
a public beach; (2) a series of popularizing events and cultural forms;
(3) the birth of a microeconomy; (4) the reinstatement of the impor-

tance of private property; and (5) major population shifts across the region.

The Los Angeles coastline underwent a marked transition as an attraction during the 1960s and '70s. Developers constructed high-rise buildings in Marina del Rey and Santa Monica, setting off a major controversy about the future of property along the Venice Boardwalk. While major city code enforcement programs required maintenance of old buildings and enabled developers to construct several new commercial and residential structures on the boardwalk, slow-growth activists averted the threat of dense high-rise development. A sprawling beach, one of the largest on the Southern California coast, stood opposite a wide mix of buildings, most of which remained neglected by landlords or completely abandoned.

Most Los Angeles commercial arteries have a built infrastructure on both sides of the street. Over sixty stores, twenty-five restaurants, and three movie theaters, including chain retail stores such as the Apple Store, Banana Republic, and Barnes & Noble, line both sides of nearby Third Street Promenade, a widely visited commercial street and car-free pedestrian walkway in Santa Monica. During the 1980s, developers, city planners, and politicians revitalized this pedestrian retail artery, investing over $500 million to gut the area and rebuild it. The Promenade's current private-property configuration attracts the public, including tourists staying within walking distance to the area at some of the most coveted hotels in Southern California. But the private-property configuration also constrains the public, with very strict surveillance of homeless panhandling and a highly scrutinized program for public performers that serves the interests of business owners.

The boardwalk's infrastructure distinguishes it from other famous Los Angeles commercial streets, like Third Street Promenade. The interface of commercial space and a public beach has anchored a particular kind of social and cultural spontaneity and openness. For decades, the boardwalk's neglect was central to Venice's bohemian reputation. With minimal redevelopment progress, the boardwalk had no centralized power holders invested in trying to transform the daily culture and control the uses of space. Certainly, some middle-class property owners who came along in the 1950s and '60s wanted to rid the area of existing cafés and especially the beatniks who could be heard pounding their drums and playing their jazz music late into the night. Not only did propertied quality of life interests lack a local consensus, but they also did not have the same degree of financial and political backing as the major development stakeholders that ultimately succeeded at transforming Santa Monica's downtown area into a prime consumption space.

The combination of a vocal and visible counterculture, long-standing property neglect, and abandonment along a major public resource—a wide open beach—made it possible for the emergence of a series of popular fads and mass cultural events that brought in droves of visitors. In the mid-1970s, an ocean-side roller-skating trend exploded into a full-fledged popular cultural craze that led then-mayor Tom Bradley to promote Venice Beach as the "roller-skating capital of the world." A subcultural interest in freestyle skateboarding originated in bordering Ocean Park, an area of Santa Monica often mistakenly referred to as part of Venice because of its similar housing stock and shared history, turning several miles of Ocean Front Walk into "Dogtown." Bodybuilding at Muscle Beach revolutionized the sport, as many of its ambassadors, including Arnold Schwarzenegger, were onetime regulars in Venice.

These popularizing events and cultural creators brought widespread attention to the boardwalk, attracting visitors from near and far. The new mass-cultural phenomenon mixed together tens of thousands of people, or some even estimate hundreds of thousands, on any given day. Where a mass public appears, an opportunity for a *microeconomy* opens up. Crowded areas, especially tourism spots, are ripe for informal economic activity.[3] The boardwalk's tourist economy emerged as a free-floating entity outside of private-property relations but directly entwined with the local bohemian culture. The now pervasive rent-paying restaurateurs and rent-paying T-shirt and sunglass salesmen were not the first to see opportunity to profit in this now-famous tourist scene. As the crowds grew larger, entertainers found an impromptu stage for their crafts. Musicians and various types of carnival performers, such as jugglers of chain saws and butcher knives, fire swallowers, comedians, and a few artists, entered into the mix, giving rise to a theme park persona (see figure 16).

Hippies, travelers, and artists also sold arts and crafts in abandoned parking lots, and other locals with an affinity for this loose public activity joined them to get rid of used items: clothes, scarves, books, furniture, and any other vintage objects that had resale value. Reggie, who first arrived to the boardwalk in the early '70s as a musician, describes the early scene as "funky," a term that refers to the unconventional character of the area:

FIGURE 16. Venice Beach carnival performer in 1979. Photograph by Alice Belkin. Copyright Los Angeles Public Library.

Things started happening because there were major crowds. The tourist thing was so much bigger. There were a hundred thousand people on any given weekend. You couldn't even walk. I mean you've seen those pictures of Venice when it was crowded like sardines. It was like head to head, body to body. And from Monday through Friday and sometimes on the weekends, but especially during the week, people even brought their stuff out and had yard sales all out on the boardwalk. . . . People would put stuff out there and sold it for a dollar fifty. It was sort of like a funky thrift store with lots of neighborhood people. That went on for a couple of years. Three or four years maybe. And then there were a lot of street performers starting out. It was pretty funky.

Franco, a long-term homeless traveler now in his seventies, first arrived in Venice in the 1970s. He was one of the early street sellers and a firsthand witness to the slowly emerging bohemian economy. He says,

> Where all the vendors are now [who rent spaces in the east side parking lots to sell knickknacks], there was nobody there. Nobody but this guy with a big blanket and sheet and he's selling stuff out of the dumpster. At that time, there was a lot of stuff people would throw away. Cameras, TVs, radios, clothes, coats, jackets, tools, knives, all kinds of gadgets. . . . Maybe two or three artists were down there on Windward. No stuff like now. Lots of musicians, a few carnival acts, that's really it. It was amazing what we'd find. Rings, jewelry, all sorts of things people throw away. We were selling cheap. The jackets were going for like two or three dollars. The pants were going like maybe three dollars. Suits, ten dollars. After a while, some guys came over and tried to collect money from us, like charge us rent for the space. Some of these guys were real con artists. And these two homeless people were working right next to me, selling stuff too. And they told me, don't give 'em nothing. They're a bunch of crooks.

As it turned out, some of the people Franco describes as "crooks" were property owners, taking back private property from its open use. *Reinstating the importance of private property*, investors sought to develop new buildings, refurbish old ones, and profit from the popular attraction. The Goodfaders bought a dilapidated, boarded-up building that had been out of use for decades. In 1976, they opened up the Sidewalk Café, which quickly became a meeting space for local artists, eventually growing into a popular restaurant and bar. They also moved their Marina-based Small World Books, an eclectic independent bookstore, into the space next door. They followed by purchasing additional adjacent lots and transforming them into over a dozen vending stalls, initially leased to artists and others selling used household items and clothing.[4] Other developers followed suit. Werner Scharff bought up property left and right, expanding and restoring buildings, including a hotel, apartments, and a wide variety of new commercial spaces, while commissioning many of the murals that now line the boardwalk.[5]

Commercial interests were not opposed to the boardwalk's reputation as a public space for the masses. Rather, these two elements worked symbiotically, as the newfound carnival stabilized the boardwalk's profit-making potential as tourists came for the free entertainment. While certain popularizing events like the roller skating craze were temporary, an eclectic mix of performers, artists, and activists sustained a new bohemian theme park. As property owners benefited from the boardwalk's growing popularity, controlling a limited supply of commercial space amidst increasing demand, *newer population changes* interacted with the local microeconomy, continuing the ecological process in which new groups entered the environment and influenced its local culture and economy. Different groups came into the boardwalk at the same time, displacing other groups and revising its public culture. Rising rental prices and the aging of the population ultimately dislocated elderly Eastern European Jews, slowly eroding the customer base of the Jewish bakeries and other institutions they supported. Likewise, as the beatnik movement faded across the region, the local cafés and hangouts supporting this culture vanished, as commercial spaces morphed into new types of establishments to meet the demand of a growing number of tourists.

Although these ethnic groups and subcultures disappeared due to changing social and economic conditions, the area did not simply transform from an inclusive site of complex heterogeneity into an exclusive site of upper-income homogeneity. Conditions outside of local control redirected the bohemian subculture into a form of popular culture. Homelessness, immigration, countercultural and artistic movements, urban development, and gentrification became interdependent as a new type of mass culture that set up multiple logics of adaptation.

Multiple Logics of Adaptation

Different populations converged in the boardwalk ecology. The attraction of property owners and rent-paying entrepreneurs was typical of a new trend of gentrification. Increased rents, as was also the case in places like New York's SoHo or Chicago's Wicker Park,[6] pushed out artists, craftspeople, and bohemian travelers. On the boardwalk, the composition of their replacements differed from the common image of a new gentry class, for they included organized bohemian and immigrant entrepreneurs. People with interests in the arts opened little stores; those with affinity to world culture and new age religions opened up others; hippies found refuge in the boardwalk as a place to make a bit more money; and Korean entrepreneurs soon discovered the potential of this untapped tourist market.

As more organized rent-paying entrepreneurs made their marks in the boardwalk ecology, other types of attachments also appeared. Los Angeles's homeless population expanded during the 1980s, and hundreds of homeless men and women concentrated on the boardwalk. In addition, unemployed and underemployed Latin American, Asian, Caribbean, and African immigrants, along with African Americans, found new vending opportunities. They distributed artwork, a range of crafts, T-shirts, hats, bags, bumper stickers, political buttons, jewelry, incense, perfume, lotions, and a wide variety of household items. Artists also used the boardwalk to stabilize and advance their careers, continuing Venice's famed artistic reputation. Five distinct logics of adaptation became commonplace: (1) rent-paying entrepreneurs, (2) artists in pursuit of career advancement, (3) entrepreneurs with a "free speech" cover, (4) homelessness masked as countercultural activism, and (5) thieves, scavengers, and stragglers.

Rent-Paying Entrepreneurs

With a growing demand and limited commercial space, property owners raised their rents. This more competitive environment squeezed out artists and hippies scratching out a living by selling paintings and used clothing in stalls and parking lots. Carole Berkson, a craftswoman and parking lot vendor between 1978 and 1980, describes the changing culture among rent-paying vendors:

> The Vendors' Lot, it was called. . . . I sat on my carpet for months, every Saturday and every Sunday. . . . The whole atmosphere in those days was very laid back. . . . Then, after a while, things got a little more hectic. A little too hectic to keep sitting on the ground. I got a table. By then I was making purses as well as belts. I had regular customers as well as regular Boardwalk-going friends who stopped to visit. I was making money. I was also paying more rent, but not more than seemed equitable in light of what I was making. By

then the whole enterprise had become more professional, tighter. But it was still primarily professional crafts people. . . . The Vendors' Lot had stopped looking like a few hippies out playing and started to look more like some sort of Moroccan bazaar. . . . Then things got more hectic. . . . By this time I had two tables and . . . I was selling beads and whatnot as well as my belts and purses, only not doing so well as I had earlier, and paying more, and enjoying it less. And some of the vendors had left and we were less of a family and a lot of the people around weren't any longer so nice and a lot of the merchandise wasn't so nice either. I was feeling more and more like a token craftsperson on the Boardwalk.[7]

Rent-paying entrepreneurs had to develop more strategic and profitable businesses to survive. Clarence was hardly a savvy corporate businessman, but in this context he took on the position of gentrifier. If his long black beard, flowing hair, dark sunglasses, and wrinkled Hawaiian shirt do not give away his bohemian identity, the fact that during the 1970s he lived in a school bus on the streets of Venice probably does. He came to own a T-shirt business on the boardwalk in the early '80s, not through any business plan but through a confluence of circumstances related to his unconventional lifestyle and his local networks.

Residing on a bus, he met a homeowner named John who supplied him with electricity, water, and occasional meals. John happened to own a silk-screening business and knew where to purchase inexpensive T-shirts. With John's assistance, Clarence and a friend started selling T-shirts in one of the vending parking lots on the boardwalk during the week for a daily fee. They wanted to expand and sell on the weekends, a far more lucrative venture due to larger crowds, but there was a waiting list. When a space opened up, the owner offered it to Clarence, but he demanded $2,800 up front. With only a thousand in hand, Clarence again called upon his local networks. John's ex-wife Sarah, also a Venice resident, loaned him the rest of the money. As the business became profitable, Clarence paid back his loans and organized more strategic plans for expanding his business, ultimately moving his parking lot T-shirt business into a store, where he has remained for over twenty-five years.

The Venice bohemian community continued to attract new entrepreneurs like Clarence and Carole, in search of a laid-back yet profitable beach lifestyle and community. As the boardwalk developed a reputation as having economic potential, Korean entrepreneurs moved in. Social scientists have found that Korean immigrants often arrive in the

United States with social and economic connections that embed them into an upwardly mobile middle-class community. In this respect, the Korean small family business has become a familiar model of immigrant entrepreneurship in contemporary urban America. It may be most pronounced in Los Angeles where individuals of Korean descent have established direct economic lines from the center of their economic organization in Koreatown into a variety of Los Angeles neighborhoods, ranging from Watts and Compton to downtown and Venice.[8]

Jae, in his midfifties, has had a business on the Venice Boardwalk for twenty-two years. When he first moved to Los Angeles from South Korea in 1980, he lived with his brother and his family and worked at their downtown business. He said, "It was a great opportunity, because I didn't really know English and I saw where to buy things. Lots of different products in downtown for very cheap." After making some money, marrying, and having children of his own, he wanted to branch out. "I wanted to open a business and a friend recommended I come to Venice. At that time, there were restaurants, some other small stores. Not too much with T-shirts and sunglasses, so I did that." Jae saw the boardwalk's untapped market as an opportunity. In this respect, he was representative of many immigrants willing to make a financial venture in a place that others might deem suspect. With financial assistance from his brother and with a deep knowledge and diverse connections with downtown merchants, he opened up a T-shirt and souvenir shop on the Venice Boardwalk. He explains, "There was lots of European visitors when I first opened, and they wanted something to remember their trip. I remember thinking to bring in more things that say Venice on them."

The economic union between Koreans and Venice Beach strengthened over time, as individuals found new opportunities, overtook the artists occupying many of the vending stalls and even, in some circumstances, took over longer-running businesses from previous owners. Kwan, a longtime boardwalk business owner, expanded his enterprise from one to two stores selling T-shirts, sunglasses, and other tourist knickknacks. Successful for almost two decades, he put his children through college and lived a comfortable life in Los Angeles. Tommy, in his midforties, moved to Los Angeles from South Korea with his wife and family in 2005 and worked for his father-in-law, an acquaintance of Kwan's. Kwan wanted to downsize his boardwalk enterprise and offered to help Tommy and his wife take over one of his stores. Kwan sold Tommy the store's stock and its system for tracking the inventory, connected him with merchants in Los Angeles and New York, and facilitated the transition with the landlord to take over the commercial lease.

While networks may have led people to initiate their business ventures, their continued success depended upon profits, leading many with less strategic business plans and less financial backing to turn to the public space for economic activity. The bohemian carnival was built upon a rent-free economy, which slowly diversified. As inexpensive rental spaces disappeared for artists, they developed a new type of economic attachment in the public space.

Artistic Advancement

Just as rent-paying entrepreneurs use the tourist space as an economic hustle, selling overpriced T-shirts and knickknacks to the masses, many artists learn to utilize the public space as a means of career advancement. Their boardwalk attachments serve as an artistic hustle. Miles, an African American artist in his early fifties, claims, "There is the art that feeds you, the art that sustains you, and the art that makes you famous." Venice Beach is a place for the "the art that feeds you." Miles refers to the fact that artists at Venice Beach compete with commercial vendors selling touristy items.

Success in the Free Speech Zone requires individuals to abide by the logic of economic adaptation. They learn to set up accounts to accept credit cards; they make their paintings into prints in order to lower costs and reduce prices; they haggle with customers over the value of a work; they create paintings of popular themes, such as Venice Beach scenery and famous musicians; and they include additional themes around holidays, like paintings of hearts on Valentine's Day or flowers on Mother's Day. Leo, in his early forties, graduated from the Columbus College of Art & Design in Columbus, Ohio, in 1998 and then moved to Los Angeles where he found his way to Venice Beach. He discusses how he adapted to the boardwalk's economic ecology as a way of advancing his career:

> You have to learn to interact with others around you and become familiar with what to do. You learn from being here, failing, and seeing what works. If it works, you do it again. If it doesn't, you don't. You find what works for others and incorporate these methods into your own method for selling. When I first came out, I was only selling originals. It seemed to work. I would make

a little bit of money. But it's hard to get ahead. My first big hurdle was getting over the idea that you need to spend money to make money. When I sold enough paintings and saved up, I bought an Epson printer and started making prints. What I found is that I could make more money with prints, because I can sell them for cheaper prices and sell more of them. And with the Epson, I can do inexpensive, nice quality ones that people like. The bottom line is that the more money I would put into the business aspect, the more I would receive and the better my chances of being successful as an artist.

Individuals seeking artistic advancement distinguish themselves in the local status hierarchy by using the boardwalk to move away from street selling into more widely accepted art world venues, such as street fairs, art conventions, independent group exhibitions, trade shows, and galleries. Miles moved to Venice when he was sixteen years old without any art school training. Instead, he developed skills he needed on the street through trial and error. He eventually expanded his repertoire by attending street fairs, conventions, trade shows, and accepting gallery representation in a number of cities in different countries. He explains,

If you're a manufacturer, who are you gonna support? Some artist on the beach that hasn't put in the time and resources? Or are you going to go to a trade show where artists set up and demonstrate that they can support themselves? They've put in the time and it's a better investment for the manufacturer to bank on someone that can put up six thousand bucks. It's not a conspiracy theory like the art world is consciously not trying to work with artists out on the beach or something like that. It's a matter of practicality.

Those who orient to the boardwalk as part of an art career both love and hate the market. Dependent on the economic opportunities that make a more legitimate career possible, they struggle to present themselves in line with their belief in "authentic artists," that is, artists with knowledge about the art world, an interest in originality rather than conformity, and an avoidance of crass commercialism. They idealize their own status by fighting off customers' perceptions of them as "vendors." Molly, a white artist in her midforties, says,

Some people are assholes that don't appreciate the work at all. This one guy came up and asked how much for the framed painting. I told him sixty dollars. Right off the bat, without any bargaining, he cuts the price in half and says, "I'll give you thirty." I looked at him and thought to myself, "he'll give me thirty?" It was like he thought he was doing me a favor. I decided right there that he wasn't going to give me anything. I told him, "I don't give bargains and for you the price is now six hundred dollars."

Regardless of their artistic ideals and narratives, they learn the ways of the local market and develop certain products that are their "hits." Mike, in his late forties, says, "Every artist out here has their hit that everyone wants. Mine is the punk poster. They even buy the display that it stands on. Every time I sell the display and make a new one, it goes that day. That's how you know you're successful on the boardwalk. You have your hit and then everyone else down the boardwalk copies it." Imitating the successful innovator is just one type of entrepreneurial cover in the boardwalk market.

Entrepreneurs with a Free Speech Cover

The Free Speech Zone allows entrepreneurs to mix with artists, performers, and craftspeople through commercial pursuits that elude legal classifications, blending into the environment and enabling them to sustain attachments over time. Many people pursuing an entrepreneurial cover are those excluded from the formal economy: immigrants, racial and ethnic minorities, and the homeless. Juan, midthirties, is an artist and immigrant from Mexico City. His mother taught him the skill of handcrafting and painting ceramic and papier-mâché skulls, an emblem of *el dia de los muertos*, the day of the dead. He and his brother design the molds and hand-paint each one. Their craft turned into a successful boardwalk enterprise that ultimately enabled them to pursue sales in additional venues beyond Venice Beach. In line with the logic of the economic ecology, however, their success spawned local copycats. "We started doing this, and then all of sudden, it was like they were everywhere. Another and another and then another. But we were the only ones making them from scratch. Everyone else was ordering them, mass-producing them, and selling them out here like they did it by hand."

Many on the boardwalk have figured out how to manufacture "free expression" as a public space business. The most pervasive commercial presence stems from groups of people who organized to purchase permits and enter the boardwalk lottery. One group consisting of over ten individuals—all family and friends with permits—arrived on the days of the lottery drawing and acquired as many spaces on the boardwalk as possible. Throughout the summer of 2006, immigrants from the Mexican region of Oaxaca set up at the same time, sometimes claiming close to ten spaces up and down the boardwalk, all of which carried the exact same reproduced ceramic skulls and wooden toys. Framing them as "original" and "handmade" crafts, they unpacked them from boxes, peeled off little golden stickers from the bottom that said "Made in Mexico," and placed them on a table for display.

Many immigrants have social ties to people already selling objects on the boardwalk, and they use these ties to learn the ins and outs of economic survival. One family of West African origin came to the boardwalk together on weekends during 2006. A family friend used to sell objects on the boardwalk and they learned of this economic opportunity through his experiences. They came to the boardwalk with the purpose of earning extra income by selling statues of giraffes and elephants that family members ship from their native country to the United States. Madou explains, "I don't want to make a career out of this. I come here to make some money and have my regular job during the week. I do not want to become like that man," pointing to one of the homeless countercultural activists who has been a regular on the boardwalk for several decades. "I am not like him. I only come to make extra money. I don't want to turn it into a political debate."

Asian immigrants, many of them Chinese, paint people's names in multiple colors, calling it "name art." Learning this complex technical skill, they reproduce it dozens of times a day to meet their customers' requests. They paint a person's name on mass-produced parchment, often with images of Disney characters. Mixing a technical skill with the sale of mass-produced items shifts their artistic identity into an entrepreneurial cover. Along with their "name art," they sell mass-produced paintings that they purchase in Chinatown and downtown Los Angeles. They label these intricately detailed works of art with natural scenery and Chinese characters as "Original Chinese Paintings," although the exact replications are found at the tables of multiple vendors up and down the boardwalk.

Selling artwork without actually having created the art, thereby becoming a "faux Venice Beach artist," is commonplace. Individuals purchase handmade art, mass-produced posters, and reproduced photographs in large quantities, and then distribute them on the boardwalk as examples of their "free expression." Manuel, a Salvadoran in his early forties, initially came to Venice as a jewelry seller. Buying inexpensive stones and beads, he strung them together and set them out on a blanket. A new boardwalk friend turned him onto a local scam about selling art. Sebastian bought inexpensive handmade paintings from a store downtown that were imported from China. Depending upon the size of the paintings, they cost between $5 and $30 and he sold them on the boardwalk for double or triple the amount. After witnessing Sebastian's profits, Manuel joined his business. At first, Sebastian would acquire the paintings and Manuel would then sell them on the boardwalk, and they had a system for dividing up their earnings. Eventually Sebastian found another job and Manuel took over the boardwalk business, learning where to purchase the paintings and improving on the scam by adding finishing touches to the work of art in front of customers in order to make it appear as though he painted the works himself.

The informal economy requires flexibility as legal changes readily force entrepreneurs to adopt new practices. Before the revised ordinance went into effect in 2005, a group of African American men sold incense, aromatherapy oils, statues, and other "religious" objects by setting up blocks of card tables with their supplies, and claiming their entrepreneurial activities as a part of their Islamic religious expression. After a new ordinance banned the sale of these items, some like Al, a black man in his early fifties, adapted to the changes, turning up and walking the boardwalk with baskets of incense, selling the same objects to the public but hiding from the regulatory forces.

Others sold items and services permitted by the ordinance, while vending prohibited objects behind the scenes to increase their returns. The "name artists" sold replicated prints; henna tattoo artists who paint designs on people's bodies sold incense or hemp jewelry out of the back of their displays using the legitimate activity as a cover. One man framed himself as a henna tattoo artist but sold marijuana out of his booth, showing that the ability to adapt to the symbolic attributes of free expression can become a mask for another type of business.

Homelessness as Counterculture

Due to the intersection of counterculture and homelessness in Venice, some believe they have developed a political connection to Venice Beach. They assert their local social positions as lifestyle prerogatives; they attain status on the boardwalk because they remain over a long period of time, some for several decades; they work tirelessly to promote their agenda as authentic boardwalk activists who represent and transmit Venice's bohemian history; and they express their identities through an antiestablishment filter, often leading them to enact territorial practices. These individuals mostly came of age during the 1960s countercultural movement, but the local ecology continuously enables newcomers, most of them homeless and of the same generation, to absorb this cultural orientation.

The link between homelessness and a countercultural identity is pervasive. Most who adapted to the boardwalk as a form of territorial resistance have suffered from tumultuous economic circumstances on the road from the '60s countercultural movement to sustained boardwalk involvement. A talented artist in her late fifties was a homeless prostitute and heroin addict before she found her way into painting on the boardwalk. A musician and political activist in his early sixties was previously a homeless alcoholic who shoplifted and panhandled in order to survive. Several men, now artists, activists, or craftsmen, were Vietnam veterans who suffered major economic and psychological setbacks in the last several decades. One in his early sixties was a homeless heroin addict and alcoholic; another in his late sixties was laid off from his longtime factory job in the mid-1990s, losing his only source of income and establishing himself on the boardwalk where he learned to survive on minimal earnings; another in his early sixties has a mental illness that has limited his ability to hold down conventional employment, forcing him to live in an RV. These individuals share a history of economic struggles and psychological traumas and they either remain homeless, were once homeless, or survive off of Supplemental Security Income, a federal program that provides minimal economic provisions to the disabled who have difficulty attaining basic needs such as food, shelter, or clothing.[9]

The boardwalk ecology sustains bohemianism as a form of territorial resistance, as individuals adopt new economic strategies to maintain their associations over extended stretches of time. Jonas, the artist and musician from the opening scene, is a Vietnam veteran. He first came to Venice in the late '60s in pursuit of a transient, bohemian lifestyle. He became a more permanent fixture in Venice in the '80s, having become homeless, addicted to drugs and alcohol, and surviving by dumpster diving for objects and selling them on the boardwalk. He met his wife, Margot, while living on the streets and together they became sober and cultivated artistic and musical skills, learning from many artists and musicians who already lived and worked on and near the boardwalk. This logic of local adaptation was passed down through interactions that transmitted the culture over time. The two of them still rely on skills developed from living on the streets, although they have upgraded to living in an RV. Jonas says that he and his wife are "outdoor artists" and brags, "I know how to find things and use them to support my art. I'm not looking to keep my art stored inside in some gallery." He turns common garbage into an artistic venture. He scrounges the neighborhood's dumpsters, sidewalks, and alleyways, finding discarded cans of latex house paint; he paints on anything from blocks of wood to old surfboards to broken skateboards; he designs political banners on found bed sheets and recycled hemp coffee-bean sacks; and he uses abandoned stepladders to display his work.

Jonas has reinvented himself: once a struggling homeless man, he has become a charismatic political leader on the boardwalk, transforming economic deprivation into a lifestyle founded upon the proper etiquette cues of bohemianism. On one occasion, as the sun is setting, I assist him in breaking down his display of art and political banners. Jonas walks with a limp, an injury from his military service, and I think my help will hasten the process. As I start folding up one of the stepladders that prop up his paintings this conversation ensues:

> Jonas says, "I got it man, don't worry about it. I got it." I tell him, "I don't mind. It's really not a problem. I can help you out." He scolds me, "No man, you don't understand! I like to take my time! I want to do it at my own pace! What do I need to rush for? What will I get if I rush to pack it all up, and then rush to get out of here, and then rush to park in the spot where I park my RV and sleep at night, and then what? I have to sit there the rest of the night and do what? This is not like a job. You don't have to rush and finish it!" I respond timidly, but probing for more. "OK, so you're not concerned about getting it done?" Jonas says, "Right, it's not like that! You're doing your own thing, so everything is in motion. The same way you set up is the same way you tear down. See because art—it's just different. It's not a job. People rushing around real quick." I ask, "So you mean, it's not about efficiency?" He replies, "Right. And then you miss out on some of the great things. Like last night, the moon was over the water. It was like there was a straight light on it. A lot of people miss everything. Sometimes I say, oh, I wish I'd gotten to bed earlier. But then you miss out. Go when it's time to go."

Reggie, like Jonas, has established a multidecade connection to Venice Beach and reinvented his economic presentation in the Free Speech Zone five times. He moved to Venice in 1974 from New York City, where he had gone through spells of alcoholism, homelessness, and panhandling to playing folk music in Greenwich Village. When he first came to Venice, he sold scarves on the boardwalk for several months before transitioning back into a musician, as part of a folk duo for close to eight years. At times homeless, Reggie was also politically active in the late '70s when the city cracked down on the use of the boardwalk as a performance space. Following his stint as a musician and activist, he turned to the healing arts, taking part in the Venice Healing Pagoda, which consisted mostly of a group of homeless men and women who learned therapeutic massage, practiced yoga on a daily basis, and adopted strict vegetarian standards. When the health department shut them down after eight years because they were unlicensed, Reggie thought his days on the boardwalk were numbered. Having been a vegan for twelve years, he decided to integrate his vegan activism into his boardwalk identity. He developed a table where he combines information, activism, and entrepreneurship, displaying posters with gruesome photos of tortured animals, distributing pamphlets and flyers about animal rights, and selling bumper stickers and pins with political slogans.

Reggie and Jonas are exemplary of a common logic of adaptation. The local ecology has enabled them to morph their identities into a consistent lifestyle and political journey. When a new law was implemented in 2005, they stood up to those imposing new classifications from the outside, believing their long-term territorial association represented a historical and authentic boardwalk culture. Whereas most boardwalk participants signed up for the lottery, Jonas, Reggie, and others who orient to the boardwalk as a form of territorial resistance attended the lottery drawings, stood to the side holding up signs, yelled at people for "selling out," and marched up and down the boardwalk in protest of those who adopted the city's new standards.

Solidifying their territorial resistance, they received dozens of tickets for not complying with the legal regulations. They believed that the city unfairly targeted them and perceived their ongoing relationships with LAPD officers as "selective enforcement." However, they also believed that receiving tickets or being arrested signified membership in an important boardwalk status group. The act of becoming a political target by resisting "official" forces is a source of belonging, strengthening ties among longtime boardwalk personalities and fueling a social movement to oppose the "unconstitutional" basis of the regulations.

As the battle over the boardwalk persisted, a number of the resisters began setting up in the same place and traveling together to city meetings and court appearances to combat their tickets to support one another. On one occasion, after several free expressionists received tickets together for displaying their items in undesignated spaces, Margot ran up as the officers were leaving and yelled, "Wait! Don't forget to give me my ticket too!" She then dropped herself down on the ground in an undesignated space with her canvas and the officers proceeded to write her a ticket as she sat with a smirk on her face.

Thieves, Scavengers, and Stragglers

All these logics of adaptation constitute viable modes of economic survival. But another segment of the boardwalk feeds off its ecological structure as thieves, scavengers, and stragglers. These individuals never get a firm foothold in the economy, and their methods of survival change from day to day. On occasion, some modify their orientation to become resisters or entrepreneurs, and others develop economic ties to both the formal and informal economies. I was sometimes unable to get such individuals to sit down and talk with me for an extended period of time because of their mental illness, alcohol and drug addiction, or for some, simply because their illegal activities made them less likely to trust me when I presented myself as a researcher and writer.

Rent-paying business attachments require a great deal of planning to maintain profits and keep up with rent; some of the other entrepreneurial attachments, such as artists and those pursuing an entrepreneurial cover, require slightly less planning but maintain a clear profit motive. The boardwalk is also a site where theft becomes a quick-turnover business. Thieves are often highly transient. They are not simply segments of the homeless population, although a number of homeless people—especially younger homeless men on the boardwalk—do steal and resell items. Thieves often walk the length of the boardwalk with a backpack, a duffle bag, rolling luggage, or even a baby carriage, trying to unload stolen goods. These range from compact discs, electronics, batteries, and paints to animals. Some build up the nerve to display their findings in the Free Speech Zone, such as Keith, a homeless white man in his early twenties, who stole a case of Zippo lighters from a store at which his friend works and unloaded each for $3 on the boardwalk.

The most common stolen objects for sale are bicycles. There is a wide range of individuals competing in the local stolen bike trade, constantly seen rolling more than one bicycle down the boardwalk at a time. They pass through Venice, in and out of alleys and streets, down to the boardwalk, where they offer a brand-new bicycle for $25. Frequently, the same person sells several bicycles in the same day. I often see young white men involved in this trade, but there are certainly others involved as well. Often, homeless people who have made a small amount of money off of the boardwalk ecology buy these bicycles, attaining a cheap source of transportation and demonstrating how the local ecology brings different elements together. I often try to discuss with these sellers where they get their bicycles, but they make up stories and provide only vague references. I ask a black man rolling a bike, "Hey, where do you get those bikes?" He responds, "I work for a bike shop, and we need to get rid of some of our bikes." I ask, "Which bike shop?" He answers: "That one, down there." I return, "Which one?" He ignores me and keeps walking away quickly. In another example, a young white man, in his early twenties, asks, "Need a bike?" I inquire, "How much?" He says, "Twenty bucks." It's a nice bicycle and looks new. I ask, "Where'd you get this bike?" He returns, "It's my friend's bike. He needs me to get rid of it."

Most thieves operate as entrepreneurs, with at least some minimal level of planning. They may start the day without knowing exactly what items they will have for sale, but they strategically seek out opportunities to take objects and turn them over for a quick profit to someone on the boardwalk. Scavenging, in contrast, is based on a logic of the right place at the right time, beggars can't be choosers, and any job is a good job: a business needs someone to help carry boxes or sweep away sand out front; someone in the Free Speech Zone wants help holding a spot or getting an additional space in the lottery; a shop needs to hire an inexpensive, but temporary part-time employee; a café wants someone to hold an advertisement billboard out front or hand out coupons to the public. The surrounding homeless population fills the void, taking a position in this unpredictable, low-wage economy.

Acquiring temporary positions in the formal economy acts as a form of scavenging, because these opportunities only come about by keeping one's eyes and ears open to the economic surroundings and immediately seizing upon them. Adolfo, a Latino man in his early forties, has been homeless on the boardwalk for two years. With no money, no place to sleep, and a criminal record (he was in prison several years ago), he has limited access to the formal economy. At first, he took a job holding a sign on the boardwalk to advertise a local pizza shop and was paid under the table. Because of limited economic options, he had no formal method of grievance when the owner took advantage of his homeless status, refusing to pay him the agreed-upon amount of $30 but underpaying him by anywhere from $10 to $20 a day. Sleeping on the boardwalk over the course of this time, a friend informed him of a new opportunity as a sales clerk in one of the rented inland stalls owned by a bohemian businesswoman. By the time I was finished with my research, he had moved on to three additional temporary positions, taking whatever options paid him for the day. Like many immersed in the boardwalk ecology, he was involved in a whirlwind of survival, being catapulted from job to job without any opportunity to plan for economic stability.

Richard, a white man whom I met one afternoon on the boardwalk while he was carrying a sign for a local business, serves as another example. A Vietnam veteran, he recently lost his factory job; his wife had lost her job the previous year, after fracturing her hip. Already living paycheck to paycheck, their lives spiraled out of control. When I met him, he and his wife had been homeless for three months, and although he was trying to make arrangements with family members to help him get back on his feet, he found a temporary job on the boardwalk. Another homeless man was unable to make it to his job holding a sign that reads "Root Beer Floats $1.99," and Richard, who was sitting nearby, filled the void. Weeks later, the former sign holder had not returned and Richard remained in this position. The job required him to stand outside in the middle of the boardwalk, paying him $25 for the day and providing food and drinks while he worked. His wife sat on a nearby bench and panhandled, holding out a handmade cardboard sign, "Disabled and Homeless," earning the couple an extra $10 to $15 per day.

Other scavengers find alternative survival methods, such as dumpster diving or searching throughout the neighborhood for discarded objects. Raymond, a white man in his midsixties, has been homeless at Venice Beach for over a decade. He is often visibly drunk, drinking whisky and smelling of it; his clothing and skin are worn and his hands and fingernails are covered with black soot; and he is rarely lucid, such that people find it difficult to have a meaningful conversation with him. Yet Raymond has the uncanny skill of finding objects that people want and he knows where to bring them for sale. Raymond knows the local area well; he has connections with many; he normally sells things for much less than they are worth; and he refuses to take more than he asks. He once found a one-hundred- year-old Bible in the trash and brought it to a person he knew as a religious scholar. Intrigued, the man purchased the Bible for $25 and later had it appraised, finding out it was worth closer to $100. On another occasion, Raymond found a handmade ceramic vase and brought it to James, who distributes information about the environment in the Free Speech Zone. Raymond offered him the vase for $3. James pulled out his wallet only to find a $5 bill for which Raymond had no change. James practically begged Raymond to take the $5. With trepidation, he eventually did. Maintaining his typical business practice, Raymond returned several hours later, after the interaction was long forgotten, with $2 in change, showing that even his scavenger activities can become a reliable survival method, though not a very profitable business, by earning the trust of repeat customers.

Commonly as I sit with an artist out on the boardwalk, a person will approach to ask, "Do you need any paints?" Some scavengers know their clientele and their activities blur the scavenger/thief distinction, finding and sometimes stealing paints to sell on the boardwalk, serving as a support system to boardwalk artists. Charlie, a white man in his early thirties, had lived on the boardwalk on and off for two years in 2004. He told me that he knew of a specific dumpster near an art store where he could find discarded, used, defective, and mislabeled paints. He searched through the dumpster and came up with dozens, sometimes hundreds of tubes of acrylic paints, and then took them to the boardwalk where he walked the beat, artist to artist, in search of interested buyers. One artist needed black paint and Charlie negotiated a "fair price" with her. Another artist needed several different colors, so Charlie went through his supplies and found the appropriate colors. They exchanged supplies and money, and Charlie moved on to his next potential client.

The availability of food and a consistent opportunity for panhandling and begging in large crowds make the boardwalk a good location for stragglers. They do not seek out economic profit, even for survival, and they often remain unnoticed. But at certain moments stragglers can become the center of attention. Nick, a white man in his early fifties, has been homeless on the boardwalk for almost two years. His personal presentation is particularly unkempt: his clothing is soiled and smells of a sour and toxic boardwalk mixture of body odor, urine, alcohol, cigarettes, and incense. On a hot July day in 2009, he stands visibly drunk in the middle of the packed boardwalk, slurring his speech and stumbling, barely able to maintain his balance, as pedestrians break up their conversations and pull their children closer to avoid contact with him.

Frank, a local renter with kind eyes and a ponytail, gives Nick an ice cream sandwich called a UFO, with a cookie on each side of the ice cream center. Nick gobbles up the UFO and holds on to the wrapper. A pedestrian approaches. Nick shows him the wrapper and says, at first barely audible, "I've eaten my UFO, how am I gonna get back to Uranus" [your anus]? Those of us who overhear start laughing. Another person passes by and Nick performs the same routine, this time a little louder. "I've eaten my UFO, how am I gonna get back to Uranus?" More laughter follows. Nick continues to perform the same bit, each time drawing in more people entertained by his antics. He does not communicate anything other than this one line, but as the laughter escalates so does the size of the crowd, instantly transforming Nick into a boardwalk character. The performance continues for almost half an hour, some people giving him dollar bills before they leave. The boardwalk, operating as a bohemian theme park, allows strangers to overlook his visible homeless condition and focus on his actions as pure entertainment value.

Free Speech Zone or Informal Economy?

As different groups converge on the boardwalk and adapt to the ecological structure, political distinctions also emerge, leading people to filter oppositions through formal and informal attachments. On the one hand, storeowners believe that rent-free vendors on the beachside of the boardwalk selling similar items in public space as those found in the rented space on the inland side have an unfair advantage. On the other hand, they struggle with the fact that the rapidly growing public space economy remains a key source of the boardwalk's popular bohemian identity, which ultimately contributes to their own profit-making potential, although no one can actually quantify this relationship. This complexity has generated an ongoing political and legal endeavor to regulate economic activity in public space without damaging its valuable symbolic resonance.

In this section I explore the delicate balance between regulating the boardwalk and sustaining its unique character as a bohemian theme park. I focus on three key factors: the rise of boardwalk policing; a transition from *regulation without parameters* to *regulation with parameters*, an important shift that institutionalized the legal distinction between commercial and free speech practices; and the penetration of the "free speech" symbol into vending and law enforcement applications, which has replaced the 1970s hippie countercultural activism as a new emblem of Venice bohemianism. These elements underpinned a multidecade series of failed regulatory attempts.

Regulations of the boardwalk's informal economy started in the late 1970s when the city assembled an LAPD substation at Venice Beach. At this time, law enforcement had no clear legal parameters. Officers just knew they were charged with ridding the boardwalk of rent-free economic activity. *Regulation without parameters* meant that there were no rules for presentation, and police officers made no attempt to distinguish between various types of commercial activities. For weeks at a time, they completely closed down the boardwalk's lively atmosphere. Reggie discusses the influx of the LAPD during the late '70s:

> They were ticketing people and fucking with them. They shut down the boardwalk at one point. They basically just scared everyone away and wouldn't let anyone take donations at all. . . . [Then-councilwoman] Pat Russell decided that there was crazy stuff going on at Venice Beach and we needed police officers down there. There were none when I first got here. For years, there was no station or anything like that, like at the end of the beatnik days and when the hippies came in.

Regulation without parameters revealed the underlying complexity of the economic ecology, a spatial dependency between the distinct forms of attachment. Intense police presence not only disabled the livelihoods of performers and vendors but to the dismay of rent-paying business owners, it also challenged the boardwalk's unusual identity as a bohemian theme park. Unlike Disneyland, the theme park has no central organization to orchestrate and manage its image. Instead, it relies on the spontaneous arrival of artists and performers to enact and reinforce Venice's bohemianism as theme-park-like characters for tourists.[10] Imagine Disneyland without Mickey Mouse and Goofy running around and posing for pictures with children. Even though people sell a wide variety of objects that compete with rent-paying businesses, when LAPD shuts down the boardwalk's free market, they also shut down the attraction:

the carnival performers, artists, and musicians that give the boardwalk its personality are forced away.

In the past, this fragile economic system operated without parameters for either enforcement or vending. When the city allowed performers and artists to return, officials quickly lost control of the types of economic activities, generating a cycle of strict regulation of all public-space economic activities followed by periods of complete deregulation in which all types of economic activities were allowed. Both long-term rent-paying storeowners and rent-free boardwalk expressionists describe this historical pattern as an unpredictable but cyclical metamorphosis. Reggie explains,

> The city just let it go by and all of a sudden, it's like, "Where'd it all come from?" I guess word of mouth, because people think they'll make money. And different people take the handle and it goes from [onetime city councilwoman] Pat Russell, to [onetime city councilwoman] Ruth Galanter, to [past city councilwoman] Cindy Miscikowski, to [current city councilman] Bill Rosendahl. They all try to get a handle on it, to control it, but they can't. It's a metamorphosis. It's always evolving. It goes up and down and down and up. New people come in, old people leave.

Dave, midfifties, whose family has owned businesses and properties on the boardwalk since the '70s, says,

> It's an ongoing struggle to deal with the commercial stuff and it's been going on since at least the '80s. Galanter and her staff wrote a law in the '80s to deal with the vending, but the police only enforced the law against the artists for some reason. So then they had to modify the law because then all the artists disappeared but the commercial vendors remained. So it goes in streaks really. Summers are much worse than the winters and harder to monitor it. But, even overall, it's really unpredictable.

During the 1980s, City Councilwoman Ruth Galanter and Los Angeles city attorneys rewrote the vending ordinance in order to distinguish between "commercial" and "free speech" activities. They sought to institute a new system: *regulation with parameters*. The new legal parameters institutionalized the boardwalk's symbolism as a bohemian theme park. In doing so, the city failed to understand three key conditions that contributed to ongoing problems on the boardwalk. First, as described with the multiple logics of adaptation, the local ecology is flexible, as people often alter and challenge it. Secondly, because of this flexibility, new legal parameters make it easier, not more difficult, for people to adapt, that is, the limits of regulation operate as more specific rules for legitimate economic presentation. Third, growing inequality in the city means that there is a continuous supply of low-income populations to reproduce a critical mass of vendors to adapt, challenge, and revise the law.

The City Attorney's Office formulated Los Angeles Municipal Code Section 42.15 (LAMC 42.15), which went through a series of revisions over the course of the next twenty years because individuals and organizations repeatedly challenged the law on constitutional grounds.[11] Galanter recalls the difficult process of defining and enforcing the parameters of legal regulations on the boardwalk:

> There's a number of reasons why it's hard to write an ordinance. The First Amendment rights of people that are handing out leaflets for animal rights or something like that have to be protected. They're entitled to the public space. If they're saying, "For the contribution, make your donation here" to whatever it is, they're allowed to do that as well. . . . Some city attorneys are really good. The guy who worked on this ordinance, I mean they tried. But they're not constitutional lawyers. The ACLU comes in at the drop of a hat and sues. So each time you do an ordinance, there's no way to enforce it. We figured out one day that the real issue is that it's not fair for the tenant businesses on the inland side to pay rent and pay business tax but have to compete with people that don't pay rent and don't pay tax. And some of them sell the same stuff.

Institutionalizing a distinction between "commercial" and "free speech" enterprises was central in sustaining the boardwalk's complex economic system. Different actors collectively made "free speech" into a symbolic practice that took over as the emblem of Venice bohemianism. It allowed people to fight against the legitimacy of enforcing the parameters of the law; it allowed newcomers to continuously adapt to the limits; and it provided law enforcement with a means to facilitate the process.

When the revised ordinance was put into practice in 1991, LAPD officers gave hundreds of tickets to boardwalk expressionists, including artists, musicians, and political activists who sold commercial objects. In addition to operating as a mode of enforcement, the legal parameters were also a mode of protection. People could challenge the legitimacy of how LAPD officers classified "commercial" and "free speech" enterprises. Constitutional attorneys James and Rhonda Fosbinder obtained an injunction that stopped enforcement of the ordinance in order to address its inequalities. With their assistance, two boardwalk plaintiffs sued the city: one was a Sikh musician who sold T-shirts and CDs related to his music and identity; the other was an animal rights activist who sold bumper stickers, buttons, and other items related to his activism. After losing in a lower court, they appealed to a Ninth Circuit Federal Court of Appeals, which ruled in their favor, claiming that people could sell objects on the boardwalk as long as "expressive parts of speech are inextricably intertwined" with the object. The judge explained the ruling in the following opinion:

> The items sold included music, buttons, and bumper stickers bearing political, religious, and ideological messages. They were expressive items, and did not lose their constitutional protection simply because they were sold. When the commercial and expressive parts of speech are inextricably intertwined, a court cannot parcel out the protected and unprotected parts. The plaintiffs' expressive activities were fully protected by the First Amendment.[12]

Influenced by this ruling, the city rewrote the ordinance, this time officially protecting the informal economy as a "Free Speech Zone." The law instituted the sale of objects that incorporated some element of "free expression," that is, objects with a message "inextricably intertwined." This legal definition made it increasingly difficult for LAPD officers to monitor the boardwalk environment, because these categories, although seemingly clear in discourse, were quite murky in practice. In daily life, people blurred the distinction between commerce and free speech. Everyone, from vendors to police officers, fell prey to the power of the boardwalk's new symbolism as a Free Speech Zone, where the representation of free speech operated as the defining symbolic economy through the sale of certain types of products.

Where crowds gather and the parameters of economic regulation are clear, financially struggling people manipulate the parameters of regulation if they can figure out a way to make money. While artists, musicians, and carnival performers continued in this space, people from all walks of life learned to frame their boardwalk identities as having a religious, ideological, or political significance that legitimated their presence in the Free Speech Zone. An African American man in his early fifties set up a huge display under a tent and sold scented lotions with a large banner behind him professing that the lotions served a "holy" purpose. A white man in his forties brought out multiple racks of factory-made hemp clothing, claiming that the use of this particular fabric was in and of itself a political act. A handful of black vendors sold mass-produced clothing couched in the national colors of Jamaica and labeled their actions as Rastafarian. An entire block's length of the boardwalk was filled with African Americans in full Muslim attire selling incense as a religious practice. African, Asian, Caribbean, and Latino immigrants sold a wide range of reproduced statues, ceramic crafts, and prints of paintings, all claiming their work as "original" and "ethnic" art. Many added any semblance of religiosity to their display: crucifixes and Buddha statues engulfed the boardwalk.

The Free Speech Zone was so dense with participants, sometimes close to three hundred vendors on a given day, that LAPD officers uncertain how to handle the situation simply facilitated it. Like the vendors themselves, they adapted to the legal parameters, explaining to naïve newcomers how to package themselves under the rubric of "free expression." Scenarios such as this one were repeated again and again: An Asian woman is selling jewelry with different chains and different silver pendants. An officer approaches her and says, "You can't sell those out here." The woman looks confused. The policeman tells her: "Just add a cross to your jewelry, then it's OK. I won't do anything now, but next time you're out here, you need to make it religious. You can't just resell jewelry."

An official classification system sought to protect the formal economic interests by distinguishing between commercial and free speech categories. Yet participants in the Free Speech Zone easily blurred the division in daily practice. They strategically molded their vending identities so that others, including city officials, interpreted their presentation of products as "free expression." Seeing the failure of the regulations, local business owners, residents, law enforcement officers, city attorneys, and politicians continued to consider how to address the boardwalk as an urban problem. They collectively communicated a new narrative about the boardwalk as a detriment to neighborhood quality of life and public safety.

Formal and Informal Redefined as Order and Disorder

At 6:00 a.m. on a Saturday morning in 2003 a group of artists stands on the inland side of the boardwalk. They smoke cigarettes and slowly unload supplies from their parked cars, vans, trucks, and RVs to get ready for the day. They have arrived early to guarantee themselves a space in the Free Speech Zone, which at this time, still operates under a first-come, first-serve system for claiming spaces. The morning starts off calmly. Small groups gather, some listening to music out of headphones and others catching up with friends. During the next three hours, many more arrive and the noise intensifies. Blasting radios mix with yelling, howling, laughing, and countless conversations. It all accumulates into a reverberating hum down a one-and-a-half-mile stretch of the boardwalk. Then 9:00 a.m. arrives—the legally designated starting time for the Free Speech Zone—and, as if someone rang a bell, people migrate from the inland side to the beach side like a herd of villagers with pushcarts, baskets, tents, and umbrellas.

Just as the changing commercial culture of rent-paying and rent-free economic activities gave way to an official division between "formal" and "informal" economies, the continuing transformation of the boardwalk's commercial and residential composition produced a struggle to redefine the distinction as one between "order" and "disorder." The Free Speech Zone was transformed from an iconic and celebrated attraction into a stigmatized problem through three processes: local residents played a part in relabeling this distinction in moral rather than economic terms; they connected with city officials to legitimate these new labels; and the city implemented new regulations that moved beyond simply commercial regulation into a more formal means of monitoring and controlling the minutiae of everyday life.

Amidst great diversity people can find almost anything if they look hard enough. Residents filtered concerns through the lenses of amplified music, fights over public space, people arriving early in the morning, territorial conflicts among individuals and groups, and continued commercial sales in public space. The police reported in meetings that they were receiving hundreds of phone calls a day from residents and business owners. Residents and business owners claimed that the hundreds of people competing for boardwalk spaces was a public safety hazard and quality of life concern. These examples speak to the problematizing discourses:

Joel, a renter on the east side of the boardwalk, complains about early arrivals: "During the summer . . . vendors begin congregating at 5 a.m. or earlier, with metal chairs, carts and supplies, often staking out spots by laying down pipes and other paraphernalia along the east side. . . . I don't want a sterile environment. . . . But I don't want to wake up to a flea market at 5 a.m."[13]

Isaac, a business owner for three years in his late forties, raises concerns about the lack of city management over selling: "Do you know who is out there [selling on the boardwalk]? Does anybody? They have no business license. Because they sell art or incense doesn't mean they are peaceful or that we know who they are and we should trust them. You need a system in place. It's about protecting the public so everybody feels safe."

Lacey, a new homeowner in her early forties, expresses her dismay about public safety issues: "When we moved here, we knew the boardwalk is right there. But when you live here, it is a bit unpredictable. Homelessness is a problem. Bicycles get stolen. Pets have been stolen. I don't want to get rid of the boardwalk and all the people, but common sense says the city should do something to make it safer."

Dave, the longtime boardwalk business owner, discusses the fighting on the boardwalk: "The police hate the fights on the boardwalk. That was the big thing. They decided it couldn't be first-come, first-serve because there were just too many fights out there. Like this guy Louis, who used to do something out there on the boardwalk, he would come over to our restaurant and threaten people eating in the restaurant. So we had to get a restraining order against him. I don't want to do that. But we have no choice if someone is coming over and harassing our customers."

Walking along the boardwalk with Madeline, a boardwalk homeowner for over a decade in her midseventies, she talks about the territoriality of vendors: "It could work if everyone would just take a little bit [of space], but this one [pointing to a boardwalk artist] . . . takes up all this space. Why should he be there and nobody else? Why should he have that much? He would say, 'You can't be here.' And they would fight, and he would say, 'No this is mine.' It was like he owned it, but it's not his. This is public."

These interpretations filtered into official political discourse, further exaggerating the claims about violent competition and early morning clamoring by vendors. Sandy Kievman, the Venice deputy for then-councilwoman Cindy Miscikowski said, "The whole place was turning into a swap meet where people were getting there as early as 4 a.m. to get a space. . . . They were physically beating each other up and hurling verbal abuse to [the point] where we constantly had to call in the police. We got lots of complaints from residents and businesspeople."[14] Gita Isagholian, then the neighborhood prosecutor, concurred with the council office prognosis: "We had a lot of complaints about morning fights between the vendors on the west side. . . . You basically have to get there at about four in the morning to get a space on the West Side. And people feel that they have entitlement to a certain space on the West Side, so if you're in their space, fights happen."

Complaints do not necessarily characterize a behavioral norm; they can easily isolate certain polemical individuals who meet the criteria they set forth. We saw this process of power labeling in previous chapters with the targeting of African Americans in Oakwood Park and the stigmatization of homelessness. Some of the boardwalk expressionists establish a routine of selling and performing in the same place. They believe that their daily presence guarantees them a right to this spot. If someone shows up earlier, an argument or even physical confrontation may erupt. Marvin has sold objects on the boardwalk on and off for a few years and in this scenario he threatens a woman playing the guitar because "she stole his space":

Harmony, a woman who plays soothing folk tunes on her guitar, arrived at 6:30 a.m. with her boyfriend to claim the space, like she has done several times this summer (2003). Marvin arrives at the boardwalk at around 11:00 a.m., walks up to her as she is performing a song in front of a handful of spectators, and tells her to move in a matter of fact way: "You're in my space. I set up here every day." She continues playing through his interruption and his intervention escalates. "Move out of my space, you fuckin' bitch!" Harmony looks shocked and stops in the middle of a tune, but several members of the crowd move closer. Her boyfriend sees the surrounding support and tells her not to move. Marvin becomes furious and screams at the top of his lungs, "If you don't move, you'll regret it! I'll fuckin' kill you!" Harmony and her boyfriend, surprised by the extreme hostility, still do not move, now with a growing number of people surrounding her performance who encourage her to stand her ground. She nervously laughs and the crowd urges her to continue to play and she resumes. Marvin does not extend his violence beyond the threat, although he has in the past, engaging in shoving matches that force police involvement. Yet every time Harmony plays her guitar and sings, Marvin walks between her and the small crowd and interrupts the performance by yelling to pedestrians to try the items he has for sale.

Although the boardwalk attracts people like Marvin, I rarely witnessed fights during my six years of fieldwork, and most of the fighting involved the same few individuals. Most boardwalk vendors never physically or verbally assaulted anyone. As Dave admits, "It's always a few bad seeds that ruin the whole lot. And that's what happened. There were a few people that were getting in fights over spaces so as a result everyone is forced to be regulated." Yet these "bad seeds" allowed the city to cite such examples as representative of a more general problem, highlighting the most negative occasions as emblematic of routine behavior. Combining the continuing concerns about unfair commercial competition with newfound complaints about quality of life, city leaders labeled the boardwalk as a problem space and showed a renewed attention to revising the ordinance in 2005. They implemented two types of restrictions that together focused on the minutiae of everyday life: restrictions on time, space, and manner; and content-based controls over what people could sell.

Restrictions on time, space, and manner allowed the city to supervise where, when, and how a person could display their items on the Venice Boardwalk, numbering spaces where people could set up and perform. Free expressionists were required to pay a onetime $25 fee in order to obtain a permit and enter a weekly lottery drawing in which they received an assigned space. Boardwalk vendors had to comply with a series of new rules that the city attorneys thought would alleviate spatial competition, emphasizing the art of legal classification: they could not display products above four feet; the sounds of their music could not extend beyond fifty feet; they could not occupy more than one space; they were restricted from claiming their assigned spaces before 9:00 a.m.; if they chose not to purchase a permit and enter the lottery, they were not allowed to occupy an open space until noon to ensure the rightful lottery owner a chance of using the assigned space; and they had to conclude their selling practices by 10:30 p.m.

The city attorneys also reframed the language of the ordinance concerning legitimacy of the content of the objects being sold. Building from legal precedent of cases involving public-space performing and selling in other cities across the country, city attorneys replaced the term *inextricably intertwined* with the phrase *nominal utility*, which prohibited the sale of items that had an additional function other than expressive communication. The free speech symbolic economy was challenged. For example, a T-shirt with a political message or a necklace with an attached crucifix—allowed by the Ninth Circuit ruling and protected under the previous ordinance—was once again outlawed due to its additional functions other than expression. The new ordinance once again attempted to cement a classification system that distinguished between "commercial" and "free expression" by strictly identifying the following items as illegal: housewares, appliances, articles of clothing, sunglasses, auto parts, oils, incense, perfume, lotions, candles, jewelry, toys, and stuffed animals.[15]

The city's classifications laid down meticulous rules for organization, identified specific objects that were illegal, and mandated sellers to purchase a permit, providing city officials with centralized information about who was using the public space. This had two major ramifications. First, the LAPD handed out dozens of tickets for minor infractions yet still failed to stop the commercial activity, leading many artists, performers, and rent-paying business owners, the very people whom the city was trying to appease and protect in the first place, to view the regulations as excessive. Secondly, requiring Free Speech Zone participants to purchase permits stigmatized those who refused, defining them as operating outside of the official political mandate. These stigmatization practices failed to take into account whether they were adhering to their initial legal distinction between "free speech" and "commercial" activity.

The LAPD focused attention on spatial parameters, as their efforts to introduce public safety concerns superseded attention to unfair commercial competition. Unanimously, every business owner whom I talked with as well as every business owner attending public meetings expressed support for artists and performers yet frustration at the continuing commercial activity in public space. Business interests commonly believe that the arts improve a place's public image and attract a wealthier customer base. One long-term business owner summed up this point of view at a neighborhood meeting, "We need regulations, but we don't want to drive out the artists. We have been facing this problem of commercial vending for decades and the city still has not successfully dealt with it. Instead, you're getting rid of the artists, the people that you should be

FIGURE 17. Homeless performer surrounded by LAPD officers for playing without a permit.

protecting. These are the people that we want. And the unfair competition doesn't go away" (see figure 17).

Instead of committing to defining and enforcing the differences between commercial and free speech products, the LAPD opted to control personal behavior. In particular, they targeted those who refused to pay to enter the lottery but displayed their wares in public space anyway. Law enforcement officials immediately focused on these self-proclaimed "resisters" who consisted mostly of artists, musicians, and political activists, people legally classified as "free speech" participants. LAPD officers directed a great deal of time and resources toward managing and controlling them, resulting in frequent ticketing of a very small group of individuals for not following the intricate rules of conduct listed in the ordinance.

At a meeting to update the public on the impact of the new ordinance, enraged business owners asked the neighborhood prosecutor about the ongoing commercial activity. She replied, "Officers spent so much time against protestors because that was a much more volatile situation, and they couldn't even get to commercial vendors." When asked by discouraged "free expressionists" about the intense scrutiny and unnecessary ticketing, the LAPD senior lead officer for Venice Beach explained that two officers were assigned to inspect whether or not people conformed to the rules and regulations, pointing out the difficult bind between enforcing the spirit of the law and the letter of the law. Visibly discouraged, he asked the public, "How many warnings am I supposed to give before you are playing me like a fool?"

City officials legitimated local interest groups' definitions of the boardwalk as a site of "social disorder," employing rigorous guidelines through official mandate. Nonetheless, troubles continued: political resistance became a time-consuming nuisance; the commercial life of the boardwalk was unrelenting; and residents, business owners, and developers remained dissatisfied with the city's efforts. The classification of the Free Speech Zone as an official site of social disorder consistently failed to control it and the cycle of new regulations and individual adaptations continues.

Conclusion

The Venice Boardwalk was transformed from a bohemian enclave, attractive to particular subcultures and voyeurs wanting to capture a glimpse of the beat and artistic lifestyles, into a bohemian theme park, one of the most popular attractions in Southern California. The symbolism of bohemianism, stemming from the lifestyle of voluntary poverty involving artists, poets, and countercultural activists, became disconnected from the social and cultural movements of decades past. Instead, it emerged as a commercial theme that people could adopt, promote, manipulate, and profit from in a symbolic economy.

Urban sociologists readily interpret commercialization as an influx of big-box stores and boutiques that reshape the look and feel of neighborhoods. Yet the boardwalk demonstrates the malleability of the urban marketplace. There is always the potential for the marketplace to draw in different groups of people and allow for invention and differentiation. The boardwalk market emerged out of Venice's particular bohemian history, yet it was also influenced by wider demographic trends and cultural and political developments, including homelessness, racial inequality, immigration, and gentrification. As new people enter the boardwalk, they build upon the particulars of the place and adapt to the conditions of regulation and competition, leading to ongoing political conflicts filtered through formal and informal interests and a narrative about urban order and disorder.

The Venice Boardwalk is a widely diverse locale that lacks corporate commerce. But markets are wild: they allow people to push and pull the historical conditions in different directions. Just as the bohemian theme park withstands regulations and maintains this unique commercial space as an integrative milieu for the masses, there is also the potential for marketplaces to maintain their independence while simultaneously becoming exclusive. Another commercial street in Venice builds upon similar historical themes just a few blocks inland, but the logics of adaptation are different. On Abbot Kinney Boulevard, Venice's *fashionable bohemia*, independent, small-scale stores, and an anticorporate mentality have transformed the street into an upscale and exclusive commercial locale.

CHAPTER SIX

Fashionable Bohemia

Venetians debate about which is the best café on Abbot Kinney Boulevard. The French Market, south of Venice Boulevard, advertises itself as more than a café. It stocks a wide variety of food products, including imported wines, pastries, and pâtés and is inviting to expats and academics alike. The French Market's outdoor seating mimics a serene backyard, featuring comfortable patio tables with umbrellas to shade customers from the fierce Southern California sun. It is a relaxing spot to read the paper, eat a buttery croissant, have a light lunch of spinach quiche and spring greens, or snack on a Nutella crepe while sipping an espresso. Their website suggests customers "can easily be convinced that they've traded their L.A. lives for the charms of the French countryside."

Venice's incoming hipster class, an assortment of artists, graphic designers, and architects, frequent Intelligentsia, the newest café on the boulevard. Those used to an efficient one-size-fits-all approach to ordering and drinking drip coffee and steeping their own tea must learn a new model. Custom-made espresso machines, a variety of coffee blends brewed by the cup, and perfectly prepared black, oolong, green, and white teas are only part of the appeal to these creative locals. With very little in the way of predesigned, permanent seating, visitors able to concentrate amidst blaring music grab loose pillows, drop them down on a concrete ledge, and pound away on their MacBooks. Intelligentsia holds public coffee tastings and offers coffee and tea reserves for customers with deep pockets. Their website describes the taste of their $22 per pound Colombian El Nogal in language that seems like a parody of a wine ad for those with the most sophisticated palates: "Complex aromatics of yellow flowers, sweet herbs and lemon drops transform into notes of Rainier cherry and cantaloupe in the cup. When you least expect it, the acidity bursts forth with Meyer lemon and clementine orange. The finish is cheerfully tart and leaves behind hints of passion fruit and fresh licorice root."

Abbot's Habit is my favorite café on the street. I lived around the corner from it and would sit there for hours on end. At this shop, I would order a sandwich on hearty multigrain bread with fresh vegetables, roasted turkey, and cranberry chutney; drink dark drip coffee; choose from an assortment of packaged and loose teas; or treat myself to a sugar-coated, chewy-on-the-inside, ginger molasses cookie. But I was not repeatedly pulled into Abbot's Habit only by its menu items or even by its standing as the oldest coffee shop on the street. It dates back only to the late '80s, its "old-timer" status suggesting the boulevard's recent reinvention as a retail center. Instead, as a sociologist studying neighborhood change, I found Abbot's Habit so attractive, because such a wide variety of locals use the space, bringing multiple layers of Venice's shifting landscape into focus in one small setting. The French Market and Intelligentsia, both of which offer appealing amenities to specific groups of Venetians, are narrower in their community functions. Their food and drink varieties, spatial layouts, and prices facilitate a process of customer self-selection. Abbot's Habit, in contrast, operates as one of the few remaining integrative spots on the street.

Although there is a sign by the cash register that reads "We reserve the right to refuse service," the staff of Abbot's Habit rarely exercises this right. Aging hippies with long stringy hair stand outside and puff on hand-rolled cigarettes. A homeless stoner in his sixties with a bushy silver beard sits at a two-seater wooden table out front and smokes marijuana out of a small wooden pipe while sipping a cup of tea. Inside, a piano is positioned in the middle of the room, amidst wobbly tables and benches. When the sound system stops booming classic rock favorites, a balding-but-ponytailed homeless man in his fifties tickles the ivories, so absorbed by his playing that he has no need for the surrounding patrons made up of aspiring models, artists, musicians, actors, designers, screenwriters and movie producers, and a range of longtime locals.

A young white woman in her twenties with long blond hair wearing a sundress fanatically checks her cell phone for new text messages to avoid working on her fashion portfolio. Feeling the rhythm of the music, she occasionally throws adoring smiles at the piano-playing homeless man. A black man in his forties sporting a stylish navy suit without a tie works around the corner at a nonprofit organization in Oakwood.

He stops in for an afternoon pick-me-up, pats a few people on the back to say hello, and is on his way. A Latino man in his fifties with a salt-and-pepper mustache wearing loose-fitting khaki shorts and a faded maroon T-shirt relaxes by drinking ginger tea and reading the newest edition of *LA Weekly*. A white man in his midthirties, his sunglasses still in place after forty-five minutes inside, brainstorms with a friend about a new script he is writing. Two women with New York accents and baby carriages block the front entrance as their husbands wait in line for cappuccinos. Fascinated by their own conversation, they have lost track of their inconvenient location, as people are forced to squeeze by them in order to get in and out. The hippies are delighted by their oblivion, as it gives them something to ridicule for the moment.

Some potential customers find the mix of people at Abbot's Habit discomfiting. A pale white woman in her early forties with long brown hair, wearing a silky flowered black dress, inspects the room for a seat. The only open table is next to one of the aging hippies. The man is not homeless, but his faded jeans are stained and ripped and his thinning gray-blond hair is long and disheveled, making it difficult for her to decipher the difference. When her friend arrives, she whispers, "The only place to sit is next to [pointing to the hippie] that homeless man or outside [pointing outside] near that guy smoking weed." Her friend laughs uncomfortably, and the pair leaves without ordering. On another occasion, a young white married couple with a young child orders coffee and toasted bagels. The woman points with her eyes to a young group of homeless punks. With mullets and Mohawks atop their heads and bodies adorned by tattoos and silver jewelry, they are acting rowdy, singing at the top of their lungs over the blasting background music. The man says, "Let's just get it to go."

Abbot's Habit has become an oasis on Abbot Kinney Boulevard where distinct worlds collide: new and old; rich and poor; white, Latino, and black; housed and homeless; clean-cut and unkempt alike share in the experience of this social space. It is one of the few respites from the boulevard's emerging exclusivity.[1] Those repelled by the live-and-let-live atmosphere of crisscrossing cultures and classes soon find that they fit in almost everywhere else on the street. The rest of Abbot Kinney Boulevard, including Intelligentsia and the French Market, draws upon a different set of aesthetic and social norms as part of a more exclusive retail environment.

Abbot Kinney Boulevard is now filled with retail spaces selling products that attract the urban lifestyle connoisseur, a segment of upper-income cultural consumers. Handmade, vintage, and craft designs are commonplace. In one store, a man picks up a pair of kelly-green suede Adidas sneakers popular in the early '80s. In another shop, a woman purchases a narrow, iron, lattice-seat chair with no cushions that serves a purely aesthetic function. Down the street, a bookstore is filled with rare, oversized, and collectible books that are handpicked by the store-owners and features first editions and other vintage works, some signed by the authors. The street incorporates a new incarnation of the "all-in-one store." Instead of the once popular five and dimes or the classic thrift shops or even the omnipresent warehouse stores of the modern era, the all-in-one theme matches the street's bohemian fashions. One shop integrates vintage clothing, works of art, and a hair salon. An arts and crafts co-op has handmade cards, jewelry, lamp shades, and other original works of art. Paintings for sale hang on the walls of various stores that claim to be both "clothing boutique and art exhibit," "coffee bar and art exhibit," "bookstore and art exhibit," or "hair salon and art exhibit."

Abbot Kinney Boulevard is neither a bohemian theme park nor a site where corporate commerce imposes universal trends on the masses. Instead, it consists of independently owned businesses that activists and merchants furiously protect, resisting the encroachment of corporate retailers, or what they call "formula retail chains." Many residents and merchants describe the street's stores and their wares as "anticorporate." When Tom, a shop owner in his early forties, began to remodel his commercial space to open in the early 2000s, he said that residents stopped by on a daily basis to voice their concerns about rumors, although untrue, that his business would become the first corporate chain. "I think the greatest fear of everybody on Abbot Kinney and maybe even in Venice," Tom said, "is that Abbot's Habit will become a Starbucks."

New residents and merchants interpret the current street scene as central to their authentic vision of Venice community life, ascribing a meaning to authenticity that is clearly distinct from the one put forth a few decades earlier. Newcomers work to sustain rituals, themes, and symbols on and around Abbot Kinney Boulevard that shape and control the aesthetic presentation, public perception, and social and economic utility of this commercial neighborhood as a site for a new wealthy class of hip urban consumers who prefer ethically and carefully manufactured products. One neighborhood newspaper celebrated the street's newfound success as "Brand Venice," defining it as "innovation, independence, and community."[2]

The branding of Abbot Kinney Boulevard is an upscale version of the one produced at Venice Beach, demonstrating both the influence of local history as well as the malleability of the marketplace. Like the boardwalk, Abbot Kinney Boulevard stands opposed to a wider trend of corporate ubiquity, as an alternative amalgam of art and commerce. Yet the boardwalk's *bohemian theme park* is overwhelmingly integrative. Abbot Kinney Boulevard, in contrast, has emerged as a *fashionable bohemia*. Its cumulative and thematic organization as a site of upscale cultural consumption facilitates a process of social exclusion. Called West Washington Boulevard prior to 1989, Abbot Kinney Boulevard was once a socioeconomic and racial mixing ground more analogous to the previous, less crowded era of the Venice Boardwalk. The boulevard's diversity has gradually disappeared, narrowed into certain spaces and corners, and its overarching reputation has been transformed from "diverse and gritty" into "safe and pure."

The merger of artistic ideals with vintage and antique material objects is a key part of the appeal to upper-income cultural consumers searching for an association with an authentic bohemian lifestyle. Such customers fetishize product diversity, overlooking the proximity to social and economic diversity once central to the street's multifunctional identity. Bohemianism once consisted of a lifestyle opposed to middle-class norms. Now bohemianism has become a commodity, one that has the potential to emerge as a tourist market for the masses on the boardwalk or one that can be packaged in ethically produced, $4 lattes, vintage chairs selling for over $1,000, and innovative multimillion-dollar artist lofts on the boulevard.[3] How did this integrative social space with multiple community functions become a fashionable commercial center oriented toward upscale and exclusive cultural consumption?

Blurred Boundary between Purity and Danger

Over the last four decades, West Washington Boulevard became Abbot Kinney Boulevard. Built upon a bourgeois classification system, the street now idealizes middle- and upper-income residential norms and divides these "pure" community practices from "dangerous" ones by imposing a clear-cut boundary between Oakwood's diversity and the fashionable boulevard's exclusivity. Its past incarnation as West Washington Boulevard supported a fundamentally different identity that housed multiple community functions and blurred the line between current conceptions of purity and danger in Venice.

Long-term residents recall black-owned businesses, a teen center for African American youth, artist studios, a literary center for poets, and affordable secondhand thrift stores. Political activists of different racial, ethnic, and socioeconomic backgrounds worked and organized in offices on the boulevard. They advocated for more affordable housing, wrote about the protection of low-income residents and antiwar protesters in the left-wing neighborhood newspaper *Free Venice Beach Head*, planned a state-wide and then national Peace and Freedom Party to counter the pro-war stances of the two major political parties, and helped to organize the countercultural movement in the Canals. The street was also home to Project Action, the African American–run nonprofit agency that helped secure federal funding for minority jobs, after-school programs, and fourteen housing projects in nearby Oakwood during the 1970s.

The networks linking this street scene with various social segments of Venice were more stable. Different groups based on race, class, political, lifestyle, and career-based associations maintained connections. African Americans who still live in Oakwood have fond memories of the street as a place where they felt comfortable spending time as recently as the 1980s. Marcella, in her late fifties, whose family has lived in Oakwood for decades, says, "There was a time when this street had a lot of artists' studios and bargain stores, and inexpensive restaurants. It wasn't all expensive stores like it is now, and there were none of those buildings, those office buildings or artist lofts. It wasn't just for rich people."

James, a black man in his late forties, grew up in Oakwood and his cousins, uncle, and grandparents still live there. He claims, "Everybody from the Oakwood, this used to be all the stomping grounds right here on Abbot Kinney. This used to be everything. Used to have the beauty salon, the night clubs, the youth foundation. It was all good." Natasha, an African American woman in her early fifties who has lived in Venice her entire life, also recalls the historical connections between Oakwood and Abbot Kinney Boulevard:

When I was a kid, Abbot Kinney had restaurants, like Lucy's restaurant. We used to have the barbeque place that's [still] there now. We used to have a haircut—the barbershop, ya know, just like the movie *Barbershop*. You could go in there and learn everything you ever wanted to know about anybody and everybody in the community. There were also artists and they would allow us kids to come in there and if we wanted to work with the paints or tempers or whatever, they'd let you. It was really a fun place to be. . . . In the '70s and early '80s. . . . [T]here was the Teen Center, which was great. We could go in there and play pool and watch movies. Kane Davis [who directed it] was good. He had books, all kinds of books on everything. . . . Any kid, free of charge [could participate]. All you had to do was sign in, because I guess he had to show to his funding that he was servicing the community, and it was somewhere to go, and it kept you out of trouble. You could go there after school, and the first thing that he wanted you to do was your homework. And that was great. Because everybody did their homework. Then after you did, he and the people that were helping him checked your homework. Then and only then could you go play pool or do the weight lifting, the dancing, the drumming. He had all kinds of activities.

Before it became a popular commercial zone, merchants had a difficult time surviving solely from retail sales. Many stores on the street were a mixture of wholesale and retail; others provided a range of services to increase their profits and consumer base. For instance, a restaurant called the Merchant of Venice (now the site of the popular and upscale Hal's Bar and Grill) combined retail, restaurant, and repair. They sold the very furniture on which people eating breakfast and lunch were sitting; and to make some extra cash, the owners would also take on furniture refinishing projects.

Leslie, a white woman in her sixties, moved her business and home from her boardwalk apartment to West Washington Boulevard in 1982 because she needed more space for her growing manufacturing and wholesale jewelry business, and she wanted to remain close to her employees. She describes the street at that time as mixed in economic activity.

LESLIE: I went looking for a commercial space to move our business into, but all my workers lived here [in Oakwood] and many of them didn't have cars. So they walked to deliver the work to me and so I was really looking for a commercial location that my workers could still access, but that I could have a regular location to do my shipping and billing and do my office work and whatever.

ANDREW: Were you among the first to do this [establish a retail store] on this street?

LESLIE: No, there were stores here when I came and they came and went and came and went and came and went. It was always changing. People trying out the street, not figuring out what it takes to make it here, and usually blowing it in some way. . . . [T]he ones who stayed the longest were like ourselves because we weren't relying on the retail business to stay here. We had this whole manufacturing business in the back and that was really the core of our business. Back in the '80s, there were like ten of us who were kind of the stable merchants here. And everybody else came and left, and we all had a wholesale business. We all had retail too, but people who didn't know about the wholesale, well, they never talked to us. They never came and said, "How do you pay the rent every month?" Because I would have said, let me show you our back room.

The transition from a multifunctional community space into one guided by a central retail theme was a slow process constrained by nearby crime in Oakwood, the street's confusing and seemingly hidden location, and its low status standing in relation to other Los Angeles shopping streets. Longtime residents and business owners describe an intertwined process of stability and change that could not solidify a new street identity. New businesses opened, some remained, and others quickly closed down. Like the boardwalk's commerce, the process has been cyclical rather than linear. Leslie says, "There is a common joke by those of us who have been here for a long time that the street has been up and coming for twenty years." Sarah, another storeowner, reiterates this point, "It [the retail activity on the street] takes three steps forward and three steps back and three steps forward and then three steps back." Robert, an interior designer and storeowner says, "They tried, I don't know how many times [since the early '90s] to get this place up and coming."

In response to a cycle of false starts, local business owners and activists proposed to change the name of the street from West Washington Boulevard to Abbot Kinney Boulevard. Naming it after the original developer of Venice, they hoped to publicize it, as one storeowner says, as "the newest street in Los Angeles." In the past, people looking to shop here would commonly get lost, because the street runs diagonally to other main roads. Often visitors traveled to the other Washington Boulevard, located just south of the Canals and separating Venice from Marina del Rey. Sharon, a white woman in her early fifties who has rented an apartment in Oakwood since 1980, explains, "I had no idea Abbot Kinney was even there. At that time it was West Washington, but for years, I didn't even know it existed."

Leslie was influential in organizing the street's name change. Here she describes how a small group with intimate knowledge of the political process was able to bring enough pressure to bear on public officials to facilitate this change. They organized locally and established connections with city representatives.

LESLIE: When it was still called West Washington that was a dilemma, because I used to do print advertising, in like the *LA Weekly* and the *LA Reader* who were the two big weekly papers at the time. And I always knew when the papers hit the streets because people would start calling and say "which Washington are you on?" . . . Then the Venice Action Committee was the one that did the main push for the name change of Abbot Kinney, and I was very, very much involved in that. There were really like three of us who did most of the work on that. And it took us two years to get the name change. Ruth Galanter was a new councilwoman at the time and she was, well, she didn't want to piss anyone off so she was very conservative. Ya know, we got all the signatures of the property owners, which is the requirement—50 percent plus 1. But then she also wanted us to get a majority of the tenants, which meant doing another additional whole campaign.

ANDREW: Getting renters?

LESLIE: Yeah. So that was a long haul and we wanted it so bad and we got all organized and went downtown to city council and had a great session with the planning and land-use committee who was hearing it. And we all came with our little thirty-second speeches so that we wouldn't bore them. And we'd give them the positive reasons why this should happen and you could see these three committee members going like, oh yeah, I've been lost down there before.

At the time of the name change, the West Washington Boulevard Association amended its name to the Abbot Kinney District Association. An open-membership neighborhood organization made up of a coalition of business owners, developers, and residents who lived on the street, the association took as its first order of business to arrange a beautification effort, much of which resulted in seventy-four palm trees lining the street. With the addition of garbage cans, bike racks, planters around the trees, cross walks, and an extensive Internet website to catalogue the stores, they facilitated an appearance of a more contained and orderly shopping atmosphere that slowly attracted new businesses and made the street more appealing to pedestrians and customers.

Setting this street transition in motion and putting forth a new definition of quality of life, these local entrepreneurs took ownership over what was previously considered public space.[4] Yet they did not quickly succeed at reinventing the street's identity and eliminating Venice's cultural and economic diversity. Storeowners of the 1980s and '90s were operating under a vastly different set of social and economic conditions than those facing merchants today. As merchants worked to redefine the street, many of the stores failed and the ones that remained often stood next to aging beach cottages, abandoned, boarded-up, and graffiti-lined buildings, and empty and overgrown lots. Such "eyesores" were still an integral part of the street in the early 2000s, when I first moved to Venice (figure 18). Moreover, storeowners faced additional complications of manufacturing an orderly retail environment on the border of Oakwood. Storeowners negotiated a fine line between adopting commercial practices that attracted upper-income cultural consumers, which benefited their own economic well-being on the street, and wiping the street clean of its relationship with the much more racially, ethnically, and socioeconomically diverse Oakwood, as well as additional countercultural organizations and marginalized populations. This was especially the case because of the traumatizing gang violence in Oakwood at the same time.

Lila, a lifelong African American resident in her sixties, says that Oakwood's citizens viewed the attempt to change the reputation and character of Abbot Kinney Boulevard to make it attractive to upper-income cultural consumers as bizarre, both a sign of the enormous social distance (if not physical distance) between the two neighborhoods and a sign of ignorance among shoppers who seemed unaware of the fact that violence readily spilled over to the commercial street. "You'd be surprised, how many people that weren't black were walking through the neighborhood [of Oakwood] when there was a race war going on. . . . And we sit there and look at them, and say, 'They are so unaware of what's going on. They just don't know, and the police are trying to keep it so quiet.' People are down here on Abbot Kinney and they're having their tea and coffee, and just kicking it and just having a grand ol' time,

FIGURE 18. One of several abandoned storefronts in early 2000s.

looking at the little boutiques, and meanwhile, there's murder going on around them. It's stupid, ya know? But it was happening."

Gang-related events in bordering Oakwood seeped into the Abbot Kinney scene, producing moments of fear and danger and impeding the street's transformation into an upscale commercial milieu. At the height of the violence during 1994, a group of Oakwood activists influenced the reputation of the street by getting people to pay attention to the internal strife in Oakwood. A local African American group called Pathfinders distributed two thousand flyers to Abbot Kinney Boulevard customers. The flyers read "WARNING UNSAFE AREA. White Customers Shopping in this Section of Venice May Be Shot Dead by Mexican Gangs—without Notice." Timothy Crayton, a lead member of the group, told a *Los Angeles Times* reporter at that time, "We're not really here to hurt anyone, but we're dying here. . . . We're tired of carrying casket after casket. The smell of death is everywhere, and we're trying to share our misery[.]"[5]

Amy, who opened up a store in the late '90s, describes the street during that time as more "hoodish" and a "dicey place" to live and work. "I would be here [at the store] 'til ten or eleven at night, painting, making things to sell, and the guy who owned the store two doors down would wait for me, because he didn't like me being in the neighborhood by myself. . . . There was a drive-by shooting when I first came here, ya know? That was some scary shit happening. . . . There was a dead guy that was right in front of this house [pointing]. And I had rented this house [right near the house she pointed to] when I had the store too. I lived here and then had the store for a while. And the things we saw. You had to be aware, much more aware, because it was definitely scary."

Creating a new street name and aesthetic character was not enough to impose a coherent border between Abbot Kinney Boulevard and Oakwood. In order to "purify" the public culture of the street from its connections with racial, ethnic, and socioeconomic diversity, and moreover, from its proximity to violence, activists and merchants publicized an official set of meanings about Abbot Kinney Boulevard as "Brand Venice." The branding of the street had a cumulative impact: it attracted new stores, enticed new development, increased rent values, and reconfigured the relationship between Oakwood and Abbot Kinney Boulevard.

Inventing Brand Venice

Political organizations helped publicize Abbot Kinney Boulevard as a unique, artisanal shopping district. Activists and merchants invented rituals that accentuated certain neighborhood historical features, while simultaneously ignoring others.[6] For instance, they endorsed the artistic and bohemian identity of Abbot Kinney Boulevard, while strategically overshadowing the lower-income surroundings and the racial and ethnic diversity of bordering Oakwood. Local events served to drown out the surrounding hype about Venice, and in particular the section of Oakwood, as a dangerous place.

By establishing neighborhood festivals, organizers broke up the monotony of everyday life and allowed certain events to stand out as representative of the street. Attracting people from beyond Venice's borders, they served as advertisements for the locality.[7] For example, the Abbot Kinney District Association established a small-scale outdoor arts and crafts festival in the late '80s, drawing attention to Venice's artistic history. A decade later, the festival grew into a large attraction. One day a year, the street is lined with tents covering artists, craftspeople, food vendors, music stages, and games for children, bringing in upward of thirty thousand people and serving as a source of recognition for local business owners. The festival became so important to merchants that in the late 2000s they renamed the district association the Abbot Kinney Festival Association.

The Venice Art Walk, a highly promoted fund-raiser for the Venice Family Clinic, in which people pay to visit studios of Venice artists who continue to reside in the area, is another important attraction. Individual studios are distributed throughout Venice; many of them are actually in Oakwood. But the entrance to the art walk, the silent auction, food vendors, and musical performances are located on Abbot Kinney Boulevard, which serves as the center of this event. The art walk directs public attention toward the narrative of Venice as an influential artistic haven while also physically bringing people into this emerging retail zone.

Kim, in her late twenties, co-owns a handcrafted furniture shop with her boyfriend. She explains the value of the events on Abbot Kinney: "The festival is really nice, because, well, it's a time when all the owners bond. Ya know? There's just such a nice atmosphere and so many people come into the store who haven't been here before. So in that way, I would say it is really a good thing for businesses on the street."

Vicky, in her midfifties, had just opened a home-furnishing store on Abbot Kinney Boulevard at the time of our interview in 2004. She discusses the benefits of the festival and reveals why she wants to participate in the art walk:

> The festival was really our first big exposure. And people were like, "We've been waiting for a store like this for twenty-five years. Thank god you're here. I'll be back when it's not so crowded." That was a great day for us. . . . And we also want to do the art walk. A lot of the photographs in here are on consignment. So we want to bring that person in and maybe another and get ourselves on the art walk. People can come in and look in—they're a different kind of client. They have money. So if we can get on that, it's like shuttling people in. And we'll have the artists in here, talking about their work. So we're trying to market ourselves in that direction.

Like middle-class residents of the Canals, residents, activists, and merchants draw upon certain themes in Venice's history to invent an authentic neighborhood identity that is disconnected from its actual history. The middle-class Canals residents invented a neighborhood theme of the quaint residential locale by restricting housing size, promoting open space, and securing a certain aesthetic character for the walls and sidewalks surrounding the waterways. On Abbot Kinney Boulevard, they highlight the history of Venice's bohemian, and in particular, artsy culture in order to legitimate the new street theme. They frame the fashionable bohemia as "anticorporate," even organizing a local political movement to ban chain stores. Two local activists, who moved to Venice in the late 1980s and late '90s, started a petition campaign called Venice Unchained to preserve the distinct street scene from the invasion of corporate commerce.[8] These activists and their local supporters worry that large-scale, corporate forces threaten the unique character of the commercial neighborhood. They gathered over four thousand signatures and received the support of the Venice Chamber of Commerce and the Venice Neighborhood Council—a city-funded, locally elected advisory board that represents Venice's interests to the Los Angeles City Council—to push for an ordinance that would ban future "formula retail" establishments. On the petition they define formula retail as "businesses that are required by contractual or other arrangements to be virtually identical to businesses in other communities including, but not limited to, businesses with standardized architecture, signs, décor, menus, food preparation policies, uniforms, or products."[9]

While activists were struggling to get this ordinance passed in the Los Angeles City Council, the first chain store, a popular purveyor of frozen yogurt called Pinkberry, opened on the street in 2007. Residents were very concerned, as rumors swirled that a Starbucks would follow. While the Starbucks rumor was untrue, political activists and residents responded by strongly opposing formula retail chains. Residents attended meetings and wrote letters to city officials. According to the editors of the local newspaper, *Venice Paper*, "No story since we began covering Venice in 2001 has catalyzed as much spontaneous e-mail and communication as the arrival of the first corporate chain on Abbot Kinney Boulevard."[10]

The response was so overwhelming because newer residents and merchants embraced an official meaning of Abbot Kinney Boulevard as the anticorporate, fashionable bohemia, despite the retail theme's short-lived history, which only emerged during the '90s following the street's name change and its new retail focus on independent creative commerce. Nevertheless, one of the founders of Venice Unchained claims, "We feel that so much of L.A. and metropolitan cities look more and more similar. . . . We want to preserve our great city [of Venice] and its originality and character."[11] These relative newcomers to Venice want to safeguard a distinct lifestyle and commercial identity as the authentic version of Venice community experience. Three years after it opened and after an informal boycott by residents, Pinkberry closed its Abbot Kinney store, claiming that it was "underperforming."[12]

The invented rituals and political movements celebrating Venice's fashionable bohemianism have contributed to strengthening the street's identity, and journalists popularize this theme at the local, national, and international levels. They provide free publicity for stores and the new cultural trends they create. According to the storeowners I interviewed, collectively they have been written up in such magazines and newspapers as *Cargo*, *Casa Brutus* (a Japanese design magazine), *Dwell*, *Interior Design*, the *Los Angeles Times*, the *New York Times*, *Travel + Leisure*, and *Western Interior and Designs*, among other print sources and countless blogs, solidifying a collective representation of Abbot Kinney Boulevard as an innovative, trendy, and upscale retail zone. For example, a *Los Angeles Times* article describes the new upscale character of the street in this passage: "Welcome to the new Abbot Kinney: upscale Abbot Kinney, a place to see and be seen, spot celebrities, eat $8 pancakes, buy $200 jeans, a $1,000 vintage wood school chair ($985 to be exact), or maybe a $2-million loft."[13]

A number of articles have been dedicated to specific businesses. The *New York Times* describes the transformation of a long-standing neighborhood bar: "In recent years it had iconic status and few customers. Now the Brig, a 40-year-old bar on Abbot Kinney Boulevard in Venice, has been transformed from a seedy dive for old-timers into a seething hangout for 20-somethings who like their beer served in an environment with attitude."[14]

Local actors reframed the identity of this commercial neighborhood as the new legitimate center of Venice. The manager of a vintage furniture store, Hillary Greene Shugrue, told a *New York Times* travel reporter in 2005, "Abbot Kinney Boulevard is the nucleus of Venice."[15] Robert, the interior designer, compared the new street scene to the famous Venice Boardwalk just a short walk away: "The boardwalk is for tourists. The *real* people from Venice hang out here." This sentiment was reinforced by the Abbot Kinney District Association's slogan in the early 2000s, when they coordinated their first retail website: "Where

Main Street meets the heart of Venice." Ironically, by reshaping Abbot Kinney Boulevard as the *real center* of Venice, merchants and activists promoted product diversity over social and economic diversity, moving further away from historic definitions of bohemianism.

Fashionable Bohemianism as a Neighborhood Homology

The merger of artistic ideals with vintage and antique material objects is a key part of the appeal to upper-income cultural consumers searching for the accoutrements of a bohemian lifestyle. Such customers fetishize product diversity as emblematic of bohemianism. Like the case of the Canals, complementary pieces fit together into a neighborhood homology between groups, styles, and space. In this case, the visible appearance of independently produced commodities and styles up and down the street creates a coherent set of high-status symbols that stands opposed to nearby surroundings of diverse and ambiguous neighborhood public cultures in Oakwood and on the Venice Boardwalk.

Different dimensions of the street are, as sociologist Pierre Bourdieu would say, "governed by the same logic," such that the types of objects on display, the spatial designs inside and outside of various stores, new cutting-edge architecture, and the street's collective reputation for ethical, vintage, and handcrafted products attract certain classes of people and repel others. Storeowners purposely organize their stores and seek out objects to sell that constitute a vintage look and feel. They are selling not only a type of product but also a particular set of values as well. In one shop, hand-fabricated, raw and unpolished wooden shelves and tables line the walls and floors, covered with the latest fashions of designer clothing and handmade jewelry. A jewelry boutique displays its one-of-a-kind products on top of a giant recycled pharmacy chest with dozens of small drawers, which the owner says she found years ago on the street. In another shop, a craftswoman has constructed display tables and wooden shelves from scratch; she then hand-painted them and skillfully scraped and damaged the wood to appear weathered and old. On these tables and shelves, the owner displays antique-like crafts, which have passed through the same process: someone hand-constructed most of the objects, including clocks, furniture, and picture frames; and then others painted the objects and sanded them down to project a vintage look. Even restaurants abide by the logic of creating a particular type of feel. *Los Angeles Magazine* reviews one new restaurant, with "broad wooden counters and wrought-iron inside and its yard sale furniture amid stone bulwarks in the courtyard" as having "an appealing frankness."[16]

In addition to handcrafted products, shop owners incorporate ethically fabricated objects and foods that synchronize with consumers' values. Boutiques carry baby clothing made of the softest organic cotton; cafés sell coffee and tea made from fair-trade beans and leaves; and restaurants abide by an etiquette of slow and whole foods, incorporating locally and organically grown produce, which the chefs try to purchase from farmers' markets. The designs of some are so carefully planned that the minimalist presentation of a clothing boutique with hardly any clothing becomes itself a work of art, and customers feel as though the storeowners had personally selected the most precious distressed leather belt for them. The most visible and obvious indicators that fashionable bohemianism has become a strategic and collective production are from the signs hanging on the outside of many shops, presenting the following store mottos: Hair. Art. More; Floral Art; Books and Gallery; Gallery and Gifts; Modern Designs, Creative Ideas; and Furniture Collection. A surfboard design shop is called The Board Gallery and its motto is "surf, skate, snow, style"; and a Japanese restaurant is called Wabi-Sabi, a whimsical play on words for an urban lifestyle connoisseur.

Some merchants have taken the stylization of bohemianism to the furthest extreme, mimicking the classic thrift store in their presentations as a way to validate the space, which serves as a shrine for carefully chosen products. For instance, figure 19 displays the last existing thrift store on the street, simply called Tony's. At one time a pervasive commercial entity, the thrift store has been superseded by its sister store-type, the antique and shabby-chic furniture shop—the one in figure 20 is called Bountiful—where vintage items are resold for hundreds and even thousands of dollars. It is interesting to notice the common presentation: neither of the stores presents its name; both line up their furniture outside for display; and each shop celebrates oldness as a style.

The difference, of course, is in their prices and reputations. Whereas Tony's is a classic thrift store model of mismatched items, used products, musty odors, and lucky finds for patient bargain hunters, Bountiful stages itself as a purified version of the thrift shop where the interior designer/shop owner carefully selects material objects. The shop has become one of the most famous home furnishing boutiques in the coun-

FIGURE 19. Last remaining thrift shop on Abbot Kinney Boulevard.

try and items thoughtfully chosen by the storeowner appear on the covers of countless design magazines. Bountiful's sweet-smelling lavender soaps distinguish its aroma from Tony's musty scent, and the very expensive objects reinforce the idea to shoppers that by walking out the door with a $3,000 white wicker chair one has purchased more than simply a place to sit. Unlike Tony's, which has no website, Bountiful's website portrays the store's aims as a perfect match for the street's fashionable bohemianism:

> Recognized as the source of the best and most unique blend of American country charm and European elegance, Bountiful attracts a wide range of clients from designers and film studios, to collectors and celebrities; all of whom faithfully turn to Sue [the owner] for her knowledge, style and enormous inventory of antiques. . . . Stroll through Bountiful's old English garden gates and discover the defining elements of Sue's signature style. Under the vaulted white ceilings of what was once an artists' loft, 19th century American and French painted furniture is paired with glamorous Italian chandeliers. Southern farm tables are draped with fine European linens. Old cast iron urns spill over with hydrangeas, and the scent of French lavender soaps fill the air. It is a journey, an experience, an inspiration . . . beginning right here.[17]

FIGURE 20. High-end shop mimicking thrift presentation.

The symbolic coherence of Abbot Kinney Boulevard as the fashionable bohemia serves as an incentive for new merchants seeking out an "offbeat" retail character unlike other popular scenes in the greater Los Angeles area: Rodeo Drive in Beverly Hills, Main Street and Montana Avenue in Santa Monica, and Robertson Boulevard and Melrose Avenue in Hollywood. The neighborhood homology between groups, prices, symbols, and retail space facilitates a process of social and economic reproduction. Whereas the boardwalk's economic ecology promotes myriad logics of adaptation, the boulevard's neighborhood homology limits potential adaptive processes.

Michael, a white man in his late thirties, owns a home-design store. He moved here from New York City in 2003, because he knew of Venice's reputation for innovative architecture, design, and artistic lifestyles. He says, "I was attracted to Venice . . . just from things I've seen in magazines, like good architecture magazines or design magazines or retail-related stuff. Just that everything that I was ever drawn to in L.A. was in Venice, so I called a friend of mine that has a business. . . . I told her what

I wanted to do and she said, 'Well, you definitely need to look at Abbot Kinney.' You know, because I told her I wanted to be at the beach. I didn't want to be in town and I also didn't want to be in the traditional home-design area."

Merchants who open up new stores on Abbot Kinney Boulevard draw upon its coherent public culture. Storefronts set the stage for how they want others who pass by, window-shop, or come into the store to interpret their commercial identities. Lily, a woman in her early thirties, moved here in 2003 from her native country of Japan with her husband. Before moving to Venice, they traveled throughout Japan and became connected with small-time producers of design products. She and her husband, upon arriving in Venice, opened a store that brought together products from these independent craftspeople:

> We wanted to create something by ourselves. So it's kind of not the goal, but the reason we wanted to leave. When we heard of Abbot Kinney, we wanted to try to have a store here. In Japan, many people like to buy a product with the brand name, but here, well, actually there is no brand name. People like to hear a story, like who makes it, like the stories behind it. So it's kind of interesting to talk with customers. Many of our customers like to create things too— artists, designers, film people, or architects—and so they like the thing itself. So they check it like this way or that way [pretending to hold up an object at different angles and squinting to get a better view of the object].

New storeowners are attracted to the no brand-name and no formula retail identity of Abbot Kinney Boulevard. Although they are relatively new to Venice and sell products that price out most middle- and lower-class residents, they strongly oppose the possible arrival of chain stores. They want to preserve their collective interests in expensive handmade products that fuse art and fashion. When I ask Kim, the furniture storeowner, if her boyfriend makes everything in the store, she replies, "Yeah, he makes everything. . . . Like we make a lot of tables like that [showing me a model], and he finally has a guy that helps him with sanding and stuff. . . . Yeah, yeah, he's down there himself doing finishing work. Which I think that's another response to the corporate thing. They [customers on Abbot Kinney Boulevard] want something that you can't recreate, so you can't Pottery Barn it."

Craig Weiss is the owner of a new trendy bar called the Otheroom and proprietor of another forthcoming café on the street. The new café will fulfill the tastes of the fashionable bohemian by including: "organic, gourmet market/café featuring specialty food . . . beer and wine, charcuterie, cheese cave, gourmet sandwiches, prepared foods, oyster bar, coal/wood fired pizza, fresh cut flowers, organic seasonal produce, organic juices, organic smoothies, organic coffees, pastries, desserts, and more."[18] Weiss recognizes the momentum of change on the street toward an overarching, harmonizing theme. He says, "It's a special moment in time to be on Abbot Kinney—it's being gentrified with integrity and I'm really excited."[19]

Artists have long been recognized as mediators of neighborhood change,[20] but it is not only artists that take on this role. The ongoing evolution of neighborhoods means that various groups step in and position themselves between more established residents and other waves of increasingly upscale newcomers. Oakwood's Latinos and white middle class have taken on this role, situating themselves between long-standing African Americans and wealthier newcomers who have recently built much larger houses. In the Canals, middle-class homeowners played a fundamental role in reconfiguring the political battles in the neighborhood, standing in between countercultural renters and speculative developers. On Abbot Kinney Boulevard, local merchants and community activists take on this middle position. As part of the middle and upper-middle classes, these local actors are unable to singlehandedly transform this commercial neighborhood into an upscale locale. While they invent cultural trends and organize large-scale events, they do not strategically coordinate economic changes with others. Individuals and groups enmeshed in disparate social and economic networks achieve results that complement one another in the cumulative process of gentrification, generating both intended and unintended consequences.

Following the merchant class and their interest in independent creative commerce, developers, property owners, and architects have renovated abandoned and graffiti-laden storefronts, and invented new mixed-use spaces on once-empty lots. Also embracing the theme of the fashionable bohemia, they design innovative buildings that are zoned for both living and working, cleverly labeling them as "artist lofts" so as to blend into the street's overall aesthetic character. These spaces do not appeal to artists, per se, at least not in the way that SoHo artists of the 1970s refurbished abandoned warehouses into now-classic Manhattan loft spaces.[21] The artist lofts on the boulevard are constructed from

FIGURE 21. New artist lofts on sale for $3.45 million each.

scratch, attracting from the outset those willing to pay higher prices to live on this newly gentrifying street. Figure 21 shows an artist loft with an asking price of $3.45 million in 2008 for a street-level work studio and a living space above it, bringing together development, commerce, and wealth through the street's cohesive lifestyle theme. As if recognizing the irony of calling them artist lofts, developer Frank Murphy claims, "Not just artists, but movie producers can work and live here. The location has everything you need: great restaurants and good commercial opportunities."[22]

Abbot Kinney Boulevard offers visitors a small-town feel, which has become central to branding this form of gentrification as one that maintains its integrity. However, the boulevard's coherent neighborhood homology still represents upper-income cultural consumption and combats countercultural activities, minority populations, and homelessness as threats to bourgeois definitions of purity. The changing commercial landscape—even if local storeowners believe they are performing an honorable version of gentrification—has reinvented bohemianism through a fetish for particular types of commodities. In turn, they have transformed race and class diversity into a marker of danger.

How a Coherent Boundary Creates Neighborhood Symbiosis

The transition of this commercial street scene from a multifunctional social and economic environment into an upscale retail district allows those who currently participate in its daily life to readily notice differences and to distinguish insiders from outsiders, typical of a small-town milieu. Often, residents who have lived in a place for a long time identify newcomers as invading their territories, labeling differences accordingly.[23] The reverse is true on Abbot Kinney Boulevard, where the creation of a neighborhood homology allows storeowners to differentiate between those who belong and those who increasingly do not fit into the narrowing public culture. The choice of products to distribute and the overarching retail theme enable storeowners to regulate their clientele by focusing on consumer preferences within a given price range. Leslie discusses the types of customers who shop at her store:

> It's just that subjectively, intuitively, there are plenty of people here with plenty of money and we've got really good restaurants which are always a constant draw. And I stay open in the evenings, because people with disposable incomes go out to dinner. Everybody goes out to lunch, but folks that go to Hal's and Joe's [two high-end restaurants on the street] they're laying out some money. They're not watching their budget. And this is, well, let's just say that the merchants on Abbot Kinney are not serving the poverty-level folks in Oakwood. It's not neighborhood serving in that regard. Lincoln Boulevard is what serves that piece of the puzzle of the economic pie.[24]

Kim reinforces this point. She says,

> To be honest, to shop with us you have to have some money. . . . We definitely, from the beginning, our big thing was that I didn't want anyone to ever feel like they were pressured into buying anything. I wanted people to feel like they could come in and browse. And if they want to come in and just get ideas, all the freakin' time, they should be able to do that. So I definitely try to have that kind of vibe going on. But yeah, the clientele, it's, well, it's more popular with people with money. We get some busloads, from like San Diego to like Redondo [another L.A. beach neighborhood, several miles south of Venice]. Like women that have these day outings because of the garden tour

and the art tour and this and that. So we sort of get that sort of crowd that thinks this is an interesting weird place and have the money to put into it.

For storeowners, craftsmen, and consumers, the changes on the street are about the incorporation of authentic products and lifestyles. But the choices they make create a more complex set of neighborhood consequences. For one, they facilitate a set of social norms, such that people can now pinpoint certain behaviors and social categories as signifying "disorder," making it easier to target activity that does not belong. This division between order and disorder on the boulevard is similar to the residential process in the Canals, but clearly distinct from the commercial processes found on the boardwalk. The boardwalk incorporates so much social, cultural, political, and economic diversity that the boundaries between order and disorder are malleable. Individuals push and pull bohemian themes to fit into the bohemian theme park, which makes it difficult for interested parties to regulate the boardwalk and transform it into an exclusive locale. On Abbot Kinney Boulevard, however, the binary classification of order and disorder is structured into the everyday common sense of local commercial life. Victor, a white artist in his early forties who works at an art gallery on the street, says,

You know, it's the homeless. I mean the last six months, I'd say, I've seen far fewer homeless people walking around Abbot Kinney. There seems to be a closer eye being kept on that sort of stuff. [Imitating an imagined yuppie, he says,] "We don't want them near our BMW or our new Porsche SUV, or anything like that." And it's a tough call. Venice has always been a very inclusive place. It's allowed very highbrow, very lowbrow. It's allowed rich and poor, and all this. Now it seems to be catering more and more to the higher class, or to the wealthier end of things. And in doing so, it means that some aspects of the old Venice get shoved out of the way. . . . Like back there [behind the store] there's always like three or four, who's to know if they're like crack addicts or whatever? But some homeless out back in the parking area. And you know, while on the one hand, where are they supposed to go and you know why is it up to us to kick these people out of the area? But on the other hand, you know, these business owners and homeowners have a right to have their areas kept free. It's a very complicated social issue. They used to hang out on the grassy area of the Vera Davis Center over there [one block into Oakwood]. I haven't seen that for a while. I think there's been a stepped-up po-

lice presence or whatever. Just shoveling them off, probably down there towards the beach.

Amy reports that she can identify "the normal crew" on the street,

> I would say, in the last three years, it had a big turnover of things that have
> made it like safer, but at the same time, it goes in waves. There are phases,
> where all of a sudden, we'll say, who are these people hangin' out? You know,
> hangin' out in the alley or on the sidewalks even. They don't look like the
> normal crew. And then there will be like, something will get stolen that day.
> We've actually had very few break-ins, but the ones that we had, like the one
> we left the window open this much [showing about an inch or two between
> her fingers] and they pulled the phone through the window.

The distinction between order and disorder is spatially organized.
Those I interviewed explicitly identify Abbot Kinney Boulevard and
Oakwood as isolated social worlds, a change from the street's bohemian
days of race, class, and cultural crossover when there was no clearly articulated border between the two. The construction of fashionable bohemianism maintains a coherent boundary, allowing newcomers to interpret
these neighborhoods as distinct spaces with opposing meanings. Olivia,
a woman who recently opened a store on the street, refers to Oakwood
as "tough" and a separate part of Venice that is "over there." She says,

> Actually last night, since we live behind there, we can hear the helicopters
> [and see] the searching light. . . . In that area [pointing across the street mean-
> ing behind Abbot Kinney in the Oakwood section], behind Electric Avenue
> that happens. Not that way though [pointing behind Abbot Kinney Boule-
> vard in the opposite direction], but this way. . . . Some people will visit here,
> and they said [they could hear gunshots] . . . in that area [again in Oakwood].
> Because that's still tough over there.

Jen, a storeowner in her midforties, tells me in disbelief that there are
subsidized housing structures in the Oakwood area, as she distinguishes
the emerging cultural and economic logic of Abbot Kinney Boulevard
from the historical trend of Venice as a multiclass neighborhood.

JEN: Also, we're the only beach community that has public housing. Like ghettos.
Ghettos! Literally, like ghettos, low-income housing, what do you call them?

ANDREW: Yeah, you mean the subsidized housing?

JEN: Yeah, but what do you call those, like what do people call those?

ANDREW: Housing projects?

JEN: Thank you—the projects! Do you know, we're the only beach community with projects and they are right over there? I mean that's [pointing toward the Oakwood part of the neighborhood] really close!

Leslie and I discuss the relationship between Abbot Kinney Boulevard and Oakwood. She says, "There's like an invisible wall along Electric [which runs parallel to Abbot Kinney, directly north of the street], and it's pretty astounding." I ask her, "Even in terms of walking on this street now, if you didn't know there was this Oakwood section, would you have a sense that it existed?" She responds simply, "No!" Paul, a storeowner in his late forties, describes the separation in moralistic terms, defining Oakwood as a site of crime and Abbot Kinney as a very safe place to live and work:

> I could be here 'til one in the morning if I'm doing projects, or midnight and I've never even been hassled. . . . The crime is in the area, they call it the hood [referring to Oakwood]. And it's just inner-city gang stuff. It doesn't have anything to do with us. . . . Here's the thing. We leave things outside all the time. We leave that glass table, we leave all the potted stuff and the round metal table. It all stays out and it's still here every morning. We've accidently left wind chimes hanging. Nothing ever happens.

The symbolic and spatial division between purity and danger becomes a social and economic boundary, which shows how power labeling and the neighborhood homology reinforce one another and increase the degree of homogeneity on the street. The coherent retail theme is not just a magnet for upper-income consumers; it also is a symbolic blockade for lower-income residents, informing them of their position as outsiders. Instead of perceiving Abbot Kinney Boulevard as an example of fashionable bohemianism, longtime Oakwood residents see the street and its commerce as a deterrent. Natasha explains,

> They say it's beautiful now, but beauty is in the eye of the beholder. I don't see it as being beautiful. I don't think walking down Abbot Kinney and looking at a three hundred dollar chair that looks like they pulled it out of the alley is beautiful. Because it's been whitewashed or whatever they call that now

[referring to the process that makes the products appear worn out]. I don't think a one thousand dollar dress on Abbot Kinney or what WE used to call Washington Boulevard is what's beautiful. I just don't. I don't get that kind of beauty and I don't want to. I liked how it was before when it really was bohemian. That's the street I liked.

Mildred, an African American woman in her late sixties who has lived in Oakwood since she was a child, understands the popular narrative about this retail space, but she does not regard the types of stores on Abbot Kinney Boulevard as more authentic than corporate formula retail chains in other places. To her, it all signifies "upscale retail." When I ask her if she ever shops on Abbot Kinney Boulevard, she responds,

No, no. It's much too expensive. It's like Melrose, those—well, any area of that style, it's sort of like, well, it's for tourists. Any place that's for tourists is always [priced] higher. People that don't live here don't know anything about Abbot Kinney, so it's like the same option as Beverly Hills and Melrose. We're at the point where we lump a lot of stuff together in our mind, and ya know, it just sells, just like those other ones do. It's just to sell the image.

When I ask Dante Miller, who has lived in Oakwood his entire life, whether he feels like Oakwood is connected to this street, he responds with cynicism:

You should ask the guy that owns Abbot's Pizza [a pizza shop on the boulevard that operates as an integrative space, similar to Abbot's Habit]. He says it all the time—the people on the street don't like it when the homies come around. [Laughing] He calls them homies, but that's because he knows. He employs a lot of kids from the neighborhood in his store. He's the only one who's really still doing that, and he's doing a good thing, and ya know, a lot of people are sayin' it about this street: if you look different, well, let's just say it's not exactly our street [he laughs].

Oakwood residents complain that even the yearly festival, which began in the 1980s, has dramatically changed. According to Cynthia, a third-generation African American woman in her sixties, the festival formerly celebrated the neighborhood's economic and cultural diversity. Now, older residents with lesser economic resources do not readily participate in the events:

You can tell the neighborhood's different now. [At the festival] there was no flavor. There were no blacks or Latinos with booths. Or even just walking around, you could see they didn't go. And the reason is it costs too much now to get a booth. Much more than it used to cost. Who can afford over two hundred dollars for one day? I went to buy my kids some burgers—six dollars! I was like, "Kids, we're not eating here today!"

During the early attempts to "purify" the street through an upscale retail theme, Oakwood's historical relationship to the street and its proximity complicated the process, as the culture of Oakwood readily seeped into Abbot Kinney Boulevard. African Americans historically established institutions on the street; their public culture included this boulevard; and proximity to detrimental violence was noticed and negotiated on a daily basis. Creating a visible separation between the two neighborhoods has redirected the relationship between them into a new neighborhood symbiosis. Abbot Kinney Boulevard, as a mounting symbol of gentrification, redefines the process of neighborhood change in Oakwood. The new public culture of this commercial neighborhood has replaced the gang narrative in the real estate industry's description of Oakwood.

I regularly attended open houses in Oakwood during the mid-2000s to get a picture of the buying/selling process, and brokers repeatedly brought up the relationship between Oakwood and Abbot Kinney Boulevard. For example, I asked one broker about the location of a house in terms of safety, and she told me that although the area has had its problems, especially with the housing projects, "Oakwood is now cleaned up." She continued to talk about the street's proximity to Abbot Kinney Boulevard, which has "all the cute shops and restaurants."[25] In fact, real estate companies now advertise Oakwood property as offering to newcomers a beachfront lifestyle that includes visits to Abbot Kinney Boulevard, quite a change from the gang narrative that overshadowed the area ten years earlier, when real estate agents, without any other selling options, would contact existing white residents to see if they wanted to purchase additional properties that were vacated. A flyer that I received at an open house in 2005, for example, describes an Oakwood home on the market for $1,089,000 in this way:

This incredibly charming 1908 Venice Beach Craftsman cottage is drenched in sunlight. From the private front yard and garden to the Zen-like backyard with gracious Ash tree, patio, and fountain pond, this home offers the perfect respite from city life! Walk to the beach or Abbot Kinney from this spacious 2+1 with skylights, hardwood and tile floors, high wood beamed ceilings, and an updated kitchen with marble counters and updated full bath. Plus there is an unpermitted detached 1+1 guest house with a secret garden.[26]

The middle position is often a precarious position, however. SoHo artists who fabricated loft living conditions in Manhattan were eventually pushed out, as they attracted suburban middle-class residents interested in a new urban lifestyle. The middle-class homeowners in the Canals may not have intended for the neighborhood to become such a high-class locale, but by buying property early on, many of them were great financial beneficiaries of the changes. Shop owners on Abbot Kinney Boulevard sometimes benefit when their stores do well, but many of the owners cannot afford to buy wholesale into the lifestyle that they advertise. Several entrepreneurs live in minute spaces in the back of their stores, and only a very small number who have been on the street for a long time own their commercial spaces or a home in Venice. Increasingly, with upkeep expenses and rapidly rising commercial leases, stores continue to go out of business and those who remain cannot afford to live in the area. Of the seventeen merchants I interviewed in 2004–2005, only seven lived in Venice and four of the seven lived in a tiny space within or behind their own stores. Kim, whose store went out of business within two years after my interview with her, describes the difficulties of finding an affordable place to live in Venice:

> We thought that we would move over here. But we have a good deal on a place over there [in Silver Lake]. . . . I mean there's nothing I would like more to just live in the neighborhood. But it's just prohibitively expensive. But I looked and looked and looked and kept thinking that maybe through word of mouth or something, but it's been two years. . . . I mean it's eighteen hundred dollars for something that's five hundred square feet or something so it's sort of hard with two cats and a dog and two people. So, it's sad.

Amy, finally able to purchase a home, moved out of Venice. "I lived in the store until recently. That was another great thing—in the back in the store, there's an office now. But it was my bedroom. And literally I lived there, since we moved two years ago, and then last year I saved enough money to buy a house, so I bought a house in Inglewood [about eight miles away], not in Venice. But it's great. It's cheap and great. You know, it was affordable and cute." While merchants have contributed to creating the retail theme of upscale cultural consumption on Abbot Kinney Boulevard, they also price themselves out of the market. They further demonstrate how the middle position varies across neighborhoods, depending on how groups become reconfigured over time within and between neighborhoods. In this case, retailers in the middle position have become service workers to a growing wealthy class of people who can afford to make use of the street's expensive amenities.

Conclusion

Many sociologists and urban planners have noted that commerce generates community vitality by drawing people into public spaces.[27] This type of vitality gives rise to a vision of community in which people idealize street-level interaction as integrative and authentic. Yet when discussing the relationship between commerce and community in a changing neighborhood, we must also ask, whose definition of community and whose preferences about commerce are privileged? The construction of a new neighborhood brand on Abbot Kinney Boulevard has had consequences for lower-income and long-term residents who are increasingly excluded from playing a role in defining the neighborhood's future.

Comparing the fashionable bohemia and the bohemian theme park also demonstrates the inherently social dynamics of markets. In both commercial neighborhoods, bohemian themes come to life in distinct ways, depending upon how different groups converge in the same space and build upon fragments of local history to shape their current public cultures. In order to create a neighborhood homology around the fashionable bohemia, individuals and groups with distinct interests have supported one another's goals, as new commerce, new rituals, economic development, and a new critical mass of consumers have parallel, though not perfectly coordinated interests, in shaping a distinct community space around anticorporate and artistic commercial themes.

A neighborhood homology between groups, prices, symbols, and space has emerged over time on Abbot Kinney Boulevard, reproducing social, cultural, and economic exclusivity. The slow construction of a coherent boundary between Abbot Kinney Boulevard and Oakwood has played a profound role in redirecting the symbiosis between these two neighborhoods. The creation of separate neighborhood public cultures—one ambiguous and diverse in Oakwood and the other coherent and exclusive on Abbot Kinney Boulevard—can now be used by the real estate industry to market the residential zone of Oakwood in a new way. The commercial theme has emerged as an autonomous symbol to promote gentrification.

This chapter detailed the processes by which Abbot Kinney Boulevard's public culture was transformed from diverse to exclusive. It also showed how distinct public cultures take form as part of a working social and symbolic order of neighborhoods, influencing the relationships between groups and proximate neighborhood spaces. The next chapter reviews the mechanisms that simultaneously maintain diverse and exclusive public cultures, providing us with a clearer understanding of how stability and change operate at the same time and reconfigure the relationships within and between neighborhoods over time.

CHAPTER SEVEN

The Future of the American City

Venice is a place in extremely high demand. Many different groups are trying to influence its future. Since the 1970s, homelessness, immigration, and gentrification have reshaped this coastal community. Stabilizing forces have also operated as a countermomentum to these changes. The interactions between broader forces and local collective actions facilitate different types of attachments and intergroup configurations in adjacent neighborhoods. People with distinct backgrounds and competing ideals about what it means to live in a neighborhood are forced together, sometimes in ways they could never have predicted and that are not always ideal for everyone involved.[1]

Any analysis of neighborhoods must artificially designate a specific period as a lens into how people become repositioned against others over time. Diverse and exclusive public cultures represent neither origins nor endpoints in this historical evolution; they are not static characteristics of neighborhoods. Instead, stability and change are intertwined social processes that contribute to relationships both within and between neighborhoods. As individuals stabilize their connections to a neighborhood and establish themselves in a place with others, waves of newcomers follow these previous residents and often come to perceive them as the "old-timers." Taking part in this historical process, people are constrained by the conditions set before them. They work within the confines of existing neighborhood infrastructures and competing groups, carrying on certain qualities of neighborhood life while altering and erasing others.

The social and symbolic order of neighborhoods comes into being as a structure of oppositions within and between neighborhoods. Configurations between groups are filtered through oppositional identities built upon race and ethnicity, housing status, political affiliations, and economic and commercial attachments. As neighborhoods change, the reconfigurations of groups, framed through such wide-ranging perspectives and identities, promote common debates about the meaning of order and disorder and raise questions about who should have a say in planning the future of their neighborhoods and who belongs in public spaces.

Gentrifiers maintain advantages in organizing their interests against others. They have greater economic resources and usually higher levels of education than previous residents. Their influence is most noticeable in their ability to link up with city officials, stigmatizing specific categories of people in a process I have called power labeling. Yet they do not easily monopolize control of local resources and instantly redirect neighborhood public cultures in their own images. Just as interventions by gentrifiers are not almighty, so too local resistance against centralized power-holders is not the core impetus of stability.[2] Upholding neighborhood attachments and continuing to influence a neighborhood's public culture involve a range of stabilizing mechanisms, such as the formation of community organizations, formal and informal economies, distinct housing infrastructures, and recognizable cultures of public and private sociality.

People of all different backgrounds collectively mark their turf. When they establish competing visible codes in the same neighborhoods, they create ambiguous and diverse public cultures. Despite demographic decline in Oakwood, African Americans' collective visibility remained pertinent to the neighborhood's identity even as the numbers of Latinos and whites increased, the latter in particular, manufacturing an alternative set of symbolic cues and political interventions. Homeless men and women have long maintained noticeable ties to the Rose Avenue neighborhood, even as gentrifiers establish their own visible culture and organize to push them out. And the Venice Boardwalk's Free Speech Zone has proved a resilient economic ecology for a wide range of people— from Latino and Asian immigrants to the homeless and the un- and underemployed—despite four decades of surrounding economic changes and ongoing political attempts to regulate this space.

Those occupying Venice's more exclusive settings also maintain differences between them. In such cases, distinctions operate like a division of labor. Complementary positions establish a cohesive public culture that demarcates the inside of these neighborhoods from their surroundings. Neighborhood homologies have emerged in the Canals and on Abbot Kinney Boulevard between groups, styles, and spaces. Although not all newcomers have the same degree of economic resources, their approaches to politics and their taken-for-granted assumptions about everyday life complement one another. The influx of middle-class residents into the Canals introduced a cultural and political order that altered the look and feel of the neighborhood. It set in motion a new configuration between two sets of property owners—middle-class homeowners and speculative developers—that pushed aside previous countercultural organizations, diverse rental options, and the overall bohemian habitat. Complementary interests also accumulated and crystallized as a new commercial theme on Abbot Kinney Boulevard: a new merchants association, savvy real estate brokers, new developers, creative entrepreneurs, and a growing supply of upscale clientele blended together into the street's fashionable bohemianism, taking distance from its former identity as a site of cross-cultural contact.

The boundaries between diverse and exclusive neighborhoods are not walled-off fortresses that forbid entrance by any specific group. The boundaries are permeable, which requires a more complex understanding of how a community like Venice maintains divisions between neighborhoods. People push and pull public cultures into action when they deem it necessary to reinforce an exclusive or diverse look and feel. A great deal of work goes into creating and maintaining these neighborhood divisions, but once a public culture hardens, it appears as a natural and taken-for-granted reality with its own carrying potential that people reproduce in relationship to their surroundings. People of many different backgrounds consistently find ways to blend into more diverse settings, in some circumstances adapting to new regulations, which allows them to continue to blur the boundaries between insider and outsider over time. In contrast, neighborhood homologies of more exclusive locales make it easier to decipher insiders from outsiders. People on both sides of the dividing line become convinced that certain types of people belong while others do not. Even without a physical barrier separating these neighborhoods, some groups learn to stay away. They recognize that the cohesive public culture means that the potential to enforce the boundaries is always present. Analyzing the social and symbolic order of these five adjacent neighborhoods in Venice calls attention to how public cultures are created, stabilized, and transformed. While Venice provides us with a focused lens into how macro- and microprocesses interact on

the ground, this approach has wider implications for the study of neighborhoods and urban life.

Rethinking Public Cultures

An ecological and relational perspective of neighborhood stability and
change has allowed us to examine how five adjacent neighborhoods in
Venice developed distinct identities through common processes. Social
interactions and collective organizations have compressed demographic
and political-economic forces into distinct inter- and intragroup configurations, giving rise to either diverse or exclusive neighborhood public
cultures. Yet this approach is neither particular to Venice nor to Los Angeles more generally. It can also help us to understand similar types of
processes within and across various cities and metropolitan regions. Local configurations between groups are dependent upon how macro- and
microprocesses converge in specific times and places, as oppositions and
associations take hold and become filtered through a wide range of perspectives and produce an array of neighborhood experiences and public
cultures both within cities and between them.

Because of regional and state differences among Mexicans and national differences among Central Americans and Asians, Los Angeles is
a city with various types of inter- and intragroup configurations, sometimes creating conflicts and separations, and other times giving rise to
coalitions and organizations, including pan-ethnic associations, such
as Chicano, Latino, and Asian collective identities.[3] Configurations of
racial and ethnic groups can differ significantly in other Latinized cities. In Miami, combinations of Cubans, Nicaraguans, Haitians, African
Americans, and whites create new political and economic affiliations,
including Latino enclaves where Cubans have a great deal of influence.[4]
The broad mix of immigrants into New York City from practically every corner of the earth—South America, Central America, the Caribbean, Europe, Africa, and Asia—position themselves in relation to more
established locals, including ethnic whites, Puerto Ricans, and African
Americans.[5] And the rise of new immigrant destinations in the southern United States has forced social scientists to reconsider how Latinos
fit into a region with historically tense divisions between African Americans and whites.[6]

Commercial adaptations and economic presentations are central to the demarcation of neighborhood public cultures. Ethnic economies are among the most distinguishing forces in urban life. European immigrants, particularly those of Jewish, Italian, Irish, and Polish descent, long played a role in marking neighborhoods through ethnic economies in Chicago, Philadelphia, Boston, and New York. Newer ethnic groups have moved in alongside these older ones, in many cases spreading out and overtaking these areas, as in the case of the slow and steady spatial expansion of Chinatown into what was once Little Italy on New York's Lower East Side. Still, ethnic economies are often central to maintaining neighborhood public cultures long after the bulk of a particular ethnic group has moved out. The prevailing local place identity does not necessarily reflect its demographic majority.[7] For example, L.A.'s Koreatown maintains its public culture as a Korean shopping district despite the fact that the residential surroundings are mostly made up of Latinos.

The layering of new groups onto the urban map complicates local relationships between ethnic identity and neighborhood differentiation. Chinatowns were once the only recognizable Asian neighborhood public culture in cities, but now Koreatowns, Little Indias, and Little Saigons also exist. It is not simply Asian ethnic economies that are diffusing into and dividing neighborhoods. Newcomers consistently move in, establish collective markers, and reshape the relationships between public spaces and groups. West Indians have constructed visible ties to multiple Brooklyn neighborhoods, manufacturing distinctions between native and foreign-born black residents as well as between various racial and ethnic groups. Ethiopians have organized a local identity on a strip of L.A.'s Fairfax Avenue and maintain a concentration of establishments on Washington, D.C.'s Eighteenth and U Streets. Vietnamese and Mexican economies quickly challenge the traditional Italian section of South Philadelphia. Mexicans, as the largest immigrant group in the United States, have slowly redefined neighborhoods throughout the nation, and their distinct regional derivations become more visible as time passes. In Los Angeles, it is not unusual for entrepreneurs to promote the origins of their Mexican cuisine from Puebla, Baja, the Gulf and Pacific Coasts, or Oaxaca.

The processes and variations of gentrification are also rapidly changing. Prior to the 1990s, gentrifiers largely moved into white neighborhoods. In recent decades, as crime rates decreased in many cities across the nation and housing prices soared beyond the reach of upper-middle-class professionals in many urban neighborhoods, white gentrifiers have started to move into black and Latino neighborhoods. If we revisit the Venice case, the Canals were always a mostly white neighborhood and, not surprisingly, Venice's earliest gentrifiers followed this trend, moving into the Canals before making an attempt to buy and build houses in Oakwood. With its well-established black community, Oakwood remained a noticeable residential holdout in terms of gentrification for decades, likely because of its distinct racial-ethnic composition and comparatively higher crime rates, which included periods of intense and deadly gang violence between black and Latino gangs.

Formerly, when African Americans moved into urban neighborhoods, established whites opposed their influx and moved out en masse. In recent years, some places have witnessed a reverse process, with whites moving into black neighborhoods. The Oakwood story is a case of historical white flight followed by a contemporary period of white return, but it is complicated by the fact that Latinos moved into Oakwood between these transformations, part of an increasingly common American urban story that suggests that whites might be more willing to move near Latinos before they move next to African Americans. Yet not all gentrification in all places involves the influx of white residents. Within all racial and ethnic categories, there are significant socioeconomic differences,[8] witnessed by the growing black middle class, a more recently visible Latino middle class, as well as a substantial number of middle- and upper-income Asians.[9] In some sections of New York's Harlem and Chicago's South Side, two of the most famous historic black communities in the United States, the established lower-income black residents encounter an influx of wealthier black people or combinations of both white and black newcomers. The Nuyorican and white middle classes are similarly reshaping the composition of the longtime, lower-income Puerto Rican neighborhood of East Harlem.[10]

Commercial changes are often the most visible clue that gentrification is on the horizon. However, it is a mistake to think that markets are predictable and gentrification follows some perfect economic order. Venice demonstrates the malleability of the marketplace and the variable ways in which people take into account historical conditions. Stabilizing forces profoundly influence how people economically adapt to their surroundings, working within the confines of existing conditions while simultaneously transforming their neighborhoods. The rise of competing bohemian commercial neighborhoods in Venice within direct walking distance from one another demonstrates the continuing influence of stabilizing forces and individual and group adaptations in the process of neighborhood change. In some neighborhoods, people of distinct socioeconomic backgrounds engage the same historical themes to produce widely different public cultures: a more integrative bohemian theme park in one place and a more exclusive fashionable bohemian locale in another. In other neighborhoods, people of the same backgrounds engage different historical themes, becoming configured in ways that produce different group identities. Gentrification becomes filtered through the lenses of race and ethnicity, housed and homelessness, conventional and bohemian cultures, informal and formal economies, among other wide-ranging oppositions. The social and symbolic order of neighborhoods—the configurations within and between spaces—crystallizes group identities and public cultures, even though the classifications of people and places are not permanent or all encompassing.[11]

The bohemian theme is so powerful in Venice that many people excluded from the labor market construct economic practices related to arts, crafts, music, and performance in order to help secure neighborhood attachments. At the same time that gentrification takes place, homelessness has become entangled in the web of local relationships and cultural narratives. Such economic adaptations among marginalized groups are commonplace in cities. Those excluded from the labor market for any number of reasons—medical problems, drug and alcohol abuse, undocumented citizenship status, lack of stable address, criminal records, neighborhood isolation, and simply high rates of unemployment—are forced to work within the confines of their surroundings, learning about and building upon particular conditions of the locale. In some cities where demand is extremely high, such as in Los Angeles, New York, and San Francisco, homelessness and gentrification often become positioned in close proximity. Nonetheless, homeless people vary their cultural performances and methods of survival. Some homeless in San Francisco become sex workers and panhandlers, while others become homeless recyclers, depending upon their racial-ethnic backgrounds, where they hang out, and with whom they associate.[12] Some of New York's homeless become book and magazine vendors in the West Village, as others build upon the economic infrastructure in other ways.[13] Likewise, some of L.A.'s homeless become artists and carnival performers on the Venice Boardwalk, while others figure out additional means of survival, including taking part in very complex and abusive relationships in Venice, Santa Monica, Hollywood, and especially in downtown skid row, the largest concentration of homeless men and women in the nation. In all of these cases, the homeless have to manage the tensions of an uncertain economy, law enforcement attempts to regulate their public activities, and daily battles ensuing from intense hierarchical relationships among the homeless themselves.

As we think about how macrotransformations of metropolitan regions become compressed into neighborhood public cultures, we cannot overlook major disparities within and between cities when it comes to the simultaneous processes of gentrification, suburbanization, and continuing neighborhood isolation. While some cities, like New York, Boston, and Washington, D.C., slowly rebuilt their economies after periods of decline and became hot spots of gentrification,[14] other cities like Philadelphia, Detroit, Newark, and Hartford have vastly different political-economic trajectories, with relatively weaker economic centers and wealthier peripheries. Some places with extremely low demand continue to experience deteriorating housing infrastructures, low property values, abandoned factories and warehouses, and spatial isolation as defining characteristics of their public cultures.[15] In such cases, people isolated from mainstream economic opportunities develop informal adaptations that do not confront local businesses, per se, such as in L.A.'s Venice and New York's West Village; they create relationships with other residents and police officers that manage and reproduce their isolation.[16] Just as inter- and intragroup configurations arise in cities and suburbs in ways that are not always planned, other times people become spatially separated, the causes of which are invisible to them in their daily lives.

The aim of this ecological and relational approach is to analyze how associations, attachments, and social and physical distances come about and change in urban spaces. Connections and oppositions between and within racial and ethnic groups, the housed and the homeless, and upper-, middle-, and lower-income urban dwellers are in motion and constant reconfiguration over time. Understanding the macro- and micro-contexts in which complementary and competing positions come into existence is central to this discussion of neighborhood public cultures. While this historical and ethnographic approach has implications for cities far and near, I also recognize that Venice is a certain type of place in high demand where competitions over space and over the right to influence its future are commonplace. I would like to once again return to this topic. Narratives about urban diversity and urban order have become intertwined in such places at the same time that they function as conflicting philosophies. Making sense of this paradox is central to understanding the future of Los Angeles, and potentially, other cities like it.

The Paradox of Diversity and Order

Many cities in the United States are facing new challenges about the possibility of making urban neighborhoods habitable for the upper classes while maintaining racial, ethnic, and socioeconomic diversity. Interest in urban diversity is not anything new. For over a century, social scientists and other commentators have placed a great deal of importance on the ideal of achieving urban diversity. Many theorists touted its significance in the United States as a new characteristic of early twentieth-century modernity, distinguishing the social and economic organization of cities from more homogeneous, rural surroundings.[17] Decades later, Jane Jacobs emerged as the most famous proponent of planning for diversity, pushing for an assortment of building sizes, mixed residential and commercial uses on the same city blocks, and social and economic diversity on sidewalks and in other public spaces. It has become commonplace to integrate and expand Jacobs's basic insights. Richard Florida has argued that politicians who want to improve their cities' economies need to advocate for assorted street uses and cultural tolerance, because the central innovators in the postindustrial economy find diversity experientially rewarding.

Social scientists have also pointed out a new demographic trend toward long-term diversity in urban neighborhoods, where people of different racial, ethnic, and socioeconomic backgrounds live side by side for decades.[18] We now know from demographers that there are many places to do detailed ethnographic research on this topic. Closer observations on the ground will help us to better address a key question: is shared space the same thing as neighborhood integration?[19] Building from my experiences and observations in Venice, I argue that the proximity of diversity does not necessitate that people come together across their differences when it comes to defining the uses of public spaces and shaping the future of their neighborhoods. Figuring out when they do and when they do not, and particularly how conflict and community change over time, is central to understanding the future of our neighborhoods and cities.

It is true that some people move into neighborhoods and break down pressing historical barriers of race and class. Some of them promote ideologies about resolving inequalities, although most make little effort to mitigate them in their daily lives. As part of a cumulative process, they alter the compositions of neighborhoods and give rise to competing stabilizing forces. Although gentrifiers do not inevitably organize to exclude others, they share cultural practices, including a penchant for privacy, devotion to their professional circles and career aspirations, and a set of assumptions about neighborhood quality of life, all of which contribute—sometimes intentionally and other times unintentionally—to building a visible challenge to neighborhood public cultures.

Newcomers, even sociologically minded newcomers like myself, cannot predict the future of their neighborhoods when they first move in. Changes involve daily negotiations with others, often producing unforeseen and unintended results such as when middle-class people set the stage for wealthier residents who have the resources to alter their neighborhoods in unimaginable ways. As individuals navigate their daily lives, they become absorbed by the existing physical, cultural, and social conditions, making it difficult to recognize the ongoing and incremental changes in which they take part. Decades later, many residents of Venice still do not realize that they played a role in the social, economic, and cultural groundswell that reconfigured the relationships between groups, because their neighborhoods did not change in the ways they thought or hoped that they would. In some cases, such as in the neighborhood of the Canals, some have come to view themselves, and are viewed by others, as old-timers amidst a wealthier set of newcomers. The meanings that people attribute to the categories *newcomer* and *old-timer* shift as groups become reconfigured and neighborhood public cultures change. We need more observers on the ground to see how these reconfigurations within and between groups and neighborhoods come about, what local mechanisms help individuals break down barriers and interact in public spaces, but furthermore, we need to better understand how collective positions and public cultures crystallize, enabling and/or preventing long-term relationships across these very differences.

Urbanites generally give lip service to their search for diversity, but when they see what it means to share spaces—especially with individuals of different socioeconomic backgrounds—they become more cautious and critical. Along with the simultaneous expansion of gentrification, homelessness, and immigration since the 1970s, we have witnessed a new paradoxical relationship between the celebration of cultural diversity and a major investment in an overpowering definition of quality of life that matches the conventions of the middle and, increasingly, upper classes. Although these narratives coexist, maintaining both at the same time in specific neighborhoods, let alone developing harmony between them, is very difficult. The celebration of cultural diversity tends to focus on ethnicity and sexuality without reference to socioeconomic distinctions; meanwhile, class-based definitions of aesthetics, methods of political organizing, and uses of public spaces shape a new quality of life agenda.

Newcomers to Venice do have legitimate anxieties: homeless men and women defecating on lawns and back alleys is a nuisance; exhaust from old RVs is environmentally hazardous and toxic for residents to breathe; amplified noise on the boardwalk is distracting to residents trying to read, write, watch television, meditate, or simply have conversations in their own apartments and houses; competition from the boardwalk's informal economy is unfair to rent-paying business owners; and drug dealing, graffiti, gang violence, and encounters with mentally ill and drug-addicted individuals on street corners, parks, and alleyways lead to emotional distress about personal safety and real risks for people walking around their neighborhoods. Upper-, middle-, and lower-income inhabitants alike have the right to feel secure in their neighborhoods. The fact that some are wealthier than others and live and work in places near people who are down and out does not excuse others' disregard for their property and personal safety, even if their methods for solving local problems differ from previous generations of residents.

In an attempt to counter powerful political narratives about creating urban order, scholars of urban studies have often denounced gentrification and any appearance of upper-income commercial amenities and housing development as a sign of oppression, a strategic plot of the changing circuits of economic capital, or even further, a direct cause of the urban crisis of increasing inequalities. The sources of these drastic inequalities are not the specific gentrifiers moving into neighborhoods, planting flowers around their homes, remodeling their kitchens, and shopping at Pottery Barn (or a vintage furniture store on Abbot Kinney Boulevard). It is not the middle-class retailers or restaurateurs opening up small shops or trendy cafés, trying to make a living by supporting craftsmen and family farms. The sources of this crisis are the macropolicies that reproduce inequalities, complicating life on the ground when diversity does actually take form in a specific place. The search for diversity has become pitted against the search for order.

The pervasive quality of life agenda for cities is a political mirage. It leads people to believe that their opposition to other locals can solve urban problems. It cannot. With the decline of federal, state, and city resources, a growing gap between the rich and the poor, and a new era of diversity in propinquity, city leaders now in office rely upon quick-hit solutions, prioritizing short-term methods of "nuisance control" instead of developing complex long-term agendas. Together, these factors reinforce taken-for-granted assumptions about the causes of neighborhood problems, blaming opposing sides, and reproducing a cycle of Band-Aid measures that never solve key problems. In Venice alone, the homeless are still on the streets; unfair competition still dominates the economic culture of the boardwalk; many remain excluded from the labor market; individuals still join gangs; and gentrifiers continue to stigmatize and displace lower-income groups at the same time that they face recurring dangers in their own daily lives. These processes have remained constant for over four decades.

In today's diverse neighborhoods, it is not enough for locals to say, "You stay in your space and we'll stay in ours," that is, to establish what Suttles called "ordered segmentation," the negotiations over space that manage interactions between distinct groups and maintain separations and peace between them.[20] When people of different racial, ethnic, and socioeconomic backgrounds comingle in the same neighborhoods and public spaces, recurring transgressions lead to overly general perceptions of individuals as part of a problem population. People see how proximity to differences affects their own lives. It is important to understand how city officials and their private partners define "problems" under such conditions and develop plans to manage them. What we see in Venice is that official methods for dealing with neighborhood problems legitimate the stigmatization of entire populations through homeless sweeps, nuisance abatement programs, code violation enforcement, community police advisory boards, new municipal codes, neighborhood quality of life courts, video surveillance, neighborhood watch movements, mobile police units, and other similar avenues of monitoring entire categories of people.

Ignoring long-term solutions and instead focusing on the immediacy of everyday troubles have generated new coalitions between specific residential groups and city officials to tackle their perceptions of disorder, relying on false assumptions that distinct neighborhood groups have fundamentally different goals. Interestingly, when it comes to neighborhood quality of life, rich and poor, black, Latino, and white, citizens and noncitizens, and housed and homeless alike are generally on the same side in principle, even if they use different methods to address their concerns. Very few people want poverty in their neighborhoods, especially those who live in poverty. Almost everyone wants personal safety for themselves and their families, including most of the homeless living on the streets. We have to be careful about holding any population, from gentrifiers to the homeless, generally responsible for today's urban ills.

City leaders, social service agencies, and law enforcement officials are also caught in the middle of these historical changes, trying to work within the confines of deepening economic and political constraints. Los Angeles City Council members are continuously searching for ways to negotiate the relationships between the convoluted and underresourced bureaucracy and the demands of their constituents, sometimes betraying the very principles to which people hold them. Former councilwoman Ruth Galanter and current councilman Bill Rosendahl, both liberal in their political ideologies and backgrounds, cannot simply oppose gentrification at every turn. While in office, they have to compromise, think about the simultaneous processes of stability and change, and mitigate the potentials of danger facing people of all political persuasions and economic backgrounds in their daily lives. This complexity leads to amazing contradictions in their decision-making processes.

Ruth Galanter is one of the strongest environmental advocates in California coastal history. She helped implement and enforce the California Coastal Act and has remained to this day a strong proponent of equal access to the coast, which includes supporting the rights of homeless people living in vehicles to park on the streets of Venice. At the same time, as a Los Angeles city councilwoman, Galanter backed a gang injunction and code enforcement program in Oakwood, key interventions in the middle-class politics of urban order. Likewise, Bill Rosendahl, a former social worker, has publicly celebrated the work of the St. Joseph Center, a major homeless service organization in Venice, and he has advocated for new housing programs, at the same time that he supports overnight parking districts and height restrictions on vehicles, both aimed to diminish the number of people living in and parking their RVs on the streets of Venice. He sees the need for more services at the same time that he understands that people have legitimate safety concerns.

When the blame game shifts from populations and politicians toward the local organizations that manage neighborhood problems, people focus on social service agencies and law enforcement officials, a highly problematic jump in our assumptions about the causes and solutions of "urban disorder." These organizations succeed at what they are set up to do; they are only equipped to resolve immediate and individual situations rather than establish long-term plans. Once again, responsibility for urban problems falls into the hands of individuals on the front lines, the visible mediators in a much larger problem that extends well beyond immediate neighborhood contexts. Social service agencies, now with complex public/private funding partnerships, were set up to protect the poor. Yet many homeowners living near these agencies blame them for maintaining the local attachments of people they label disorderly, most commonly homeless men and women. Likewise, law enforcement agents have adapted to the shifting demographic composition, as institutionalized protectors of middle- and upper-class quality of life. However, anti-poverty activists and homeless advocates criticize them for criminalizing entire populations.

These organizations address individual transgressions as they erupt, which cannot prevent the historical reproduction of social and economic problems over time, as such problems return days, weeks, or months after each incident. These organizations certainly offer some evidence of their successes, which allows for continued investment into their agendas. Social services celebrate when individuals break out of poverty, calling attention to their plans to help ten, twenty, or even one hundred people get off the streets. Specific homeless individuals find their ways into new jobs and new housing; some undocumented immigrants find necessary health care services for their children; and several gang members escape their affiliations with a turbulent group identity. We should not discount the importance of helping individuals achieve their goals and improve their health and safety when in need, but we should be wary of calling these interventions long-term solutions to historical problems. As individuals become representative examples of successful interventions, the pervasive collective dilemma of urban poverty continues, whether it takes place in Venice or somewhere else in the city.

Law enforcement agents operate in the reverse. Forced into neighborhood quality of life management over the last four decades, they are trained in preventing crimes, not in addressing and solving the conditions of poverty and mental health. They have their own constraints. They remove specific individuals causing residential problems, hoping that each dislocation improves the neighborhood quality of life in some way. Identifying neighborhood dislocation of specific men and women as a solution to neighborhood disorder is troubling. Police officers break down houses, for one. Looking for criminals, they destroy property and worsen already unstable conditions for certain residents with complicated family dynamics and historical circumstances. These methods underpin long-standing racial divisions and distrust without an eye toward long-term solutions. Additionally, scrutinizing urban spaces for homeless men and women breaking municipal codes, such as sleeping in undesignated spaces, leads individuals to lose modest possessions and pushes them further away from any possibility to move out of homelessness.

The management of neighborhood oppositions is intertwined with political-economic and spatial inequalities, sometimes shifting people around the urban landscape, such that one neighborhood's solution can become another neighborhood's problem. These hidden power dynamics are severely underexplored. Decades ago, interest groups working to clean up the Canals succeeded at pushing out people living and sleeping in empty lots. More recently, some homeowners in the Canals have found ways to limit public parking in their own neighborhood, demarcating public alleyways as private driveways. The limited parking in the Canals neighborhood means that residents never have to face concerns about the high volume of RVs on their streets. Yet both street homelessness and mobile homelessness remain heavily concentrated in the neighborhood of Rose Avenue. While conflicts between housed and homeless or between homeowners and social service agencies are commonplace in the Rose Avenue neighborhood, conflicts between residents of the Canals and residents of Rose Avenue do not exist. Furthermore, residents of other coastal communities like Santa Monica and Pacific Palisades have addressed their RV parking problems by implementing overnight parking restrictions without permission of the California Coastal Commission. Venice was left behind as the only coastal location without regulations to absorb hundreds of people sleeping in their vehicles.

We tend to describe inequalities by their most visible manifestations: they appear to us as conflicts within neighborhoods between the housed and the homeless, rent-free vendors and rent-paying storeown-

ers, or old-timers and newcomers. But unequal conditions within and between neighborhoods and communities—both proximate and distant—
also shape public cultures. We need to better understand how we, as
individuals, become absorbed by our immediate surroundings, adapt to
the conditions that appear in front of us, and overlook the wide-reaching
webs of associations and inequalities that influence our own daily lives.

Venice's public appeal may not stem from its distinctiveness. In an
exaggerated way, Venice represents universal themes about urban life.
Its diverse composition, neighborhood divisions, and passionate political
contestations enable processes of self-discovery, ingenuity in establishing and maintaining attachments to places, and various filters through
which neighborhood conflicts and public cultures come about. History
impinges on the present, but people are also actively carving out spaces
where they belong amidst the backdrop of political regulations, transgressions on the street, and intergroup conflicts in neighborhoods. Tensions between exclusivity and diversity in close proximity are just the
latest incarnation in a long string of oppositions about the right to use
public spaces, mark territories, and influence the future direction of public culture. Such tensions, like the historical evolution of neighborhoods
and cities themselves, are without concrete endpoints. Rather, the search
for stability in the context of an ever-changing city is itself central to establishing a meaningful urban experience.

Notes

Preface

1. In this respect, I follow some classic examples (recent and not so recent), such as Whyte (1943); Gans (1967); Kornblum (1974); and Bourgois (1996).

2. See Kusenbach's (2003) account of the "go-along" as an ethnographic tool in neighborhoods.

Introduction

1. Ellen (2000) finds that almost one-fifth of neighborhoods in the United States were racially mixed in 1990, and three-quarters of the neighborhoods that were racially mixed in 1980 remained that way in 1990, revealing a stable pattern of diversity rather than rapid succession. Also see Logan and Zhang (2010) who call attention to two simultaneous patterns, a new ethnic diversity in "global neighborhoods" coupled with the continued segregation of African Americans. Others point to neighborhood diversity in terms of culture, sexuality, and creative lifestyles. Florida (2002) defines tolerant cities by calculating correlations between bohemian and gay populations and the postindustrial "creative economy." However, this approach to diversity raises unanswered questions about the distinctions between lifestyle diversity and socioeconomic diversity, given that the gay population is notable in its high household median income. New investigations of urban diversity need to raise questions about the competing influences of identity politics (diversity in cultures and sexuality) and class politics (economic diversity). In recent years, scholars have complicated our understandings of the intentions of gentrifiers (Caulfield 2004; Brown-Saracino 2010), many of whom seek out some form of diversity. It is extremely important to highlight new social patterns and complicate any specific group identity as these authors have

done, but we also need to better understand how the distinctions between cultural variations and socioeconomic positions take form, as well as to make sense of the historical development of the relationships between them.

2. We are used to hearing about gangs marking turf to defend territories from outsiders (e.g., Thrasher 1927; Suttles 1968; Venkatesh 2000). We also commonly hear about "growth machine" alliances between developers and politicians (Logan and Molotch 1987) who aim to reinvent places through branding (Greenberg 2008), theming (Gottdiener 1997; Sorkin 1992; Zukin 1991), or by constructing symbolic economies that intertwine "cultural symbols and entrepreneurial capital" (Zukin 1995). It is not only gangs and power alliances that mark spaces. A wide variety of groups stabilize attachments to and in turn influence neighborhood spaces, which often leads to conflicts over them. The interest in the character of places in American sociology dates back to early Chicago School accounts of concentric circles, community areas, and distinct urban zones (Park, Burgess, McKenzie 1925). Yet Burgess's famous definition of Chicago community areas demonstrates an effort to impose labels on places, contradicting the Chicago School's conceptual emphasis on internal attributes. According to Venkatesh (2001, 276–277), Burgess's effort to "prescribe" stable community areas in Chicago was at odds with his sociological efforts to "describe" the "uncertainty, fluidity, and discordance" in the city's settlement patterns. Nonetheless, many of these "symbolic communities" have continued to influence how residents build their mental maps of territories in the city (Hunter 1974). This distinction between place identity and the fluctuation of internal characteristics raises key points about the ongoing relationships between stability and change and the ways that people come to understand what makes any given neighborhood distinct from its surroundings. Neighborhood distinctions emerge through everyday struggles over the definition of space. While there are observable qualities that allow people to filter their perceptions through a storied lens (Firey 1945; Lynch 1960; Strauss 1976; Suttles 1984; Pattillo-McCoy 1999; Molotch et al. 2000), oppositions within and between spaces harden these identities as practical categories.

3. The tour provides an account of what one might potentially see. Such an exercise presents interesting methodological challenges. As an ethnographer, I approach the subject matter based on what I have seen or heard. I observed firsthand each of these circumstances as recurring interaction patterns, including specific types of individuals and groups described in the account. I then compiled them into a cohesive walk around even though the accounts were from fragmented moments, weaving together events and encounters at different times and days to give the reader a sense of what they might encounter.

4. Quotation cited in Bulmer (1984, 97).

5. Park (1952, 47).

6. Urban ethnographers tend to describe diversity as moments of contact

rather than as stable components of everyday life. Suttles's (1968) classic account of ordered segmentation in Chicago's Addams area paints such a portrait, but we also see more recent accounts, such as Anderson's (2011) "cosmopolitan canopy," about the spaces of the city where differences appear in public settings, allowing people to conduct "folk ethnography" of differences only to return to more homogeneous or segregated residential settings. There are certainly particular cities and types of neighborhoods where diversity rarely takes hold as part of everyday life. However, Venice presents a case, increasingly common in many American cities, where the relationship between diversity and exclusivity is in constant tension. Diversity, in this case, is not merely built upon moments of contact at the edges, but exists as a central component of daily interaction.

7. Zukin's ([1982] 1989) classic account of gentrification in New York is among the first to think through the multidimensional forces behind urban change, looking at how state interventions, cultural forces, and population movements intersect. Also see Schwirian's (1983) review where he identifies different forces of change and raises the potential for a new agenda in urban sociology. Recent sociological accounts have finally followed this lead, investigating multidimensionality in a variety of contexts. Halle (2003) shows multiple population flows in New York and Los Angeles, and Pattillo (2007) locates the simultaneous processes of gentrification and low-income housing construction in a lower-income black neighborhood of Chicago. Hyra (2008) looks across cities—Chicago and New York—to trace out the complex causes of neighborhood change. Katz (2010) and Katz et al. (unpublished manuscript) are detailing multiple processes in Hollywood to highlight different types of neighborhoods emerging across the Los Angeles landscape. Locating simultaneous population movements, such as immigration and gentrification, could be a key difference between doing research in cities like New York, Los Angeles, San Francisco, Boston, and Washington, D.C.—places now deemed in "high demand," where population growth and multiple industries have emerged over the last several decades—versus conducting research in Philadelphia, Newark, Detroit, or Hartford, where the population continuously declined or stagnated over several decades and where employment options are much more constrained by limited industry. I thank Philippe Bourgois for pointing this out.

8. Ruth Glass (1964) coined the term *gentrification*, referring to a movement of the middle class from the suburbs into the central city. More recently, the idea of gentrification as a return to the city movement by the middle and upper classes has become increasingly obsolete. Individuals often move between neighborhoods within the same city. There are ongoing ecological interconnections between places in close proximity, changing the dynamics of how gentrification operates in many of today's cities and changing the relationships between exclusivity and diversity. Historically, wealthier whites moved into lower-income white places, following artists and students into neighborhoods (Simpson 1981;

Zukin [1982] 1989; Abu-Lughod 1994). Yet, for the first time in history, white and black middle and upper classes are moving into lower-income black neighborhoods, especially in New York (Jackson Jr. 2001; Taylor 2002; Freeman 2006; Hyra 2008), but also in Chicago (Pattillo 2007; Hyra 2008), raising questions about the future meaning of diversity in cities and communities where there is an increasing demand for property.

9. I refer to the city of Los Angeles as "prismatic" (Bobo et al. 2002) rather than paradigmatic. Dear (2001, 2002) identified a loosely connected group of mostly geographers as the L.A. School, a response to the classic Chicago School, claiming that Los Angeles serves as a new model of urban growth in the twenty-first century. Many have criticized his claim that L.A. is paradigmatic on two basic counts. First, critics reject the idea that one place can serve as a paradigm that drives urban growth in other places. Brenner (2003) argues that this approach draws upon stereotypes to express superiority of one place over another without adopting objective measurements to understand their similarities and differences. Gottdiener (2002) notes that a focus on urban processes instead of superlative claims about particular regions shows that others have already found similar phenomena in different cities. Halle's (2003) edited volume adopts objective measurements to compare New York and Los Angeles on many different counts, finding that these cities with great geographic distance and even more elaborate stereotypes between them often converge in demographic, cultural, and political patterns. Secondly, the L.A. School approach contrasts Los Angeles as a model of the twenty-first-century city with Chicago as a model of the twentieth-century city by using Burgess's (1925) spatial model of concentric circles. Many have pointed out that Burgess's geographic model was imprecise. Hoyt's (1939) "sector analysis" and Harris and Ullman's (1945) "multiple nuclei model" are just two of the earliest examples of urban planning. But maybe more important, it misrepresents the intellectual endeavor of what sociologists and anthropologists have come to identify as the Chicago School. It replaces the wide variety of grounded investigations with only the geographic component and content. Specific cities have particularities in geography and demographics, but Park (1925) and his collaborators also developed complex approaches to examining place-making, community differentiation, and subcultural formation and transition, processes certainly relevant to most cities, including Los Angeles. See Hannerz (1980) and Abbott (2002).

10. Whereas Chicago School urban ethnographers tend to interpret diversity as the differentiation of homogeneous spaces, urban scholars focusing on power and culture tend to adopt an inverse perspective about the increasing homogenization of diverse spaces. Important examples by Davis ([1990] 1992, [1998] 1999) in Los Angeles and Zukin (2010, 1995, 1991, [1982] 1989) and Mele (2000) in New York look at how gentrification, corporate commerce, media images, architectural designs, and the privatization of public spaces organize and influence the

visible wealth of cities by constructing new high-class symbols and eradicating the presence of urban diversity. Smith (1996) explicitly argues that gentrification rids neighborhoods of their cultural significance and social histories through dislocation and redevelopment across the globe. He writes, "[If] the past is not entirely demolished it is at least reinvented—its class and race contours rubbed smooth—in the refurbishment of a palatable past." Such accounts locate gentrification and class power as a uniform economic force, building upon an assumption about markets as perfect in their relationship between process and outcome. While gentrification can certainly dislocate people and make neighborhoods more homogeneous over time, it is difficult to capture how and why this takes place and to understand why it happens more dramatically and quickly in some places than others. Urban markets are unpredictable, which forces us to take into account both the particularity of places and their relationships to large-scale historical events. The recent housing crisis is simply the most visible widespread marker of this unpredictability. Even without a housing crisis, sometimes old homeowners sell their property at the same time that some—usually renters—are forced out. These are very different causes of population movement. Studying these changes requires a complex set of longitudinal research methods to trace individual and collective processes over time.

11. Elias and Scotson (1965). The relationship between "established and outsiders" is part of a larger project by Elias to understand how psychogenetic and sociogenetic processes unfold together, absorbing and bridging both macro- and microprocesses through changing configurations at particular times and places.

12. According to Molotch, Freudenburg, and Paulsen (2000, 816, 793), urban sociologists have given too little thought to the mechanisms that govern the coherence and continuity of place character, that is, the perception of a place's features that distinguishes it from other places. In their comparative study of Santa Barbara and Ventura, two proximate Southern California coastal cities with similar geographies and climates, they describe how early collective responses to powerful forces—Ventura embraced the role of big oil and Santa Barbara limited its influence—set in place local conditions in each city that people have continued to draw upon, reinforcing and reproducing divergent place identities over time. To explore how "place differences develop and persist," they examine how "physical and social elements cohere" at particular times and places, giving rise to the perception of local character, and they also show how people have actively drawn upon the "existing conditions" of a place, creating continuity in each city's character over time.

13. Competing and complementary configurations are distinct social forms. Attention to social forms builds from Simmel ([1908] 1959), and more recently Vaughan (2004) and Zerubavel (2007). They argue that a key approach to developing theory is to locate the form across cases, that is, to analyze the general patterns of social life, what Vaughan identifies as "analogous circumstances"

between different levels of analysis or what Zerubavel calls the "sociohistorical configurations as mere instantiations of such patterns." Despite employing thick descriptions in each of the following chapters to display complex historical narratives about the construction of neighborhood attachments and conflicts, this formal approach moves each of these seemingly different cases in terms of content beyond a grounded theoretical perspective. Instead of taking the points of view of local actors as the definitive theory-building tool, emphasizing the folk perceptions and local interpretations in each case, this book builds a model for explaining the process of stability and change in neighborhoods by focusing on more general patterns and mechanisms about how competing and complementary forms give rise to diverse and exclusive public cultures and a social and symbolic order of neighborhoods.

14. It is easy to bound race, ethnicity, and class differences as cohesive "groups" with clear boundaries of belonging, but we have to be careful about seeing collective units as natural and permanent. Collective identities are always under construction, and oppositions both within and between neighborhoods crystallize visible cohesiveness, creating both the appearance of distinct-group coherence and the appearance of neighborhood public cultures. There is nothing natural about black, white, homeless, Latino, vendor, merchant, developer, or any other local identity as a cohesive unit of analysis, nor are exclusive and diverse public cultures innate characteristics of places. They become seen as cohesive units of analysis in specific times and places, under particular conditions, according to emerging oppositions of groups and places.

Simmel (1955) claimed that groups do not create conflicts; rather conflicts give rise to cohesion and the appearance and enactment of groups. Abbott (1995, 862) further argues that boundaries come before entities, that is, "differences in character" exist before people set out to define "set membership." In Venice, common characteristics of boundaries emerge in various changing settings, but people enact membership through particular filters that give the appearance of distinct entities. The relationship between group, neighborhood formation, and transformation needs more scrutiny in urban sociology, where we tend to simplify this process of making differences. Differences between people do not automatically entail unification in every set of circumstances on each side of the opposition. We need to think closely about how differences in character turn into intergroup and politicized contestations by examining the conditions that shape the visibility of collectivity and moments of cohesion. I believe the structure of oppositions within and between neighborhoods is central to reinforcing and reproducing these distinctions.

15. Broken windows policing is built upon taken-for-granted assumptions about the relationships between disorderliness and diversity in public spaces. For an account from the perspective of police authority, see Bratton (1998). There are a number of critical schools challenging this model. Neo-Marxist per-

spectives are most recognized for criticism about controlling public space, such as Harvey (1973); Davis ([1990] 1992); Mitchell (2003); and Wacquant (2009), but there is also a vibrant tradition of investigations of social control in planning and public space, including Whyte (1988); Lofland (1998); Duneier (1999); and Vitale (2008). Also, some studies of disorder have demonstrated new ways of testing the relationships between race, poverty, and perceptions of "broken windows," finding that contexts with higher proportions of racial minorities and poverty conditions amplify these perceptions. See, for example, Sampson and Raudenbush (2004).

16. Becker (1963) claims that people collectively label behaviors that do not fit their own in-group conventions as "outsiders." According to Goode and Ben-Yehuda (1994), some in-group conventions carry more weight due to their relationship to legislative and law enforcement practices in establishing "moral panic." They argue that "the more power a group or social category has, the greater the likelihood that it will be successful in influencing legislation which is consistent with the views, sentiments, and interests of its members, which its members support." I thank Harvey Molotch for suggesting the term *power labeling* for this process.

17. Neighborhood homologies are different from what Davis ([1990] 1992, 257) has called "semiotic barriers." Semiotic barriers, in this definition, refer to the design of the space itself. Davis argues that architects (and I presume planners too) design buildings and public spaces that guide the masses in specific routes, which then makes them easier to control. He writes, "They enclose the mass that remains, directing its circulation with behaviorist ferocity." Davis is part of a larger critical discussion focusing on planned privatization of public spaces. I agree with Davis that planning, politics, and policing often seek to restrict public activity, but I also think that "privatization" and "enclosure" are not universal outcomes. In fact, top-down planning, as Jane Jacobs (1961) pointed out, does not automatically lead to the adoption of strategic outcomes in everyday life. Locals often adapt to their surroundings in ways that contradict the intensions of planners and developers. Because of the ability to circumvent social structure and adapt over time, the concept of neighborhood homology is more precise than semiotic barriers, because it also draws upon the intricate and constructive processes that enable people to establish complementary relationships.

The sociological use of the term *homology* stems from the work of Willis (1978, 2000), who describes homology in terms of group identity, focusing on the interconnected elements of style, image, and meaning in everyday life. He studied working-class subcultures, such as hippies and bikers, by looking at how they construct lifestyles, consume and use material objects, and create a system of symbols that allows members of the group to make sense of their relations to others. Actions, objects, values, and styles mesh together as a coherent way of life and allow those taking part in the subculture to establish a meaningful sense of belonging. Bourdieu (1977; 1984, 175, 232) extends this discussion to class positions and inequalities. He identifies everyday lifestyles and practices as adaptive everyday practices and interactions that emerge in particular contexts with others, but operate as mirrors of more general class positions. Cultural practices such as the types of foods people consume, how they decorate their homes, the traditions and manners they hold sacred, and what musical genres they enjoy reflect parallel class positions that reproduce the class structure. Similar to the construction of a subculture as a coherent way of life, such "practices and goods" become "associated with the different classes" and are "governed by the same logic." Bourdieu argues that the concept of class homology is best analyzed as a structure of oppositions: the array of cultural "tastes" found among members of a specific class can be understood in relation to others in a "field" of economic stratification.

18. Early gentrifiers often refer to themselves as "pioneers," viewing the uncharted city—unexplored at a particular moment in history by somewhat wealthier whites compared to the current residents—as a great frontier. Smith (1996) critically dissects this frontier metaphor and its applications in a wide range of places.

19. Boundary processes have played a major role in sociological theorizing over the last decade (see Lamont and Molnár 2002 for an extensive review). Sennett (2008) argues that the focus on boundary processes largely assumes a territorial limit. He adds the concept of "border" to emphasize that some edges are interactive zones. Sennett's sensitivity to ecological metaphors and processes, similar to the Chicago School, calls attention to interconnected relationships between distinct groups and spaces, or what I have labeled as public cultures. In Venice, the relations between these neighborhood public cultures are interactive. Diversity and exclusivity are interdependent at the same time that they are distinct, and neither of them operates as permanent and all-encompassing characteristics at every single moment of every single day. These are really public cultures "in action," and by that I mean that they are produced and maintained either by competing groups upholding connections to a space in the face of ongoing changes or by complementary groups upholding separations between spaces by building and enacting coherent collective representations. Venice may be an extreme case, although increasingly such types of places are found in many cities, where the interdependence between diversity and exclusivity occurs in adjacent neighborhoods and is therefore noticeable to the casual observer in daily life. Creating and sustaining neighborhood exclusivity and diversity requires understanding the opportunities and constraints facing an array of groups, whether they live near each other or not, and how they are limited in their movements across spaces. Cases like Venice open up the possibility to make these analytic comparisons.

20. This separation of commercial and residential public cultures may seem awkward to residents and observers of cities where mixed-use development has a long history, like in New York and Chicago. Mixed-use planning has only recently emerged as a common planning approach in Los Angeles. Historically, L.A.'s commercial and residential settings were planned as separate, although proximate, features of community life, comparable to many American suburbs.

Chapter One

1. Fogelson (1967, 137–138).
2. Fishman (1987); Avila (2004).
3. Fogelson (1967); Bottles (1987).
4. Banham (1971).
5. See Dear (2001); Soja (1996); Soja and Scott (1996). Also see Garreau (1992).
6. It is not only the postindustrial city that has emerged as an "entertainment machine" (Clark 2004). Cities have long been entertainment machines, organizing a wide range of amenities, leisure events, and nightlife activities as sources of place identification, consumer outlets, and modes of development. Certainly, there are important distinctions between so-called industrial and postindustrial phases of urban development, but it is not that one is singularly production-oriented and the other consumer-oriented. Even in this age of industry, Venice was a consumer and entertainment driven locale.
7. Cunningham (1976, 9–10).
8. Stanton ([1993] 2005, 6).
9. Warren (1934); Springer (1992); Stanton ([1993] 2005). Venice actually remained under the political authority of Ocean Park until 1910, at which time it became its own, if only short-lived, municipality.
10. McWilliams (1943, 131); Walker (1976); Starr (1985, 80).
11. Abu-Lughod (1999, 141–142).
12. Adler (1969); Dully (1970, 5).
13. For listings of Venice in films, the following websites are informative: (1) http://www.imdb.com/List?endings=on&&locations=Venice,+Los+Angeles,+California,+USA&&heading=18%3Bwith+locations+including%3BVenice,+Los+Angeles,+California,+USA&&skip=200; (2) http://www.westland.net/venicehistory/articles/movies.htm; (3) http://hubpages.com/hub/Venice—California-and-Movies; (4) http://www.virtualvenice.info/media/film.htm.
14. Cunningham (1976, 32–33); Dully (1970, 7); Schwieterman (2004, 74–75).
15. Reese-Davis (2006).
16. Kinney is part of the local lore in Oakwood's black community. One story

is that Kinney was among the most open-minded whites of his era. When he was on the road he reportedly refused to stay in hotels that did not allow his personal chauffeur, an African American man, to stay there. They claim that he had such principled beliefs about it that he would sleep in the car with his chauffeur instead of staying in the more comfortable hotel room.

17. Logan and Molotch (1987).

18. Venice I, No 7. July 1912. Los Angeles Public Library, Venice Branch.

19. Starr (1985, 80).

20. Abu-Lughod (1999, 154).

21. Stanton ([1993] 2005, 117).

22. Gray (2006); Cunningham (1976, 56–57, 66); Stanton ([1993] 2005).

23. Scott (2004, 102); Stanton ([1993] 2005, 140); Cunningham (1976, 71).

24. Springer (1992, 8–15).

25. *Los Angeles Times* (1929).

26. Cunningham (1976) and Stanton ([1993] 2005) both provide compelling accounts of this history.

27. Sabin (2005b, 56–70); Sabin (2005a, 95–114).

28. The Los Angeles Public Library houses a wonderful photo collection of remaining oil derricks and environmental conditions during this period.

29. Bradbury (1999, 1).

30. *Billboard* (1946, 62); Stanton ([1993] 2005, 229–230); Weller (2005, 167).

31. The iconic beat culture that made West Coast bohemianism so famous was not the first wave of California bohemianism. Hurewitz (2007) details the rise of a bohemian culture around arts, sexuality, and lifestyle politics in L.A.'s Silver Lake, then called Edendale, during the three decades prior to the rise of the beat movement in Venice and San Francisco.

32. The hobo culture gave rise to legendary writers like Jack London and Carl Sandburg, while the beat culture brought fame to the likes of Jack Kerouac and Allen Ginsberg.

33. Burgess (1925, 54) locates hobos in a specific place right outside the central business district, the center of "Hobohemia," calling attention to its transient residential patterns. Also see Anderson (1923).

34. Lipton, the father of *Inside the Actor Studio* host James Lipton, wrote one of the classic books on the beat movement, in which he recounts the culture and biographies of the established Venetian beats, including their encounters with some of the most famous cultural entrepreneurs of the era—Allen Ginsberg, Dylan Thomas, and Lawrence Ferlinghetti.

35. See Maynard (1991, 114–120).

36. Groves (2010).

37. Lipton (1959, 15–16).

38. Recorded interview with Rick Davidson, California State University, Long Beach, Venice Archives.

39. Haag (1978).

40. Ibid.

41. Ibid.

42. See the documentary directed by Morgan Neville (2008).

43. Quoted in Webb (2007, 13–17).

44. The use of mixed media and industrial materials and the blurring of boundaries between sculpture and painting inspired the future of both art and architecture. Some see this innovative artistic community as the major influence on superstar architect Frank Gehry's characteristic postmodern style. In fact, Gehry has attributed much of his creative technique to learning from his artistic friends in Venice. Gehry has even served as curator for exhibitions about the relationship between his own innovative work and Venice artists. The Weisman Museum at the University of Minnesota described one exhibit as follows: "Focused on blurring the boundaries between different media—such as painting and sculpture or sculpture and architecture—and playing with non-traditional materials—such as industrial metals, plastics, and junk—this community of artists provided the inspiration and support that Gehry was not able to garner from the local architectural establishment." See http://www.weisman.umn.edu/exhibits/west/comm.html. Artist Guy Dill said of Gehry: "Frank learned from artists adding, gutting, and exposing the structure, rather than going through a long, agonizing process of ground-up design and construction" (Quoted in Webb 2007, 17).

45. Szántó (2003, 402); Webb (2007).

46. Schrank (2009).

47. Overend (1976).

48. Banham (1971, 142).

49. Abu-Lughod (1999, 245).

50. Abu-Lughod (1999, 247–248); Sides (2006, 111).

51. Abu-Lughod (1999); Avila (2004).

52. Avila (2004, 49).

53. Sociologists are increasingly paying attention to this changing color line. See Farley and Frey (1994); Abu-Lughod (1999); Gans (1999); Bobo et al. (2002); Logan, Stults, and Farley (2004); Iceland (2004); Charles (2006); Lee and Bean (2007); Iceland (2009).

54. Sabagh and Bozorgmehr (2003, 102).

55. Bobo et al. (2002).

56. See Calavita 1992; Sánchez 1993; Waldinger and Bozorgmehr 1996; Sabagh and Bozorgmehr 2003.

57. Sabagh and Bozorgmehr (2003, 102).

58. Sabagh and Bozorgmehr (2003).

59. Halle, Gedeon, and Beveridge (2003, 29).

60. Laslett (1996).

61. Myers (2007, 127).

62. Changing census categories for identifying "Hispanics" and the miscal-culation of the undocumented population make it nearly impossible to know ex-actly when Latinos became the largest foreign-born population in Venice. Cun-ningham (1976, 133) claims that the Jewish ghetto by the beach was the "first departure from the white, Anglo-Saxon Protestant majority." This is not exactly true. Black residents, as I've already discussed, lived in the Oakwood section, and there were several hundred listed as "other races," which were likely Japa-nese and Mexican residents as recounted by longtime residents. Many of the Jap-anese residents worked as vegetable growers south of Venice and were interned during World War II, forced to give up their stake in the community.

63. See Light and Bonacich (1988, 3). We are used to thinking that the major-ity of a neighborhood's residents develops the identity of a place. Suttles (1968, 20) found that Italians made up the majority of the Addams area in Chicago, an otherwise racially and ethnically diverse setting, "and the surrounding city also tend[ed] to authenticate their claim by referring to the area as an Italian commu-nity[.]" Pattillo-McCoy (1999, 40–43), in her account of a Chicago neighborhood, discusses how race and class signifiers lead outsiders to interpret its identity as both a "black" and "middle class" locale. She concludes that this "sweeping por-trayal [of local identity] can blur the diversity within the neighborhood in an at-tempt to highlight the common interests of the majority of . . . residents." Yet Latinos make up over 70 percent of the population in Koreatown, and they also comprise over 60 percent of the population in Watts, the city's most famous "black neighborhood." Contradictions between neighborhood identity and de-mographic composition are increasingly common as population shifts reshape an urban landscape with stable racial and ethnic groups already in place.

64. Light and Bonacich (1988); Zhou and Kim (2004); Horton (1995).

65. Light and Bonacich (1988, 3–6).

66. Ibid. Also see Ong, Bonacich, and Cheng (1994).

67. See Lopez (2005), part of a series of his penetrating articles on downtown L.A.'s skid row.

68. Snow and Anderson (1993); Wolch and Dear (1993, 31).

69. Jencks (1994) draws the distinction between homeless who slept in shel-ters and those who slept in public places. He shows that the former have been easier to track due to more consistent counting methods, while the latter are dif-ficult to tally because of unclear criteria for deciphering homeless individuals, as many are not readily visible to the public eye.

70. Wolch (1996, 390–406).

71. Wolch and Dear (1993, xxiii, 219).

72. According to Rossi (1989, 20), during the nineteenth century, transient individuals—almost always men without stable residency—became institution-alized and segregated in American cities. Anderson (1923, 4–15) argued in his

study of hobos that every city had an area where the homeless congregated, creating isolated cultural areas called Hobohemias. He writes, "Here characteristic institutions have arisen—cheap hotels, lodging-houses, flops, eating joints, outfitting shops, employment agencies, missions, radical bookstores, welfare agencies, economic and political institutions—to minister to the needs, physical and spiritual, of the homeless man."

73. Dear and Wolch (1987); Los Angeles Homeless Services Authority (2007).

74. Los Angeles Homeless Services Authority (2007).

75. Wolch and Dear (1993) refer to the area as "Skid Rose" in an investigation from several decades ago, employing a local folk category that homeowners and business owners continue to use to make sense of their "homeless problem."

76. Fishman (1987, 167); Banham (1971, 79).

77. Venice is not an anomaly, even along the Southern California coast, in its struggle over community identity and residential and public space inclusion. Santa Monica was famous for its fierce struggles to maintain affordability (Čapek and Gilderbloom 1992) and still struggles with its large homeless population (Wolch 1996). Ventura and Santa Barbara, despite similar landscapes, had different historical conditions that limited economic investment in Ventura while Santa Barbara became a well-known haven for wealth (See Molotch et al. 2000). But even Santa Barbara continues to struggle with homelessness, a condition of its liberal past that haunts many newcomers to the area expecting a more serene environment (Rosenthal 1994; Wakin 2005, 2008). This trend of rebuilding the coast followed by periods of decline is commonplace on the East Coast as well. In the famed Long Island community of the Hamptons, wealthy homeowners overtook the beach lifestyle after long struggles to sustain its economic diversity (Dolgon 2005), and in Asbury Park developers invoke eminent domain laws to force long-term property owners out of their houses and businesses to make room for a new wave of development (Eliopoulos 2009). But there are also quite a number of coastal places that have been far less successful. Simon's (2004) account of Atlantic City portrays a dramatic decline and a "devil's bargain" to rebuild it into a gambling oasis that hides continuing residential poverty.

78. See Zukin ([1982] 1989); Logan and Molotch (1987); Smith (1987); Mele (2000).

79. Sherman and Pipkin (2005, 431–439).

80. Gans (1962).

81. Lipton (1959) called Venice the "slum by the sea" in his classic book, using the surrounding infrastructural deterioration as a source of pride, demonstrating his commitment to bohemian ideals.

82. Quoted in Cunningham (1976).

83. Maynard (1991).

84. Harris (1966, 68–70).

85. Myerhoff (1978) claims that thousands of Jews were dislocated due to up-grading measures. It is likely that some were uprooted, but it is unlikely that the number of evictions was as great and as quick as she claims. The beachfront area around the Israel Levin Center still struggles to rebuild its identity as upscale, with a mix of housing types and both wealthy and affordable housing located in close proximity. Santa Monica, where I can only guess that many of the elderly men and women resided, has done a relatively decent job at securing affordable housing for seniors along the beach. It is likely that many were forced away in this gentrification process, but my guess is that the disruption of this community was more complicated due to the age of her subjects and variation in types and degrees of economic support from family far and near.

86. Ley (1980, 1996) draws close attention to the standard of "livability" used by the New Left to guide collective action against growth machine politics. He finds that this new political ideology, framed as a new social justice paradigm, was an early introduction of quality of life initiatives central to middle-class po-litical movements.

87. Interview with former L.A. councilwoman and state coastal commissioner Ruth Galanter. Also see http://www.power-la.org/news.html.

Chapter Two

1. For an inside perspective about how the Oakwood gang war started and different efforts to quell it, see Umemoto's (2006) penetrating study.

2. The 2000 census reported that Oakwood had over 8,500 residents. The loss of 1,200 residents reflects a major decline in total population over the time span between the 2000 census and the current 2005–2009 American Commu-nity Survey data. I would hypothesize that this shift has to do with development patterns and the increase of residents who are much more likely to build larger single-family dwellings, along with a simultaneous movement of immigrants out of Oakwood to other areas of the region.

3. Throughout this chapter, I use Latino to refer to individuals of Hispanic origin. The reader will notice, however, that when people identified as Mexi-can American or Chicano, or used other terms, I adopted their categories. In addition, I use the racial classifications of black/African American and white throughout the chapter as a reference to non-Hispanic black/African American and non-Hispanic white respectively. Again, I adopted these terms because of the ways that neighborhood residents employ racial-ethnic categories as a system of local classifications.

4. Quoted in Alexander and Alexander (1991, 215).

5. Interview with Sonya Reese Davis about her grandfather and the history

of Venice, by Farai Chideya for National Public Radio, July 4, 2005, available at http://www.npr.org/templates/story/story.php?storyId=4728758.

6. See Cunningham (1976).

7. Adler (1969).

8. For an in-depth investigation of the role that churches play in the building and sustaining community among African Americans see McRoberts (2003).

9. Wilson (1987, 1996) argues that structural shifts in the national economy produced consequences for African American urban communities as meaningful work opportunities rapidly disappeared. His analysis shifts explanations of black poverty from racism, which has always existed, to a combination of historic patterns of racism with current patterns of economic restructuring. Notwithstanding the advances won by the civil rights movement, the contraction of employment opportunities for less educated African Americans, particularly a substantial loss of jobs in manufacturing industries, led to sharp declines in economic resources available in black urban communities. It's not completely clear whether Wilson's model perfectly coheres in Oakwood. The aviation industry, which had provided previous generations of Oakwood residents with reasonably stable and relatively well-paying jobs, certainly contracted and some Oakwood residents lost jobs. But I also found that many of the younger generation who fell into a life of crime, including drug distribution, gang violence, and prison, had working parents with a stable income. This greatly complicates the causes of poverty and crime in Oakwood. I don't have the space in this book to engage this topic in close detail, but certainly the debate about socioeconomic differentiation and racial homogeneity has become central to ethnography. Pattillo-McCoy's (1999) investigation of the intersection of racial homogeneity and class heterogeneity highlights similar points about middle-class black youth living in close proximity to lower-income black youth. Gregory (1998, 9) also contends, "In the binary 'ghetto' versus 'mainstream' conceptual economy, which continues to drive much of the research on black urban life, working- and middle-class people are either absent or taken to be unproblematically integrated into the vague topography of 'mainstream society.'" The trend to overlook the black working and middle classes, Gregory claims, dates back to Rainwater's (1970) identification of an opposition between ghetto culture and mainstream culture, an either/or model of social separation or integration that posits a problematic moral binary between good and evil as if individuals have one or another essence.

10. Cunningham (1976).

11. Interview recording with Castile from Long Beach State University, Venice Archives.

12. Castile claims that the buildings were foreclosed upon and fell into receivership, but it's unclear what the conflict was behind the process. According

to Castile, investors backed out during the construction of the last six buildings, leaving the management of the buildings to Project Action, which had limited resources.

13. Collins (2004, 7).

14. The LAPD put together a report called the "Oakwood Plan" during the 1980s. See Umemoto (2006).

15. Anderson (1999).

16. Garcia and Hill-Holtzman (1990).

17. For a thorough accounting of the paradox between Latino cultural branding and political invisibility, see Dávila (2001).

18. Calculating the proportion of residents from distinct geographic regions is nearly impossible through research without a representative sample. My fundamental goal is to highlight variations within and across social categories. Based on impressionistic observations, talking to different people, finding out their origins, and asking them their perceptions of what different geographic backgrounds other people have, I believe Oaxaca is a common point of origin.

19. This is consistent with Quillian and Prager (2001), who find that whites are averse to moving into black neighborhoods due to stereotypes of African Americans, and young black men more specifically, as dangerous. Latinos, it seems, also commonly hold this view, but they maintain fewer options of mobility.

20. Doherty (1992).

21. The CSO, a barrio-based self-help group movement founded in 1947 by Saul Alinsky and Anthony Rios, a mentor to Cesar Chavez (no relation to Flora), was probably the most significant organization that served individuals of Latino origin in Oakwood. The fact that a white woman headed it further speaks to the limits of living without citizenship.

22. For more information, see Woo (2003). Also one can download a comprehensive multihour oral history interview with Flora Chavez at http://salticid.nmc .csulb.edu/cgi-bin/WebObjects/OralAural.woa/wa/interview?pt=109&bi=1&col =a1000&ser=a1006&prj=a1174.

23. The 1990s gang war is covered by Umemoto (2006). She provides a rich, detailed account about the rise of this violent event and the local methods of initiating a truce between the sides.

24. Katz (2003) argues that organized public activity in Los Angeles is often labeled as "gang-related," despite any clearly articulated definition of the term. The meaning of gang has less to do with criminal organizations, and more to do with the naming of a group and the use of this name in a variety of circumstances. Individuals who affiliate with a named group—Venice 13 and Shoreline Crips in Oakwood—become labeled as gang members in all of their activities, even when the activities are not motivated by or influenced by their participation within this named group. Katz (1988) notes in other work that crime is often the outcome of spontaneous and sensual attractions in the moment that draw people

to commit acts with others. In one interview, a former gang member describes his participation in criminal activities, selling drugs or breaking into cars, as a "cat and mouse game," in which he and his friends knew that the police officers were out there looking for criminal activities, but they played off of the feeling they got from hiding from LAPD officers. These actions were not organized by any group, but occurred as a spur of the moment event. However, because of their affiliations with a named group—a "gang"—such criminal acts became labeled as "gang-related crimes."

25. Hastings (1994).

26. Zukin's ([1982] 1989) classic account of loft living in lower Manhattan provides a comparable example of how an art walk contributed to opening up a neighborhood to outsiders, presenting to them the possibility of a new urban lifestyle. In Oakwood, the art walk opened up the public to an "up-and-coming" neighborhood by the beach and the laid-back coastal lifestyle typical of Los Angeles beachfront communities. At the same time, it required that newcomers take a risk in a neighborhood with a history of drug dealing and violence.

27. See Fanucchi (1984b). Local black activists still purport that "neighborhood watch" does not engage the police, but rather continues as an independent venture. One black activist told me that the goal of the current neighborhood watch is not "to do the work of the police," but instead to keep the neighborhood safe. For instance, she has directly moved dealers off her street by explaining to them that senior citizens live there. Typically, she has received a positive response when she expresses it in these terms. Under no circumstance will she call the police or engage in activity that she perceives as "dangerous police work."

28. Doherty (1992).

29. Umemoto (2006, 47) finds similar evidence. She writes, "New property owners . . . cooperated with police to videotape criminal activity from their homes at the risk of their personal safety."

30. See http://www.lapdonline.org/gang_injunctions.

31. Ehrenreich (1999).

32. California Gang Node Advisory Committee (2007).

33. *Argonaut Newspaper* (2006).

34. Holiday Venice is now owned by GH Capital LLC. In 2010, the company engaged in another effort to prepay the mortgage, leading to a range of lawsuits against HUD filed by Holiday Venice residents.

35. These battles are ongoing. With the contracts coming due, there are struggles about if and how they will remain affordable, calling upon HUD to intervene. Affordable housing developers have tried to purchase the buildings, but as of the writing of this chapter, there is still no clear resolution about the future. This scenario about the place of large-scale affordable housing developments is familiar to Venice residents, as the 790-unit Lincoln Place, located less than one mile away from Oakwood (east of Lincoln Boulevard), fell prey to a simi-

lar process. Corporate condo conversions allowed them to carry out the largest mass eviction in the history of Los Angeles. Even with small-scale legal successes to bring back some of the residents into Lincoln Place, it is a clear shift in overall affordability and access. With the recent battles over Lincoln Place, affordable housing advocates, community organizers, and longtime Oakwood locals interpret their ongoing fight to preserve these buildings as the last chance of maintaining a cluster of affordable housing in Venice, especially west of Lincoln Boulevard.

36. Discussions of the "privatopia" and "fortress lifestyle" of protection and privacy in suburban life have become central to urban studies. See Davis ([1990] 1992); McKenzie (1994); Soja (1996); Blakeley and Snyder (1997); Caldeira (2000); and Low (2003). Specifically related to this trend of privatizing wealthy spaces in proximity to lower-income surroundings, see Caldeira's (2000, 256–296) discussion of enclosed "fortified enclaves" as a new pattern of separation between economic classes living in close proximity in São Paulo.

37. Anderson (1976, 1999); Gregory (1998); Duneier (1999); Pattillo (1999, 2007).

Chapter Three

1. De Certeau (1984, 29–30) makes the distinction between "tactics" and "strategies," arguing that strategies are used to make places conform to more abstract models, "produc[ing], tabulat[ing], and impos[ing] these spaces . . . whereas tactics can only use, manipulate, and divert these spaces." Venice's residential setting is defined by the strategic political and law enforcement enterprise of normalizing middle-class values, which makes deviations from these values seem suspect. The homeless are then forced into a reactive, adaptive, and tactical mode of survival.

2. Douglas (1966).

3. Lipton (1959, 16).

4. The hatred of the duck population by certain Canal residents underscores correlations in the use of language, definitions of uses of public space, and even suggestions for how to solve public space "problems." While space does not allow for a close investigation of this correlation, one possible explanation is that cultural repertoires unify interpretations of any and all "matter out of place" across cases, as a mode of dehumanization.

5. Lamont and Thévenot (2000).

6. Gentrifiers rarely complain about health hazards of dog feces and urination, despite regular concern about duck and human feces. African American activists commonly complain about people using Oakwood Park as a dog park, describing the potential exposure of children to the remains as unhealthy. This

distinction further highlights how social positions are tied up with interpretive and oppositional frameworks. In the former example, incoming gentrifiers interpret human feces as dirty and dangerous as a method of stigmatization, never calling attention to dogs, which are an accepted part of middle-class convention. In the latter example, the position of old-timers in Oakwood leads to interpretations of dog feces as dirty and dangerous, as a technique to challenge new uses of the park by gentrifiers.

7. In 2010, activists spotted someone living in their vehicle dumping waste on the streets. It turned into a media frenzy. Living in Philadelphia at the time, I received countless e-mail updates about this situation, and followed it in almost every major news source, including national coverage in televised and print news. The media never criticized city and state policies for giving rise to and prolonging the existence of such a huge homeless problem, putting the blame squarely on the individuals responsible for the dumping and stigmatizing the homeless in general as a result.

8. Homelessness generally gives rise to what Rowe and Wolch (1990) call "time-space discontinuity." They show how the homeless "lack . . . locationally fixed stations in the daily path." Discontinuity techniques are the modes of breaking up these connections to place by political and social forces, but as I also show, these techniques are situated in a complex tension between labeling the homeless as "people out of place" and creating conditions in Venice that makes it a "home for the homeless."

9. The Citywide Nuisance Abatement Program (CNAP) is a program under the auspices of the City Attorney's Office that works with Los Angeles Departments of Police, Building and Safety, and City Planning. Together they work to stop blight in neighborhoods, focusing on abandoned buildings, "nuisance properties," and other local neighborhood problems. For more information, see http://atty.lacity.org/OUR_OFFICE/CriminalDivision/CNAP/index.htm.

10. Duneier (1999) shows how broken windows policing affects a specific segment of the homeless population who sell magazines and books in New York's West Village, pointing out that a significant transformation in the Village involves the influx of black homeless vendors on the streets. He identifies "space wars" between storeowners and the street book vendors. But I would also add to his point that the Village, like the rest of Manhattan, is no longer the working class "urban village" of Jane Jacobs's era. There have been major demographic shifts to the surrounding neighborhoods since Jacobs published her monumental work in 1961, the surrounding neighborhoods becoming beacons of upper-income cultural norms about quality of life while still touting the importance of cultural diversity and open-mindedness, quite similar to Venice. This contradiction is key to this new era of privatization.

11. Quoted in DiMassa and Pfeifer (2005). The distinction between behaviors and populations is significant to sociologists. For one, Bratton seems to have re-

versed what Foucault (1991) called the "art of government," in which the state's purpose is to fulfill the "needs" and "aspirations" of "populations" as well as make them "the object in the hands of the government." The claim that law enforcement focuses on "behaviors" rather than "populations" assumes an artificial abstractness to law that privileges private over public rights. The same behaviors conducted in private spaces inside one's home evade the eye of law enforcement; some are even legal, i.e., drinking alcohol. Secondly, the move from populations to behaviors takes the perception of solutions out of the hands of legislators. Laws cannot isolate any specific category of people in the language, but law enforcement agents can manage behaviors that disproportionately influence the target of enforcement. This new management strategy also artificially pushes the police into the front lines and makes them perceived as responsible for solutions. This logic is commonplace. The gang injunction, nuisance abatement codes, and code enforcement programs operate in similar ways in Oakwood. They were written as abstract and general, but how they are applied in certain circumstances privileges some positions. My own observations support those by elderly African Americans who point out in neighborhood meetings that it is usually young white people who purchase drugs from black sellers, while attention to law enforcement almost exclusively focuses on the black sellers, raising an entirely different set of issues. If we really want to better explain the processes of "criminalization," we need to trace how, when, and why laws are created, conduct ethnographies of the legislative processes, and follow the diffusion of new laws and ordinances into law enforcement practices.

12. The Official City of Los Angeles Municipal Code can be found in the searchable database of the American Legal Publishing Corporation. See http://www.amlegal.com/nxt/gateway.dll?f=templates&fn=default.htm&vid=amlegal:lamc_ca.

13. Most crimes by the homeless are minor, but I also knew others who committed serious crimes: possession of an illegal weapon, assault, theft (bicycle theft is prevalent), dumping of sewage, and one person I know was arrested and convicted for rape. There were also cases reported of murders committed by so-called transients. Such outstanding and widely reported cases give credence to stereotypes that homeless people are problems.

14. Khan (2010).

15. The issue of lifestyle choices complicates the homeless/bohemian category. How do we know whether someone wants to remain on the streets or if the routine that they have established on the streets limits other possible understandings that would lead them off the streets? Venice's homeless readily claim that they have made a choice, but further investigation reveals complex biographies, usually involving intense drug use or other medical difficulties. A comparison with Duneier's (1999) case highlights that a common search for dignity through a classic American repertoire of free choice has invaded people strug-

gling on the streets. It seems as if Americans of all backgrounds and conditions, including the homeless, are antagonistic to sociological explanations of life course, believing in models of strategy and freedom rather than social, political, and economic explanations.

16. Geertz (1983, 167) argues that there are particular systems of meaning that are practiced in local places and that in order to "to know a city" one must get to "know its streets."

17. Many homeless people believe that shelters are more dangerous than streets, as theft and violence are commonplace. Also, there are firm restrictions on the number of items one can bring into a shelter, which requires that people risk leaving most of their belongings somewhere in public. Notwithstanding negative experiences with the system, the Ninth Circuit ruling that made it no longer acceptable to arrest a homeless person for sleeping on the sidewalk pointed out another pertinent fact: there are not nearly enough shelter beds in Los Angeles for the number of homeless people. This fact makes the discussion of the safety of shelters less poignant, as most do not even have the option of testing the stereotypes of shelters against the facts.

Chapter Four

1. The '60s countercultural movements are what sociologists now call "new social movements." Having a say over one's own identity and producing it together with others became central to the politicization of everyday life. See Cohen 1985.

2. See Jackson (1985).

3. Hansen (1965b).

4. Hansen (1965a).

5. Smith (1961); Hansen (1965a).

6. Smith (1961).

7. Hansen (1965a).

8. See (1967).

9. *Los Angeles Times* 1969.

10. Ferderber (1971).

11. Davidson (1981).

12. Davidson (1983).

13. Rosen and Binder (1969).

14. *Los Angeles Times* September 1972.

15. Ibid.

16. *Los Angeles Times* 1964.

17. Oral history from Venice Archives, Long Beach State University.

18. Zadeh (1974).

19. Maryjane (2005, 29) is one of many Venetians who has written a memoir of her own life and involvement in the community. Hers is a detailed account of various Canals political and cultural actions, which also includes excellent drawings of the houses in which people she knew resided, basically outlining her own social networks. Such resources are priceless for neighborhood ethnographers.

20. Venice Archives, Long Beach State University.

21. Faris (1975).

22. When sociologists write about middlemen, they often refer to immigrant minorities who occupy an "intermediate position" in the dichotomy between the high-status "white" groups and low-status "black" groups. Most refer to those who have taken risks to open up businesses in economically unstable areas (See Blalock 1967; Bonacich 1973). Pattillo (2007) has expanded this concept in her work about the black middle class who moved into a poor black neighborhood in Chicago. These middle-class newcomers hold conventional forms of knowledge and distinct skill sets, types of cultural capital that enable them to straddle the worlds of a mostly white workforce and mainstream political affairs while also living among poor black neighbors excluded from these same economic, cultural, and political opportunities.

The middle position I describe here is not exclusively about race and ethnicity and it is fundamentally about historical positioning between groups. It is central to the more general historical process of evolving relations between people. All types of neighborhood transformation involve a middle position, and it may be most visible and polemical in studies of gentrification. Thus, even though some move into a place and have good intentions to preserve previous residents (Brown-Saracino 2010), the temporal order positions them against others and provides a visible intersection between socioeconomic status and cultural practices. Students, artists, black, white or Latino middle-class residents, immigrants of distinct ethnic backgrounds, and other types of people can also occupy this middle position. The key, however, is to untangle the webs of association over time as people become reconfigured against others.

23. The classic inquiry into unanticipated consequences of "purposive action" is Merton (1936). Tilly (1996) links these unanticipated consequences to the durability of social structures. Admittedly, the notion of the middle position requires an artificial breaking off of a period of history. One could easily contend that all movements are middle positions between two other points in time. I agree with this proposition. My point is simply to highlight how reconfiguration takes place, and in order to do that, I highlight a period of history in which a significant transition took place by redirecting taken-for-granted political and cultural norms.

24. See Small (2004).

25. See Simpson (1981); Zukin ([1982] 1989). Jager (1986) refers to this as "sweat equity."

26. Long Beach State University, Venice Archives.

27. Fanucchi (1984a).

28. Ibid.

29. From California Coastal Zone Conservation Commission Meeting Minutes, December 1, 1976; and California Coastal Commission Meeting Minutes, November, 3, 1975.

30. Faris (1976).

31. Fanucchi (1984a).

32. Kaplan (1987).

33. Citron (1986).

34. Fanucchi (1984a); Citron (1986).

35. Doherty (1991).

36. Ibid.

37. See, for example, http://www.betsysellsvenice.com/convertedpages/real estatesalesneighborhoodpage.html, accessed September 8, 2011.

38. http://www.sandyberens.com/listings.html, accessed June 18, 2010.

39. Thornburg (1999).

Chapter Five

1. For those with particular historical interests in Los Angeles and Venice, I highlight Springer's (1992) work on the early construction of Venice. He points out that during the early 1900s, with the birth of the amusement pier on Venice Beach, sellers arrived in wagons and competed with the pier's established economic enterprises by setting up on the boardwalk. In other words, the distinction between formal and informal economies is central to the boardwalk's history. One difference between now and then, however, is the current informal economy has become an institutionalized feature of the boardwalk.

2. This thesis takes a number of forms, from the analysis of theme parks, shopping malls, and other "themed environments" (Sorkin 1992; Crawford 1992; Gottdiener 2001) to the standardization of suburbia as a "geography of nowhere," in which everything takes the same commercial and architectural form (Kunstler 1993). Most recently, Zukin (2010) has described the widespread invasion of chain stores in New York City as the destruction of "authentic spaces."

3. This trend appears in cities throughout the world, taking place in varied types of locations, from the Eiffel Tower to the World Trade Center, the latter example highlighting that even horrific acts can stimulate microeconomies by opening up new opportunities for vendors to sell New York paraphernalia to tourists visiting the World Trade Center site.

4. Stanton ([1993] 2005, 272).

5. *Venice Paper* (2006).

6. Zukin ([1982] 1989); Simpson (1981); Lloyd (2006).

7. Berkson (1982).

8. Light and Bonacich (1988); Lee (2002).

9. For more information see http://www.ssa.gov/notices/supplemental-security-income. Last accessed, August 21, 2006.

10. Not all "theming" is the outcome of top-down strategies. While Disneyification speaks to the imposition of the theme park motif on the public (e,g, Zukin 1995; Gottdiener 2001), Venice Beach presents a combination of forces, many of them local, contributing to thematic identity that pressures specific logics of adaptation.

11. For an overview, see "Perry v. LAPD," case number 96–55545, U.S. Court of Appeals for the Ninth Circuit. August 25, 1997. Also see Woody Mulligan, and Robert "Jingles" Newman against the City of Los Angeles, Case Number CV05–4998, U.S. District Court, Central District of California, Western Division. There is also a history of draft documents of the ordinance and its numerous revisions, some of which contain overviews of the law, available from the city council office.

12. "Perry v. LAPD," case number 96–55545, U.S. Court of Appeals for the Ninth Circuit. August 25, 1997.

13. Groves (2004).

14. Wood (2005). In fact, vendors—aside from the homeless who slept on the boardwalk—were not commonly arriving as early as they say. During the dozens of times I went out to the boardwalk at 5:00 a.m., I never found people waiting around and making lots of noise. The earliest arrival time was generally 6:00 a.m., and most started arriving after 8:00 a.m.

15. *Los Angeles Municipal Code Section 42.15* revised and approved on January 31, 2006.

Chapter six

1. Oldenburg (1999) refers to such spaces as "third spaces," the accessible, open, and affordable spaces that allow for more creative interactions. Anderson (2011) more recently calls such spaces "cosmopolitan canopies," where individuals of different racial backgrounds test out their assumptions about others.

2. Rothman (2004). Branding has recently become a major concept in the social sciences. See Greenberg (2008) for a discussion of branding a city.

3. This claim is a revision of Brooks's (2000) famous thesis about "bourgeois bohemians" (bobos). While I agree, in principle, that the liberal elite evokes an ideology of acceptance and tolerance, their practices still point to exclusive lifestyles, conspicuous consumption, and a cohesive material culture of previous eras. The attention to bobos, and similarly to Florida's "creative class," tells only

part of a very complex story about consumption and neighborhood change. Focusing on these practices and cultural themes in neighborhood life allows a comparative perspective, to show how one set of lifestyles and practices directly and indirectly impacts other sets of lifestyles and practices, in this case, attributed to lower-income residents.

4. They took on a similar function as Business Improvement Districts (BIDs) in that private interests gained control over publicly owned land (Lofland 1998, 212). However, unlike BIDs, which literally provide business and property owners with formal controls and certain formal responsibilities, like taxing themselves to raise money and ultimately improve the landscape and hire security and private maintenance (Zukin 1995, 33; Duneier 1999, 231–233), the collective organization of Abbot Kinney Boulevard operated as an informal advocacy process through a nonprofit organization. These entrepreneurs campaigned for a new street aesthetic based on personal and group preferences that privileged their own definitions of quality of life. They raised money from independent sources, membership drives, and fund-raisers, and attracted government interests, while still remaining free of formal associations with the city.

5. Kramer (1994).

6. See Hobsbawm and Ranger (1983) for a discussion of inventing tradition; also see Zukin (1995) for a discussion of the politics of cultural identity and how some groups have a privileged role in defining space.

7. See especially Williams (1988). Warner (1959); Small (2004); and Brown-Saracino (2010) also discuss the role of festivals in shaping local area identity.

8. See website at: www.veniceunchained.org, accessed June 2006.

9. Echavaria (2006).

10. *Venice Paper* (2007).

11. Echavaria (2006).

12. Walker (2010).

13. Komaiko (2003).

14. Anderton (2001).

15. Brown (2005).

16. Kuh (2009).

17. http://www.bountifulhome.com/home.html.

18. http://www.yovenice.com/forum/eat-drink/local-1205-abbot-kinney-opening-soon/.

19. http://blogs.laweekly.com/squidink/bars/the-otheroom-beer-and-wine-cra/.

20. See, for example, Simpson (1981); Zukin ([1982] 1989); Lloyd (2006).

21. See Zukin ([1982] 1989).

22. Wedner (2008).

23. Both Rieder (1985) and Jackson Jr. (2001) find that old-timers have antagonistic tendencies toward newcomers. This is also the case in Oakwood, where African Americans sustain territorial control in the face of demographic

changes. However, in Oakwood, like Abbot Kinney Boulevard, newcomers develop strategies that demonstrate how positioning against others can lead to power differentials.

24. In Venice, Lincoln Boulevard is filled with corporate retail chains. It includes Ralphs and Whole Foods supermarkets, banks, Staples, inexpensive chain shopping outlets like Ross Dress for Less, and a wide range of corporate and local fast food establishments, smaller independently owned restaurants, and local thrift shops. Many of these stores, including the corporate chains, integrate a wide range of consumers, raising questions about both near and distant causes of social exclusion and whether it matters that places take on the same look and feel. On Lincoln Boulevard, stores are priced in a way that attracts lower-income residents to shop on the street. In this case, corporate commerce is not uniformly dominating to consumers and we need to identify different types of inequalities that emerge through configurations within and between spaces. On one hand, inequalities remain between different types of stores, as many small stores, like independent groceries, certainly cannot compete with large supermarket corporations like Ralphs or Whole Foods. But on the other hand, inequalities remain between different types of consumption spaces. Regardless of the type of store and owner of it, price point shapes where people will shop and how integrative spaces are.

25. Throughout the '80s and '90s, Oakwood was slowly becoming gentrified. The median home value grew from $150,000 in 1979 to $280,000 in 1989 (Umemoto 2006). However, the gang violence in the mid-1990s impacted the gentrification process as the median price of houses sold in Oakwood dramatically decreased. In 1997, for instance, the median sale price was $161,000, over $100,000 less than the median household value eight years earlier. (For year by year housing sales by neighborhood see: http://www.betsysellsvenice.com/convertedpages/realestatesalesneighborhoodpage.html.) Real estate agents had a difficult time selling properties because of the area's reputation for violence and fear, and with limited selling options they contacted existing homeowners to see if they had an interest in purchasing additional properties.

Yet after the intense gang war subsided, the relationship between Abbot Kinney Boulevard and Oakwood was reconfigured. A combination of local community action, economic development, and city-led accomplishments during the late '90s and early 2000s helped to transform Oakwood into a safer location. Increased police presence, including the organization of community policing and Oakwood neighborhood watch groups, led to more arrests. In addition, Ruth Galanter, the city councilwoman for the district at that time, worked closely with the Los Angeles City Attorney's Office and the Los Angeles Police Department in order to implement a confrontational gang injunction. Complementary actions created a safer environment, which allowed real estate brokers to reframe their selling angle.

26. Document acquired at open house in Oakwood.

27. See Jacobs (1961); Oldenburg (1999); Florida (2002); and, most recently, Anderson (2011).

Chapter Seven

1. Attention to the intersection of population changes and neighborhood relations parallels Park, Burgess, and McKenzie's (1925) classic ecological perspective to explain the growing city of Chicago during the early twentieth century. They focused on how population shifts, in their time largely involving the absorption of new European immigrants by the city, facilitated a process of neighborhood invasion and succession. Park and others argued that newcomers challenged the established local cultures by their sheer volume, gave rise to their own neighborhood institutions, and ultimately succeeded the former residents. Yet they also believed that the process of invasion/succession was part of a natural economic order of cities. As a result, they failed to scrutinize the internal neighborhood compositions and social configurations between distinct groups, making it impossible to know what roles different groups played in influencing the momentum of change and fundamentally buying into the idea that economic forces promote a racial and ethnic order of community differentiation. By this logic, race and ethnicity serve as concrete categories solidified by economic competition. As we have seen in Venice, the sheer numbers of people do not necessarily result in control of neighborhood public cultures. Stabilizing mechanisms, even if benefiting only a small proportion of the overall population, possess their own carrying potential and operate as a unique type of local power.

The Chicago School did not stop with inquiries into ecological processes as a natural order of cities, however. Robert Park (1915, 1952) also championed a tradition of grounded empirical observations of the formation of subcultures and intergroup dynamics in American cities. In studies of interaction patterns between different groups, ethnographers working within this tradition have performed the arduous task of closely observing neighborhoods, taking copious field notes, and finely detailing the daily negotiations between people in various urban settings. We have learned a tremendous amount about the inner workings of cities from ethnographers, who have provided us with snapshots of particular eras from the points of view of the people whom they have studied. While urban ethnographers capture the tensions within neighborhoods and even within groups, they have shied away from one of the key Chicago School tenets; that is, neighborhoods and cities are constantly in flux.

Privileging the study of stasis and order over change and unrest, urban ethnographers tend to isolate settled peoples, times, and places. They paint portraits of constant demographic compositions, continuous inter- and intragroup configurations, consistent moral positions, and repetitive uses of local spaces. Finding "order" amidst commonly upheld conceptions of "chaos" or "disorder" has long remained one of the most important ethnographic warrants, as a tool to debunk stereotypes and urban myths about the most marginalized peoples and places (Katz 1997). The importance of this perspective notwithstanding, it strategically tells part of a story. Neither conflict nor community is constant in neighborhood relations; each is called into action at given moments under particular conditions. Adding a historical approach to the ethnography of neighborhoods and groups allows us to capture the variations within and between groups over time.

2. Social scientists often conceptualize stability in the face of change as "resistance," especially in regard to gentrification. See Williams (1988); Abu-Lughod (1994); Smith (1996); Mele (2000); Newman and Wyly (2006); and Slater (2006, 2008). Certainly resistance is part of the gentrification story, but I am cautious of relying on it as an overarching perspective about stabilizing forces. History is an ongoing process, and strategic political action contributes to neighborhood development and inter- and intragroup configurations through constant transitions of places over time. It is unclear whether or not African American senior citizens in Oakwood are resisting gentrification on a daily basis or whether they are sustaining their own local culture, built up over time, and in the process entering into politicized struggles. I think it is the latter. Their durable local culture is not the outcome of strategic political action against white gentrifiers alone. On the contrary, their resistance to white gentrifiers is possible because they already established a local culture, an outgrowth of previous struggles, including struggles based on segregation rather than gentrification. They build upon the past. Mechanisms are already in place for them to act as a political group: knowledge and access to resources, networks with other African Americans, knowledge and availability of meeting spaces, a stable segment of homeowners, and a history of organizing. The influx of gentrifiers solidifies contestations in moments, making it seem like organized resistance is the impetus of action. Likewise, in the case of the Venice Boardwalk, I find it difficult to make the case that the formation and continuation of this economic culture are based upon resistance, even though some certainly mobilize politically on occasion. Some of the most marginalized members of society, such as low-income African Americans, undocumented immigrants, and homeless men and women, build upon the boardwalk's opportunities, become comfortable with them over time, and some of the participants then organize and fight to sustain them in the face of challenges. Resistance is not the only force in sustaining the boardwalk ecology. It is part of a cyclical process: the economic ecology supports opportunities for political resistance, which on occasion play a part in challenging the constitutionality of regulations and help to sustain the economic ecology.

3. See Espiritu (1992); Sanchez (1993); and Saito (1998).

4. See Portes and Stepick (1993); and Stepick et al. (2003).

5. See Sanjek (1998); Sabagh and Bozorgmehr (2004); Smith (2005); Kasinitz et al. (2006); Foner (2007); Kasinitz et al. (2008).

6. See McClain et al. (2006); McClain et al. (2007).

7. See Stanger-Ross (2010).

8. At the same time that some members of distinct racial-ethnic categories experience upward mobility, others experience separation, stagnation, and downward mobility. My point is not to say that there is any single trajectory, but instead that socioeconomic differences—including different trajectories of mobility—are occurring at the same time. One new agenda for urban sociology is to take count of the simultaneity of trajectories and rethink how we talk about race, ethnicity, and class in American neighborhoods. A one-size-fits-all approach to any social category and neighborhood public culture is obsolete; in fact, it's unclear if this approach ever really had a legitimate place at the table. In-group differences were central to two of the most important classics on African Americans, W. E. B. DuBois's (1903) *The Souls of Black Folks* and Drake and Cayton's ([1945] 1993) *Black Metropolis*, but also to more modern sociological classics, such as Anderson's (1976) *Place on the Corner*, Wilson's (1978) *Declining Significance of Race*, and Pattillo-McCoy's (1999) *Black Picket Fences*.

9. For more on the black middle class, see Jackson Jr. (2001); Pattillo (2007); Hunt (2010); for more on the Latino middle classes see Agius Vallejo and Lee (2009); for more on the Asian middle classes see Horton (1995), Saito (1998), and Zhou and Kim (2004).

10. For a study of gentrification in Harlem see Jackson Jr. (2001); for a study of gentrification in the South Side of Chicago, see Pattillo (2007); for a comparative study of the two, see Hyra (2008). For a report on Latino gentrification in Spanish Harlem, see Berger (2002). For a multifaceted exploration of Latino spaces, inter- and intragroup dynamics in Spanish Harlem, see Dávila (2004)

11. Urban sociologists should privilege neither political-economic nor ecological processes. They are both fundamental to the ways people become configured in time and space. These macroprocesses do not give rise to objective racial and ethnic groups that operate the same in all times and places. Racial and ethnic groups are put together in ways that are often outside of their control, having to do with population flows and the political economy of the city. Thomas and Znaniecki's (1918–1920) study of the Polish peasant migrating to Chicago is a classic example. The creation of the category "Polish" involved the fitting together of people of different regions of Poland in a new context in which they became positioned in close proximity to other ethnic groups. The same was the case with the emergence of Italians, Irish, Germans, and other ethnic whites as categorical identities. We are now seeing similar processes take place with the classifications of groups and neighborhoods as Mexican, Chinese, Japanese, or Korean, once again overshadowing previous differences in their places/regions

of origin. The crystallization of groups and neighborhoods is further exaggerated when we label them as Latino and Asian. The key to understanding these
classifications of neighborhoods and groups is to dissect the coercive processes
by which they come together and differentiate.

12. For San Francisco cases, see Bourgois and Schonberg (2009) and Gowan
(2010).

13. For a case in New York's West Village, see Duneier (1999).

14. See Greenberg (2008) for an account of rebranding New York City. Immigration is commonly a major driver of urban population growth, but the 2010
U.S. Census shows that growth in Washington, D.C., a city long recognized as
having a majority black population, stems from the influx of wealthier whites.
This significant event speaks to a major transformation to the meaning of the
American urban center, one that has been taking place for several decades
across the country in other major cities.

15. The so-called ruins found in center cities like Detroit have become definitive markers of their public cultures. Detroit in particular has become the representative case of the durable imagery of urban decline, giving rise to a number of photo essays, websites, documentaries, and books on the visibility of its
abandonment. For the definitive history of Detroit's postwar decline, see Sugrue
(1996). As places rebuild their center cities, we also cannot ignore the fact that
new visible pockets of poverty emerge, including suburban locations beyond the
classic urban core. For studies of the recently changing and declining inner-ring
suburbs in the United States, see Frey (2001) and Murphy (2010).

16. See Bourgois (1996); Anderson (1999); Venkatesh (2000); Fairbanks II
(2009); Goffman (2009); and Wacquant (2009).

17. Park, Burgess, and McKenzie (1925) or Wirth (1938) were, of course, not
the first to theorize this shift, although they did it with great attention to the spec-
ificity of "place," i.e., Chicago. But the shift from community to society (Tönnies
1887), mechanical solidarity to organic solidarity (Durkheim [1893] 1997), and
feudalism to capitalism (Marx [1859] 1978) remain central categories to account
for the macrofoundations of urbanization. Moreover, as Sennett (1974) reminds
us, tensions stemming from urban diversity long preceded the rise of the American metropolis. The crowding of the European capital cities of the eighteenth
century generated a new "public region" that was built upon "diverse, complex
social groups . . . brought into ineluctable contact."

18. See Ellen (2000); Alba (2009); and Logan and Zhang (2010).

19. Almost forty years after Molotch (1972) defined the process of "managed
integration" due to the propinquity of whites and blacks, a new era of population shifts requires that we still think about similar sets of issues, not just in the
United States, but also on a global scale. I would argue that new difficulties of
integration are fundamentally class based, although race and ethnicity are often
visible lenses through which class differences emerge in many situations. Cal-

deira (2000) has called attention to a new "city of walls," arguing that the proximity of classes is giving rise to a new type of urban segregation of fortified enclaves in São Paolo. Uncovering this mechanism—and others like it throughout the world—requires detailed investigations of places and the processes of sharing space.

20. See Suttles (1968).

Bibliography

Abbott, Andrew. 1995. "Things of Boundaries." *Social Research* 62(4): 857–882.
———. 2002. "Los Angeles and the Chicago School." *City and Community* 1(1): 33–38.
Abu-Lughod, Janet (editor). 1994. *From Urban Village to East Village: The Battle for New York's Lower East Side.* Oxford: Blackwell.
———. 1999. *New York, Chicago, Los Angeles: America's Global Cities.* Minneapolis: University of Minnesota Press.
Adler, Patricia. 1969. *A History of the Venice Area.* Los Angeles: Department of City Planning.
Agius Vallejo, Jody, and Jennifer Lee. 2009. "Brown Picket Fences: The Immigrant Narrative and Patterns of Giving Back among the Mexican Origin Middle-Class in Los Angeles." *Ethnicities* 9 (1): 5–23.
Alba, Richard. 2009. *Blurring the Color Line: A New Chance for an Integrated America.* Cambridge, MA: Harvard University Press.
Alexander, Schell, and Carolyn Elayne Alexander. 1991. "Interview with Mercier Reese." In Carolyn Elayne Alexander (editor), *Abbot Kinney's Venice-of-America.* Vol. 1, *The Golden Years: 1905–1920,* p. 215. Los Angeles: Los Angeles Westside Genealogical Society.
Anderson, Elijah. 1976. *A Place on the Corner.* Chicago: University of Chicago Press.
———. 1990. *Streetwise: Race, Class, and Change in an Urban Community.* Chicago: University of Chicago Press.
———. 1999. *Code of the Street: Decency, Violence, and the Moral Life of the Inner City.* New York: W. W. Norton.
———. 2011. *The Cosmopolitan Canopy: Race and Civility in Everyday Life.* New York: W. W. Norton.
Anderson, Nels. 1923. *The Hobo: The Sociology of the Homeless Man.* Chicago: University of Chicago Press.

Anderton, Frances. 2001. "A Modernist Temple Replaces a Dive." *New York Times*, September 13, p. F3.

Argonaut Newspaper. 2006. "Oakwood House Declared Public Nuisance; Owners Barred from Site." January 28.

Astvasadoorian, Raffy. 1998. "California's Two-Prong Attack against Gang Crime and Violence: The Street Terrorism Enforcement and Prevention Act and Anti-Gang Injunctions." *La Verne Law Review: Journal of Juvenile Law* 19: 272.

Avila, Eric. 2004. *Popular Culture in the Age of White Flight: Fear and Fantasy in Suburban Los Angeles*. Berkeley: University of California Press.

Banham, Reyner. 1971. *Los Angeles: The Architecture of Four Ecologies*. Berkeley: University of California Press.

Becker, Howard S. 1963. *Outsiders: Studies in the Sociology of Deviance*. New York: Free Press.

Berger, Joseph. 2002. "A Puerto Rican Rebirth in El Barrio; After Exodus, Gentrification Changes Face of East Harlem." *New York Times*, December 10.

Berkson, Carole. 1981. "Street Vendor's Blues." *Free Venice Beachhead*, no. 135 (March).

Beveridge, Andrew A., and Susan Weber. 2003. "Race and Class in the Developing New York and Los Angeles Metropolises, 1940–2000." In David Halle (editor), *New and Los Angeles: Politics, Society, and Culture*, pp. 49–78. Chicago: University of Chicago Press.

Billboard: The World's Foremost Amusement Weekly. 1946. "Venice Pier, Calif: Spot Will be Razed." January 26, p. 62.

Blakeley, Edward J., and Mary Gail Snyder. 1997. *Fortress America. Gated Communities in the United States*. Washington, D.C.: Brookings Institution Press and Lincoln Institute of Land Policy.

Blalock, Hubert M. Jr. 1967. *Toward a Theory of Minority Group Relations*. New York: John Wiley.

Bobo, Lawrence D., Melvin L. Oliver, James H. Johnson Jr., and Abel Valenzuela Jr. 2002. *Prismatic Metropolis: Inequality in Los Angeles*. New York: Russell Sage Foundation.

Bonacich, Edna. 1973. "A Theory of Middleman Minorities." *American Sociological Review* 38 (October): 583–594.

Bottles, Scott L. 1987. *Los Angeles and the Automobile: The Making of the Modern City*. Berkeley: University of California Press.

Bourdieu, Pierre. 1977. *Outline of a Theory of Practice*. Cambridge: Cambridge University Press.

———. 1984. *Distinction: A Social Critique of the Judgment of Taste*. Cambridge, MA: Harvard University Press.

Bourgois, Philippe. 1996. *In Search of Respect: Selling Crack in El Barrio*. Cambridge: Cambridge University Press.

Bourgois, Philippe, and Jeff Schonberg. 2009. *Righteous Dopefiend*. Berkeley: University of California Press.

Bradbury, Ray. 1999. *Death Is a Lonely Business*. New York: HarperCollins.

Bratton, William J. 1998. *Turnaround: How America's Top Cop Reversed the Crime Epidemic*. New York: Random House.

Brenner, Neil. 2003. "Stereotypes, Archetypes, and Prototypes: Three Uses of Superlatives in Contemporary Urban Studies." *City and Community* 2(3): 205–216.

Brooks, David. 2000. *Bobos in Paradise: The New Upper Class and How They Got There*. New York: Touchstone.

Brown, Janelle. 2005. "Venice, Calif., Is Turning into Sunrise Boulevard." *New York Times*, November 20.

Brown-Saracino, Japonica. 2010. *A Neighborhood That Never Changes: Gentrification, Social Preservation, and the Search for Authenticity*. Chicago: University of Chicago Press.

Bulmer, Martin. 1984. *The Chicago School of Sociology: Institutionalization, Diversity, and the Rise of Sociological Research*. Chicago: University of Chicago Press.

Burgess, Ernest. 1925. "The Growth of the City: An Introduction to a Research Project." In Robert E. Park, Ernest W. Burgess, and Roderick D. McKenzie (editors), *The City*, pp. 47–62. Chicago: University of Chicago Press.

Calavita, Kitty. 1992. *Inside the State: The Bracero Program, Immigration, and the I.N.S.* New York: Routledge.

Caldeira, Teresa P. R. 2000. *City of Walls: Crime, Segregation, and Citizenship in São Paulo*. Berkeley: University of California Press.

Čapek, Stella M., and John I. Gilderbloom. 1992. *Community versus Commodity: Tenants and the American City*. Albany: State University of New York Press.

Caulfield, Jon. 1994. *City Form and Everyday Life: Toronto's Gentrification and Critical Social Practice*. Toronto: University of Toronto Press.

Charles, Camille Zubrinsky. 2006. *Won't You Be My Neighbor? Race, Class, and Residence in Los Angeles*. New York: Russell Sage Foundation.

Citron, Alan. 1986. "Summer Start Seen for Long-Stalled Project Council OKs Canal Restoration Plan." *Los Angeles Times*, February 9, p. WS1.

Clark, Terry Nichols (editor). 2004. *The City as an Entertainment Machine*. Amsterdam: JAI/Elsevier.

Cohen, Jean. 1985. "Strategy versus Identity: New Theoretical Paradigms and Contemporary Social Movements." *Social Research* 52(4): 663–716.

Collins, Randall. 2004. *Interaction Ritual Chains*. Princeton, NJ: Princeton University Press.

Crawford, Margaret. 1992. "The World Is a Shopping Mall." In Michael Sorkin (editor), *Variations on a Theme Park*, pp. 3–30. New York: Hill and Wang.

Cunningham, Lynn. 1976. *Venice, California: From City to Suburb*. UCLA. Unpublished PhD dissertation.

Davidson, Rick. 1981. "Free Venice—Myth or Reality." *Free Venice Beachhead*, no. 141 (September).

———. 1983. "Free Venice; On Stage or Off." *Free Venice Beachhead*, no. 163 (July).

Dávila, Arlene. 2001. *Latinos Inc.: Marketing and the Making of a People*. Berkeley: University of California Press.

———. 2004. *Barrio Dreams: Puerto Ricans, Latinos and the Neoliberal City*. Berkeley: University of California Press.

Davis, Mike. (1990) 1992. *City of Quartz: Excavating the Future in Los Angeles*. New York: Vintage Books.

———. (1998) 1999. *Ecology of Fear: Los Angeles and the Imagination of Disaster*. New York: Vintage Books.

Dear, Michael (editor). 2001. *From Chicago to LA: Making Sense of Urban Theory*. Thousand Oaks, CA: Sage.

———. 2002. "Los Angeles and the Chicago School: Invitation to a Debate." *City and Community* 1(1): 5–32.

Dear, Michael J., and Jennifer R. Wolch. 1987. *Landscapes of Despair: From Deindustrialization to Homelessness*. Cambridge: Polity Press.

De Certeau, Michel. 1984. *The Practice of Everyday Life*. Berkeley: University of California Press.

DiMassa, Cara Mia, and Stuart Pfeifer. 2005. "2 Strategies on Policing Homeless: LAPD Chief Touts Arrests for Crimes Downtown. Sheriff Says Sweeps Won't Solve the Big Problem." *Los Angeles Times*, October 6, p. A1.

Doherty, Shawn. 1991. "Changing Channels Plan to Renovate Venice Waterways OK'd after 30 Years." *Los Angeles Times*, November 17, Metro, p. 1.

———. 1992. "Not Welcome," *Los Angeles Times*, March 5, p. 1.

Dolgon, Corey. 2005. *End of the Hamptons: Scenes from the Class Struggle in America's Paradise*. New York: New York University Press.

Douglas, Mary. 1966. *Purity and Danger: An Analysis of the Concepts of Pollution and Taboo*. London: Routledge.

Drake, St. Clair, and H. Cayton. (1945) 1993. *Black Metropolis: A Study of Negro Life in a Northern City*. Chicago: University of Chicago Press.

DuBois, W. E. B. (1903) 1989. *The Souls of Black Folk*. New York: Penguin Books.

Dully, Larry. 1970. *An Analysis of the Forces Affecting Low-Income Housing in Venice, California*. Department of Urban and Regional Planning, University of Southern California. Unpublished manuscript.

Duneier, Mitchell. 1999. *Sidewalk*. New York: Farrar, Straus and Giroux.

Durkheim, Emile. (1893) 1997. *The Division of Labor in Society*. New York: Free Press.

Echavaria, Vince. 2006. "Groups Want Chain Store Ban on Boardwalk, Abbot Kinney." *Argonaut*, June 22.

Ehrenreich, Ben. 1999. "Crips and Bloods Unite: Nation of Islam Steps in to Challenge Gang Injunction." *Los Angeles Weekly*, July 7.

Elias, Norbert. 1994. *The Civilizing Process*. Oxford: Blackwell.

Elias, Norbert, and J. L. Scotson. 1965. *The Established and the Outsiders: A Sociological Enquiry into Community Problems*. London: Frank Cass.

Eliopoulos, Christina (writer and director). 2009. *Greetings from Asbury Park*. Tribeca Film Institute Reframe Collection.

Ellen, Ingrid Gould. 2000. *Sharing America's Neighborhoods: The Prospects for Stable Racial Integration*. Cambridge, MA: Harvard University Press.

Espiritu, Yen Le. 1992. *Asian American Panethnicity: Bridging Institutions and Identities*. Philadelphia: Temple University Press.

Fairbanks II, Robert P. 2009. *How It Works: Recovering Citizens in Post-Welfare Philadelphia*. Chicago: University of Chicago Press.

Fanucchi, Kenneth. 1984a. "Canal Rebuilding Plan Gains." *Los Angeles Times*, July 12, p. WS1.

———. 1984b. "Oakwood Determined to Stamp Out the Pushers." *Los Angeles Times*, August 5, p. WS1.

Faris, Gerald. 1975. "Venice Canals—A Slum Minus Misery." *Los Angeles Times*, June 1, p. WS1.

———. 1976. "Future of Venice: Status Quo? Growth? Rollback?" *Los Angeles Times*, February 8, p. WS1.

Farley, Reynolds, and William H. Frey. 1994. "Changes in the Segregation of Whites from Blacks during the 1980s: Small Steps Towards a More Integrated Society." *American Sociological Review* 59(1): 23–45.

Ferderber, Skip. 1971. "Meeting Fails to Unite Canal Property Owners, Tenants." *Los Angeles Times*, June 13, p. WS1.

Fishman, Robert. 1987. *Bourgeois Utopias: The Rise and Fall of Suburbia*. New York: Basic Books.

Firey, Walter. 1945. "Sentiment and Symbolism as Ecological Variables." *American Sociological Review* 10(2): 140–148.

Florida, Richard. 2002. *The Rise of the Creative Class*. New York: Basic Books.

Fogelson, Robert M. 1967. *The Fragmented Metropolis: Los Angeles, 1850–1930*. Berkeley: University of California Press.

Foner, Nancy. 2007. "How Exceptional Is New York? Migration and Multiculturalism in the Empire City." *Ethnic and Racial Studies* 30(6): 999–1023.

Foucault, Michel. 1991. "Governmentality." In Graham Burchell, Colin Gordon, and Peter Miller (editors), *The Foucault Effect: Studies in Governmentality*, pp. 87–104. Chicago: University of Chicago Press.

Freeman, Lance. 2006. *There Goes the 'Hood: Views of Gentrification from the Ground Up*. Philadelphia: Temple University Press.

Frey, William H. 2001. "Melting Pot Suburbs: A Census 2000 Study of Suburban Diversity." Washington, D.C.: Brookings Institution.

Gans, Herbert J. 1962. *The Urban Villagers: Group and Class in the Life of Italian-Americans*. New York: Free Press.

———. 1967. *The Levittowners: Ways of Life and Politics in a New Suburban Community*. New York: Alfred A. Knopf.

———. 1999. "The Possibility of a New Racial Hierarchy in the Twenty-First-Century United States." In Michèle Lamont (editor), *The Cultural Territories of Race: Black and White Boundaries*, pp. 371–389. Chicago: University of Chicago Press.

Garcia, Kenneth J., and Nancy Hill-Holtzman. 1990. "Terror Takes Brief Holiday: Drugs, Gangs Resurface in Oakwood Neighborhood Only Hours after Bush Visit" (Home Edition). *Los Angeles Times*, May 24, p.1.

Garreau, Joel. 1992. *Edge Cities: Life on the New Frontier*. New York: Anchor Books.

Geertz, Clifford. 1983. *Local Knowledge: Further Essays in Interpretive Anthropology*. New York: Basic Books.

Glass, Ruth. 1964. Introduction to *London: Aspects of Change*. London: Centre for Urban Studies and MacKibben and Kee.

Goffman, Alice. 2009. "On the Run: Wanted Men in a Philadelphia Ghetto." *American Sociological Review* 74(3): 339–357.

Goode, Erich, and Nachman Ben-Yehuda. 1994. *Moral Panics: The Social Construction of Deviance*. Oxford: Blackwell.

Gottdiener, Mark. 2001. *The Theming of America: Dreams, Visions, and Commercial Spaces*. Boulder, CO: Westview Press.

———. 2002. "Urban Analysis as Merchandising: The 'LA School' and the Understanding of Metropolitan Development." In John Eade and Christopher Mele (editors), *Understanding the City: Contemporary and Future Perspectives*, pp. 159–180. Malden, MA: Blackwell.

Gowan, Teresa. 2010. *Hobos, Hustlers, and Backsliders: Homeless in San Francisco*. Minneapolis: University of Minnesota Press.

Gray, Fred. 2006. *Designing the Seaside*. London: Reaktion Books.

Greenberg, Miriam. 2008. *Branding New York: How a City in Crisis Was Sold to the World*. New York: Routledge.

Gregory, Steven. 1998. *Black Corona: Race and the Politics of Place in an Urban Community*. Princeton, NJ: Princeton University Press.

Groves, Martha. 2004. "Sore Spots on a Split Venice Boardwalk: L.A. Ordinance Would Require Vendors on the 'Free' Side to Pay for Privilege of Peddling." *Los Angeles Times*, October 26, 2004, p. A1.

Groves, Martha. 2010. "Seeking Establishment Recognition of Beat Hangout's Importance." *Los Angeles Times*, January 7. http://articles.latimes.com/2010/jan/07/local/la-me-venice-west7–2010jan07.

Haag, John. 1978. "The Venice Peace and Freedom Party." *Free Venice Beachhead*, no. 100 (April).

Halle, David (editor). 2003. *New York and Los Angeles: Politics, Society, and Culture*. Chicago: University of Chicago Press.

Halle, David, Robert Gedeon, and Andrew A. Beveridge. 2003. "Residential Separation and Segregation, Racial and Latino Identity, and the Racial Composition of Each City." In David Halle (editor), *New York and Los Angeles: Politics, Society, and Culture*, pp. 150–191. Chicago: University of Chicago Press.

Hannerz, Ulf. 1980. *Exploring the City: Inquiries Towards an Urban Anthropology*. New York: Columbia University Press.

Hansen, Ken. 1965a. "Bright Future Seen in Rejuvenation of Venice." *Los Angeles Times*, December 26, p. WS1.

———. 1965b. "City Pledges No Apartments for Venice Canal Improvement Area." *Los Angeles Times*, December 2, p. WS1.

Harris, Chauncy D., and Edward L. Ullman. 1945. "The Nature of Cities." *Annals of the American Academy of Political and Social Sciences* 242(1):7–17.

Harris, Robert J. 1966. *Venice, California: Urban Rehabilitation in a Small American Community*. UCLA. MA thesis.

Harvey, David. 1973. *Social Justice and the City*. Baltimore: Johns Hopkins University Press.

Hastings, Deborah. 1994. "Venice's Oakwood District: 'Los Angeles at Its Worst.' " *Los Angeles Sentinel*, January 27.

Hobsbawm, Eric, and Terence Ranger (editors). 1983. *The Invention of Tradition*. New York: Cambridge University Press.

Hopper, Kim. 2003. *Reckoning with Homelessness*. Ithaca, NY: Cornell University Press.

Horton, John. 1995. *The Politics of Diversity: Immigration, Resistance, and Change in Monterey Park, California*. Philadelphia: Temple University Press.

Hoyt, Homer. 1939. *The Structure and Growth of Residential Neighborhoods in American Cities*. Washington, D.C.: Federal Housing Administration.

Hunt, Darnell. 2010. "Introduction: Dreaming of Black Los Angeles." In Darnell Hunt and Ana-Christina Ramón (editors), *Black Los Angeles: American Dreams and Racial Realities*, pp. 1–17. New York: New York University Press.

Hunter, Albert. 1974. *Symbolic Communities: The Persistence and Change of Chicago's Local Communities*. Chicago: University of Chicago Press.

Hurewitz, Daniel. 2007. *Bohemian Los Angeles and the Making of Modern Politics*. Berkeley: University of California Press.

Hyra, Derek. 2008. *The New Urban Renewal: The Economic Transformation of Harlem and Bronzeville*. Chicago: University of Chicago Press.

Iceland, John. 2004. "Beyond Black and White: Metropolitan Residential Segregation in Multi-Ethnic America." *Social Science Research* 33: 248–271.

———. 2009. *Where We Live Now: Race and Immigration in the United States.* Berkeley: University of California Press.

Jackson, John Jr. 2001. *Harlemworld: Doing Race and Class in Contemporary Black America.* Chicago: University of Chicago Press.

Jackson, Kenneth T. 1985. *Crabgrass Frontier: The Suburbanization of the United States.* New York: Oxford University Press.

Jacobs, Jane. 1961. *The Death and Life of Great American Cities.* New York: Vintage Books.

Jager, Michael. 1986. "Class Definition and the Esthetics of Gentrification: Victoriana in Melbourne." In Neil Smith and Peter Williams (editors), *Gentrification of the City*, pp. 78–91. Boston: Allen and Unwin.

Jencks, Christopher. 1994. *The Homeless.* Cambridge, MA: Harvard University Press.

Jonas, A. E. G., and D. Wilson (editors). 1999. *The Urban Growth Machine: Critical Perspectives Two Decades Later.* Albany: State University of New York Press.

Kaplan, Tracey. 1987. "Residents Resume Old Feud over New Plan to Upgrade Venice Canals." *Los Angeles Times*, March 15, p. WS1.

Kasinitz, Philip, John H. Mollenkopf, Mary C. Waters (editors). 2006. *Becoming New Yorkers.* New York: Russell Sage Foundation.

Kasinitz, Philip, John H. Mollenkopf, Mary C. Waters, and Jennifer Holdaway. 2008. *Inheriting the City: The Children of Immigrants Come of Age.* Cambridge, MA: Harvard University Press.

Katz, Jack. 1988. *Seductions of Crime.* New York: Basic Books.

———. 1997. "Ethnography's Warrants." *Sociological Methods and Research* 25(4): 391–423.

———. 2003. "Metropolitan Crime Myths." In David Halle (editor), *New and Los Angeles: Politics, Society, and Culture*, pp. 195–224. Chicago: University of Chicago Press.

———. 2010. "Time for New Urban Ethnographies." *Ethnography* 11(1): 25–44.

Katz, Jack, Peter Ibarra, and Margarethe Kusenbach. *Seven Hollywoods: Resident Biographies and Neighborhood Transformation, Street Life and Social Inequalities, 1880–2010.* Unpublished manuscript.

Khan, Amina. 2010. "Venice Beach Sweep Nets Nearly 50 Violators; Social Services Offered." *Los Angeles Times*, February 12. http://latimesblogs.latimes.com/lanow/2010/02/venice-beach-sweep-nets-nearly-50-violaters-social-services-offered.html.

Komaiko, Leslee. 2003. "Between Yesterday and Today." *Los Angeles Times*, September 25, p. E34.

Kornblum, William. 1974. *Blue Collar Community*. Chicago: University of Chicago Press.

Kramer, Jeff. 1994. "Venice Leaders Call Warning Flyers Racist Activism." *Los Angeles Times*, June 26, p. B18.

Kuh, Patric. 2009. "Fired Up." *Los Angeles Magazine*, February.

Kunstler, James Howard. 1993. *Geography of Nowhere: The Rise and Decline of America's Manmade Landscape*. New York: Simon and Schuster.

Kusenbach, Margarethe. 2003. "Street Phenomenology: The Go-Along as Ethnographic Research Tool." *Ethnography* 4(3): 455–485.

Lamont, Michèle, and Virág Molnár. 2002. "The Study of Boundaries in the Social Sciences." *Annual Review of Sociology* 28:167–195.

Lamont, Michèle, and Laurent Thévenot. 2000. "Introduction: Toward a Renewed Comparative Cultural Sociology." In Michèle Lamont and Laurent Thévenot (editors), *Rethinking Comparative Cultural Sociology: Repertoires of Evaluation in France and the United States*. Cambridge: Cambridge University Press.

Laslett, John H. M. 1996. "Historical Perspectives: Immigration and the Rise of a Distinctive Urban Region, 1900–1970." In Roger Waldinger and Mehdi Bozorgmehr (editors), *Ethnic Los Angeles*, pp. 39–75. New York: Russell Sage Foundation.

Lee, Jennifer. 2002. *Civility in the City: Blacks, Jews, and Koreans in Urban America*. Cambridge, MA: Harvard University Press.

Lee, Jennifer, and Frank D. Bean. 2007. "Reinventing the Color Line: Immigration and America's New Racial/Ethnic Divide." *Social Forces* 86(2): 1–26.

Ley, David. 1980. "Liberal Ideology and the Post-Industrial City." *Annals of the Association of American Geographers* 70(2): 238–258.

———. 1996. *The New Middle Class and the Remaking of the Central City*. Oxford: Oxford University Press.

Light, Ivan, and Edna Bonacich. 1988. *Immigrant Entrepreneurs: Koreans in Los Angeles, 1965–1982*. Berkeley: University of California Press.

Lipton, Lawrence. 1959. *The Holy Barbarians*. New York: Julian Messner.

Lloyd, Richard. 2006. *Neo-Bohemia: Art and Commerce in the Post-Industrial City*. New York: Routledge.

Lofland, Lyn. 1998. *The Public Realm: Exploring the City's Quintessential Social Territory*. New York: Aldine de Gruyter.

Logan, John R., and Harvey L. Molotch. 1987. *Urban Fortunes: The Political Economy of Place*. Berkeley: University of California Press.

Logan, John R., and Charles Zhang. 2010. "Global Neighborhoods: New Pathways to Diversity and Separation." *American Journal of Sociology* 115(4): 1069–1109.

Lopez, Steve. 2005. "Now Comes the Heavy Lifting." *Los Angeles Times*, October 23.

Los Angeles Homeless Services Authority. 2007. *2007 Greater Los Angeles Homeless Count*. Los Angeles: Los Angeles Homeless Services Authority.

Los Angeles Times. 1929. "Venice Canals to Be Filled." June 12, p. 8.

———. 1964. "City Begins Cleanup of Venice Canal System." October 15, p. I2.

———. 1969. "Canal Area Renters May Not Get to Speak at Next Hearing." March 30, p. WS1.

———. 1972. "Trial Under Way on Venice Canal Suits." September 20, p. B1.

Low, Setha. 2003. *Behind the Gates: Life, Security and the Pursuit of Happiness in Fortress America*. New York: Routledge.

Lynch, Kevin. 1960. *The Image of the City*. Cambridge, MA: MIT Press.

Marx, Karl. (1859) 1978. "Preface to A Contribution to the Critique of Political Economy." In Tucker, Robert C. (editor), *The Marx-Engels Reader*, pp. 3–7. New York: W. W. Norton.

Maryjane. 2005. *A Sea Shore Memoir Celebrating Venice: 100th Anniversary, 1905–2005*. Los Angeles: self-published by Maryjane.

Maynard, John Arthur. 1991. *Venice West: The Beat Generation in Southern California*. New Brunswick, NJ: Rutgers University Press.

McClain, Paula D., Niambi M. Carter, Victoria M. DeFrancesco Soto, Monique L. Lyle, Jeffrey D. Grynaviski, Shayla C. Nunnally, Thomas J. Scotto, J. Alan Kendrick, Gerald F. Lackey, and Kendra Davenport Cotton. 2006. "Racial Distancing in a Southern City: Latino Immigrants' Views of Black Americans." *Journal of Politics* 68(3): 571–584.

McClain, Paula D., Monique L. Lyle, Niambi M. Carter, Victoria M. DeFrancesco Soto, Gerald F. Lackey, Kendra Davenport Cotton, Shayla C. Nunnally, Thomas J. Scotto, Jeffrey D. Grynaviski, and J. Alan Kendrick. 2007. "Black Americans and Latino Immigrants in a Southern City: Friendly Neighbors or Economic Competitors?" *Du Bois Review: Social Science Research on Race* 4(1): 97–117.

McKenzie, Evan. 1994. *Privatopia: Homeowner Associations and the Rise of Residential Private Government*. New Haven, CT: Yale University Press.

McLung, William Alexander. 2000. *Landscapes of Desire: Anglo Mythologies of Los Angeles*. Berkeley: University of California Press.

McRoberts, Omar. 2003. *Streets of Glory: Church and Community in a Black Urban Neighborhood*. Chicago: University of Chicago Press.

McWilliams, Carey. 1943. *Southern California: An Island on the Land*. Layton, UT: Gibbs Smith.

Mele, Christopher. 2000. *Selling the Lower East Side: Culture, Real Estate, and Resistance in New York City*. Minneapolis: University of Minnesota Press.

Merton, Robert K. 1936. "The Unanticipated Consequences of Purposive Social Action." *American Sociological Review* 1(6): 894–904.

Mitchell, Don. 2003. *The Right to the City: Social Justice and the Fight for Public Space*. New York: Guildford Press.

Molotch, Harvey. 1972. *Managed Integration: Dilemmas of Doing Good in the City.* Berkeley: University of California Press.

Molotch, Harvey, William Freudenburg, and Krista E. Paulsen. 2000. "History Repeats Itself, But How? City Character, Urban Tradition, and the Accomplishment of Place." *American Sociological Review* 65(6): 791–823.

Murphy, Alexandra K. 2010. "The Symbolic Dilemmas of Suburban Poverty: Challenges & Opportunities Posed by Variations in the Contours of Suburban Poverty." *Sociological Forum* 25(3) (September): 541–569.

Myerhoff, Barbara. 1978. *Number Our Days.* New York: Simon and Schuster.

Myers, Dowell. 2007. *Immigrants and Boomers: Forging a New Social Contract for the Future of America.* New York: Russell Sage Foundation.

Neville, Morgan (director and producer). 2008. *The Cool School: How LA Learned to Love Modern Art.* New York: Arthouse Films.

Newman, Kathe, and Elvin Wyly. 2006. "The Right to Stay Put, Revisited: Gentrification and Resistance to Displacement in New York City." *Urban Studies* 43(1): 23–57.

Oldenburg, Ray. 1999. *Great Good Places: Cafes, Coffee Shops, Bookstores, Bars, Hair Salons, and Other Hangouts at the Heart of a Community.* New York: Marlowe.

Ong, Paul, Edna Bonacich, and Lucie Cheng (editors). 1994. *The New Asian Immigration in Los Angeles and the Global Restructuring.* Philadelphia: Temple University Press.

Overend, William. 1976. "Behind the Scenes at Bohemia-by-the-Beach." *Los Angeles Times,* July 20, p. G1.

Park, Robert E. 1915. "The City: Suggestions for the Investigation of Human Behavior in the City Environment." *American Journal of Sociology* 20(5): 577–612.

———. 1952. *Human Communities.* Glencoe, IL: Free Press.

Park, Robert E., Ernest W. Burgess, and Roderick D. McKenzie. 1925. *The City.* Chicago: University of Chicago Press.

Pattillo, Mary. 2007. *Black on the Block: The Politics of Race and Class in the City.* Chicago: University of Chicago Press.

Pattillo-McCoy, Mary. 1999. *Black Picket Fences: Privilege and Peril among the Black Middle Class.* Chicago: University of Chicago Press.

Portes, Alejandro, and Alex Stepick. 1993. *City on the Edge: The Transformation of Miami.* Berkeley: University of California Press.

Quillian, Lincoln, and Devah Prager. 2001. "Black Neighbors, Higher Crime? The Role of Racial Stereotypes in Evaluations of Neighborhood Crime." *American Journal of Sociology* 107(3): 717–767.

Rainwater, Lee. 1970. *Behind Ghetto Walls: Black Families in a Federal Slum.* Chicago: Aldine.

Reese-Davis, Sonya. 2006. *Arthur L. Reese: The Wizard of Venice*. Los Angeles: Venice Historical Society.

Rieder, Jonathan. 1985. *Canarsie: The Jews and Italians of Brooklyn against Liberalism*. Cambridge, MA: Harvard University Press.

Rosen, Albert, and David Binder. 1969. "News from Western Center on Law and Poverty at the University of Southern California Law Center." August 22.

Rosenthal, Rob. 1994. *Homeless in Paradise: A Map of the Terrain*. Philadelphia: Temple University Press.

Rossi, Peter. 1989. *Down and Out in America: The Origins of Homelessness*. Chicago: University of Chicago Press.

Rothman, Tibby. 2004. "Brand Venice." *Venice Paper* (September/October edition).

———. 2008. "Gang Crackdown or Police Overkill?" *Los Angeles Weekly*, March 7–13: 30–34.

Rowe, Stacy, and Jennifer Wolch. 1990. "Social Networks in Time and Space: Homeless Women in Skid Row." *Annals of the Association of American Geographers* 80(2): 184–204.

Ryon, Ruth. 1999. "Four Houses Are Better Than One for Venice Residents Orson Bean and Actress-Wife Alley Mills, Who Turned One Home on Their Adjoining Lots into a Kitchen." *Los Angeles Times*, Real Estate Section, p. 1.

Sabagh, Georges, and Mehdi Bozorgmehr. 2003. "From 'Give Me Your Poor' to 'Save Our State.' " In David Halle (editor), *New York and Los Angeles: Politics, Society, and Culture*, pp. 99–123. Chicago: University of Chicago Press.

Sabin, Paul. 2005a. "Beaches versus Oil in Greater Los Angeles." In William Deverell and Greg Hise (editors), *Land of Sunshine: An Environmental History of Metropolitan Los Angeles*, pp. 95–114. Berkeley: University of California Press.

———. 2005b. *Crude Politics: The California Oil Market, 1900–1940*. Berkeley: University of California Press.

Saito, Leland T. 1998. *Race and Politics: Asian Americans, Latinos, and Whites in a Los Angeles Suburb*. Urbana: University of Illinois Press.

Sampson, Robert J., and Stephen W. Raudenbush. 2004. "Seeing Disorder: Neighborhood Stigma and the Social Construction of 'Broken Windows.'" *Social Psychology Quarterly* 67(4): 319–342.

Sánchez, George J. 1993. *Becoming Mexican American: Ethnicity, Culture, and Identity in Chicano Los Angeles, 1900–1945*. Oxford: Oxford University Press.

Sanjek, Roger. 1998. *The Future of Us All*. Ithaca, NY: Cornell University Press.

Schrank, Sarah. 2009. *Art and the City: Civic Imagination and Cultural Authority in Los Angeles*. Philadelphia: University of Pennsylvania Press.

Schwieterman, Joseph P. 2004. *When the Railroad Leaves Town: American*

Communities in the Age of Rail Line Abandonment. Kirksville, MO: Truman State University Press.

Schwirian, Kent P. 1983. "Models of Neighborhood Change." *Annual Review of Sociology* 9: 83–102.

Scott, Paula. 2004. *Santa Monica: A History on the Edge.* San Francisco: Arcadia.

See, Carolyn. 1967. "Venice Last Poor Beach." *Los Angeles Times*, November 5, p. B20.

Sennett, Richard. 1974. *The Fall of Public Man.* New York: W. W. Norton.

———. 2008. "The Public Realm." http://www.richardsennett.com/site/SENN/Templates/General2.aspx?pageid=16.

Sherman, Douglas, and Bernard Pipkin. 2005. "The Coast of Southern California: From Santa Monica to Dana Point." In Gary Griggs, Kiki Patsch, and Lauren Savoy (editors), *Living with the Changing California Coast.* Berkeley: University of California Press.

Sides, Josh. 2006. "A Simple Quest for Dignity: African American Los Angeles since World War II." In Martin Schiesl and Mark M. Dodge (editors), *City of Promise: Race and Historical Change in Los Angeles*, pp. 109–136. Claremont, CA: Regina Books.

Simmel, Georg. (1908) 1959. "The Problem of Sociology." In Kurt H. Wolff (editor), *Georg Simmel, 1858–1918: A Collection of Essays with Translations and Bibliography*, pp. 310–335. Columbus: Ohio State University Press.

———. 1955. *Conflict.* New York: Free Press.

Simon, Bryant. 2004. *Boardwalk of Dreams: Atlantic City and the Fate of Urban America.* Oxford: Oxford University Press.

Simpson, Charles. 1981. *Soho: The Artist in the City.* Chicago: University of Chicago Press.

Slater, Tom. 2006. "The Eviction of Critical Perspectives from Gentrification Research." *International Journal of Urban and Regional Research* 30(4): 737–757.

———. 2008. " 'A Literal Necessity to Be Re-Placed': A Rejoinder to the Gentrification Debate." *International Journal of Urban and Regional Research* 32(1): 212–223.

Small, Mario Louis. 2004. *Villa Victoria: The Transformation of Social Capital in a Boston Barrio.* Chicago: University of Chicago Press.

Smith, Jack. 1961. "Venice May Revive Its Canal Dream," *Los Angeles Times*, February 27, p. B1.

Smith, Neil. 1987. "Gentrification and the Rent-Gap." *Annals of the Association of American Geographers* 77 (3): 462–465.

———. 1996. *The New Urban Frontier: Gentrification and the Revanchist City.* London: Routledge.

Smith, Robert Courtney. 2005. *Mexican New York*. Berkeley: University of California Press.

Snow, David, and Leon Anderson. 1993. *Down on Their Luck: A Study of Homeless Street People*. Berkeley: University of California Press.

Soja, Edward. 1996. *Thirdspace: Journey to Los Angeles and Other Real-and-Imagined Places*. Oxford: Blackwell.

———. 2000. *Postmetropolis: Critical Studies of Cities and Regions*. Oxford: Blackwell.

Soja, Edward W., and Allen J. Scott. 1996. "Introduction to Los Angeles: City and Region." In Allen Scott and Edward Soja (editors), *The City: Los Angeles and Urban Theory at the End of the Twentieth Century*, pp. 1–21. Berkeley: University of California Press.

Sorkin, Michael. 1992. *Variations on a Theme Park: The New American City and the End of Public Space*. New York: Hill and Wang.

Springer, Arnold. 1992. *History of Venice of America*, Vol. 1. Venice, CA: Ulan Bator Foundation.

Stanger-Ross, Jordan. 2010. *Staying Italian: Urban Change and Ethnic Life in Postwar Toronto and Philadelphia*. Chicago: University of Chicago Press.

Stanton, Jeffrey. (1993) 2005. *Venice California: "Coney Island of the Pacific."* Los Angeles: Donahue.

Starr, Kevin. 1985. *Inventing the Dream: California through the Progressive Era*. Oxford: Oxford University Press.

———. 1990. *Material Dreams: Southern California through the 1920s*. Oxford: Oxford University Press.

Stepick, Alex, et al. 2003. *This Land Is Our Land: Immigrants and Power in Miami*. Berkeley: University of California Press.

Strauss, Anselm. 1976. *Images of the American City*. New Brunswick, NJ: Transaction Books.

Sugrue, Thomas J. 1996. *The Origins of the Urban Crisis: Race and Inequality in Postwar Detroit*. Princeton, NJ: Princeton University Press.

Suttles, Gerald. 1968. *The Social Order of the Slum: Ethnicity and Territory in the Inner City*. Chicago: University of Chicago Press.

———. 1972. *The Social Construction of Communities*. Chicago: University of Chicago Press.

———. 1984. "The Cumulative Texture of Local Urban Culture." *American Journal of Sociology* 90(2): 283–304.

Szántó, András. 2003. "Hot and Cold: Some Contrasts between the Visual Art Worlds of New York and Los Angeles." In David Halle (editor), *New York and Los Angeles: Politics, Society, and Culture*, pp. 393–422. Chicago: University of Chicago Press.

Taylor, Monique M. 2002. *Harlem between Heaven and Hell*. Minneapolis: University of Minnesota Press.

Thomas, W. I., and Florian Znaniecki. 1918–1920. *The Polish Peasant in Europe and America*. Chicago: University of Chicago Press.

Thornburg, Barbara. 1999. "Open to Interpretation; Building Light, Space and Soul into a House on the Venice Canals." *Los Angeles Times Magazine*, February 21, p. 26.

Thrasher, Frederic. 1927. *The Gang: A Study of 1,313 Gangs in Chicago*. Chicago: University of Chicago Press.

Tilly, Charles. 1996. "Invisible Elbow." *Sociological Forum* 11(4): 589–601.

Tönnies, Ferdinand. (1887) 1957. *Community and Society*. Translated by C. P. Loomis. New York: Harper.

Umemoto, Karen. 2006. *The Truce: Lessons from an LA Gang War*. Ithaca, NY: Cornell University Press.

Vaughan, Diane. 2004. "Theorizing Disaster: Analogy, Historical Ethnography and the Challenger Accident." *Ethnography* 5(3): 315–347.

Venice Paper. 2006. "A Venice Goodbye: Werner G. Scharff, Venice Patriot (1916–2006)." August 23. http://www.venicepaper.net/pmt_comments.php?id=282_0_1_0_C.

Venice Paper. 2007. "This Ain't No Disco—Venice Ain't Loving That Chain Story Feeling." June 1. http://www.venicepaper.net/pmt_more.php?id=347_0_1_0_M.

Venice Publicity Bureau. 1912. Venice I, No 7. (July). Los Angeles Public Library, Venice, Abbot Kinney Memorial Branch.

Venkatesh, Sudhir. 2000. *American Project: The Rise and Fall of a Modern Ghetto*. Cambridge, MA: Harvard University Press.

———. 2001. "Chicago's Pragmatic Planners: American Sociology and the Myth of Community." *Social Science History* 25(2): 275–317.

———. 2006. *Off the Books: The Underground Economy of the Urban Poor*. Cambridge, MA: Harvard University Press.

Vitale, Alex. 2008. *City of Disorder: How the Quality of Life Campaign Transformed New York Politics*. New York: New York University Press.

Wacquant, Loïc. 2008. "Relocating Gentrification: The Working Class, Science and the State in Recent Urban Research." *International Journal of Urban and Regional Research* 32(1): 198–205.

———. 2009. *Punishing the Poor: Neoliberal Government of Social Insecurity*. Durham, NC: Duke University Press.

Wacquant, Loïc, and William J. Wilson. 1989. "The Cost of Racial and Class Exclusion in the Inner City." *Annals of the American Academy of Political and Social Science* 501 (January): 8–25.

Wakin, Michele. 2005. "Not Sheltered, Not Homeless: RVs as Makeshifts." *American Behavioral Scientist* 48(8): 1013–1032.

———. 2008. "Using Vehicles to Challenge Anti-Sleeping Ordinances." *City and Community* 7(4): 309–327.

Waldinger, Roger. 1986. *Through the Eye of the Needle: Immigrants and Enterprise in New York's Trades*. New York: New York University Press.

Waldinger, Roger, and Mehdi Bozorgmehr. 1996. "The Making of a Multicultural Metropolis." In Waldinger and Bozorgmehr (editors), *Ethnic Los Angeles*, pp. 3–37. New York: Russell Sage Foundation.

Walker, Franklin. 1976. "Abbot Kinney's Venice." In John Caughey and LaRee Caughey (editors), *Los Angeles: Biography of a City*, pp. 235–239. Berkeley: University of California Press.

Walker, Gary. 2010. "Venice: Effectiveness of Pinkberry Boycott by Anti-Chain Group Debated after Frozen Yogurt Store Closes Its Abbott Kinney Location." *Argonaut*, May 5.

Warner, Lloyd W. 1959. *The Living and the Dead: A Study of the Symbolic Life of Americans*. Westport, CT: Greenwood Press.

Warren, Charles S. 1934. *History of the Santa Monica Bay Region*. Santa Monica, CA: A. H. Cawston.

Webb, Michael. 2007. *Venice, CA: Art + Architecture in a Maverick Community*. New York: Abrams.

Wedner, Diane. 2008. "The Art of the Venice Art Loft." *Los Angeles Times*, February 17, Real Estate Section, K4.

Weller, Sam. 2005. *The Bradbury Chronicles: The Life of Ray Bradbury*. New York: HarperCollins.

Whyte, William Foote. 1943. *Street Corner Society: The Social Structure of an Italian Slum*. Chicago: University of Chicago Press.

Whyte, William H. 1988. *City: Rediscovering the Center*. New York: Doubleday.

Williams, Brett. 1988. *Upscaling Downtown: Stalled Gentrification in Washington, D.C.* Ithaca, NY: Cornell University Press.

Willis, Paul. 1978. *Profane Culture*. London: Routledge and Kegan Paul.

———. 2000. *The Ethnographic Imagination*. Cambridge: Polity Press.

Wilson, J. Q., and G. L. Kelling. 1982. "Broken Windows: The Police and Neighborhood Safety." *Atlantic Monthly* 249 (March): 29–38.

Wilson, William J. 1978. *Declining Significance of Race: Blacks and the Changing American Institutions*. Chicago: University of Chicago Press.

———. 1987. *The Truly Disadvantaged: The Inner City, The Underclass, and Urban Social Policy*. Chicago: University of Chicago Press.

———. 1996. *When Work Disappears: The World of the New Urban Poor*. New York: Random House.

Wirth, Louis. 1938. "Urbanism as a Way of Life." *American Journal Of Sociology* 44 (July): 1–24.

Wolch, Jennifer R. 1996. "From Global to Local: The Rise of Homelessness in Los Angeles During the 1980s." In Allen Scott and Edward Soja (editors), *The City: Los Angeles and Urban Theory at the End of the Twentieth Century*, pp. 390–425. Berkeley: University of California Press.

Wolch, Jennifer R., and Dear, Michael J. 1993. *Malign Neglect: Homelessness in an American City.* San Francisco: Jossey-Bass.

Woo, Elaine. 2003. "Obituaries: Flora Chavez, 85, Longtime Westside Activist, Volunteer." *Los Angeles Times,* September 14, p. B18.

Wood Daniel. 2005. "In Bohemian Zone of Free Spirits, Can Spaces Be Assigned?" *Christian Science Monitor,* March 28, p. 1.

Zadeh, Stellah. 1974. "Venice Canals Crackdown Due." *Evening Outlook,* October 31.

Zahniser, David. 2006. "Welcome to Gentrification City." *Los Angeles Weekly,* August 24.

Zerubavel, Eviatar. 2007. "Generally Speaking: The Logic and Mechanics of Social Pattern Analysis." *Sociological Forum* 22(2): 131–145.

Zhou, Min, and R. Kim. 2004. "A Tale of Two Metropolises: Immigrant Chinese Communities in New York and Los Angeles." In David Halle (editor), *New York and Los Angeles: Politics, Society, and Culture,* pp. 124–149. Chicago: University of Chicago Press.

Zorbaugh, Harvey Warren. 1929. *The Gold Coast and the Slum: A Sociological Study of Chicago's Near North Side.* Chicago: University of Chicago Press.

Zukin, Sharon. (1982) 1989. *Loft Living: Culture and Capital in Urban Change.* New Brunswick, NJ: Rutgers University Press.

———. 1991. *Landscapes of Power: From Detroit to Disneyland.* Berkeley: University of California Press.

———. 1995. *The Cultures of Cities.* Cambridge, MA: Blackwell Publishers.

———. 2010. *Naked Cities.* Oxford: Oxford University Press.

Zukin, Sharon, and Ervin Kosta. 2004. "Bourdieu Off Broadway: Managing Distinction on a Shopping Black in the East Village." *City and Community* 3(2): 101–114.

Index

Abbot Kinney Boulevard, 6, 7, 10, 13, 17, 42, 44, 204–34; coherence of culture, 219–25; festival, 215–16, 230–31; relation to Oakwood, 15, 18, 209, 215, 228

Abbot Kinney District Association, 212, 215, 218

Abbot's Habit (coffee shop), 6, 205–6

African Americans, 5, 16, 22, 31–33, 40, 46, 55–56; impact on neighborhood public culture, 48–59; migration of, 8; stigmatization of, 70, 76, 92; see also segregation

Anderson, Elijah, 58, 253n6

artist lofts, 3, 29, 30, 141, 208, 224–26, 232, 267n26

artists, 1, 3, 6, 29–30, 125, 139, 141, 169, 173, 189; as gentrifiers, 70–71, 224, 232; exploiting Free Speech Zone market, 178–180, 199–200; influence on architecture, 261n44

authenticity, 169, 179, 183, 185, 207, 208, 216, 218, 227, 230, 233, 273n2

Ballona Wetlands, 20

Banham, Reyner, 31, 38

beatniks, 26–27, 28, 40, 170, 174

boardwalk, xi, 1, 2, 3, 10, 12, 16, 21, 35, 88, 164–203; business cycle, 192, 202; homeless use, 90, 100, 111; see also Free Speech Zone

bohemianism, 8, 13, 17, 20, 26–27, 29–30, 31, 33, 89, 112, 139, 142, 173, 202, 217, 260n31; see also counterculture

Bonin, Mike, 73–74

Bourdieu, Pierre, 219, 258n17

boutiques, 1, 207, 220–24

Bradbury, Ray, 25–26

Bradley, Tom, 171

Brand Venice, 208, 215–19, 233

Bratton, William J., 101–2

Breezes Del Mar. See Holiday Venice

broken windows strategy, 88, 101, 256n15, 269n10

Brooks, David, 274n3

building codes, 126, 148–49, 155–56

Burgess, Ernest, 252n2, 254n9, 260n33; see also Chicago School

Bush, George H. W., 59

Business Improvement Districts (BIDS), 275n4

California Coastal Act and Commission, 41–42, 115–16, 148–52, 247

campers. See RVs

canal compounds, 155–56

Canal Festivals, 139

canals (waterways), 21, 24, 27, 125, 159; cleanup campaigns, 136–37; restoration, 131–34, 150–52

Canals (neighborhood), 7, 10, 13, 15, 16, 40, 42, 90, 124–63; middle-class inmigration, 125, 139–40, 142–43, 237

carnival performers, 171–73, 192

Castile, Bob (activist), 53

categorization (of groups and places), 72, 89, 123, 257n16, 269n11, 270n15, 279n8, 279n11

Chaplin, Charlie, 21

Chautauqua, 21

Chavez, Flora, 65–66

Chicago, xiii, 9, 38, 239, 240, 252n2
Chicago School, 252n2, 254n9, 254n10,
    277n1
code enforcement, 28, 40–41, 75–76, 134,
    138, 170, 246–47
coffee shops, xiv, 1, 5, 204–6
collective identity, 55, 56, 162, 238, 256n14
collective visibility and invisibility, 59, 60,
    65, 67, 70, 84, 236
Collins, Randall (interaction ritual chains),
    55
commercialism, 17, 21–22, 169–70, 173–78,
    179–82, 202–3, of independent busi-
    nesses (in contrast to corporations), 18,
    173, 203, 207, 217, 223, 276n24; see also
    Free Speech Zone
Community–Police Advisory Boards
    (C–PABs), 98–99; see also nuisance
    abatement
Compton, 34, 177
configuration (of social and political
    groups), 10–15; as complementary posi-
    tions, 13–14, 126, 140, 146, 149, 152–53,
    159, 162, 200–202, 219–20, 236–37;
    as conflict between formal and infor-
    mal attachments, 165–66, 167–68, 189,
    193, 197–98; through housed/home-
    less proximity, 87–88, 91–98, 109–10,
    111–13, 117, 120, 122; as intragroup
    dynamics, 57–59, 60, 64–65, 119–21,
    198–99; as racial/ethnic oppositions,
    47–48, 50–51, 60, 62–64, 67–70, 72,
    80–81, 84–85; as renter/owner tensions,
    125, 132–35, 136–41, 143
counterculture, 28, 129–31, 135, 138, 147,
    182–83
criminalization of homelessness. See dis-
    continuity techniques
cultural repertoires, 92–98
Culver City Boys (gang), 68, 73

danger, perceptions of, 56, 63, 71, 73,
    81–82, 94–96, 116, 120–21, 126, 128–31,
    209–15
Davidson, Rick (activist), 28–29
Davis, Mike, 117, 254n10, 257n17
discontinuity techniques, 98–108, 269n8
diversity, 1, 2, 8, 9, 10, 12, 13, 18, 20, 30, 154,
    213, 227, 235, 251n1, 252n6; in opposi-
    tion to order, 243–46, 254n10

Douglas, Mary, 88
drug dealing and distribution, 5, 13, 16,
    56–57, 63, 72, 75, 82, 125
drug use, xi, 8, 13, 183, 186; see also
    marijuana
ducks, 126, 137, 149, 268n4
Duneier, Mitchell, 166, 269n10, 270n15

ecology: of affluence, 38; of commercial
    competition and adaptation, 20, 22,
    174, 178, 180, 185, 190; of interdepen-
    dent populations, 19, 108, 167, 174, 175,
    187, 238, 242, 258n19; see also Chicago
    School
Elias, Norbert, 10, 255n11; see also
    configuration
entrepreneurs, 175–78; with free speech
    cover, 180–82
eviction, 65, 77, 264n85, 267n35
exclusivity, 2, 8, 10, 14, 20, 157; see also
    neighborhood homology

fences, 6, 47, 79, 83
Fine Art Squad, 29
Florida, Richard, 243, 251n1, 274n3
Foucault, Michel, 269n11
Free Speech Zone, 3, 12, 17, 165, 168,
    178–82, 185, 236; regulation of, 167,
    185, 190–95, 199–202
Free Venice movement. See Peace and
    Freedom Party
freeways, 19, 26, 28

Galanter, Ruth, 73–74, 76, 151–52, 192,
    212, 247
gangs, xiv, 13, 15, 45, 56–57, 67, 82, 240,
    246, 252n2; injunctions against, 73–75,
    247; sweeps, 77
gang war of 1990s, 45, 68–69, 70, 71,
    213–14, 264n1
Gas House, 28, 40
gentrification, xiii, 9, 10, 15, 16, 19, 69–83,
    84, 87–88, 167, 224, 231, 239–40,
    244–46, 253n8; as racialized public cul-
    ture, 69–70, 72, 79–83; in tandem with
    homelessness, 91, 241
graffiti, 6, 13, 56, 57, 74, 75, 82, 213, 224,
    245
Great Depression, 20, 24
growth machine, 41, 252n2

Haag, John (activist), 29, 134
Hal's Bar and Grill, 6
hippies, 29, 90, 112, 130–32, 137, 146, 206
history. *See* stabilizing forces
hobos, 27–28, 260n32, 260n33, 262n72
Holiday Venice, 52–54, 76–77
Holiday Venice Tenant Action Committee, 77
Hollywood, 37, 241
homelessness, xi, xii, xiii, xiv, 3, 4, 7, 9, 15–17, 19, 30, 36–38, 65–66, 164–65, 225, 227, 235; as counterculture, 182–86; resources for social integration, 108–16; on Rose Avenue, 86–123; shelters, 117; sweeps, 105–8, 246; tied to mental illness, 95–97, 186
homeowners, 10, 17, 91, 93, 95, 97–98, 146; black, 50, 77–79; middle-class, 143, 147, 149, 150, 151; new, 83, 131, 138, 145, 158, 244
homogeneity. *See* neighborhood homology
housing: affordable, xii, 41–42, 76, 150; remodeling of, 14, 47, 141, 157
housing projects, 5–6, 26, 41, 228–29, 231; *see also* Holiday Venice
housing stock, 40

identities: of groups, xii, 10, 11, 82, 183, 185, 194, 195, 235, 256n14; of places, 1, 8, 236, 238–43, 252n2, 255n12; as racial/ethnic classification, 238, 279n11; of stores, 223; *see also* collective identity; public culture
immigrants, xi, xiii, 8, 17, 19, 30, 33–36, 235; Asian, 9, 35; as entrepreneurs, 167, 181–82; Korean, 35, 166–67, 176–77, 239; Latin American, 9, 34; Mexican, 60, 165, 239; use of public space, 61–62, 181
incarceration, 4, 59, 71, 102, 106
industrialization, 8, 31–32
inequality, 28, 193, 245, 249–50
informal economy, 17, 35, 196–202; *see also* Free Speech Zone
institutionalization, 29, 37, 52, 55, 113, 191–93, 262n72, 277n1
integration: of neighborhoods, 1, 12, 243, 280n19; across social categories, 29, 36, 112, 137, 276n24

Jacobs, Jane, 243, 257n17, 269n10
Jews, 40–41, 174, 264n85

Katz, Jack, 253n7, 266n24, 278n1
Kievman, Sandy, 198
Kinney, Abbot, 20–21, 23, 32, 48–49, 125, 127, 259n16
Korean War, 27

L.A. School, 254n9
Latinos, 15, 31, 32, 34–35, 59; invisibility of, 67, 84; in Oakwood, 45, 47, 53, 59–69, 83, 84, 236
Lipton, Lawrence, 28
Lopez, Steve, 36
Los Angeles City Council, xiii, 13, 59, 115, 135, 217; *see also* Galanter, Ruth; Miscikowski, Cindy; Rosendahl, Bill; Rundberg, Karl; Russell, Pat; Timberlake, L. E.
Los Angeles Department of City Planning, 40, 79, 149, 156
Los Angeles Department of Parks and Recreation, 101, 167, 168
Los Angeles Human Relations Commission, xiii, 45, 59, 75
Los Angeles Police Department (LAPD) *see* police
Los Angeles, population, 21, 30, 32

macro– and microprocesses, interactions of, 9–11, 18, 19, 237, 238, 242, 245, 255n11, 279n11
manufacturing industries, 31–32, 50, 210–11
Manzarek, Ray, 26–27, 28
marijuana, 4, 58, 103, 106, 182, 205
Marina del Rey, 1, 24, 40, 42, 125, 132–33, 170
markets, xii, 179, 202–3, 240; *see also* Free Speech Zone
Marsh, Norman, 20
mass culture, 169
media representations (of neighborhoods), 22, 68, 128, 139, 140, 208, 218
Mello Act, 42
Mexicans, 34, 35
middle position, 115, 140–41, 145, 232, 272n22
Miscikowski, Cindy, 81, 107, 192, 198

Mlikotin, Alex, 146
Molotch, Harvey, 10, 255n12, 280n19
Morrison, Jim, 26–27, 28
musicians, 3, 7, 164–65, 171, 185, 193, 198–99, 205

Namco Capital Group. *See* Holiday Venice
Nation of Islam, 74
neighborhood boundaries, 6, 15, 159, 209, 229, 237; as division between diversity and exclusivity, xii–xiii, 2, 8, 9, 11–12, 15, 228–31, 235, 253n6, 258n19; as division between insider and outsider, 157–59, 226, 229, 237
neighborhood homology, 14–15, 126, 162, 219, 233, 257n17
neighborhood symbiosis, 226–33
New York, xi, 28, 38, 238, 239, 240, 253n7
nuisance abatement, 76, 88, 99–100, 246

Oakwood (neighborhood), 5, 10, 12, 15, 22, 30, 32, 40, 41, 44–85, 236; homeownership, 52, 55; population, 46, 59; public culture, 47–48; *see also* Abbot Kinney Boulevard
Oakwood Beautification Committee, 72
Oakwood Park, 55, 56, 66, 67, 81; *see also* Oakwood Recreation Center
Oakwood Recreation Center, 45, 56, 57, 58, 67, 74, 82
Ocean Front Walk. *See* boardwalk
Ocean Park, 20–21, 23, 27, 40
oil drilling, 24–25, 128, 140
outsiders, 10, 15, 132, 157, 159, 161, 226, 229, 237, 257n16
Overnight Parking Permit. *See* parking regulation

Park, Robert, 9, 277n1; *see also* Chicago School
parking regulation, as control of homeless population, 94, 97–98, 102, 115–16, 160
parks, xiv, 55–56, 66–67, 81; unofficial, 124, 138, 160; *see also* Oakwood Park
Pattillo, Mary, 253n7, 262n63, 265n9, 272n22
Peace and Freedom Party, 113; Free Venice movement, 134, 139
police, 3, 4, 5, 12, 13, 44–45, 50–51, 56, 68, 115, 135, 185, 248–49; enforcement of

gang injunctions, 74–75; response to homelessness, 87, 100–108, 120–22, 161, 227–28; role in gentrification, 71–73, 213
political organizations, 11, 12, 29, 215
Poulson, Norris, 133
power labeling, 12–13, 43, 70, 82, 198, 229, 236
privacy, 153, 155, 157; as middle-class practice, 12, 79–81, 83, 144; of homeless, 117
Prohibition, 23
Project Action, 41, 52–54, 76, 209
public culture, 8, 9, 10–12, 20, 235, 238–42, 250; African American, 55, 64, 79, 81, 84; ambiguous, 1–2, 12, 14, 47–48, 85, 123, 236; of scenic neighborhood, 124, 125–26, 152, 153–62; *see also* neighborhood homology
public space, xii, 1, 11, 13, 61, 88, 213; privatization of, 254n10, 257n17
public transportation, 19, 22, 24, 61

quaintness, 146–62
quality of life politics, 12, 13, 24, 85, 88, 98, 115, 158, 168, 196–97, 199, 213, 244–45, 246–49, 264n86, 269n10, 275n4

real estate: abandoned property (empty lots) 90, 129, 131, 132, 134, 137, 146–47, 155, 157, 160, 213, 214, 249; brokers, 18, 76, 78–79, 143; developers, xii, 12, 17, 19, 53, 70, 76, 146–47, 166, 170, 173–74; prices, 38–39, 50, 53–54, 71, 146, 154, 225, 231–32, 276n25; speculation, 125, 147, 149
recreational vehicles. *See* RVs
Reese, Arthur, 48–49
rental occupancy, 16, 52–54, 76–77, 129, 131–32, 134–35; *see also* Holiday Venice
Resident and Non-Resident Property Owners Association. *See* Venice Canal Association
restaurants, 1, 6, 170, 173, 210, 219–20
restrooms, public, 100–101
retail chains, 170, 207, 217, 223, 230, 273n2, 276n24
retailers, 18, 207, 210–11, 216, 220–24
Rose Avenue, 4, 10, 12, 15, 16, 38, 86–123, 236
Rosendahl, Bill, 45, 166, 192, 247

Rundberg, Karl, 133
Russell, Clarence, 21
Russell, Pat, 41, 150, 151, 191, 192
RVs, xii, 16, 27, 87, 90, 94, 98, 100, 109, 112, 118–20, 183–84, 196, 245, 247, 249

San Francisco, 27, 28, 241
Santa Barbara, 38, 255n12, 263n77
Santa Monica, 1, 21, 23, 37, 42, 67, 84, 170–71, 241
Save the Canals Committee, 134–35
scavenging, 187–89
segregation, xiii, 15, 30, 32, 47, 50, 70, 84, 251n1
Sennett, Richard, 258n19
Seventh Avenue, 6
Shoreline Crips (gang), 68, 71, 73
sidewalks of canals, 127–28, 133, 154, 158
single-family homes, 4, 19, 42, 130
skid row (downtown L.A.), 36, 37, 113; see also Lopez, Steve
smells (in neighborhoods), xi, 124, 127, 189–90, 205–6
social service agencies, 4, 16, 36–37, 88, 99, 113, 123, 247; see also St. Joseph Center; Venice Family Clinic
Sponto Gallery, 112
sports, 59, 171
sprawl, xi
St. Joseph Center, 92–93, 97, 113, 114–15, 247
stabilizing forces, 11, 236; of African American visibility, 48, 50–56; as conditions for bohemian theme park, 168; of countercultural resistance, 134–135; as homeless attachments, 108–20; of invented history, 125–26, 145–46, 162, 216–17; in relation to change, 11, 162, 211, 235, 240–44
stigmatization. See cultural repertoires; power labeling
Stone, Oliver (The Doors film), 26
suburban ideals, 19, 26, 38, 130, 131, 142, 144–45, 259n20
surveillance, 5, 13, 45, 81, 84, 100, 153, 160, 170; as mode of stigmatization, 246
Suttles, Gerald, 246, 252n6, 262n63

Tabor, Irvin, 49
theft, 186–87

themed environment, 21, 22, 273n2; see also Brand Venice
thrift stores, 209, 220–21
Timberlake, L. E., 133
Topanga, 27
tourism, 38, 39, 106, 159, 171, 208

unintended consequences, 140, 224, 244, 272n23
urban pioneers, 14, 258n18
urban planning, 22, 24, 39, 40, 42, 125, 133, 149, 243, 254n9
urban renewal, 39–41, 136

Venice: amusement pier, 24, 49; consolidation with Los Angeles, 20, 22–24; municipal independence, 19; population, 32–35
Venice 13 (gang), 68, 71, 73
Venice Art Walk, 70, 216
Venice Boardwalk. See boardwalk
Venice Boulevard, 7
Venice Canal Association, 147, 150–52, 158
Venice Canal Resident Homeowner Association, 146–47
Venice Canals Improvement Association, 132
Venice Chamber of Commerce, 217
Venice Community Housing Corporation, 41–42, 158
Venice Family Clinic, 70–71, 113, 114–15, 216
Venice Neighborhood Council, xiii, 97, 113, 217
Venice Town Council, 41, 113, 147, 148
Venice Unchained, 217–18
Venice West Café, 28, 112
Ventura (California city), 24, 255n12, 263n77
Vera Davis Center, 55, 67, 108, 227
Vietnam War, 27, 29; veterans, 183
Villaraigosa, Antonio, 36
Voice of the Canals, 152, 158

Watts (neighborhood), 32, 34, 177, 262n63
Welles, Orson, 25
West Washington Boulevard, 29, 208, 210; black-owned businesses, 209; name change, 211–13; see also Abbot Kinney Boulevard

white flight, 49–50, 79, 240
white people, 44, 162; in Oakwood, 47,
  69–70, 82–83, 236
wildlife, 126
Willis, Paul, 257n17
Wilson, William Julius, 265n9
World War II, 31–32

Yorty, Sam, 133

zoning, 77
Zorbaugh, Harvey, xii–xiii
Zukin, Sharon, 253n7, 254n10, 267n26,
  273n2, 274n10